THE ACADEMY OF INTERNATIONAL BUSINESS
Published in Association with the UK Chapter of the Academy of International Business

Titles already published in the series:

International Business and Europe in Transition (Volume 1)
Edited by Fred Burton, Mo Yamin and Stephen Young

Internationalisation Strategies (Volume 2)
Edited by George Chryssochoidis, Carla Miller and Jeremy Clegg

The Strategy and Organization of International Business (Volume 3)
Edited by Peter Buckley, Fred Burton and Hafiz Mirza

Internationalization: Process, Context and Markets (Volume 4)
Edited by Graham Hooley, Ray Loveridge and David Wilson

International Business Organization (Volume 5)
Edited by Fred Burton, Malcolm Chapman and Adam Cross

International Business: Emerging Issues and Emerging Markets (Volume 6)
Edited by Carla C. J. M Millar, Robert M. Grant and Chong Ju Choi

International Business: European Dimensions (Volume 7)
Edited by Michael D. Hughes and James H. Taggart

Multinationals in a New Era: International Strategy and Management (Volume 8)
Edited by James H. Taggart, Maureen Berry and Michael McDermott

International Business (Volume 9)
Edited by Frank McDonald, Heinz Tusselman and Colin Wheeler

Internationalization: Firm Strategies and Management (Volume 10)
Edited by Colin Wheeler, Frank McDonald and Irene Greaves

The Process of Internationalization (Volume 11)
Edited by Frank MacDonald, Michael Mayer and Trevor Buck

International Business in an Enlarging Europe (Volume 12)
Edited by Trevor Morrow, Sharon Loane, Jim Bell and Colin Wheeler

Managerial Issues in International Business (Volume 13)
Edited by Felicia M. Fai and Eleanor J. Morgan

Anxieties and Management Responses in International Business (Volume 14)
Edited by Rudolf Sinkovics and Mo Yamin

Corporate Governance and International Business (Volume 15)
Edited by Roger Strange and Gregory Jackson

Contemporary Challenges to International Business (Volume 16)
Edited by Kevin Ibeh and Sheena Davies

Resources, Efficiency and Globalization (Volume 17)
Edited by Pavlos Dimitratos and Marian V. Jones

DOI: 10.1057/9781137367204.0001

Firm-Level Internationalization, Regionalism and Globalization (Volume 18)
Edited by Jenny Berrill, Elaine Hutson and Rudolf Sinkovics

International Business (Volume 19)
Edited by Simon Harris, Olli Kuivalainen and Veselina Stoyanova

The Changing Geography of International Business (Volume 20)
Edited by Gary Cook and Jennifer Johns

International Business and Institutions after the Financial Crisis (Volume 21)
Edited by Yama Temouri and Chris Jones

DOI: 10.1057/9781137367204.0001

International Business and Institutions after the Financial Crisis

Edited by

Yama Temouri and Chris Jones
Economics and Strategy Group, Aston Business School, UK

DOI: 10.1057/9781137367204.0001

First published 2014 by
PALGRAVE MACMILLAN

Palgrave Macmillan in the UK is an imprint of Macmillan Publishers Limited,
registered in England, company number 785998, of Houndmills, Basingstoke,
Hampshire RG21 6XS.

Palgrave Macmillan in the US is a division of St Martin's Press LLC,
175 Fifth Avenue, New York, NY 10010.

Palgrave Macmillan is the global academic imprint of the above companies
and has companies and representatives throughout the world.

Palgrave® and Macmillan® are registered trademarks in the United States,
the United Kingdom, Europe and other countries

ISBN: 978–1–137–36719–8

This book is printed on paper suitable for recycling and made from fully
managed and sustained forest sources. Logging, pulping and manufacturing
processes are expected to conform to the environmental regulations of the
country of origin.

A catalogue record for this book is available from the British Library.

A catalog record for this book is available from the Library of Congress.

Contents

DOI: 10.1057/9781137367204.0001

DOI: 10.1057/9781137367204.0001

List of Figures

List of Tables

DOI: 10.1057/9781137367204.0003

DOI: 10.1057/9781137367204.0003

DOI: 10.1057/9781137367204.0003

Foreword

The 40th Annual Conference of the Academy of International Business, UK and Ireland (UKI) Chapter, was held at a snowy Aston Business School on the 21–23 March 2013. This book reflects the contributions to the conference, and its theme – International Business: Institutions and Performance after the Financial Crisis – has offered the book a suitable title. The book is the 21st volume in the Palgrave Macmillan AIB UK and Ireland International Business series.

The theme of the conference revolved around the importance of institutions and how they relate to the thorny issues of how governments, with decidedly more limited funds since the crisis, still attract and retain internationally mobile investments, and maximize the benefits of internationalization. The two keynote speeches of the conference featured two distinguished professors. Saul Estrin, Professor of Management and Head of the Department of Management at The London School of Economics and Political Science, presented in his keynote a fascinating insight into the internationalization of firms from emerging markets, their location choice and the impact of state ownership. The second keynote featured Professor John Cantwell of Rutgers Business School and Editor-in-Chief of the *Journal of International Business Studies*, who gave a thought-provoking talk on the crucial role of international business in the global spread of technological innovation.

The 40th Annual Conference attracted 142 delegates from 20 countries, including Australia, Europe, Japan, New Zealand, Scandinavia, South Korea, Taiwan and Thailand. The delegates presented 102 papers in the conference tracks and 29 doctoral students participated in the doctoral colloquium, which reflects the continuing commitment of the AIB-UKI Chapter to promote and develop doctoral work in international business. The work at the annual conference, which is reflected in the chapters in this book, confirms the commitment of the Chapter to promote and develop international business research in the UK and Ireland and is linked to work in the wider Academy of International Business community. The Chapter is continuing to expand its involvement in the development of international business research by organizing future annual conferences and providing resources and information to enhance the quantity and quality of international business research. Please visit our website (http://www.aib-uki.org) which provides more details of the Chapter's work.

Heinz Tüselmann
Chair, Academy of International Business,
UK and Ireland Chapter

DOI: 10.1057/9781137367204.0004

Acknowledgements

Many thanks to the Aston Business School for hosting the 40th Annual Conference of the Academy of International Business, UK and Ireland Chapter. Particular thanks to Professors Nigel Driffield and Jim Love who brought this prestigious conference to Aston Business School. Special thanks also to Maria Podsiadly, the conference coordinator, for organizing the conference and the gala dinner; the reviewers of the papers of the conference; fellow staff members in the Economics and Strategy Group and doctoral students at Aston University for their kind support. Thanks are also due to Virginia Thorp at Palgrave Macmillan for overseeing the smooth production of the volume.

DOI: 10.1057/9781137367204.0005

Notes on the Editors and Contributors

Editors

Yama Temouri is Lecturer in International Business at Aston Business School, UK. His research interests are in international economics and trade, particularly the economics of multinational enterprises and its impacts on host and home economies. He is particularly interested in issues to do with productivity, outsourcing/offshoring activities and employment dynamics. He is currently working on the links between institutional quality, FDI and firm performance. His research has been published in journals such as the *Journal of Comparative Economics, Futures* and *The Review of World Economics*.

Chris Jones is Senior Lecturer in International Economics and Business at Aston Business School, UK. He gained his PhD from Nottingham University in the Department of Economics. His main research interests are in the broad areas of trade and foreign direct investment with a focus on developing countries. In 2011 Chris won the Economics Network's student nominated award for learning and teaching.

Contributors

Chiara Amini completed a PhD in Economics at University College London in 2012. Her thesis analysed three key issues of economic development: foreign direct investment, human capital and poverty. She is currently working on CSR, FDI and the economics of education in low- and middle-income countries. She joined London Metropolitan University as Senior Lecturer in Economics in 2011 and she has also worked as a research consultant for the European Bank of Reconstruction and Development, and the World Bank.

Dolores Añón-Higón is Associate Professor at the Department of Applied Economics II and Research Fellow at ERI-CES, Universitat de València (Spain). She received her MSc and PhD from the University of Warwick. Her research interests include the internationalization of R&D, and the relationship between innovation, trade, information technology and productivity.

Suma Athreye is Professor of International Strategy at Brunel Business School and Founding Director of the Centre on International Business and Strategy in Emerging Markets. Her research focuses on internationalization and its impact on technology management in developed and in emerging economies. Some of her well cited publications are on knowledge markets and the growth of international licensing, foreign investment into India, the growth of the Cambridge high tech cluster, the software and pharmaceutical industries in India and the internationalization of Chinese and Indian firms. She has won several grants for her research, which has also been recognized by national and international media.

Petra Bouvain is Assistant Professor at the University of Canberra and is currently completing her PhD at Macquarie University on CSR in the financial services sector. Her primary research interests are in the areas of CSR, branding and financial services marketing. Her research has been published in journals such as the *Journal of Business Ethics* and the *International Journal of Bank Marketing*.

Randolph Luca Bruno received his PhD in Economics and Management in 2006 from LEM., Sant'Anna School of Advanced Studies, Pisa. He has been a visiting scholar at Berkeley (University of California), research assistant at the Centre for New and Emerging Markets (London Business School) and an intern at the European Bank for Reconstruction and Development (London). He worked as a short-term consultant for the World Bank and joined Fondazione Rodolfo DeBenedetti (Milan, Italy) as an Affiliate in 2002. Between 2006 and 2009 he was Research Fellow at the University of Bologna, Italy and between September 2009 and June 2010 he was Teaching Fellow in Economics at University College London. He was appointed Lecturer in Business Economics at the University of Birmingham in July 2010 and he moved to UCL, School of Slavonic and East European Studies in September 2012, where he is now a Lecturer in Economics. He also joined IZA as a Research Affiliate in March 2007 and became a Research Fellow in April 2010.

John Cantwell is Distinguished Professor of International Business at Rutgers University, New Jersey, USA. He was previously Professor of International Economics at the University of Reading in the UK. His research focuses on technological innovation and multinational corporations. His earliest work helped to launch a new literature on multinational companies and international networks for technology creation, beyond merely international technology transfer. John Cantwell has published twelve books, over 65 articles in refereed academic journals, and over 80 chapters in edited collections. His published research spans the fields of international business and management, economics, economic history, economic geography and innovation studies. He is the Editor-in-Chief of the *Journal of International Business Studies* (2011–16). He has been an elected Fellow of the Academy of International Business (AIB) since 2005 and a Founding Fellow of the European International Business Academy (EIBA) since 2001.

Stephen Chen is Professor of International Business and Head of the International Business Discipline at the University of Newcastle, UK. He

DOI: 10.1057/9781137367204.0006

obtained his PhD from Imperial College, London, his MBA from the Cranfield School of Management and his BSc from King's College, London. His primary research interests are in the areas of global strategy and CSR. His research has been published in journals such as *Management International Review, Journal of World Business* and the *Journal of Business Ethics*.

Maria Cipollina received her MSc in Economics in 2003 from Birkbeck College London and a PhD in 2006 from the University of Molise at Campobasso, Italy. Between 2005 and 2009 she was a Research Assistant and Teaching Fellow in Economics at the University of Molise. In 2009 she became Lecturer in Economics at the University of Molise, Department of Economics, in Campobasso.

Gary Cook is Professor of Economics and Head of Economics, Finance and Accounting at the University of Liverpool Management School. His principal areas of research are industrial clusters, with particular emphasis on media industries and financial services, multinational location, innovation and internationalization. He also researches in the area of law and economics, focusing on the insolvency and turnaround of small firms.

Nigel Driffield is Professor of International Business and Regional Economics at Aston Business School, and has recently completed a year as Interim Executive Dean. By training he is an applied industrial economist with experience of working on a wide range of issues relating to inward investment and the impact of internationally mobile capital on host locations. He has published two books and over 60 academic papers. In addition to having had four ESRC funded projects, has also carried out consulting work for DTI, UKTI, OECD, UNCTAD, the European Commission and the World Bank, all on projects relating to inward investment and firm performance. Beginning in September 2013 he has a two-year Leverhulme fellowship that will allow him to research the relationships between international business and local economic development. On a more local level, he led the team that performed the inward investment analysis as part of the Manchester Independent Economic Review and more recently, he was one of the core executive team who delivered the 'Greater Birmingham Project' – a pilot project conducted by the Greater Birmingham and Solihull Local Economic Partnership (LEP) for how the LEPs may respond to the Heseltine Report.

Jun Du is a Reader of Economics at the Economics and Strategy Group, Aston Business School, and a visiting research fellow of Stockholm China Economic Research Institute, Stockholm School of Economics, Sweden. Jun is interested in the economics of industrial organization in emerging economies and the role of institutions as a determinant or mediating factor. Jun has published in the *International Journal of Industrial Organization, Kyklos, Research Policy,*

DOI: 10.1057/9781137367204.0006

Empirical Economics, Journal of Productivity Analysis, and *Entrepreneurship Theory and Practice.*

Saul Estrin is a Professor of Management and Head of the Department of Management at The London School of Economics and Political Science. His areas of research include labour economics, economic development and entrepreneurship. He is best known for his work on privatization and foreign direct investment. He was formerly Adecco Professor of Business and Society at London Business School where he was also Deputy Dean (Faculty and Research) for six years and the Director of the Centre for New and Emerging Markets, which analyses private sector development and business opportunities in emerging markets, notably Brazil, China, India, Russia and Central and Eastern Europe. Saul has published more than one hundred scholarly articles and books. His publications include the widely cited *Privatization in Central and Eastern Europe; Foreign Direct Investment into Transition Economies;* and recently, *Investment Strategies in Emerging Markets.* He has also published numerous papers in scholarly journals including *Quarterly Journal of Economics, European Economic Review, Journal of Public Economics, Journal of Industrial Economics* and *Journal of Comparative Economics.* He also writes for policy journals such as *Economic Policy and Business Strategy Review,* of which he was for some years the editor. Saul has considerable practitioner experience. He is currently on the Board of Barings Emerging Markets and has been a consultant to the World Bank, European Union,OECD, DfID and NERA. He has taught executive programmes for a large number of major companies including BA, BT, Lloyds TSB, Marks and Spencer, PWC, Vauxhall, Powergen, Deutsche Bank, ING Barings, Swedbank and ABN-AMRO Bank.

Pervez Ghauri is Professor of International Business at King's College London. He obtained his PhD from Uppsala University, Sweden, where he has also taught for several years. He has published 25 books and numerous journal articles. He has consulted to a number of organizations such as BP, Airbus Industries and Ericsson. He is Editor-in-Chief of the *International Business Review* and Editor (Europe) of the *Journal of World Business.*

Sourafel Girma is Professor of Industrial Economics at the University of Nottingham. He joined the Centre on Globalisation and Economic Policy as a Post-Doctoral Research Fellow in 1998. He took up a Senior Lectureship at the University of Leicester in 2002, before joining the Nottingham University Business School in 2005, as an Associate Professor and Reader in Industrial Economics. He was promoted to Professor in 2007 and has now re-joined the Nottingham School of Economics as Professor of Industrial Economics. He is affiliated to GEP as an Internal Research Fellow.

Yundan Gong is a Senior lecturer in Economics and Innovation at Aston Business School, UK. Before joining Aston she worked as a Research Fellow in

DOI: 10.1057/9781137367204.0006

the Leverhulme Centre for Research on Globalisation and Economic Policy (GEP) and completed her PhD at the Nottingham University Business School. She also worked as a manager in a Chinese commercial bank before embarking on her academic career. Her main research interests are in firm performance analysis, firm level response to globalization, innovation and R&D and applied Micro-econometric analysis.

Holger Görg is Professor of International Economics at Christian-Albrechts-University Kiel, and Head of the Research Group 'The Global Division of Labour'at the Kiel Institute for the World Economy. Before joining Kiel he was at University College Cork, University of Ulster, and Nottingham University, where he still retains an affiliation as research fellow in the Leverhulme Centre for Research on Globalisation and Economic Policy (GEP). He is also affiliated with CEPR and IZA. He completed a PhD in Economics in 1999 at the University of Dublin, Trinity College. His main research interests are in applied international trade issues, in particular relatingto foreign direct investment, international outsourcing, trade and labour markets.

Börje Joansson is Professor of Economics at the Jönköping International Business School (JIBS) and research fellow of CIRCLE at Lund University. He is also affiliated with the Centre of Excellence for Science and Innovation Studies (CESIS) at the Royal Institute of Technology (KTH), where he remained director of CESIS between 2004 and 2012. He received his PhD at Gothenburg University in 1978 and was acting professor in Regional Economics at the University of Umeå in 1979. At the same university he has been director of the Centre of Regional Science (CERUM) and professor of Regional Economics. Between 2000 and 2003 he was president of the European Regional Science Association ERSA. He has published a wide set of journal articles, books, and edited books. In 2013 he was awarded the EIB-ERSA prize for contributions to regional science.

Ewa Kaliszuk is a professor at the Institute for Market, Consumption and Business Cycles Research (Instytut Badań Rynku, Konsumpcji i Koniunktur – IBRKK). She is also a Head of the European Integration Unit at the IBRKK and an editor-in-chief of the bi-monthly "European Union.pl". Her research interests focus on international economics, with special attention given to foreign trade and regional integration and their interactions with FDI. She is an author of numerous publications on the WTO and EU trade issues and their impact on Poland's economy. She has supervised and participated in several research projects on trade- and investment-related issues conducted for the Polish government and parliament, the European Commission, and the OECD.

Palitha Konara is a PhD student at the York Management School, University of York. His main research interest is foreign direct investment (FDI), with a

DOI: 10.1057/9781137367204.0006

strong focus on determinants of inward FDI and the impact of FDI on host economies.

Sandra Lancheros is an Assistant Professor in Economics at the University of Nottingham Ningbo China. Sandra joined the School of Economics in 2013 after working for two years as a Research Fellow at Aston University. She completed her PhD at the University of Nottingham in 2012. Her research interests are in the areas of international trade and foreign direct investment, innovation and technology transfer, and applied microeconomics.

Hans Lööf is Professor of Economics, Division of Entrepreneurship and Innovation, Department of Industrial Economics and Management, KTH. He is also deputy director at the Centre of Excellence for Science and Innovation Studies, Royal Institute of technology, Stockholm Sweden. His main research interest is the economics of innovation and growth which includes a number of quite disparate economic fields, including macroeconomics (international trade), industrial organization (the strategies and interactions of innovative firms), public finance (policies for encouraging private sector innovation), economic development (innovations systems) and the economics of geography (agglomerations and accumulation of knowledge and spillover).

Sushanta Mallick is a professor at the School of Business and Management at Queen Mary, University of London. Prior to Queen Mary, he spent nearly three years as a Lecturer at the Department of Economics, Loughborough University. He previously worked as a Sovereign Research Analyst covering Asian emerging markets at JPMorgan Chase, based in Hong Kong. He began his research career in the early 1990s at the Institute for Social and Economic Change, followed by a Commonwealth Scholarship to study for a PhD in Economics at the University of Warwick. He has published numerous journal articles and is the author of *Modelling Macroeconomic Adjustment with Growth in Developing Economies* (1999). His main research interests include issues in international macroeconomics and finance.

Miguel Manjón-Antolín is Associate Professor at the Department of Economics, Rovira i Virgili University, Spain. He has also held visiting positions at the Netherlands Bureau for Economic Policy Analysis and the Universities of Warwick (UK), Tilburg (the Netherlands) and KU Leuven (Belgium). His research interests include applied microeconometrics, new firm formation and empirical industrial organization.

Pardis Nabavi graduated from the Master's Program in Economics of Innovation and Growth at the Royal Institute of Technology in Stockholm in 2010. She is currently a PhD student at the Division of Entrepreneurship and Innovation at the Royal Institute of Technology, Sweden. Her research interest is mainly

DOI: 10.1057/9781137367204.0006

innovation and economic growth, export and productivity, entrepreneurship, regional economics and spatial econometrics.

Rekha Rao Nicholson is a Lecturer in International Management at the University of Bath. She obtained her PhD in Economics and Management from Sant'Anna School of Advanced Studies, Italy. Her research interests are strategy in emerging economies and the economics of innovation. She has published in *Research Policy, International Business Review, Journal of Evolutionary Economics, Economics of Innovation* and *New Technology and Industry and Innovation.*

Abubakr Saeed is Assistant Professor at the Department of Business and Economics at Foundation University, Pakistan. He received his MPhil from Brunel Business School, Brunel University. His thesis focused on the impact of financial reforms in emerging economies. In addition, he holds an MBA in Finance (Blekinge Tekniska Högskola, Sweden) and an MSc in Computer Sciences (Umeå University, Sweden). His research interests include corporate investment, financial reforms and emerging economies.

Julie Salaber is a Lecturer in Finance at the University of Bath where she teaches courses in international finance, investment banking and investment management. She received her PhD in Management from the University of Paris-Dauphine, France. Her research interests range from finance (empirical asset pricing, behavioural finance), economics (macroeconomics, religion) to international business (cross-border mergers and acquisitions). She has recently published in *International Business Review* and *European Journal of Political Economy.*

Meng Song is a PhD student from Aston Business School at Aston University. She is interested in firms' internationalization strategies. Part of her thesis is on how firms' characteristics determine their choice of strategies when expanding to overseas markets using a Chinese dataset. She is also interested in technology transfer from FDI. The second part of her thesis is to investigate how domestic firms can benefit from technology transfer from FDI using a comprehensive Chinese firm level dataset. She uses innovation performance of firms as the direct evidence of technology transfer.

Misagh Tasavori is a Lecturer in Entrepreneurship and International Business at Essex Business School, University of Essex. She obtained a PhD in Business Administration from Manchester Business School. Her research interests focus on international business, social entrepreneurship and socially entrepreneurial behaviour among multinational corporations.

Agata Wancio is a PhD candidate in International Economics at the Warsaw School of Economics and research fellow at the Institute for Market,

DOI: 10.1057/9781137367204.0006

Consumption and Business Cycle Research in Warsaw. Her research focuses on foreign trade and investment, with special emphasis on MNEs from emerging markets and the outward FDI-innovation relationship. She also has research experience in the areas of FTA deals and European integration and participated in several projects in these fields for the Polish government.

Yingqi Wei is Professor of International Business, York Management School, University of York. Her main research interests are foreign direct investment (FDI), international trade and economic development, with a particular focus on the determinants and impact of inward FDI in China and the internationalization of Chinese firms. She has published in *Journal of International Business Studies, Journal of Business Research, Management International Review,* and *Regional Studies.*

Yong Yang joined the University of Sussex in October 2012 as a Senior Lecturer in Strategy. Before joining Sussex, he was a lecturer in International Business and Entrepreneurship at the University of Essex. He worked, for a year, on a FP7 project funded by the European Commission at Brunel University, UK. He obtained his PhD in Business and Management from Queen Mary University of London. His research interests are in the internationalization process of firms, location choice of foreign direct investment, international knowledge transfer, and exporting and firm performance.

Reza Zaefarian is a Lecturer in Entrepreneurship at the Faculty of Entrepreneurship, University of Tehran. He obtained his PhD from Sharif University of Technology. His research interests include networks, new product development and information systems in entrepreneurial firms.

DOI: 10.1057/9781137367204.0006

Introduction: International Business and Institutions after the Financial Crisis

Yama Temouri and Chris Jones

The theme for the Academy of International Business (UK and Ireland chapter) 2013 Conference was *International Business, Institutions and Performance after the Financial Crisis.* Developed economies are still reeling from the aftermath of the worst financial crisis since the Great Depression. The bursting of the US housing bubble triggered huge losses in securities, led to questions regarding bank solvency, and tightened credit, all of which forced large declines in international trade and foreign direct investment (FDI). As the effects fed through into the real economy, unemployment began to rise and bank bailouts had a huge impact on public finances, with countries recording large deficits and debt ratios approaching 100 per cent of gross domestic product (GDP). This has been compounded by the effects of the Eurozone crisis and the bailouts afforded to countries on the periphery such as Greece and Cyprus. Furthermore, unpredictable macroeconomic policy via unconventional monetary policy and the controversy surrounding the use of fiscal policy to control the public finances has created much uncertainty for international business. Indeed, OECD outward and inward FDI flows in 2012 still rest at 45 per cent and 54 per cent below their peak levels in 2007 respectively.

Since the financial crisis of 2008, governments have been wrestling with the difficult task of how to attract international investment despite their much-reduced resources. This issue and events have put the spotlight on the importance of institutions for the global economy. On the one hand, governments in old and new markets are increasingly attuned to the need to provide an appropriate institutional environment in terms of market efficiency and property rights. On the other hand, international firms are realizing that they are required to adapt to the prevailing market conditions. This is particularly important when one considers the sections of the global economy that are expected to be the engines of growth. At the macro level, emerging and transition countries, powered by high levels of technical efficiency, are expected to generate growth and provide new markets for western producers while allying

DOI: 10.1057/9781137367204.0007

1

their productivity with frontier technology. At a micro level, western governments are looking to new business formation, often linked to global frontier
technology through niche markets and as suppliers to global firms, to deliver
growth that large firms seem unable to do.

The chapters in this volume are drawn from contributions given at the 40th
Academy of International Business (UK and Ireland Chapter) conference that
was held at Aston Business School in Birmingham on the 21–3 March 2013, and
was chaired by Nigel Driffield and Jim Love. We begin the book with two chapters, in Part I: Keynotes, from the keynote speakers: Saul Estrin, Professor and
Head of the Department of Management at The London School of Economics
and Political Science, and John Cantwell, Professor of International Business
at Rutgers Business School and Editor-in-Chief of the *Journal of International
Business Studies*.

Chapter 1 is based on Professor Saul Estrin's keynote speech, where he gives
a fascinating insight into how the pattern of FDI has changed to reflect the
increasing maturity of emerging markets. He offers two ways that the emphasis
of research might change to reflect this pattern. Firstly, he questions the
eclectic paradigm when one thinks about emerging market multinationals;
and secondly, he discusses the role of source country characteristics in the
internationalization process. Chapter 2 is based on Professor John Cantwell's
thought-provoking keynote speech on the crucial role of international business
in the global spread of technological innovation. The first part of his chapter
emphasizes the historical perspective with which one can view the relationship
between the globalization of business and the international location of technological innovation. This is then linked, in the second part, with evidence on
the relationship between the two in the most recent phase of global economic
development since 1950.

The remainder of the volume is divided into two further parts. Part II:
Institutions and Foreign Direct Investment focuses on the conference's main
theme. There are six chapters containing research looking at the entry of multinationals at the base of the pyramid; FDI and property rights in resource-rich
countries; the impact of the financial crises on the performance of European
acquisitions; internal capital markets and outward FDI from India and China;
the investment and development path (IDP) in the context of Poland's accession to the EU; and the adoption of the Global Reporting Initiative (GRI) by
FT500 firms.

Part III: Knowledge Flows and Firm Performance focuses on other areas that
were central to the conference proceedings. There are seven chapters based on
research looking at inward investment, technology transfer and innovation;
knowledge sources of persistent exporters; financing patterns and multinational
performance; the role of language in bilateral FDI; a meta-regression analysis
on the impact of FDI on economic performance; the drivers of technology

DOI: 10.1057/9781137367204.0007

upgrading via foreign acquisitions in China; and international research and development (R&D) spillovers.

Part II – Institutions and Foreign Direct Investment

The chapters in Part II all exemplify the importance of institutions for understanding international business activity and reflect the main theme of the conference.

In Chapter 3, Tasavori, Ghauri and Zaefarian examine the fact that multinational corporations (MNCs) have traditionally ignored low-income markets, usually referred to as the base of the pyramid (BOP). They state that despite the dominant poverty in this market, a growing number of MNCs are attempting to learn about successful strategies for entering this market segment. By focusing on relationships between MNCs and non-governmental organizations (NGOs) and trying to explain how they facilitate MNCs' entry into this market the authors use a network perspective, which has been adopted and used to analyse the relationship between MNCs and NGOs. Interviews with two MNCs and their NGO partners in India suggest that corporations can enter the BOP market by building trust in their relationships with NGOs, and thus demonstrating their commitment and strengthening their legitimate position among NGOs and BOP communities.

In Chapter 4, Amini explores whether natural resource endowments moderate the property rights–FDI relationship. Based on a panel of 92 low- and middle-income countries, she finds that the sensitivity of foreign investors to local institutions varies both across countries and types of investment. Indeed there is novel evidence that, in resource-rich countries, the positive effect of property rights on FDI is undermined. However the type of resource endowment matters. Out of the three resources analysed – oil, minerals and agricultural products – it is found that only oil production has a significant moderating impact on the FDI–property rights relationship.

In Chapter 5, Nicholson and Salaber look at the impact of the recent financial crisis on the short-term performance of European acquisitions. They use institutional theory and transaction cost theory to study whether bidders derive lower or higher returns from acquisitions announced after 2008. Looking at shareholders' stock price reaction to 2245 deals that occurred during 2004–12 across 22 European Union (EU) countries, the results, using both univariate and multivariate analysis, show that the deals announced in the post-crisis period, corresponding to the period of economic recession, generate higher returns to shareholders as compared to acquisitions announced in the pre-crisis period.

In Chapter 6, Saeed and Athreye investigate how internal capital markets affect firm investments in emerging economies. In particular, they examine

DOI: 10.1057/9781137367204.0007

two aspects of internal capital markets: (1) business group affiliation and (2) state ownership. By employing a simultaneous equations approach to estimate the role of these organizational characteristics on the joint determination of domestic and foreign investment decisions, they find that these firms face considerable financial constraints to domestic and foreign investment. However the organizational forms are able to mitigate credit constraints in both domestic and foreign investments.

In Chapter 7, Kaliszuk and Wancio examine whether Poland has entered the third stage of the IDP using the theoretical framework provided by John H. Dunning. Then they go on to analyse the channels through which the two external factors – Poland's accession to the EU and the global financial and economic crisis of 2008–9 – have influenced the Polish IDP. They conclude that there are several indications that suggest Poland has entered the third stage of the IDP and that EU membership has been the catalyst for this transition.

In Chapter 8, Chen and Bouvain examine the effects of the national institutional environment as well as the influence of exports and inward FDI in the home country on the adoption of the GRI by firms in the FT500. Their results suggest that the adoption of the GRI is negatively correlated with exports of the country of origin and institutional development of the country. Furthermore there is a significant positive interaction effect between corporate sustainability performance and national institutional development.

Part III – Knowledge Flow and Firm Performance

The chapters in Part III cover a range of topics that are of great interest to scholars in international business. They are an eclectic mix including such topics as technology transfer and R&D spillovers.

In Chapter 9, Song, Driffield and Du study the technology transfer of inward FDI to domestic firms by using innovation as direct evidence of technological benefits. They analyse how domestic firms can learn from FDI to produce patents. The initial part of the chapter reviews the main channels of technology transfer. The authors then statistically analyse the trend of FDI penetration and domestic firms' patents production using Chinese firm-level data during 2000–8. They find that patent production of indigenous firms accompanies the changes of FDI in different sectors and that this correlation is more pronounced in technology-intensive sectors compared with labour-intensive sectors.

In Chapter 10, Lööf, Nabavi, Cook and Joansson examine the economic performance difference between persistent exporters and other firms. The chapter shows that such differences can be associated with how the firms combine internal and external knowledge. A firm's internal knowledge is measured by its accumulation from recurrent R&D and patenting engagement, while the

DOI: 10.1057/9781137367204.0007

firm's external knowledge is measured by its distance-discounted access to the supply of knowledge-intensive producer services. In the investigation the authors apply linear and non-linear panel data models to a sample of 4000 Swedish manufacturing firms with at least one employee that persistently exported every year between 1997 and 2008. The results show how a composite knowledge variable positively affects a persistent exporter's export intensity and scope as well as its growth in value added, productivity and employment.

In Chapter 11, Mallick and Yang's main purpose is to provide new empirical evidence on the effects of financing patterns by firms, focusing on two related questions. Firstly, do sources of financing matter for firm performance; and secondly, do multinationals' performance and leverage get transmitted to their overseas affiliates?

The chapter draws on firm-level data covering over 10,000 firms from 47 countries in order to address these questions. The authors find that, while retained earnings and equities have a positive effect on productivity, bank and non-bank loans tend to negatively influence productivity. Furthermore while the multinational parents' performance significantly influences the subsidiaries' performance, higher debt ratios of parents do not matter for the productivity of subsidiaries.

In Chapter 12, Konara and Wei examine the role that language plays in affecting the FDI location decision. They state that language distance (LD) between home and host countries can lead to high information costs, making legitimacy building in the host country difficult and creating complications in the transfer of core competencies. The chapter makes a preliminary attempt to develop a conceptual framework and empirically tests the relationship between LD and FDI using bilateral FDI flows between 29 OECD countries and 111 partner countries during the period 1986–2008. The authors find strong evidence of dynamic and negative effects of LD on bilateral FDI.

In Chapter 13, Bruno and Cipollina explain and summarize a large number of empirical results on the indirect effect of FDI on economic performance in the Enlarged Europe by means of a meta-regression analysis. The chapter discusses some of the more recent findings from the empirical literature focusing on the FDI–growth relationship – horizontal vs. vertical at the firm level. It does this by collecting all the relevant quantitative studies to run a regression of regressions focused on the Enlarged Europe. The authors show three main results: first, the existence of a positive indirect impact of FDI on productivity and ultimately on economic growth in the EU; second, that the positive impact is limited in magnitude; and third, that the effect of FDI on growth is stronger for new member states, compared to the old EU-15 members after 2001.

In Chapter 14, Girma, Gong, Görg and Lancheros study the impact of foreign ownership structure on firms' technological upgrading using Chinese manufacturing firm-level data from 2001 to 2007. Using an approach that combines

DOI: 10.1057/9781137367204.0007

difference-in-differences with propensity score matching, the authors find that the injection of inward FDI has a direct impact on technology upgrading via R&D and new product development. However when foreign investors own the majority of capital, the impact on technology upgrading is diminishing. Moreover the estimates provide evidence not only on the year of the acquisition, but the impact up to two years post-acquisition.

In Chapter 15, Añón Higón and Manjón-Antolín examine the extent to which domestic firms can reap productivity gains from R&D spillovers due to the innovation activities of foreign affiliates in the same industry. Foreign R&D spillovers are measured as a weighted sum of the R&D conducted by foreign affiliates, where the weights reflect the institutional distance between the home country of the affiliates and the host country. The results, which use a sample of UK innovative firms, show the presence of positive FDI-transmitted R&D spillovers. The overall findings suggest that UK firms benefit more from the innovation conducted by institutionally close foreign enterprises.

Conclusion

The book examines various issues from different viewpoints, particularly that of institutions, and draws on research conducted in different country settings. We hope that it will provide useful ideas for further research in seeking to understand the evolution of international business activity and how organizations cope in the aftermath of crises.

DOI: 10.1057/9781137367204.0007

Part I
Keynotes

DOI: 10.1057/9781137367204.0008

Part 1

Keynotes

1

Internationalization of Firms from Emerging Markets: Location Choice and the Impact of Institutions and State Ownership*

Saul Estrin

Introduction

Since its early days in the 1960s, the literature on foreign direct investment (FDI) has always sought to understand and explain observed phenomena (Caves, 1996; Dunning, 1980, 1998). Between the 1960s and 1990s, most actual FDI took the form of the creation of subsidiaries by American firms in Europe, or European firms in America. From the 1970s, investments by Japanese firms in both America and Europe also became significant (Yang et al., 2009). This might all be regarded as 'north–north' investments; and the theorizing to explain it focused on 'ownership advantages' (Dunning, 1980) of source firms, often based around technology or brands, or firm specific advantages (Rugman, 1982) that can be developed by careful corporate strategy. Even in this period, of course, there was also FDI, for example, between firms based in developed and less developed economies – 'north–south' investments – to exploit natural resources; captured by Dunning as resource seeking as a motivation for FDI (Dunning, 1980). However, the period between 1990 and 2008 saw increasing movements of FDI between developed and developing countries and for motives including efficiency seeking and market seeking. This was the era of emphasis on 'emerging markets', where growth and development was seen to be concentrated in a small group of countries termed the BRICs (Brazil, Russia, India, China) by Goldman Sachs economist Jim O'Neill (O'Neill, 2012).

* This chapter is a version of the keynote address to the UK Association of International Business Conference held at Aston University on March 22nd 2013. It draws on research projects with Klaus Meyer, Bo Nielson and Sabina Nielson. Comments from conference participants are also gratefully acknowledged, though errors are all mine.

DOI: 10.1057/9781137367204.0008

In 2010, the flows of FDI to developing economies for the first time exceeded the flows to developed economies. The FDI literature shifted from issues of ownership and internalization advantages towards also analysing in-depth location issues, in particular questions of institutional quality and risk (e.g. Habib and Zwawick, 2002; Khanna and Palepu, 2000; Khanna and Rivkin, 2001; Meyer et al., 2009).

In recent years, the pattern of FDI has begun to shift once again to reflect the increasing levels of wealth and maturity in emerging markets. We are now beginning to see yet another form of FDI influencing the literature, namely investment flows by companies domiciled within developing economies. These flows are both south–north and south–south; for example, widely reported activities by Chinese multinationals in African countries related to their needs for secure supplies of raw materials. In the same way that previous major shifts in the form of FDI have influenced the literature, it seems likely that these changes will impact greatly on our understanding of the FDI process and this is already reflected in the literature (e.g. Cuervo-Cazurra and Genc, 2008; Yiu, Lau, and Bruton, 2007). While the scale of FDI from emerging markets remains relatively small in comparison with north–north and north–south investments, it is very fast growing (UNCTAD, 2011) and likely to become increasingly significant over time as the BRICs and other emerging markets play an increasing role in the international division of labour (O'Neill, 2012).

There are many ways that the emphasis of research might change in response to this shifting FDI pattern, but I will focus only on two. The first concerns the global strategies of emerging market multinationals. Clearly, north–north and north–south FDI can be understood using traditional tools; for example, resource-seeking, market-seeking and efficiency-seeking motives. Emerging market multinationals may have resource-seeking motives, as noted already, but the latter two motives at first sight seem less convincing. These firms already operate in economies that are amongst the largest and fastest growing in the world. Moreover their growth has been driven to a significant extent by the exploitation of cost advantages, notably labour costs, which cannot easily be replicated in developed economy host environments. Indeed the fundamentals of the eclectic paradigm might be brought into question when one thinks about emerging market multinationals, because their ownership advantages for a global economy are not as clearly delineated in the technologies, brands, distribution networks and other intangible assets that can explain how developed economy multinationals have overcome the 'liability of foreignness' (Zaheer, 1995).

A second issue raised by the growth of south–north FDI is the role of home country characteristics in the internationalization process. Until now, this has been a less important issue for the literature because the variation in source

DOI: 10.1057/9781137367204.0008

economy characteristics is relatively modest when one considers either north–north or north–south FDI. Though developed economies clearly differ in many important respects (Hall and Soskice, 2001), these variations are rarely considered as important determinants of the nature and pattern of investment. Attention has instead been focused on host country characteristics, especially institutions such as corruption, when considering the locational choice of FDI, which is almost always implicitly assumed to derive from a developed economy. However it seems likely that the impact of the local institutional environment will be comparably important for the domestic internationalization process of emerging market multinationals as is it for the locational choice of developed economy multinationals. One example will suffice to make the point. When considering FDI choices by firms based in developed economies, we rarely if ever consider the impact of ownership and governance arrangements, for the simple reason that there is more or less no variation; multinational firms are typically privately owned by large numbers of shareholders. However such arrangements are not the norm in emerging markets (Morck, Wolfenson and Yeung, 2005). Rather we find ownership concentrated in family hands, often within complex business groups, or in the hands of the state (Young et al., 2008). Such arrangements are likely to imply that the standard principal–agent problems that bedevil incentive structures in developed economies will instead be replaced in emerging markets by principal–principal conflicts concerning the objectives of the organization. Firms may not therefore always follow the logic of the search for profit, instead seeking to satisfy the aims of their state or family owner. Thus the state as owner may pursue long-term development goals using their owner's firms as proxies in the process, thereby introducing additional motivations for FDI.

The study of emerging market multinationals is likely to be a lengthy and fascinating process. My objective in this short chapter is simply to highlight a few issues about the theoretical issues raised by the phenomenon, as a pointer to future research, hopefully both theoretical and empirical. My comments will draw on research with Klaus Meyer (Estrin and Meyer, 2012) and with Klaus Meyer, Bo Nielson and Sabina Nielson (Estrin et al., 2013).

The strategies of emerging market multinationals

There is scope for researchers to reconsider the entire range of global strategies through the lenses of foreign multinational enterprises (MNE). Some scholars argue that MNEs from emerging economies (EEs) are systematically different from MNEs originating from a developed economy (DC) and thus call for the development of new theory to explain their characteristics (Child and Rodgriguez, 2005; Guillén and Garcia-Canal, 2009; Rui and Yip, 2008). In contrast, others propose that the established theories should not be prematurely

DOI: 10.1057/9781137367204.0008

abandoned since they retain the capacity to explain the principal features of EE MNEs (Hennart, 2009; Narula, 2012; Ramamurti, 2012).

As noted previously, most EE MNEs lack the famous brands and leading-edge technologies that are usually viewed as the drivers of MNEs' overseas FDI. The location decision of a firm is usually argued to depend on the inter-action of its firm specific advantages (FSAs) (Rugman, 1982) with the specific locational advantages at potential host locations (Dunning, 1998; Narula, 2012). Firms therefore expand internationally where they can redeploy their internationally-transferable proprietary resources and capabilities to both exploit and explore their resource base (Barney, 1991) and the choice of investment location is determined by the interaction of the firm with the host context.

The EE MNE literature suggests that two types of FSAs could be driving their internationalization. First, studies identify a range of operational capabilities of particular relevance to EE contexts (Verbeke and Kano, 2012). For example, EE MNEs may possess capabilities in 'process innovations' that allow them to lower production costs without necessarily reducing product quality (Zeng and Williamson, 2007) and 'frugal innovation' generating new products initially designed for the needs of an EE, but also enabling entry into niches in advanced economies. Other EE MNEs develop capabilities in managing dispersed value chains and labour-intensive manufacturing processes (Ramamurti, 2012), or 'the ability to manage institutional idiosyncrasies' (Henisz, 2003), which helps EE MNEs to compete in other EEs and provides them with a competitive advantage in those contexts (Cuervo-Cazurra and Genc, 2008).

Second, the FSAs of EE MNEs may be grounded in their preferential access to country-specific advantages of their home country (Hennart, 2012; Narula, 2012). This preferential access may arise from close network relationships in the home country, or from ownership and governance forms that provide access to external resources. As we have seen, many EE MNEs belong to business groups that share resources and internalize markets. Their FDI may be driven by their role within the business group and supported by resources shared within the group (Khanna and Rivkin, 2001). Other firms access resources through state ownership and other forms of association with the home country government, for example, by obtaining finance from state-owned banks on comparatively favourable terms. Therefore firms aligning themselves with governmental policy agendas are reportedly finding it easier to attract resources that facilitate outward FDI, notably in China (Buckley et al., 2007; Morck, Yeung and Zhao, 2008). This preferential resource access enables them to be less averse to political risk, and to seek resources of national rather than of purely corporate interest (Ramasamy et al., 2012).

Thus EE MNEs internationalize with different sorts of FSAs than a typical DC MNE, be they internal to the firm (such as operational capabilities) or in

DOI: 10.1057/9781137367204.0008

the form of preferential access to country specific advantages of the home country. These differences in starting points are likely to affect their outward FDI strategies. Recent literature has proposed two innovative theoretical ideas to explain differences between MNEs from EEs and DCs respectively, namely strategic asset seeking (or springboard) perspectives (Li, Li and Shapiro, 2012; Luo and Tung, 2007) and institutional perspectives (Cuervo-Cazurra and Genc, 2008; Cui and Jiang, 2012; Holburn and Zelner, 2010). To date, empirical contributions in this literature are mostly based on single country studies, and hence provide insights regarding the distinct features of the particular country but offer limited advancement of knowledge into the comparative aspect of the research question. Finally I present a learning perspective (Li, 2010; Meyer and Thaijongrak, 2013), which suggests that lower levels of maturity in internationalization may be the distinguishing feature of EE MNEs.

Strategic asset-seeking perspective

A common thread in the empirical literature is the observation that EE MNEs tend to acquire strategic assets overseas by purchasing firms in DCs that are more advanced in terms, for example, of technology, distribution skills and even management than they are themselves (Deng, 2009; Peng, 2012; Rui and Yip, 2008). This observation led to theoretical work suggesting that FDI by EE MNEs primarily aims to *create* FSAs, rather than to exploit them (Rugman, 2009). These acquired assets are strategic in the sense that they strengthen the capabilities of the acquirer not only in the local market, but in its global operations, providing, for example, advanced technologies or international brand names that strengthen the firm's competitive position vis-à-vis its competitors back home. Hence, the 'strategic asset seeking' or 'springboard' perspective (Li et al., 2012; Luo and Tung, 2007) suggests that EE MNEs would use such acquisitions to acquire resources abroad that are then combined with existing resources to create FSAs that enable them to compete more effectively both at home and abroad.

This motive mainly applies to FDI by EE MNEs into DCs, where such internationally transferable assets are likely to be found. It suggests that investments by EE MNEs in DCs are primarily designed to accomplish a catch up with global leaders, and target locations where complementary assets such as technology are most available (Li et al., 2012).

Institutional perspective

Firms in EE face business environments of extensive market imperfections, also known as institutional voids (Khanna and Rivkin, 2001; Meyer et al., 2009). Hence they develop practices and capabilities that enable them to fill or overcome such voids, and to succeed under such conditions. Once developed, such capabilities can become a foundation both for domestic diversification

DOI: 10.1057/9781137367204.0008

(Khanna and Palepu, 2000) and for international expansion into other EEs with similar market imperfections, and hence where such capabilities contribute to attaining competitive advantages locally. This institutional perspective thus suggests that the capabilities developed by EE MNEs in their domestic markets enable them to expand most easily where they find similar institutional conditions (Curvo-Cazurra and Genc, 2008; Henisz, 2003) and political risks (Holburn and Zelner, 2010).

A related institutional argument focuses on the close association of many EE MNEs with their home government. State ownership is relatively more widespread in emerging markets, in part because of former socialist legacies (Estrin et al., 2009) and the weakness of private capital markets (Globerman and Shapiro, 2002). Even where the state does not own firms, governments influence company decision-making directly through state ownership and more subtly through personal ties between managers and government officials (Lin, 2011). These relationships facilitate access to certain types of resources, but also create pressures to align firm strategies with government policy. For example, government-associated firms gain preferential access to guarantees, bank loans and information about the foreign business environment, as well as collaboration with research institutes and universities (Morck et al., 2008; Peng, 2012; Ramasamy et al., 2012).

As already noted, governmental support in the provision of resources comes at a price in terms of blurring corporate objectives, with SOEs in particular in a position of resource dependence and therefore required to align their FDI strategies to their government's policy goals. These policy goals vary from country to country; in the case of China, scholars emphasize acquiring natural resources and advanced technologies (Luo et al., 2010). Governmental financial support also makes the strategies of MNEs from EEs less sensitive to institutional deficiencies in the local environment, such as political risk or corruption, because the additional costs that these conditions impose are offset by implicit guarantees or the attainment of the non-material goals. Both arguments suggest that EE MNEs may have capabilities that are particularly suited for competing in less advanced institutional environments and they may be able to accept higher levels of political and economic risks than their DC competitors.

Learning perspective

To these established frameworks, Estrin and Meyer (2012) have added a third based on the relative inexperience of EE MNEs in global markets. Thus they argue that EE MNEs begin internationalization from a position of relative weakness compared to global leaders. They lack knowledge of how to overcome various barriers to entry that MNEs face when entering 'foreign' locations because they lack experience in both its general and its host country-specific forms (Clarke, Tamaschke and Liesch, 2012). Since EE MNEs are still in the early stages of their 'internationalization process' (Johansen and Vahlne, 2009), despite their often considerable size in their home country, their first challenge is to overcome barriers to entry given their limited experiential knowledge on how to operate under 'foreign' conditions (Autio, Sapienza and Almeida, 2000). Hence, many of the activities of EE firms outside their own country may perhaps be understood with reference to their contribution to the firm's capability-building process and learning trajectory (Li, 2010; Mathews, 2006).

The internationalization process is driven by both internal, experiential learning (Tsang, 2002) and external learning through knowledge sharing in business networks (Johansen and Vahlne, 2009; Meyer and Thaijongrak, 2013). Embeddedness in business networks shapes their processes of international learning and growth. At the early stages of internationalization, they thus tend to invest in locations where they can tap into existing networks of compatriots that facilitate their learning processes and operations (Tan and Meyer, 2012). Moreover EE MNEs use acquisitions of small firms abroad strategically to accelerate their internationalization processes and to overcome barriers to entry.

In the learning perspective, each FDI project is viewed in terms of its contribution to the firm's process of building a portfolio of competences that will eventually enable it to compete in its chosen markets internationally. EE MNEs have less international experience, and can draw on experience shared in their home community. Translated to the country-of-origin level, this 'maturity perspective' thus suggests that learning how to overcome high barriers to market entry in host economies and creating learning opportunities that assist in building capabilities would be key drivers of EE MNEs strategies.

Host economy characteristics and emerging market multinationals

I have argued that the diversification of national origins of MNEs has increased the heterogeneity of their organizational forms and ownership. In this chapter, I will concentrate on state owned enterprises (SOEs); that is, commercial organizations, which are majority or entirely owned by the state. SOEs are especially significant in the major emerging markets – BRICS – and increasingly compete on international markets. For example, out of ten Chinese firms in the Fortune Top 100 in 2012, nine were majority state owned. Brazil had two firms in the top 100, both of which were majority state owned. Similarly, the 2011 World Investment Report charts the increasing internationalization of SOEs. The number of outward FDI projects by SOEs increased from around 88,000 in 2003 to 146,000 in 2010, and their share in FDI outflow reached about 14 per cent in 2009 (UNCTAD, 2011). This raises the question of whether these firms will behave similarly or differently to privately owned MNEs.

DOI: 10.1057/9781137367204.0008

How does state ownership impact on firms' internationalization? SOEs differ from private, profit-oriented firms in terms of, for example, the objectives of the organization (Estrin and Perotin, 1991), management's attitude to risk (Borisova et al., 2012) and the firm's access to resources (Wang et al., 2012). The consequences of these differences are also influenced by the specific institutional environment in which SOEs operate. As Peng, Wang and Jiang (2008) emphasize, it is important to understand *how* specific institutions affect the behaviour of particular types of firms. While researchers have recognized the importance of both home and host country institutions, most empirical work has focused on host country characteristics (e.g. Meyer et al., 2009) or the distance between home and host countries (e.g. Tihanyi, Griffith and Russell, 2005). In contrast, the influence of home country institutions has been largely neglected; though it has been shown that country-of-origin factors exert important influences on firm strategies especially for EEs (Henisz and Zelner, 2010; Morck, Yeung and Zhao, 2008).

Views of the SOEs vary substantially with a key distinction being between benevolent contributions of SOEs to societies and non-benevolent actions of SOEs that are to the detriment of society at large. For example, Acemoglu and Robinson (2012) distinguish between inclusive and extractive states, whereas Shleifer and Vishny (1994) distinguish between the state's 'helping hand' and the state's 'grabbing hand'. Visions of benevolent impact of SOEs – the helping hand – underlie a number of roles that governments assign to them, depending on the political economy of a country (Hall and Soskice, 2001). Consistent with the free market model, SOEs serve specific purposes where pure market outcomes are considered either inefficient or socially undesirable. A social democratic vision views the state as being concerned with the distribution of income as well as with economic efficiency. For example, objectives of social welfare may be pursued by ensuring some degree of equality in the distribution of income and of opportunity. A third benevolent vision attributes to the state a direct role in economic development with SOEs strategically deployed to achieve the political objectives of a national or provincial government (Wang et al., 2012). Indeed, state ownership may enable funding of key industrialization or infrastructure projects that otherwise may remain unfunded (Prebisch, 1950). In transition economies like China or Vietnam, and market economies such as Singapore, the leading political traditions envision the state as guiding the process of market-driven economic development (Lin, 2011; Tipton, 2009).

In contrast, some scholars of SOEs emphasize the grabbing hand of the state, and view the strategies of SOEs as non-benevolent. Specifically, SOEs are seen to be used by politicians to exploit the state apparatus to achieve their personal goals; for example, providing benefits for their own supporters or extracting private rents (Faccio, 2006; Krueger, 1990; Shleifer and Vishny, 1994). Political economy studies suggest that elites can manage to capture and exploit SOEs

DOI: 10.1057/9781137367204.0008

for their own purposes, including for the extraction of rents, even in market economies (Acemoglu and Robinson, 2012). Under such a scenario, rather than follow strategies that maximize shareholder value, SOEs may seek to enable elites of the country, or the managers leading SOEs, to extract personal benefits. Such extractable rents are generated by dominant positions held by some SOEs within the domestic economy, and the domestic institutions supporting them, providing SOEs with some degree of protection from competition and monitoring. For example, SOEs may be used to create or maintain employment among politically influential groups, such as voters in critical political constituencies.

The essence of these arguments is that SOEs are subject to contrary pressures of benevolent and non-benevolent motivations. The balance of these two pressures varies across countries. If benevolent motives dominate, SOEs will act in many ways like private enterprises, yet with some specific objectives added. If, on the other hand, non-benevolent motives dominate, SOEs may be used by elites or managers for their personal ends, in particular to extract rents. These rents are normally found and extricated domestically, having been carefully constructed and protected by policy and regulation (Applebaum and Katz, 1987). Hence non-benevolent SOEs are probably associated with lower levels of internationalization. To what extent SOEs are following benevolent or non-benevolent motives will depend on a more detailed specification of the institutional context in which they are operating.

It is therefore not straightforward to predict the impact of state ownership on MNE internationalization strategies. In some situations, the emphasis on the domestic economy, either for the state to address market failures or for elites to extract rents, will lead state-owned firms to undertake less FDI than would be done in a comparable private firm. On the other hand, the state as owner might use its firms to spearhead an internationalization drive in order to achieve its development goals. Moreover, as Estrin et al., (2013) have stressed, the outcome will depend on other aspects of the country-of-origin business environment, notably the institutional structure. The fundamental point remains that the standard models of MNE strategy will have to be adapted to take account of factors such as ownership and institutional arrangements when FDI from emerging markets is the subject of analysis.

Conclusions

I have argued that MNEs from emerging markets are indeed a new and significant phenomenon that researchers in international business will have to take increasingly seriously in the future. There is no doubt that our existing theories and models provide a solid framework for analysing their behaviour. But there are also a number of important factors that will need to be taken into

DOI: 10.1057/9781137367204.0008

account as our theories evolve to address these challenges. I have outlined two factors in this chapter: the strategic motives of EE MNEs in undertaking FDI and the increasing significance of country-of-origin factors, for example concerning ownership and governance. Future research should develop deeper theorizing on the relationship between the source country context, MNE resources, strategy, governance and host economy context. These new and enriched theories will then require validation by empirical testing, which highlights the need for more and higher quality data on EE MNEs, in a form that allows the literature to proceed beyond single-country studies to identify the complex interrelationships between source and host country effects. At the same time there remains much space for country-specific studies that could explore in-depth the dynamics of the way firm-specific resources and institutions interact to influence the process of internationalization. There is much to be done and so the study of emerging economy multinationals seems likely to be an important subject for researchers in international business for many years to come.

References

Acemoglu D. and Robinson, J. (2012) *Why Nations Fail*. New York: Crown Publishing.
Autio, E., Sapienza, H.J. and Almeida, J.G. (2000) Effects of age at entry, knowledge intensity, and imitability on international growth. *Academy of Management Journal*, 43: 909–24.
Barney, J. (1991) Firm resources and sustained competitive advantage. *Journal of Management*, 17: 99–120.
Borisova, G., Fotak, V., Holland, K. and Megginson, W. (2012) Government ownership and the cost of debt: evidence from government investments in publicly traded firms, working paper, SSRN no. 2127397.
Buckley, P.J., Clegg, J., Cross, A., Liu, X., Voss, H. and Zheng, P. (2007) The determinants of Chinese outward FDI. *Journal of International Business Studies*, 38(4): 499–518.
Caves, R. (1996) *Multinational Enterprise and Economic Analysis*. 2nd edn. Cambridge: Cambridge University Press.
Child, J. and Rodrigues, S.B. (2005) The internationalization of Chinese firms: a case for theoretical extension? *Management and Organization Review*, 1(3): 381–410.
Clarke, J.E., Tamaschke, R. and Liesch, P. (2012) International experience in international business research: a conceptualization and exploration of key themes. *International Journal of Management Reviews*, advance online.
Cuervo-Cazurra, A. and Genc, M. (2008) Transforming disadvantages into advantages: developing country MNEs in the least developed countries. *Journal of International Business Studies*, 39(6): 957–79.
Cui, L. and Jiang, F. (2012) State ownership effect on firms' FDI ownership decisions under institutional pressure: a study of Chinese outward-investing firms. *Journal of International Business Studies*, 43(3): 264–84.
Deng, P. (2009) Why do Chinese firms tend to acquire strategic assets in international expansion? *Journal of World Business*, 44(1): 74–84.
Dunning, J.H. (1980) Towards an eclectic theory of international production: some empirical tests, *Journal of International Business Studies*, 11: 9–31.

DOI: 10.1057/9781137367204.0008

Dunning, J.H. (1998) Location and the multinational enterprise: A neglected factor? *Journal of International Business Studies*, 29(1): 45–66.

Estrin, S., Hanousek, J., Kocenda, E. and Svejnar, J. (2009) The effects of privatization and ownership in transition economies. *Journal of Economic Literature*, 47(3): 699–728.

Estrin, S. and Meyer, K. (2012) How Different are Emerging Economy MNEs? A Comparative Study of Location Choice. LSE mimeo.

Estrin, S., Meyer, K., Nielson, B. and Nielson, S. (2013) The Internationalization of State Owned Enterprises: An Institutional Perspective. LSE mimeo.

Estrin, S. and Perotin, V. (1991) Does ownership always matter? *International Journal of Industrial Organization*, 9(1): 55–72.

Faccio, M. (2006) Politically connected firms. *American Economic Review*, 96(1): 369–86.

Globerman, S. and Shapiro, D. (2002) Global foreign direct investment flows: the role of governance infrastructures. *World Development*, 30(11): 1899–919.

Guillén, M.F. and Garcia-Canal, E. (2009) The American model of the multinational firm and the 'new' multinationals from emerging economies. *Academy of Management Perspectives*, 23(2): 23–35.

Habib, M. and Zurawicki, L. (2002) Corruption and foreign direct investment. *Journal of International Business Studies*, 33: 291–307.

Hall, P.A. and Soskice, D.W. (eds) (2001) *Varieties of Capitalism*. Cambridge: Cambridge University Press.

Henisz, W.J. (2003) The power of the Buckley and Casson thesis: the ability to manage institutional idiosyncrasies. *Journal of International Business Studies*, 34(2): 173–84.

Henisz, W.J. and Zelner, B.A. (2010) The hidden risks in emerging markets. *Harvard Business Review*, 88: 88–95.

Hennart, J.F. (2009) Down with MNE-centric theories! Market entry and expansion as the bundling of MNE and local assets. *Journal of International Business Studies*, 40(9): 1432–54.

Hennart, J.F. (2012) Emerging market multinationals and the theory of the multinational enterprise. *Global Strategy Journal*, 2(3): 168–87.

Holburn, G.L.F. and Zelner, B.A. (2010) Political capabilities, policy risk, and international investment strategy: evidence from the global electric power generation industry. *Strategic Management Journal*, 31(12): 1290–315.

Johanson, J. and Vahlne, J.E. (2009) The Uppsala internationalization process model revisited: from liability of foreignness to liability of outsidership. *Journal of International Business Studies*, 40(9): 1411–31.

Khanna, T. and Palepu, K. (2000) The future of business groups in emerging markets: long run evidence from Chile. *Academy of Management Journal*, 43(3): 268–85.

Khanna, T. and Rivkin, J. (2001) Estimating the performance effects of business groups in emerging markets. *Strategic Management Journal*, 22: 45–74.

Krueger, A.O. (1990) Government failures in development. *Journal of Economic Perspectives*, 4(3): 9–23.

Li, P.P. (2010) Toward a learning-based view of internationalization: the accelerated trajectories of cross-border learning for latecomers. *Journal of International Management*, 16: 43–59.

Li, J., Li, Y., Shapiro, D. (2012) Knowledge seeking and outward FDI by emerging market firms: the moderating effect of inward FDI. *Global Strategy Journal*, 2(4): 277–95.

Lin, N. (2011) Capitalism in China: a centrally managed capitalism (CMC) and its future. *Management Organization Review*, 7(1): 63–96.

Luo, Y.D. and Tung, R.L. (2007) International expansion of emerging market enterprises: a springboard perspective. *Journal of International Business Studies*, 38(4): 481–98.

DOI: 10.1057/9781137367204.0008

Luo, Y.D., Xue, Q. and Han B. (2010) How emerging market governments promote outward FDI: experience from China. *Journal of World Business*, 45(1): 68–79.

Meyer, K.E. and Thaijongrak, O. (2013) The dynamics of emerging economy MNEs: how the internationalization process model can guide future research. *Asia Pacific Journal of Management*, online advance.

Meyer, K.E., Estrin, S., Bhaumik, S.K. and Peng, M. (2009) Institutions, resources, and entry strategies in emerging economies. *Strategic Management Journal*, 30(1): 61–80.

Morck, R. Wolfenzon, D. and Yeung, B. (2005) Corporate governance, economic entrenchment, and growth. *Journal of Economic Literature*, 43(3): 655–720.

Morck, R., Yeung, B. and Zhao, M. (2008) Perspectives on China's outward foreign direct investment. *Journal of International Business Studies*, 39(3): 337–50.

Narula, R. (2012) Do we need different frameworks to explain infant MNEs from developing countries? *Global Strategy Journal*, 2(3): 188–204.

O'Neill, J. (2012) *The Growth Map*. London: Penguin.

Peng, M.W. (2012) The global strategy of emerging multinationals from China. *Global Strategy Journal*, 2(2): 97–107.

Peng, M.W., Wang, D. and Jiang, Y. (2008) An institution-based view of international business strategy: a focus on emerging economies. *Journal of International Business Studies*, 39: 920–36.

Prebisch, R. (1950) *The Economic Development of Latin America and its Principal Problems*. New York: United Nations.

Ramamurti, R. (2012) What is really different about emerging market multinationals? *Global Strategy Journal*, 2(1): 41–7.

Ramasamy, B., Yeung, M., Laforet, S. (2012) China's outward foreign direct investment: location choice and firm ownership. *Journal of World Business*, 47(1): 17–25.

Rugman, A.M. (1982) *New Theories of the Multinational Enterprise*. New York: Taylor and Francis.

Rugman, A.M. (2009) Theoretical aspects of MNEs from emerging economies, in: R. Ramamurti and J.V. Singh (eds) *Emerging Multinationals in Emerging Markets*. New York: Cambridge University Press, pp. 42–63.

Rui, H. and Yip, G.S. (2008) Foreign acquisitions by Chinese firms: a strategic intent perspective. *Journal of World Business*, 43(2): 213–26.

Shleifer, A. and Vishny, R.W. (1994) Politicians and firms. *Quarterly Journal of Economics*, 109: 995–1025.

Tan, D. and Meyer, K.E. (2012) Country of origin and industry FDI agglomeration of foreign investors in an emerging economy. *Journal of International Business Studies*, 42: 504–30.

Tihanyi, L., Griffith, D.A. and Russell, C.J. (2005) The effect of cultural distance on entry mode choice, international diversification, and MNE performance: a meta-analysis. *Journal of International Business Studies*, 36: 270–83.

Tipton, F.B. (2009) Southeast Asian capitalism: history, institutions, states, and firms. *Asia Pacific Journal of Management*, 26(3): 401–34.

Tsang. E. (2002) Acquiring knowledge by foreign partners from international joint ventures in a transition economy: learning by doing and learning myopia. *Strategic Management Journal*, 23(9): 835–54.

UNCTAD (2011) *World Investment Report*. Geneva: United Nations.

Verbeke, A. and Kano, L.L. (2012) No new theory needed to study MNEs from emerging economies. AIB Conference, Washington DC, June.

DOI: 10.1057/9781137367204.0008

Wang, C.Q., Hong, J.J., Kafouros, M. and Wright, M. (2012) Exploring the role of government involvement in outward FDI from emerging economies. *Journal of International Business Studies*, 43: 655–76.

Yang, X.H., Jiang, Y., Kang, R.P. and Ke, Y.B. (2009) A comparative analysis of the internationalization of Chinese and Japanese firms. *Asia Pacific Journal of Management*, 26(1): 141–62.

Yiu, D.W., Lau, C.M. and Bruton, G.D. (2007) International venturing by emerging economy firms: the effects of firm capabilities, home country networks, and corporate entrepreneurship. *Journal of International Business Studies*, 38(4): 519–40.

Young, M.N., Peng, M.W., Ahlstrom, D., Bruton, G.D. and Jiang, Y. (2008) Corporate governance in emerging economies: a review of the principal-principal perspective. *Journal of Management Studies*, 45(1): 196–220.

Zaheer, S. (1995) Overcoming the liability of foreigness. *Academy of Management Journal*, 38(2): 341–63.

Zeng, M. and Williamson, P. (2007) *Dragons at Your Door*. Boston: Harvard Business School Press.

DOI: 10.1057/9781137367204.0008

2
The Role of International Business in the Global Spread of Technological Innovation

John Cantwell

Background: revisiting Marx and social evolution

This chapter considers the relationship between the globalization of business and the international location of technological innovation in historical perspective. These processes, globalization and innovation, are the two key mechanisms through which capitalism has developed and progressed as an economic system over the past 200 years or so. Somewhat ironically, in view of the anti-capitalist political and social movements that have been founded in his name, it was Marx who clearly identified how these two main drivers of the forces of production under capitalism work in tandem with one another to generate enormously powerful economic development, relative to the standards of any pre-capitalist society. So I begin by revisiting Marx's argument in order to better appreciate the historical context for globalization and innovation as key elements in modern social evolution, before turning in the latter part of the chapter to some evidence on the relationship between the two in the most recent phase of global economic development since 1950. Two quotations will serve to illustrate how, according to Marx, capitalist economic progress is characterized by a combination of ever deepening internationalization and continuous technological development.

> The bourgeoisie has through its exploitation of the world market given a cosmopolitan character to production and consumption in every country. To the great chagrin of Reactionists, it has drawn from under the feet of industry the national ground on which it stood. All old-established national industries have been destroyed or are daily being destroyed. They have been dislodged by new industries, whose introduction becomes a life and death question for all civilized nations, by industries that no longer work up

DOI: 10.1057/9781137367204.0009

indigenous raw material, but raw material drawn from the remotest zones; industries whose products are consumed, not only at home, but in every quarter of the globe. In place of the old wants, satisfied by the productions of the country, we find new wants, requiring for their satisfaction the products of distant lands and climes. In place of the old local and national seclusion and self-sufficiency, we have intercourse in every direction, universal inter-dependence of nations. (Marx and Engels, 1848, pp. 46–7)

The bourgeoisie cannot exist without constantly revolutionizing the instru-ments of production, and thereby the relations of production, and with them the whole relations of society.…. Constant revolutionizing of production, uninterrupted disturbance of all social conditions, everlasting uncertainty and agitation distinguish the bourgeois epoch from all earlier ones.…. The bourgeoisie, during its rule of scarce one hundred years, has created more massive and more colossal productive forces than have all preceding genera-tions together. Subjection of Nature's forces to man, machinery, application of chemistry to industry and agriculture, steam navigation, railways, electric telegraphs, clearing of whole continents for cultivation, canalization of rivers, whole populations conjured out of the ground – what earlier century had even a presentiment that such productive forces slumbered in the lap of social labour? (Marx and Engels, 1848, pp. 45, 45–6 and 48)

Despite the greater attention that is generally paid (both by Marxists and their critics) to Marx's view of the role of class antagonisms as a driver of social change, and to his belief in a revolutionary transition from capitalism to socialism leading ultimately to communism, the central underlying mech-anism in Marx's theory of history remains a continuous process of inherent evolution of the entire system of production and the society within which it is embedded in response to the development needs of each epoch. Building especially upon the insights found in Hegel's philosophy of history, Marx's approach held that the basis for any new society is gradually built up within the old. Occasional historical transitions from one society to another occur when an existing society has essentially exhausted its potential to develop effectively the forces of production, giving impetus to some newer social for-mation that is capable of initiating and sustaining more powerful economic development, and which emerges steadily and gains momentum within the old society. Thus, this perspective on social evolution contends:

No social order ever disappears before all the productive forces, for which there is room in it, have been developed; and new, higher relations of pro-duction never appear before the material conditions of their existence have matured in the womb of the old society itself. Therefore, mankind always

DOI: 10.1057/9781137367204.0009

sets itself only such tasks as it can solve; since, looking at the matter more closely, we will always find that the task itself arises only when the material conditions necessary for its solution already exist or are at least in the process of formation. (Marx, 1859, pp. 12–13)

Now taking this social evolutionary perspective from the vantage point of the present day, unlike that of the nineteenth century when Marx was writing, I believe it is clear that what he termed the capitalist mode of production has subsequently evolved through different types. I suggest that there are three forms of capitalism that have followed one another in an historical sequence since the time of the first industrial revolution, and they are sufficiently different from one another that they might even be considered as distinct, new modes of production. While this is not the place to develop this argument more fully, I would also draw attention in this context to Marx's view that (in more modern terminology) the technology of production, organizational forms and institutions co-evolve such as to collectively mark out and distinguish any given society from others that have existed historically.

> Social relations are closely bound up with productive forces. In acquiring new productive forces men change their mode of production; and in changing their mode of production, in changing their way of living, they change all their social relations. The hand-mill gives you society with the feudal lord; the steam-mill, society with the industrial capitalist. The same men who establish their social relations in conformity with their material productivity, produce also principles, ideas and categories, in conformity with their social relations. ..... Labour is organized, is divided differently according to the instruments it disposes over. The hand-mill presupposes a different division of labour from the steam-mill. (Marx, 1847, pp. 95 and 116)

Marx used the term 'modern industry' to distinguish the most advanced form of capitalism that had emerged up until the time he was writing in the aftermath of the industrial revolution in the late eighteenth century, from the earlier forms of handicraft (the putting out system) and then manufacture (the earliest factory system). This transition to 'modern industry' occurred between the middle of the eighteenth century and the middle of the nineteenth, as reflected in the reference to 'its rule of scarce one hundred years' in Marx and Engels' from writing 1848. To reflect the centrality of technological innovation and international business coordination as drivers of each phase of capitalist development since the industrial revolution, as I argued at the start, I suggest distinguishing now between the following types of capitalism: machinery-based and trade-based capitalism, from the late eighteenth to the late nineteenth century (which was the type of capitalism analysed by

DOI: 10.1057/9781137367204.0009

Marx as 'modern industry'); science-based and managerially-coordinated capitalism, from the late nineteenth to the late twentieth century; and information-based and internationally-networked capitalism, which has emerged since the late twentieth century. To build on Marx's analogy, if the steam-mill was representative of machinery-based and trade-based capitalism, the oil-powered electro-mechanical plant was representative of science-based and managerially-coordinated capitalism, while the micro-electronic computer is representative of information-based and internationally-networked capitalism. It is surely not hard for any objective observer to see that the nature of society and the system of production today is very different to that of 70 years ago, let alone to that of 170 years ago. Despite some commonalities over time, each new phase of capitalist development has been the outcome of some major transformations of its predecessor that emerged from within.

The changed nature of technology and organization in the techno-socio-economic paradigms for innovation with which each of these three forms of capitalism has been associated has been well documented by Freeman and Perez (1988), von Tunzelmann (1995) and Freeman and Louçã (2001). The central role of mechanization in the first paradigm from roughly the 1770s to the 1870s was reflected in the representation of technological change by Ricardo and Marx as the introduction of machinery into production, and the acquisition of steadily more sophisticated and improved machinery. In the second paradigm from roughly the 1870s to the 1970s the relationship between science and technology became closer and more direct, as discussed by Bernal (1954), Mowery and Rosenberg (1989) and Rosenberg and Nelson (1996), and which can be represented by the electrification of industry and the emergence of organic chemistry, in systems of mass production especially driven by new large industrial firms, as documented by Chandler (1990). In the most recent paradigm since around the 1970s, the pervasiveness of information and communication technologies has been associated with the computerization of production processes in every industry, the fragmentation of production and decomposition or modularization of the value chain, and more flexible and cooperative networked organizational forms, as discussed by Freeman (1987), Lazonick (1992) and Freeman and Louçã (2001).

The one point I wish to emphasize here is that the classical theories of industrial growth pioneered by Smith, Ricardo and Marx largely reflected conditions and trends that were characteristic of the machinery-based and trade-based capitalism of their day. Unlike the institution-free and ahistorical approaches found in much neoclassical economics, which proceed by way of logical deduction from a priori axioms of rational human behaviour in general, it cannot be supposed that the classical theories remain equally applicable to the analysis of the information-based and internationally-networked capitalism of today. In particular, in moving between the three different phases of

DOI: 10.1057/9781137367204.0009

capitalism identified, the processes of technological accumulation have become steadily more separated from the processes of capital accumulation that in classical theories had been largely treated as synonymous. Marx devoted a good deal of attention to the social processes in modern industry that made technological change a path-dependent cumulative process (see e.g. Rosenberg, 1976), and this argument retains its perceptive validity through to the present. Yet in the era of mechanization in his day most technological improvements were embodied in new machinery, so it was feasible to draw a direct parallel between technological accumulation and the accumulation of investments in machinery. Thus, Marx related technological change in machinery-based capitalism to a rise in the volume of machinery per worker (the technical composition of capital), and to a consequent belief in a tendency towards an increase in the value of machinery used up in production relative to the wage bill, or what he termed the ratio of dead to living labour (the organic composition of capital).

In science-based capitalism instead technological change became increasingly disembodied in knowledge and expertise, and a growing proportion of problem-solving efforts went 'off-line' in the form of corporate research and development (R&D). As is well known, the managerial coordination of this epoch was also founded on a separation between the ownership of capital (the means of production) and the control of production. Today, in information-based and internationally-networked capitalism matters have gone much further, and achieving disembodied technological change (improvements in the state of technological knowledge and its operationalization) relies upon the capacity to access and coordinate a range of complementary capabilities whose ownership and location may be quite widely dispersed, rather than depending upon the direct ownership of the means of production. Crucially, this has meant that the processes of technological accumulation have also been moved increasingly to an international level, as I argued some years ago (Cantwell, 1989).

So to return to the second key driver of productivity growth alongside technological innovation, namely globalization, the nature of international business too has been transformed over the past 200 years. Following the expansion of international trade in the era of machinery-based capitalism, the significance of which is noted in the quotes from Marx and Engels with which I began, the era of science-based capitalism ushered in what is these days sometimes termed the 'first wave' of globalization, while the arrival of information-based capitalism more recently has been associated with a 'second wave' of globalization. The term 'globalization' used in this context implies the proactive managerial coordination of distant production facilities, which became feasible only with the transport and communication technologies that were developed in the mid-nineteenth century, as explained by Chandler (1990) and Wilkins (2009).

DOI: 10.1057/9781137367204.0009

In other words, it includes the foreign direct investment (FDI) of modern multinational corporations (MNCs), and not just international trade and the interdependence of markets internationally. A drawback of some of the historical comparisons of the first and second waves of globalization is that they are overly focused on the relatively impressive historical scale of globalization, using indicators such as the ratio of FDI or trade to gross domestic product (GDP) at a country level (see e.g. O'Rourke and Williamson, 1999). More to the point here is the way in which the character of globalization has evolved, owing to the fragmentation of production and the orchestration of global production networks, associated with a substantial rise in trade in intermediate products relative to final products.

The focus of attention in what remains in this chapter is on another related aspect of how globalization has changed when moving into this new phase of capitalist development. In each new wave of globalization a gradually broader range of countries has been brought into the industrialized and innovative group, as they have caught up with the leading locations for technological development. Yet as capitalism has evolved from one type to another the conditions for catching up have changed, and hence the mechanisms by which catch up has been achieved – where it has – have undergone an equivalent transformation. In the first wave of globalization with the arrival of science-based capitalism, the USA and Germany caught up through the emergence and rapid growth of firms in the science-based industries, in which they were leaders and benefited from first mover advantages, as discussed by Chandler (1990). Later in this era, Japan and subsequently South Korea caught up by building entire national industrial systems grounded on machinery-based innovation then steadily integrated with science-based industries, through the span of domestic activities organized by large business groups – the zaibatsu, and then the keiretsu and the chaebols. By the time of the catch up of Korea, which began late in the science-based era of mass production, and with the emergence of information-based internationally-networked capitalism, subcontracting was vital to their technological learning from foreign multinationals (Hobday, 2000), just as licensing had been for Japanese firms earlier in the post-war period (Ozawa, 1974).

With the arrival of information-based and internationally-networked capitalism the most prominent and striking technological catch up experiences have been those of China and India. These latest countries catching up have relied more extensively still on the global connections that have become associated with the second wave of globalization. Rather than focusing on building large scale domestic inter-industry networks, these countries have been able to grow rapidly in specialized positions or nodes in a steadily changing international division of labour, as value chains have become further decomposed and globally redistributed. In the remainder of this chapter I examine some evidence

DOI: 10.1057/9781137367204.0009

for the connections between globalization and the technological catch up of some selected countries in the recent period.

Technological catch up with the emergence of the information age

Not so long ago it was quite commonplace to argue that with the tightening of World Trade Organization (WTO) rules and intellectual property rights (IPR) enforcement strategies, less developed countries would find themselves locked into an unfavourable international division of labour. Having been blocked from protecting the growth of their infant industries, or from using strategies of technological imitation, no newcomer country would be able to replicate the successful development experience of Korea or Japan – let alone the USA or Germany in a still earlier era. Each of these countries had used selective protection and imitation as part of a wider strategy for industrialization and technological development. Yet the strong role attributed to these aspects of catch up in the past relied on the evidence of what had been achieved in an earlier era under different conditions more generally (not just in the world trade policy environment), and in which protection and imitation had to be understood in each case in the context of a supporting raft of national institutional structures well suited to the demands of the period in question. In the USA the foundation of mass production systems with interchangeable parts on the basis of a large domestic market was vital (Chandler, 1990). In Germany the connections of science-based industry with university research and professional associations especially in chemistry proved critical (Murmann, 2003). In Japan and Korea the support for imitation and innovation provided by the domestic business groups and their foreign technology licensing and subcontracting has already been mentioned (Freeman, 1987; Ozawa, 1974).

More often during the science-based and managerially-coordinated era, the national institutional framework within which trade protection occurred made that protection a recipe for inefficiency and backwardness, owing to the reduction in the competitive impetus for innovation. Such was the general experience of Latin America with so-called import substitution industrialization (ISI). On average, Latin American countries moved backwards or failed to advance in the relative development ranks of countries, comparing their position by the start of the twenty-first century with that around the turn of the twentieth century. While the Latin American average GDP per capita was about 43 per cent of the equivalent western European average in 1913, it had fallen to around 29 per cent by 2003 (Maddison, 2007). Compared to the USA on the same index of economic development, Latin America declined from 28 per cent to under 20 per cent over the same period, 1913–2003. In other words, during this era of capitalism Latin America did not catch up, but

DOI: 10.1057/9781137367204.0009

fell further behind. Clearly, even for those that have espoused ISI strategies for development, these strategies were very far from being sufficient to ensure catch up, even during the period when such policies may have been a part of some more successful development experiences.

The conventional wisdom that it would be harder to catch up in a new environment of tighter enforcement of WTO rules and IPR regimes ignored two other crucial changes associated with the emergence of the information age. First, there has been an increasing international spread of scientific establishments, which geographical dispersal has made viable localized science-technology connections (university-industry relationships) in the process of building corporate technological capabilities in a wider array of locations (Mazzoleni and Nelson, 2007). Related to this phenomenon of better local training and research support in what have become known as the emerging market economies, the upside of having IP markets that are internationalized as they have begun to function more reliably across national borders is the opportunity this has created for new players to obtain returns on IP creation from international licensing. While dominant incumbent firms may continue to retain their position in the technologies behind the mainstream products of an industry (e.g. personal computer operating systems such as MS Windows in the case of software) and can extract more effectively the rents associated with such a position, many new niche applications can be developed by independent firms, which build up the relevant expertise in various other locations that have particular kinds of specialized knowledge (e.g. software customized for the needs of selected other industries or business functions). The more effective operation of international IP markets has made it feasible for some new players to get returns from innovation without depending on a substantial domestic production base and product market. I will report further on supportive evidence of this having occurred.

Second, and as already alluded to, as flexible specialized systems came to adapt and transform those of mass production, with the emergence of information-based capitalism from within science-based capitalism, production became steadily more fragmented. The decomposition of value chains that in the previous era had become more integrated now became associated with modularization, outsourcing and the continual geographical redistribution and shift in the ownership patterns of activities in global production networks (GPNs). The operation of these GPNs has widened the dispersion of knowledge both across actors and countries, and it has facilitated the emergence of some new knowledge-creating nodes, where local capabilities have been built up to fulfil specialized roles within GPNs. While GPNs are still at an early stage of development, the rapid growth in the presence of foreign-owned R&D facilities in China and India is indicative of the changed environment they are cultivating. In a recent study I co-authored, we found a reversal of an earlier trend

DOI: 10.1057/9781137367204.0009

towards a rising cross-country concentration of technological resources, and we examined how globalization has been connected to this shift (Athreye and Cantwell, 2007). We looked at the impacts of both international trade and FDI on the international location of technological activity.

Part of this story involves a more direct connection between international trade and FDI with the emergence of information-based and internationally-coordinated capitalism. While some theoretical models at the firm level had postulated a substitution effect (a choice) between home country exports and outward FDI in the market-seeking case, various studies have demonstrated the existence of a complementary relationship between international trade and FDI in the aggregate (e.g. Lipsey and Weiss, 1981). Even market-seeking FDI has always tended to be positively related to both home and host country trade (see Cantwell, 1994, for a fuller discussion). As FDI has become more internationally integrated in the form of GPNs, the positive association with trade (and jobs) has been reinforced – since with geographically dispersed value chains, the share of intermediate product trade associated with the orchestration of GPNs has risen sharply relative to trade in final products. As a further reflection of this changing structure of trade in a period of falling transport and communication costs, the greatest barrier to trade today is inventory holding costs, rather than protectionism or transport costs. The cost of warehousing or storage outweighs the cost of shipping in a poorly managed GPN, and this is where the effective use of information technology in managing stocks at each stage has become vital. Keane and Feinberg (2006) have shown that improved technology and logistics including just in time (JIT) systems explain much of the rapid growth in intra-firm trade that has been observed.

So as MNCs innovate and gradually develop better systems to manage international business networks, trade increases within their GPNs. Yet this in turn feeds back into increased FDI, and so an ever closer association between FDI and trade. GPNs associated with MNCs account for about 80 per cent of world trade, according to a recent UNCTAD report (UNCTAD, 2013). Around 28 per cent of gross exports consist of the value of imported intermediate products that are then incorporated into exported goods and services from the same country (UNCTAD, 2013). The same source has shown that the share of emerging market economies (EMEs) in world trade associated with GPNs has climbed from around 20 per cent in 1990 to about 30 per cent in 2000, and over 40 per cent today. In EMEs, trade connected to GPNs accounts for about 28 per cent of a country's GDP on average, compared to 18 per cent for mature industrialized countries. This illustrates the role of this new form of the internationalization of business in contemporary catch up processes in the information age.

In our analysis, Athreye and I reasoned in terms of two stages of development in countries catching up, each associated with a different level of capabilities on the part of firms in the host country. In an earlier stage of technological

DOI: 10.1057/9781137367204.0009

catch up firms rely on simpler capabilities, small companies may play a more prominent independent entrepreneurial role, and there is less dependence upon international knowledge connectedness. We suggested that such basic capabilities will be reflected in the wide range of intellectual property for which licensing revenues can be earned, which international licensing receipts thus offer a measure of the extent of foundational capabilities developed by firms in a country. Instead, higher levels of technological development require sustained international knowledge interdependencies especially in the current era, and the more advanced capabilities associated with international knowledge exchange are generally needed for a country to become a significant inventive source of patents. Therefore we used patents invented in a country as our measure of such later stage development, taking patents granted in the USA but invented abroad as a common benchmark for international comparisons.

We argued that the relationship between the globalization of business and technological catch up in a country is likely to differ for early stage and later stage development. Openness to product trade is likely to be helpful for attaining earlier stages of development – a capacity to create simpler knowledge-based outputs that can be licensed – since openness provides potential access to markets for higher quality products. Inward FDI is less likely to matter for earlier phases of development – countries becoming sources of licensing revenues – for which the growth of technology trade matters more. Conversely, an expansion of inward FDI is more likely to matter for higher stages of development – countries becoming sources of patenting – as it fosters the international knowledge connections on which more complex technologies depend. When considering where to locate their foreign subsidiary activity, MNCs require good local capabilities and infrastructure in a host country site. Having been attracted once development passes the critical threshold, FDI then facilitates the consolidation of higher level capabilities, even though it isn't usually the means by which lower level capabilities are initially built.

As just mentioned, two indices of the technological ability of nations are their share of international licensing revenues, and of the foreign origin patents issued by the US Patent and Trademark Office (USPTO). From each of these measures we can calculate a Herfindahl index of concentration (of licensing revenues or patent shares) across countries as a summary measure of the extent of unevenness in the varying technological ability of nations at any point in time. A chart illustrating the trends in this index since 1950 is shown in Figure 2.1. It can be seen that as depicted by a downward trend in the index of geographical concentration, a technological catch up process began in terms of basic capabilities (licensing revenues) from around the mid-1970s onwards, and in terms of more advanced capabilities (patents) from the early 1990s onwards.

We examined the relationship between a decline in each of these indices of geographical concentration of innovative efforts, or technological catch

DOI: 10.1057/9781137367204.0009

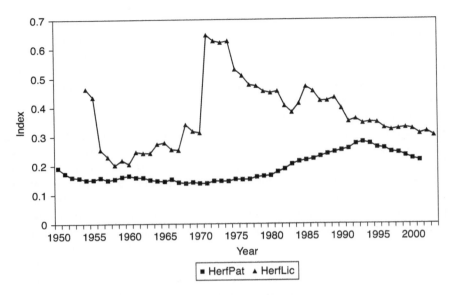

Figure 2.1   Herfindahl index of patents and licensing revenues
Source: Athreye and Cantwell (2007).

up, and our indicators of the globalization of business. Our statistical analysis revealed that increasing inward FDI (which implies existing international
knowledge connectedness of locations) leads to the emergence of new higher
level technology producers capable of patenting. For earlier level development
associated with the emergence of new licensors, greater openness to trade is
helpful, but what matters most is the opportunities created for new participants by the tremendously rapid growth of IP markets (see Figure 2.2), and the
fragmentation of production (GPNs).

These findings indicate that in the earlier stages of capability development,
catch up tends to rely mainly on a localized and indigenous learning that isn't
closely interconnected with current knowledge creation elsewhere in the world
through FDI. However it has been stimulated by more informal institutional
channels for IB connections, such as trade, subcontracting and especially the
recent growth of IP markets. Instead, in the later stages of catch up in higher
order types of innovative activity, acquiring sufficient absorptive capacity to
join existing international knowledge networks by attracting an expansion of
FDI (an extension of MNC networks) is more likely to be a precondition.

In GPNs, the middle stages of value chains (including assembly and some
elementary processing tasks) may migrate to emerging market economies,
assisting the migration of simpler innovation reliant on basic capabilities, with
the support of trade and GPN connections (see Mudambi, 2008). In this case

DOI: 10.1057/9781137367204.0009

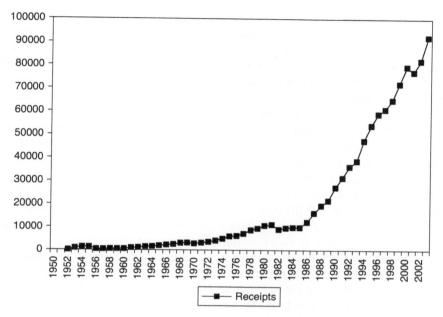

Figure 2.2 Royalty and licensing fees (1950–2003) ($ millions)
Source: Athreye and Cantwell (2007).

innovation is more widely geographically dispersed (or 'the world is flat' in the terminology of Friedman, 2005). By developing basic capabilities firms in emerging market economies can lay the basis for more technical capabilities, and hence may be able to begin to move up or down along the value chain, in either direction from the low point in the middle of the 'smile' of value creation and towards R&D on the one side or product design and branding on the other. In this phase, the local embeddedness of subsidiaries evolving towards competence-creating activities can become a driver or support for the development of a local host country innovation system into more advanced capabilities. In this case innovation is more clustered in key poles of development (or 'the world is spiky' in the language of Florida, 2005). GPNs permit catch up with a narrower range of national specialization than in the earlier historical era of mass production systems locally connected to a spectrum of science-based industries (see Cantwell and Vertova, 2004). Moreover the current increasing informality of GPN relationships requires closer connections between the internal and external networks of MNCs, for example, in project teams, which create new opportunities for partner organizations located elsewhere.

Indeed, the competitive advantage of mature MNCs increasingly stems from their ability to integrate GPNs in ways that facilitate the development of new

DOI: 10.1057/9781137367204.0009

capabilities across the nodes they coordinate over time. The locus of new capability building is now more widely distributed and decentralized in many MNCs, and knowledge flows are increasingly reciprocal. The dispersion of innovation implies a dispersion of control in the MNC network. International MNC networks for innovation have evolved towards an enhanced differentiation of subsidiary capabilities (Cantwell and Mudambi, 2005). Parent-subsidiary knowledge relationships have become stronger, and the 'dual embeddedness' of subsidiaries in both their internal MNC group and external networks are more pronounced still as the extent of local creativity rises. Thus sharply separating the treatment of internal and external networks may now often be misleading (see Cantwell, 2013), counter to the common choice theoretic frameworks (through reference with respect to e.g. the make or buy decision) generally still utilized in transaction cost economics, much of the alliance literature and so on. Informal crossover networks combine internal and external diversity to foster greater creativity and innovation. This is one of the most pertinent illustrations of how analytical frameworks and assumptions must be changed as the nature of capitalism shifts once more, calling for some reconsideration of where we should focus our scholarly attention, and for a better and deeper appreciation of some of the new realities.

References

Athreye, S.S. and Cantwell, J.A. (2007) Creating competition? Globalisation and the emergence of new technology producers. *Research Policy*, 36(2): 209–26.

Bernal, J.D. (1954) *Science in History*. London: Faber and Faber (later editions published by Cambridge, Mass.: MIT Press).

Cantwell, J.A. (1989) *Technological Innovation and Multinational Corporations*. Oxford: Basil Blackwell.

Cantwell, J.A. (1994) The relationship between international trade and international production, in D. Greenaway and L.A. Winters (eds) *Surveys in International Trade*. Oxford: Basil Blackwell.

Cantwell, J.A. (2013) Blurred boundaries between firms, and new boundaries within (large multinational) firms: the impact of decentralized networks for innovation. *Seoul Journal of Economics*, 26(1): 1–32.

Cantwell, J.A. and Mudambi, R. (2005) MNE competence-creating subsidiary mandates. *Strategic Management Journal*, 26(12): 1109–28.

Cantwell, J.A. and Vertova, G. (2004) Historical evolution of technological diversification. *Research Policy*, 33(3), 511–529.

Chandler, A.D. (1990) *Scale and Scope: The Dynamics of Industrial Capitalism*. Cambridge, Mass.: Harvard University Press.

Florida, R. (2005) The world is spiky. *The Atlantic Monthly*, October, 48–51.

Freeman, C. (1987) *Technology Policy and Economic Performance: Lessons from Japan*. London: Frances Pinter.

Freeman, C. and Louçã, F. (2001) *As Time Goes By: From the Industrial Revolutions to the Information Revolution*. Oxford and New York: Oxford University Press.

DOI: 10.1057/9781137367204.0009

Freeman, C. and Perez, C. (1988) Structural crises of adjustment, business cycles and investment behaviour, in G. Dosi, C. Freeman, R.R. Nelson, G. Silverberg and L.L.G. Soete (eds) *Technical Change and Economic Theory.* London: Frances Pinter.

Friedman, T.L. (2005) *The World Is Flat: A Brief History of the Twenty-First Century.* New York: Farrar, Straus and Giroux.

Hobday, M. (2000) East versus southeast Asian innovation systems: comparing OME- and TNC-led growth in electronics, in Kim, L. and Nelson, R.R. (eds) *Technology, Learning and Innovation: Experiences of Newly Industrializing Economies.* Cambridge and New York: Cambridge University Press.

Keane, M.P. and Feinberg, S. (2006) Accounting for the growth of MNC-based trade using a structural model of U.S. MNCs. *American Economic Review*, 96(5): 1515–58.

Lazonick, W. (1992) Business organization and competitive advantage: capitalist transformations in the twentieth century, in G. Dosi, R. Giannetti and P.A. Toninelli (eds) *Technology and Enterprise in a Historical Perspective.* Oxford and New York: Oxford University Press.

Lipsey, R.E. and Weiss, M.Y. (1981) Foreign production and exports in manufacturing industries. *Review of Economics and Statistics*, 63(4): 488–94.

Maddison, A. (2007) *Contours of the World Economy, 1–2030 AD: Essays in Macroeconomic History.* Oxford and New York: Oxford University Press.

Marx, K. (1847) *The Poverty of Philosophy.* Reprint of 1973 edition, Moscow: Progress Publishers.

Marx, K. (1859) Preface to *A Contribution to the Critique of Political Economy.* Reprint of 1904 edition, Chicago: Charles H. Kerr and Company.

Marx, K. and Engels, F. (1848) *Manifesto of the Communist Party.* Reprint of 1969 edition, Moscow: Progress Publishers.

Mazzoleni, R. and Nelson, R.R. (2007) Public research institutions and economic catch-up. *Research Policy*, 36(10): 1512–28.

Mowery, D.C. and Rosenberg, N. (1989) *Technology and the Pursuit of Economic Growth.* Cambridge and New York: Cambridge University Press.

Mudambi, R. (2008) Location, control and innovation in knowledge-intensive industries. *Journal of Economic Geography*, 8(5): 699–725.

Murmann, J.P. (2003) *Knowledge and Competitive Advantage: The Coevolution of Firms, Technology, and National Institutions.* Cambridge and New York: Cambridge University Press.

O'Rourke, K. and Williamson, J.G. (1999) *Globalization and History: The Evolution of a Nineteenth Century Atlantic Economy.* Cambridge, Mass.: MIT Press.

Ozawa, T. (1974) *Japan's Technological Challenge to the West, 1950–1974: Motivation and Accomplishment.* Cambridge, Mass.: MIT Press.

Rosenberg, N. (1976) Marx as a student of technology. *Monthly Review*, 28, July–August, 56–77.

Rosenberg, N. and Nelson, R.R. (1996) The roles of universities in the advance of industrial technology, in R.S. Rosenbloom and W.J. Spencer (eds) *Engines of Innovation: US Industrial Research at the End of an Era.* Boston, Mass.: Harvard Business School Press.

UNCTAD (2013) *Global Value Chains and Development.* New York and Geneva: United Nations.

von Tunzelmann, G.N. (1995) *Technology and Industrial Progress: The Foundations of Economic Growth.* Aldershot: Edward Elgar.

Wilkins, M. (2009) The history of multinational enterprise, in A.M. Rugman (ed.) *The Oxford Handbook of International Business.* Oxford and New York: Oxford University Press.

DOI: 10.1057/9781137367204.0009

Part II
Institutions and Foreign Direct Investment

DOI: 10.1057/9781137367204.0010

3
The Entry of Multinational Companies to the Base of the Pyramid: A Network Perspective

Misagh Tasavori, Pervez Ghauri and Reza Zaefarian

Introduction

One of the markets that has attracted the attention of business leaders and consequently international business researchers in recent years is the base of the economic pyramid (BOP) (Hammond and Prahalad, 2004; Hart and Christensen, 2002; Lodge, 2006; Lodge and Wilson, 2006; London and Hart, 2004; Prahalad, 2009; Prahalad and Hammond, 2002; Seelos and Mair, 2007). This market, which comprises people with a daily income of less than $2 a day, has mainly been ignored by multinational corporations (MNCs) up until now (Hammond et al., 2007). However faced with saturated markets at the top of the economic pyramid, MNCs are increasingly diverting their attention to the BOP and developing strategies to enter this market and sell their products or services to this segment. Recent studies illustrate that corporations have to revise the way they do business in order to fit the specific characteristics of the BOP (London and Hart, 2010). One of the factors found to distinguish successful from unsuccessful MNCs in this market is the building of relationships with non-traditional partners such as non-governmental organizations (NGOs) (Teegen, Doh and Vachani, 2004). While the role of NGOs has been corroborated in several international business studies (Doh and Teegen, 2002; Parker, 2003; Teegen et al., 2004; Teegen, 2006), and specifically at the BOP (London and Hart, 2004; Prahalad, 2009), we still know very little about how NGOs help MNCs to enter the BOP (Perez-Aleman and Sandilands, 2008). To explain the relationship between MNCs and NGOs and its effect on the former's entry to the BOP market, this research adopts a network perspective. While the business network approach has been extensively employed in the fields of industrial marketing (Ghauri, 1999; Hakansson and Snehota, 1995) and international business (Forsgren et al., 2005; Johanson and Vahlne, 2003), there

DOI: 10.1057/9781137367204.0010

are few studies applying this theoretical perspective to the study of MNCs and social actors (Hadjikhani and Ghauri, 2001). Therefore we extend the boundaries of network theory to analyse the relationship between MNCs and NGOs at the BOP.

This chapter is organized as follows. First, the literature related to the characteristics of the BOP, the challenges facing MNCs at the BOP and the collaboration of MNCs and NGOs at the BOP are briefly reviewed. Then we elaborate the network perspective and its dimensions that will be used in this study. After that the research method is described and the findings of the research presented. The chapter concludes with managerial implications, research limitations and future research directions.

MNCs, the BOP and NGOs

Though MNCs benefit from a superior ability to confront a variety of challenges, evidence shows that being a large MNC does not necessarily guarantee success at the BOP. Specifically, the concept of doing business with the poor calls for additional focus and significant changes in business models (London and Hart, 2004). At the BOP, companies will not have access to the usual infrastructure and support systems. In contrast to the top of the economic pyramid, where corporations are concerned with willingness to consume (Hammond and Prahalad, 2004; London and Hart, 2004; Prahalad, 2004), consumers in low-income markets are often willing to use products but lack sufficient money to pay for them (Seelos and Mair, 2007). The income constraints of the poor present a severe challenge to MNCs, in terms of how they design their products and manage costs (Seelos and Mair, 2007). At the same time, MNCs are expected to bring world-class products, with corresponding quality and safety standards, to less developed economies. However providing high quality at a low price is not possible using traditional ways of doing business (Prahalad, 2009). A further challenge to the MNCs comes from the numerous, geographically dispersed villages without proper transportation infrastructures, which demands innovative strategies for the distribution of products and services (Velayudhan, 2007). The promotion of products also needs to be different, as illiteracy among many of the consumers in BOP markets constrains the use of print media (Velayudhan, 2007).

In addition, companies have to find solutions that will empower the poor and offer sustainable changes in their lifestyles (London et al., 2009), as poor communities will be more likely to embrace the products of those firms that not only serve them well but also improve their standard of living (Wood et al., 2008). Due to these characteristics of the BOP market, researchers have revealed that corporations addressing four particular aspects will be most successful in this market, namely awareness, affordability, availability and acceptability of products or services (Anderson and Billou, 2007).

DOI: 10.1057/9781137367204.0010

As a result of these specific BOP conditions, many corporations have found collaboration with NGOs to be a helpful solution to the challenges embedded in this market (Hammond et al., 2007; London and Hart, 2010). London and Hart (2004) study a number of corporations at the BOP and highlight that successful firms have established relationships with non-traditional partners, including NGOs. Simanis and Hart (2009) examine product development at the BOP and report that innovation in this market should involve local NGOs. Perez-Aleman and Sandilands (2008) elaborate on how MNC–NGO partnerships benefit the poor and facilitate the inclusion of poorer producers in global supply chains. Doh and Teegen (2002) point out the role of NGOs in defining the institutional environment and influencing the interaction between businesses and other entities.

Theoretical background

The theoretical perspective of this research goes beyond the business networks of MNCs and focuses on their non-traditional partners. This is in line with prior studies revealing that corporations are embedded in business networks as well as social-political networks that have proved crucial to the success of firms (Hadjikhani et al., 2008; Hadjikhani and Ghauri, 2001; Keillor and Hult, 2004). To explain the business relationships between MNCs and NGOs and how they impact on MNCs' entry into the BOP market, this research builds its argument upon three concepts: commitment, trust and legitimacy (see Figure 3.1).

The concepts of commitment and trust have been widely used by business network researchers (Hausman, 2001; Walter and Ritter, 2003). In addition, some researchers have suggested that legitimacy is a useful concept for examining the relationships between corporations and social and political partners (Hadjikhani et al., 2008; O'Higgins and Morgan, 2006; Walter and Ritter, 2003). This is mainly because of the differences in the nature of relationships

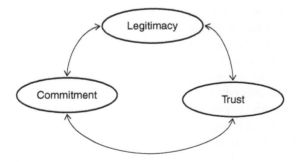

Figure 3.1   Dimensions of the relationship
Source: based on Hadjikhani et al., 2008.

DOI: 10.1057/9781137367204.0010

among business networks and socio-political networks. While technological and/or financial interdependency is the key reason for collaboration between business partners, they may be less relevant when corporations work with socio-political entities (Hadjikhani et al., 2008).

Legitimacy is defined as the perceived need to gain society's acceptance by complying with dominant norms, values and beliefs (Suchman, 1995). Accordingly, legitimacy is a socially constructed position of a firm recognized by its networks. Since legitimacy has become a critical issue for MNCs (Kostova and Zaheer, 1999), they are increasingly seeking new forms of legitimacy (Palazzo and Scherer, 2006) by entering into domains that have traditionally been considered the realm of governments or NGOs (Matten and Crane, 2005). By collaborating with them, and incorporating their expectations, MNCs can improve their legitimacy (DiMaggio and Powell, 1983) and as a result obtain and maintain the required resources (Oliver, 1991). At the BOP, MNCs can enhance their legitimacy by demonstrating how their initiatives can create mutual benefits for corporations, NGOs and ultimately the BOP population.

Commitment is defined as believing that an on-going relationship with another party is so important that the partners will make as much effort as possible to maintain it (Morgan and Hunt, 1994); that is, committed MNCs and NGOs believe their relationship is worth investing in, to ensure that it endures for a long time. Through their interactions with NGOs, MNCs can obtain information and experience about the BOP market and use that knowledge to enter the market themselves (Johanson and Vahlne, 1977). When MNCs increase their collaboration with NGOs, their perceived risk of investing in the market declines and their market commitment increases. The commitment of MNCs can be measured by the size of their tangible and intangible investments and their actions towards NGOs or other actors connected to them (e.g. BOP community) (Scott, 1994). Specifically, MNCs demonstrate their commitment when they invest in developing products or services for the BOP population and when they accept the long-term nature of their investment.

Trust, as the driving force behind commitment or an outcome of commitment, is defined as 'the firm's belief that another company will perform actions that will result in positive outcomes for the firm as well as not take unexpected actions that result in negative outcomes' (Anderson and Narus, 1990, p. 45). Trust is fostered when one party is confident of the other party's reliability and integrity, which is related to qualities such as competence, honesty, responsibility, helpfulness and benevolence (Morgan and Hunt, 1994). Han et al. (1993) suggest that perceived mutual trust is a principal characteristic of a good relationship. Rodríguez and Wilson (2002) note that trust is dependent on the goal congruency of the partners. Therefore, to improve the trust in their relationships with NGOs, MNCs have to pursue initiatives that will benefit the BOP population. MNCs use their resources to develop trust in the BOP and

DOI: 10.1057/9781137367204.0010

reach NGOs in order to gain special treatment (Hadjikhani and Ghauri, 2001). Commitment and trust dissuade exchange partners from sacrificing expected long-term benefits of working with existing partners for attractive short-term alternatives (Morgan and Hunt, 1994).

Trust in MNC–NGO relationships can affect the commitment and legitimacy in them. The higher the commitment between an MNC and an NGO, the higher will be the trust in the relationship and the legitimacy of the MNC.

Research method

This study used a qualitative case study approach to explore the relationships between MNCs and NGOs at the BOP. Yin (2009) proposes using the case study method to understand real-life phenomena in-depth, and also to understand important contextual conditions. A multiple case study approach was employed in this research to enhance the generalizability of the findings (Ghauri and Gronhaug, 2010; Stake, 1995). The study was conducted in India as the majority of the world's BOP population live in this country (Hammond et al., 2007) and an increasing number of MNCs are trying to enter the BOP market there. The MNCs selected for the research were all serving the needs of the BOP population through their products or services and had collaborated with NGOs in order to enter this market. In each MNC, we interviewed managers who were directly involved in the BOP projects of the firm. The number of interviewees in each company varied as we used snowball sampling (Bryman, 2008). The use of multiple interviewees in each case can reduce subjective bias (Eisenhardt and Graebner, 2007). Additionally some of the NGO partners of the MNCs were identified and interviews carried out. In total 13 interviews were conducted, 11 with MNCs and two with NGOs. Table 3.1 gives some information about the MNCs. The interviews were semi-structured and based on an interview guide addressing the theoretical concepts of this study.

Table 3.1 Overview of interviewed MNCs

Company	Year founded	Year of establishment of subsidiary in India	Field of activity	Revenue of MNC in 2010 (€ billion)	Number of employees in 2010
HR Consult	1960	1992	Human resources consultancy	14.2	27,500
Tel Co.	1985	2007	Mobile telecommunication	51	85,000

DOI: 10.1057/9781137367204.0010

In addition to the primary data collected from the interviews, we used secondary data for identification and corroboration purposes (Ghauri and Firth, 2009). The major sources of secondary data included company websites, company reports, articles from newspapers and magazines, videos of presentations by executives (e.g. press conferences or speeches) as well as other online sources. The collected data were analysed using pattern matching and systematic case comparisons (Yin, 2009; Ghauri and Gronhaug, 2005).

MNC cases

HR Consult

As a human resource consultancy, HR Consult provides a range of services, including regular temporary staffing and permanent in-house placements, search and selection, and human resource solutions. It registers the information of applicants who are looking for new jobs and collects a database of job opportunities in corporations. It then tries to match candidates to vacancies in companies, helping job seekers to find the best position and employers to identify the best talent for roles across various levels. The company also offers training to applicants to enhance their employability, and to corporations to improve their productivity.

In 2007, HR Consult decided to establish a foundation in India to employ its core capabilities and bring poor people out of poverty by increasing their earnings. In particular, the foundation aims to create sustainable change in the lives of children, women and youths from disadvantaged backgrounds. It focuses on several aspects of poverty but, for the purposes of this research, two will be discussed:

(1) Providing empowerment and employability for women.
(2) Building the capacities of NGOs that work at the grass-roots level.

First of all, the foundation aimed to empower disadvantaged women to earn extra money for their families and become more independent and self-reliant. As a starting point, HR Consult identified NGOs that were pursuing the same goal: namely, the empowerment of poor people. The company then invited NGOs to collaborate with it in offering entrepreneurial education to poor women. The aim of these simple training courses was to help the attendees to learn how to start a micro-business. Each year, the company donates part of its profits to the foundation. This has enabled the foundation to help microfinance NGOs to provide loans to these disadvantaged women so that they can start their own businesses.

DOI: 10.1057/9781137367204.0010

Finally, building upon its database of available job opportunities, and the needs of different industries, HR Consult is offering training programmes to enhance disadvantaged groups' employability and marketable skills. These programmes are aimed at improving the skills and knowledge of youths and women to enable them to work for companies.

The foundation realized that, in order to scale up its initiatives, it would need the support and collaboration of NGOs. It therefore started another initiative to improve the visibility, connectivity and capacity of local grass-roots NGOs. It has created a facilitative platform where NGOs, companies and individuals with common social concerns can come together for mutual learning, sharing and the collective espousal of social causes. The programme is aimed at providing visibility, connectivity and capacity to NGOs working at the grass roots level. Currently, it has a strong network of 256 NGOs, 300 individuals and 14 corporations.

Since HR Consult is not pursuing any profits from these activities at this stage, and has aligned its goals with those of the NGOs, it is finding it easy to attract the trust of local NGOs. The investment of the company's resources, such as giving employees the opportunity to volunteer, offering free training to poor women and donating money to micro-finance NGOs, demonstrates the firm's commitment towards changing poor people's lives. Similarly, the NGO capacity-building initiatives have contributed significantly to strengthening the relationships between HR Consult and the NGOs. Finally, since HR Consult's activities at the BOP have enabled NGOs to achieve their goals of reducing poverty, and poor people to earn money and improve their lives, the company has gained legitimacy in the eyes of the NGOs and poor communities, and thus gained their support.

Tel Co.

Tel Co. is a global telecommunications company headquartered in Europe. It is one of the world's largest mobile companies in terms of revenue and number of subscribers. It operates in over 30 countries and has partner networks in more than 40 others.

As a mobile network provider, the activities of Tel Co. at the BOP are related to investing in disadvantaged areas to build mobile network infrastructure. The company also offers a variety of schemes aimed at making telephone conversations fairly affordable. However despite the low call rates, poor people were still unable to use mobile technology because they could not afford to purchase even the simplest handsets. Therefore the company decided to address this barrier by introducing a new affordable handset. In addition, to enable the poor to benefit from the advantages of mobile phones, and in order to increase

DOI: 10.1057/9781137367204.0010

its sales, Tel Co. invited micro-finance NGOs to work with it and offer loans for purchasing handsets. In the words of one of the managers:

> We are working with micro-finance organizations that are also NGOs. They give people financing or rural consumer financing for very small purchases such as Rupees 300, Rupees 500; they get Rupees 50 per month or Rupees 20 per month as a kind of pay back. So we do have that kind of arrangement in some places where these groups exist, where we get them to fund the purchase of our handsets or our service, and we educate them through this.

Another challenge was the distribution of mobile phones and a system for adding credit to them. For this, the company decided to seek the help of NGOs, asking them to put them in touch with poor women from their self-help groups. The company then trained these women in commercial operations. They now work as representatives for the firm and sell mobile services in their villages. This strategy has led to the opening of many mini-stores to provide mobile services in a number of widely dispersed areas.

Another challenge that Tel Co. faced at the BOP came from the lack of infrastructure and widespread illiteracy among people in rural areas. Because of the former, the reach of media such as cable TV and satellite was very low. As a result, the company could not advertise its products and services using the methods common in urban areas, mainly TV advertisements. Meanwhile, illiteracy meant that flyers and newspapers would be ineffective. Therefore communication had to be mostly verbal or visual, which required extensive physical reach into rural areas. So, the company developed several short audio-visual films showing a villager becoming an entrepreneur and creating a small company through his access to mobile communication methods. These films were shown at village gatherings, and helped the company build great awareness of its services and the benefits they could bring to the lives of the villagers.

Tel Co. also understood that offering mobile technology is not enough at the BOP, as people are constrained by their low incomes. Therefore, in collaboration with NGOs, the company started to educate people about how they could develop micro-enterprises based on mobile communication. In partnership with its distributors, the company is also taking vans into rural villages and educating rural consumers about how mobile technology can enhance the social and economic lives of the poor. One of the interviewees described the thinking behind this idea:

> We go and show the rural people how mobile telephones can make their lives more comfortable, can help them grow in their businesses and help them keep in touch with loved ones living in the towns, and that is something that will help them grow as individuals and in their financial lives.

DOI: 10.1057/9781137367204.0010

In this case, the trust in the relationship between Tel Co. and the NGOs developed through the alignment of their goals and the resulting creation of mutual value. Tel Co. aimed to enter the BOP market by selling its handsets and mobile network to the BOP population and encouraging people to use mobile phones. Meanwhile the NGOs were trying to help women find a way out of poverty, through self-help groups. As a result, when Tel Co. suggested making these women sales representatives, the idea was very much welcomed by the NGOs.

Tel Co. also demonstrated its commitment to the BOP population by investing resources in building infrastructure in rural areas, and bringing the advantages of mobile phones to the poor. The company also invested in training poor women to work as its sale representatives. These contributions, in providing jobs for poor women and improving the lives of those on low incomes by giving them access to mobile phones, has brought about a higher acceptance of Tel Co.'s initiatives at the BOP and legitimacy for the firm.

Discussion

The case studies in this research highlight the necessity of establishing relationships with actors outside traditional business networks in order to achieve business goals. This is in line with prior studies expressing the need to include social actors in MNCs' networks (Hadjikhani et al., 2008), especially at the BOP (London et al., 2004; London and Hart, 2004). However this research adds to the previous understanding by elaborating on the role that establishing relationships with NGOs plays in helping MNCs to enter the BOP market. A summary of the MNC–NGO relationships and how they facilitated the case MNCs' entry to the BOP is presented in Table 3.2.

In line with prior studies (Anderson et al., 1994; Rodríguez and Wilson, 2002), the findings of this research illustrate that defining mutually beneficial goals can strengthen trust in a relationship. Both of the case companies in this study pursued this strategy and designed their entry into the BOP in such a way that also allowed NGOs to achieve their social goals, improving the lives of the BOP population. HR Consult provided education and training skills for the poor to enhance their employability chances. Tel Co. offered jobs to poor women whom the NGOs were already trying to help. In collaboration with NGOs, Tel Co. also developed some business ideas based on the use of mobile phones, to improve micro-entrepreneurship among the poor.

The establishment of trust among the MNCs and NGOs also improved the commitment of both. The MNCs' market entry into the BOP created benefits for the NGOs and the BOP, which strengthened the NGOs' commitment to the relationships. This is in line with the findings of Morgan and Hunt (1994), highlighting that in a committed relationship each party will invest in maintaining the relationship. The findings of this research also confirm

DOI: 10.1057/9781137367204.0010

Table 3.2 Summary of the MNC–NGO relationships and their role in the BOP market entry of the MNCs

	HR Consult	Tel Co.
Initiatives for building trust	– Offering non-profit initiatives – Offering solutions to increase the earnings of poor women (training workshops to start a micro-enterprise, developing poor women's skills to improve their employability) (Alignment of HR Consult's goals with those of the NGOs)	– Bringing the advantages of mobile phones to poor communities – Offering job creation for self-help group women (Alignment of Tel Co.'s goals with those of the NGOs)
Initiatives for demonstrating commitment	– Dedicating resources to the provision of training workshops for poor women – The donation of money to microfinance NGOs to support the poor in the starting of micro-enterprises – Dedicating resources to building the capacity of NGOs	– Developing the telecommunication infrastructure in rural areas of India – Developing an affordable handset – Training women to establish micro-enterprises
Enhancement of legitimacy	– Reducing poverty by generating incomes for poor women – Enhancing the employability of the poor – Building the capacity of the NGOs – Obtaining support from the NGOs to scale up the initiatives at the BOP	– Empowerment of self-help group women – Providing access to mobile phones in rural areas – Obtaining the support of NGOs for Tel Co.'s initiatives at the BOP
Consequences of building relationships with NGOs and BOP market entry	– The NGOs helped HR Consult to gain access to the BOP communities, offering training workshops and scaling up initiatives	– The NGOs encouraged women form their self-help groups to work as the firm's sales representatives – The NGOs provided microfinance for the purchase of handsets

the necessity of establishing a win-win relationship at the BOP, as suggested by international business scholars in the past few years (London et al., 2010; London and Hart, 2004; Prahalad, 2009).

By contributing to the reduction of poverty and the enhancement of poor people's lives, companies' initiatives at the BOP will be more easily accepted

DOI: 10.1057/9781137367204.0010

and the organizations will increase their legitimacy (Bowen et al., 2010; Chen and Roberts, 2010). In line with prior understandings, the MNC cases in this research engaged in several initiatives to improve their legitimacy. Both Tel Co. and HR Consult attempted to understand the real needs of the poor people in their target markets and to incorporate the NGOs' aims to improve the lives of these people. HR Consult, for example, offered training to improve the earnings of the poor, either through increasing their employability or their chances of starting new micro-businesses. In addition, HR Consult's investment in the capacity of the NGOs, which were then able to help the company to scale up its activities, enhanced its acceptability among both the poor and the NGOs. Tel Co., in addition to offering an affordable handset, sought the collaboration of micro-finance NGOs in giving loans to the poor to purchase these handsets. Changing the lives of the poor by suggesting ways they could earn money using their mobile phones also made the company's activities more acceptable at the BOP.

Conclusion

This research sought to reveal how the collaboration of MNCs and NGOs at the BOP can contribute to the market entry of MNCs. We adopted network theory and highlighted the necessity of developing trust, commitment and legitimacy in the relationships between MNCs and NGOs, and provided some insights, based on our empirical findings, into how these factors can facilitate the entry of MNCs into the BOP.

The findings of this research contribute to theory by extending the boundaries of business to non-business networks and providing a theoretical understanding of the interaction between MNCs and NGOs at the BOP. Therefore the findings corroborate prior studies emphasizing the necessity of incorporating social actors in the analysis of MNCs' behaviour (Hadjikhani et al., 2008; Hadjikhani and Ghauri, 2001).

This research also has several implications for the managers of both MNCs and NGOs. The findings reveal that entering the BOP market requires different strategies and MNCs should learn to collaborate with NGOs and seek their help and advice. They should first develop trust, illustrate their commitment and improve their legitimacy in the eyes of the NGOs and then the BOP population. NGOs should also appreciate the contribution MNCs can make to improving the lives of the poor and collaborate with them to develop products and services that meet the specific unmet needs of the poor.

This research is not without limitations. Like any other qualitative study, the generalizability of the findings is limited. Future studies can thus focus on the BOP in different countries, and collaborations between MNCs and NGOs in a variety of industries and on a larger scale.

DOI: 10.1057/9781137367204.0010

References

Anderson, J. and Billou, N. (2007) Serving the world's poor: innovation at the base of the economic pyramid. *Journal of Business Strategy*, 28(2): 14–21.

Anderson, J.C., Håkansson, H. and Johanson, J. (1994) Dyadic business relationships within a business network context. *Journal of Marketing*, 58(4): 1–15.

Anderson, J.C. and Narus, J.A. (1990) A model of distributor firm and manufacturer firm working partnerships. *Journal of Marketing*, 54(1): 42–58.

Bowen, F., Newenham-Kahindi, F. and Herremans, I. (2010) When suits meet roots: the antecedents and consequences of community engagement strategy. *Journal of Business Ethics*, 95(2): 297–318.

Bryman, A. (2008) *Social Research Methods*. Oxford: Oxford University Press.

Chen, J. and Roberts, R. (2010) Toward a more coherent understanding of the organization–society relationship: a theoretical consideration for social and environmental accounting research. *Journal of Business Ethics*, 97(4): 651–65.

Dimaggio, P.J. and Powell, W.W. (1983) The iron cage revisited: institutional isomorphism and collective rationality in organizational fields. *American Sociological Review*, 48(2): 147–60.

Doh, J.P. and Teegen, H. (2002) Nongovernmental organizations as institutional actors in international business: theory and implications. *International Business Review*, 11(6): 665–84.

Eisenhardt, K.M. and Graebner, M.E. (2007) Theory building from cases: opportunities and challenges. *Academy of Management Journal*, 50(1): 25–32.

Forsgren, M., Holm, U. and Johanson, J. (2005) *Managing the Embedded Multinational: A Business Network View*. Cheltenham: Edward Elgar.

Ghauri, P.N. (ed.) (1999) *Advances in International Marketing: From Mass Marketing to Relationships and Networks*. Greenwich, CT: JAI Press.

Ghauri, P.N. and Firth, R. (2009) The formalization of case study research in international business. *Der Market: Journal for Marketing*, 48(1–2): 29–40.

Ghauri, P.N. and Gronhaug, K. (2005) *Research Methods in Business Studies: A Practical Guide*. Harlow: Prentice Hall.

Ghauri, P.N. and Gronhau, K. (2010) *Research Methods in Business Studies: A Practical Guide* (Harlow: Financial Times/Prentice Hall).

Hadjikhani, A. and Ghauri, P.N. (2001) The behaviour of international firms in socio-political environments in the European Union. *Journal of Business Research*, 52(3): 263–75.

Hadjikhani, A., Lee, J.-W. and Ghauri, P.N. (2008) Network view of MNCs' socio-political behavior. *Journal of Business Research*, 61(9): 912–24.

Hakansson, H. and Snehota, I. (1995) *Developing Relationships in Business Networks*. London: Routledge.

Hammond, A.L., Kramer, W.J., Tran, J., Katz, R. and Walker, C. (2007) *The Next 4 Billion: Market Size and Business Strategy at the Base of the Pyramid*. Washington, DC: World Resources Institute, International Finance Corporation and the World Bank.

Hammond, A.L. and Prahalad, C.K. (2004) Selling to the poor. *Foreign Policy*, 142(May/June): 30–8.

Han, S.-L., Wilson, D.T. and Dant, S.P. (1993) Buyer supplier relationships today. *Industrial Marketing Management*, 22(4): 331–8.

Hart, S.L. and Christensen, C.M. (2002) The great leap: driving innovation from the base of the pyramid. *MIT Sloan Management Review*, 44(1): 51–6.

DOI: 10.1057/9781137367204.0010

Hausman, A. (2001) Variations in relationship strength and its impact on performance and satisfaction in business relationships. *Journal of Business & Industrial Marketing*, 16(6/7): 600–16.

Johanson, J. and Vahlne, J.-E. (1977) The internationalization process of the firm: a model of knowledge development and increasing foreign market commitments. *Journal of International Business Studies*, 8(1): 23–32.

Johanson, J. and Vahlne, J.-E. (2003) Business relationship learning and commitment in the internationalization process. *Journal of International Entrepreneurship*, 1(1): 83–101.

Keillor, B.D. and Hult, G.T.M. (2004) Predictors of firm-level political behavior in the global business environment: an investigation of specific activities employed by US firms. *International Business Review*, 13(3): 309–29.

Kostova, T. and Zaheer, S. (1999) Organizational legitimacy under conditions of complexity: the case of the multinational enterprise. *Academy of Management Review*, 24(1): 64–81.

Lodge, G.C. (2006) *The Corporate Key: Using Big Business to Fight Global Poverty*, in S.C. Jain and S. Vachani (eds) *Multinational Corporations and Global Poverty Reduction*. Northampton, MA: Edward Elgar.

Lodge, G.C. and Wilson, C. (2006) Multinational corporations and global poverty reduction. *Challenge*, 49(3): 17–25.

London, T., Anupindi, R. and Sheth, S. (2009) Creating mutual value with base of the pyramid producers, in G.T. Solomon (ed.) *Academy of Management Best Paper Proceedings*. Chicago, Illinois: Academy of Management.

London, T., Anupindi, R. and Sheth, S. (2010) Creating mutual value: lessons learned from ventures serving base of the pyramid producers. *Journal of Business Research*, 63(6): 582–94.

London, T. and Hart, S.L. (2004) Reinventing strategies for emerging markets: beyond the transnational model. *Journal of International Business Studies*, 35(5): 350–70.

London, T. and Hart, S.L. (2010) *Next Generation Business Strategies for the Base of the Pyramid*. Wharton: Wharton School Publishing.

London, T., Rondinelli, D.A. and O'Neill, H. (2004) Exploring uneasy learning alliances between corporations and non-profit organizations, in D.H. Nagao (ed.) *Academy of Management Best Paper Proceedings*. New Orleans: Academy of Management.

Matten, D. and Crane, A. (2005) Corporate citizenship: toward an extended theoretical conceptualization. *Academy of Management Review*, 30(1): 166–79.

Morgan, R.M. and Hunt, S.D. (1994) The commitment-trust theory of relationship marketing. *Journal of Marketing*, 58(3): 20–38.

O'Higgins, E.R.E. and Morgan, J.W. (2006) Stakeholder salience and engagement in political organisations: who and what really counts? *Society and Business Review*, 1(1): 62–76.

Oliver, C. (1991) Strategic responses to institutional processes. *Academy of Management Review*, 16(1): 145–79.

Palazzo, G. and Scherer, A.G. (2006) Corporate legitimacy as deliberation: a communicative framework. *Journal of Business Ethics*, 66(1): 71–88.

Parker, R. (2003) Prospects for NGO collaboration with multinational enterprises, in D.A. Teegen (ed.) *Globalization and NGOs: Transforming Business, Governments and Society*. Westport, CT: Praeger Books.

Perez-Aleman, P. and Sandilands, M. (2008) Building value at the top and the bottom of the global supply chain: MNC–NGO partnerships. *California Management Review*, 51(1): 24–49.

DOI: 10.1057/9781137367204.0010

Prahalad, C.K. (2004) *The Fortune at the Bottom of the Pyramid: Eradicating Poverty Through Profits*. Upper Saddle River, NJ: Wharton School Publishing.

Prahalad, C.K. (2009) *The Fortune at the Bottom of the Pyramid: Eradicating Poverty Through Profits*. Upper Saddle River, NJ: Wharton School Publishing.

Prahalad, C.K. and Hammond, A.L. (2002) Serving the world's poor, profitably. *Harvard Business Review*, 80(9): 48–57.

Rodríguez, C.M. and Wilson, D.T. (2002) Relationship bonding and trust as a foundation for commitment in U.S.–Mexican strategic alliances: a structural equation modeling approach. *Journal of International Marketing*, 10(4): 53–76.

Scott, J. (1994) *Social Network Analysis: A Handbook*. London: Sage Publications.

Seelos, C. and Mair, J. (2007) Profitable business models and market creation in the context of deep poverty: a strategic view. *Academy of Management Perspectives*, 21(4): 49–63.

Simanis, E. and Hart, S. (2009) Innovation from the inside out. *MIT Sloan Management Review*, 50(4): 77–86.

Stake, R.E. (1995) *The Art of Case Study Research*. Thousand Oaks, CA: Sage Publications.

Suchman, M.C. (1995) Managing legitimacy: strategic and institutional approaches. *Academy of Management Review*, 20(3): 571–610.

Teegen, H. (2006) *Achieving the Millennium Development Goals: Ways for MNCs to Effectively Interface with NGOs*, in S.C. Jain and S. Vachani (eds) *Multinational Corporations and Global Poverty Reduction*. Northampton, MA: Edward Elgar.

Teegen, H., Doh, J.P. and Vachani, S. (2004) The importance of nongovernmental organizations (NGOs) in global governance and value creation: an international business research agenda. *Journal of International Business Studies*, 35(6): 463–83.

Velayudhan, S.K. (2007) *Rural Marketing*. New Delhi: Sage Publications.

Walter, A. and Ritter, T. (2003) The influence of adaptations, trust, and commitment on value-creating functions of customer relationships. *Journal of Business & Industrial Marketing*, 18(4/5): 353–65.

Wood, V.R., Pitta, D.A. and Franzak, F.J. (2008) Successful marketing by multinational firms to the bottom of the pyramid: connecting share of heart, global 'umbrella brands', and responsible marketing. *Journal of Consumer Marketing*, 25(7): 419–29.

Yin, R.K. (2009) *Case Study Research: Design and Methods*. Thousand Oaks, California: Sage Publications.

DOI: 10.1057/9781137367204.0010

4
FDI and Property Rights in Resource-Rich Countries

*Chiara Amini**

Introduction

International organizations and policymakers have often promoted foreign direct investment (FDI) as a necessary instrument for economic development. The theoretical literature in support of this view argues that FDI can trigger growth and development by generating knowledge and technological spillovers. However the empirical evidence on this is rather mixed (Alfaro et al., 2009). Scholars have shown that positive effects arising from FDI are likely to depend on host country characteristics, such as the level of human capital, financial markets and the institutional frameworks (Blomström and Kokko, 2003; de Mello, 1999). Moreover the activities of multinational companies (MNCs) have aroused controversy and concern, especially in the case of the extractive industry and natural commodities sectors, where resources are often located in conflict-prone regions. Recent research has highlighted that in some cases foreign companies in the extractive industry have aggravated violence and conflict, for example, by providing arms or finance (Ballentine and Nitzschke, 2004). In such cases, the beneficial effect of FDI is likely to be limited due to the potential effects on the real exchange rate and loss of competitiveness (Le Billon, 2005; Sachs and Warner, 2001), worsening social inequality (Renner, 2002; Ross, 1999) and instability (Collier, 2004). In addition, recent research highlights that in resource-rich economies the role played by host country characteristics in attracting foreign investors differs compared to other economies. New empirical studies have shown that the relationship between democracy and FDI in the primary sector may be atypical (Aisedu and Lien, 2011; Shultz, 2007). In this instance, there is no evidence of the expected positive relation between foreign investment and democracy. However the theoretical and

* I am grateful to Chris Gerry, Tomek Mickiewicz, Photis Lysandrou and the reviewers of the AIB UK&I conference for providing very useful comments and feedback.

DOI: 10.1057/9781137367204.0011

empirical literature on the drivers of FDI in resource-rich economies remains limited. In light of the issues and concerns related to investments in natural resources, understanding the interplay between institutions and foreign investors in resource-rich countries seems particularly important. To address this gap in knowledge, we focus on low- and middle-income countries, and examine the effect of property rights, as measured by the 'law and order' indicator from the International Country Risk Guide (ICRG), on FDI inflows using a dataset of up to 92 developing and emerging countries from 1996 to 2008. A model of FDI determinants is estimated using the Blundell-Bond system GMM (Generalized Method of Moments) estimator (Blundell and Bond, 2000).

The contribution of this chapter is threefold. This is the first study that focuses on the interplay between property rights, FDI and natural resources using aggregate data. The results provide broad support for the argument developed in the chapter that the presence of natural resources affects the property rights–FDI relationship. Namely, in resource-rich countries, where investments are concentrated principally in the primary sector,[1] property rights are less important for attracting FDI. While existing research stresses that institutional weakness is negatively correlated with FDI, the proposition here is that the risk posed by frail institutions can be offset by the investment potential and by the MNCs' ability to negotiate favourable entry conditions with the host government.

We also contribute to the discussion on the impact of different types of natural resources on economic development. We find that only oil, and not minerals or agricultural products, has a robust and significant moderating impact on the FDI–property rights relationship.

Finally, while existing studies focus on resource export intensity as a proxy of resource endowment, we make use of alternative measures of natural resources, namely resources production and rent relative to gross domestic product (GDP).

The structure of this chapter is as follows. The second section discusses the relationship between property rights, FDI and natural resources and formulates the key hypothesis to be tested. The third and fourth sections present the econometric model and the data used in estimations. The final part discusses the results and draws some conclusions.

FDI, natural resources and institutions

The economic literature has largely discussed how the characteristics of the legal system, in particular property rights, are vital components of a

---

[1] The assumption that resource-rich economies attract mainly resource-seeking investment is confirmed by recent empirical research. For instance, Poelhekke and van der Ploeg (2010) find that natural resource production significantly decreases non-resource FDI.

DOI: 10.1057/9781137367204.0011

country's institutional set up and therefore matter for both domestic and foreign investment (Demsetz, 1967; Libecap, 1989; North, 1990). This theoretical proposition has been tested empirically in a growing body of cross-country studies. While there seems to be some consensus that the overall institutional environment can significantly increase FDI inflows (Bénassy-Quéré et al., 2007; Globerman and Shapiro, 2003), the same cannot be said about specific aspects of that environment. For instance, while several empirical studies find that better property rights have a significant and positive effect on FDI (Ali et al., 2010; Biglaiser and Staats, 2010; Gani, 2007), others do not find robust evidence in support of this hypothesis (Asiedu, 2002; Daude and Stein, 2007; Jung and Sing, 1996).

Conflicting findings on the effects of the efficiency of the legal system may be due to differences in time and country coverage, which in turn may reflect differences in the composition of FDI flows. In fact, FDI can be market, efficiency or resource seeking (Caves, 1996) and this may affect the interactions between host countries' characteristics and FDI. The following section reviews the existing literature on foreign investments in natural resources and tries to establish whether the relationship between the host country's property rights and foreign investment is affected by the composition of FDI.

The first discussion on MNCs in natural resource industries stems from Vernon's (1971) obsolescing bargain model (OBM). This framework aimed at explaining the wave of expropriation of natural resources-based FDI that occurred in the 1970s in developing countries by analysing the relationship between MNCs and the host country's bargaining power. Vernon (1971) and his followers (Moran, 1974; Tugwell, 1975) argued that the bargaining power of MNCs in extractive industries is relatively weaker than that in other industries because these firms incur high fixed costs, which transfer bargaining power to the host country's government. A recent take on the OBM argues that the risk of expropriation is particularly important to MNCs in natural resource industries because of the high asset specificity of locations with large sunk costs and long gestation periods associated with these types of ventures (Asiedu and Lien, 2011; Nunnenkamp and Spatz, 2003; WRI, 2007). This view can be criticized on several grounds. First, it is only partly correct to assume that the government has a stronger position than the MNC, as the withdrawal of FDI and technical expertise may lead to disruption of income for the host government. Therefore what we see is a mutual dependence where, using Williamson's (1987) terminology, the cost of breaking a transaction is high for both sides. Second, the OBS has overestimated the power of the local government because MNCs can put pressures on host countries' governments to protect their interests (Jenkins, 1986). Several case studies have shown that MNCs have been able to retain some bargaining power and prevent

DOI: 10.1057/9781137367204.0011

government expropriation (Eden et al., 2004).[2] Critics of Vernon's predictions have also noted that in recent times the MNC–host country relationship is more cooperative than conflictual, hence today the OBS framework is less relevant (Dunning, 1993; Luo, 2001).

Recently, a small but growing body of empirical studies has investigated the interplay between FDI, natural resources and institutions. Ali et al. (2010) analyse a panel of 45 developing countries between 1981 and 2005 and find that institutions, measured with the 'investment profile' index and the 'law and order' indicator from ICRG, do not have a significant impact on primary sector FDI. Schulz (2007), using data on industry-level FDI, finds some evidence that the relationship between formal institutions (democracy vs. autocracy) is sector-dependent and that resource-seeking FDI is less sensitive to democracy. When sectoral data are not available, studies rely on the assumption that a high resource endowment is associated with FDI concentrated in the primary sector (Asiedu and Lien, 2011). Asiedu and Lien (2011) find that democracy is positively correlated with FDI only if the share of minerals and oil in total exports is less than a critical value. Kolstad and Wiig (2012) analyse aggregate Chinese outward FDI over the period 2003–6 and find that Chinese investors in non-OECD countries are driven by a combination of high natural resources and low institutional quality (as measured by the Rule of Law index from the World Bank Institute Governance Indicators). The finding that resource-seeking investors may display an inclination towards autocratic regimes can be explained in three ways. First, the stability that characterizes autocracy facilitates the development of close relationships between investors and the host government (Asiedu and Lie, 2011). The development of close ties is a necessary condition to access natural resources, which are usually tightly controlled by the local government. In connection with this point, Li and Filer (2007) also note that deficiencies of the legal system do not necessarily prevent MNCs from setting up foreign operations. In fact, when societies lack a system of fair and transparent rules, investors often rely on relational capital to carry out economic transactions. This allows them to minimize the risk of expropriation and to circumvent institutional weaknesses. Second, some transaction costs induced by weak institutions may be balanced out by expected returns (Agarwal and Ramaswami, 1992; Asiedu, 2002). Hence the institutional framework is not a precondition to attract investment: if the comparative advantage of the host country is high (e.g. because of abundant natural resources or because of a large domestic market), investors may be willing to accept the risks associated with

---

[2] For example, Kramer and von Tulder (2009) mentioned the agreement between the Libyan government and Mittal Steel as an example of a foreign investor having been able to negotiate favourable conditions. The agreement includes tax incentives and the facilitation of corporate rights over those of local communities, and forbids the application of new law to the company.

DOI: 10.1057/9781137367204.0011

a weak legal system and institutions. Third, given the need to access resources that are not readily available in other countries, investors have no choice but to accept the host country institutions (Bayulgen, 2010; Spar, 1999). In connection to the latter point, it should be noted that FDI in natural resources tends to have few linkages to local product and labour markets (Nunnenkamp and Spatz, 2003). This feature of natural resources-based FDI can explain the limited spillover from this type of investment (Poelhekke and van der Ploeg, 2010). However a lack of linkages to other sectors of economic activity may also imply that FDI in the natural resource sector may be less sensitive to the general institutional framework shaping economic interactions across most of the economy.

To summarize, institutional weakness, such as frail property rights, should have less impact on FDI in natural resources because (a) the latter can be isolated from most of the other sectors in the economy; (b) institutional risk may be decreased by colluding with a local government; and (c) high transaction costs can be compensated for by higher returns results from participating in the resource rents.

Hence the hypothesis that we wish to test is the following:

Hypothesis 1: when FDI is concentrated in the primary sector this is expected to attenuate the effect of property rights on FDI.

Data and methodology

Model estimated and data

To test the effect of natural resources on the FDI-property rights relation, we estimate the following model:

$$LFDI_{it} = \beta_0 + \beta_1 LFDI_{it-1} + \beta_2 propertyrights_{it} + \beta_3 resources_{it}$$
$$+ \beta_4 propertyrights_{it} * resources_{it} + \beta_k X_{kit} + e_{it} \tag{1}$$

where $LFDI_{it}$ is the logarithm of FDI inflow as share of GDP, in country i at time t, 'propertyrights' and 'resources' are two indicators of the effectiveness of the legal system and the level of resource endowment and X_{kit} is a matrix of k control variables which are thought to affect FDI. To test H1 we are interested in the parameter β_4, which captures the effect of property rights conditional on the value of natural resources. Equation (1) models the inflow of FDI as a dynamic process where the dependent variable in year t depends in part on its value in year $t–1$.[3]

---

[3] This follows Cheng and Kwan (2000) and Noorbakhsh et al. (2001).

DOI: 10.1057/9781137367204.0011

The empirical analysis uses a panel data of 92 low- and middle-income countries over the period 1996–2009.[4] Details of the variables and the sources of data can be found in the appendix in table A1.[5]

For the period analysed (1996–2009), a number of institutional indicators are available from the ICRG. Amongst other institutional measures, the dataset supplies an index of the effectiveness of the legal system. Our property rights indicator is the ICRG's 'law and order', which measures both the strength and impartiality of the legal system, and the extent to which the law is observed. Moving to natural resources, the economics literature has traditionally measured resource endowments using the amount of natural resources produced or exported (Hodler, 2005). As the main measure of natural resources we use the shares of three primary commodities in merchandise exports: fuel and oil, ores and metals, and agricultural goods (Asiedu and Lien, 2011; Sachs and Warner, 1995). As a robustness check we also employ resources production and resources rent as share of GDP. Data on oil production, oil rent and mineral rent are available from the World Bank.[6] Oil production, calculated as the unit price multiplied by total production, provides a measure of the economic importance of resource extraction. Natural resources rent is calculated as the unit rent, that is, price net of cost, multiplied by the amount of resource extracted. Some scholars argue that rents are a better measure than resource exports, especially when analysing the interplay between institutions and resources (de Soysa and Neumayer, 2007). This is because rents are a direct measure of the gains from natural resources. Moreover, resource rents are strongly correlated with the value of reserves, in which case rents can be taken as a good proxy for sub-oil assets (Poelhekke and van der Ploeg, 2010).

The choice of the control variables is based on the existing empirical literature. The empirical literature on the determinants of FDI inflows is large and the evidence on the effects of many variables is mixed. Where consensus has emerged it is around the finding that country-level variables such as GDP (Brewer, 1993; Chakrabarti, 2001; Crenshaw, 1991; Globerman and Shapiro, 2003; Grosse, 1997; Lipsey, 1999), GDP per capita (Bénassy-Quéré et al., 2007), inflation (Satyanath and Subramanian, 2004), trade openness (Liu, Wang and Wei, 2001; Stone and Jeon, 2000) and institutions (Globerman and Shapiro, 2002) are important determinants of FDI inflows. For what concerns

---

[4] We defined low- and middle-income countries using the distribution of GDP per capita in PPP. Low-income countries are those in the lower 20 per cent of the income distribution; lower-middle-income countries are between the 20 per cent and 50 per cent of the income distribution; and symmetrically, upper-middle-income countries are between the 50 per cent and the 80 per cent of the income distribution.

[5] Descriptive statistics and a correlation table are available from the author on request.

[6] Minerals included in the calculations of rent are the following: tin, gold, lead, zinc, iron, copper, nickel, silver, bauxite and phosphate.

DOI: 10.1057/9781137367204.0011

institutions, we control for democracy and political stability. Legal system, political stability and democracy are closely interrelated, so not taking the latter into account may cause an omitted variable problem.

Estimation strategy

The empirical estimation of the model presented here is problematic as the lagged dependent variables as well as some of the regressors are endogenous. We therefore estimate the model with Systems GMM, a method designed for fixed effects-idiosyncratic errors that are heteroskedastic and correlated within but not across individuals. When implementing GMM estimates particular attention should be given to the Arellano-Bond test for autocorrelation in the differenced residuals and to the Sargan and Hansen tests for over-identifying restrictions. In the estimates reported we use two sets of instruments: 'GMM' style instruments, which can be predetermined variables (i.e. correlated with the past but not the present values of the error term), and 'IV' style instruments, which should be strictly exogenous variables. External instruments are not used. We estimate two models. In the first model, all variables except the lag of the dependent variable are assumed to be exogenous and thus are used as IV instruments. The second model relaxes the exogeneity assumption and it allows all the regressors, except the year dummies, to be endogenous. In this instance, all endogenous variables are included as GMM instruments. This is clearly a realistic assumption, as all independent variables (GDP, inflation, trade, resource export and institutions) suffer from reverse causality. It is well-known that foreign investors are not passive agents but they can affect the economic and institutional characteristics of the host countries. However, introducing many variables as GMM instruments has the drawback of creating a large number of instruments, which can cause concerns (Roodman, 2006). In order to limit the number of instruments, the estimates have been performed using the 'collapse' option where one instrument is created for each variable and lag distance, instead of one for each time period, variable and lag distance. For consistency, we limit the number of instruments when assuming the explanatory variables to be exogenous. Finally, we control for heteroscedasticity between countries by using the robust standard errors.

Descriptive statistics

Unconditional correlations provide a first glance of the relationship between FDI and property rights. FDI and the 'law and order' indicator have a correlation of 0.106,[7] which is positive and significant as expected. We then ask

---

[7] Full correlation table available from the author on request.

DOI: 10.1057/9781137367204.0011

whether this correlation is affected by the presence of natural resources. We divide countries according to the export intensity of two types of natural resources: fuel and oil and ores and metals; and agricultural raw materials. Following UNCTAD (2011), countries are defined as major natural-resource exporters if the share of natural resource exports to total exports is greater than 50 per cent. In our sample, this corresponds roughly to the 80th percentile of the distribution of the export intensity variables (e.g. fuel and oil and ores and metal to total export; agricultural raw material to total export). Thus throughout the analysis the sectors fuel and oil and ores and metals are concatenated.

Figures 4.1 and 4.2 indicate that there is a significant difference in the correlation between FDI and 'law and order' depending on the degree of export intensity. For major natural-resource exporters, the correlation between FDI and institutions seems much weaker compared to other countries. The preliminary analysis confirms that the relation between the strength of the legal system and foreign investors is conditional on natural resource endowments, here proxied by resource export intensity. This point will be further investigated in the following econometric analysis.

Results

The regression analysis aims to shed some light on how natural resources endowments – here, measured by natural resource export intensity – affect the

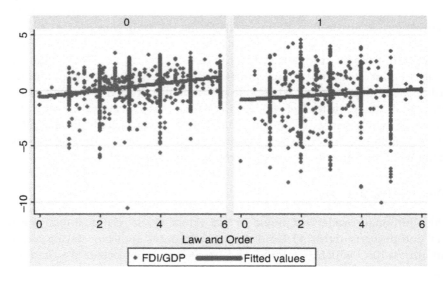

Figure 4.1   Property rights and oil and metal export

DOI: 10.1057/9781137367204.0011

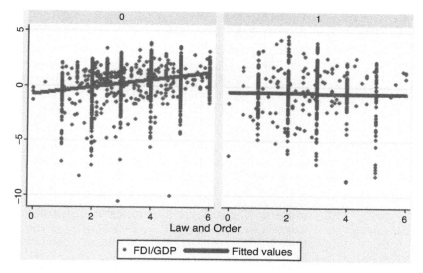

Figure 4.2   Property rights and agricultural export

FDI–property rights relationship. We distinguish between export intensity in fuels and oil, ores and metal and agricultural raw material. Table 4.1 analyses the effect of oil and metal export on FDI. In columns 1 and 2 all variables except the lagged dependent variables are exogenous, while the specifications reported in columns 3 and 4 allow all independent variables, except the year dummies, to be endogenous. In all columns the lagged values of FDI and trade openness are positive and highly significant, confirming that FDI and trade are very much complements rather than substitutes, and also that FDI is a dynamic process, characterized by persistence. GDP and GDP per capita are positive, while inflation, as expected, is consistently negative, although these variables are not significant. The variable 'nat', which stands for fuels and oil and ores and metal export intensity, has a positive and at times significant effect on FDI flows. The estimates reported show that property rights, political stability (ICRG) and democracy (polity2) are positively correlated with FDI. 'Law and order' and the democracy indicator have a robust and significant effect, while political stability is significant in only one instance. In columns 2 and 4, we explore whether the relationship between FDI and institutions is affected by the natural resources endowment by introducing an interactive term. The results indicate that the interaction between natural resources and 'law and order' is negative and significant. This result indicates that for increasing levels of fuels and oil and ores and metal exports the impact of the legal system on FDI decreases, thus confirming our hypothesis that an increasing level of natural resources decreases the positive effect of property rights on FDI.

DOI: 10.1057/9781137367204.0011

Table 4.1 Effect of oil and metal export on FDI

Variables	(1)	(2)	(3)	(4)
L.LFDI	0.335***	0.347***	0.388***	0.425***
	(0.0734)	(0.0743)	(0.0879)	(0.0936)
Ltrade	0.378***	0.347***	0.717	0.673
	(0.128)	(0.125)	(0.897)	(1.119)
LGDP	−0.0352	−0.0417	0.313*	0.297*
	(0.0361)	(0.0323)	(0.166)	(0.179)
LGDP per capita	−0.00913	0.0107	−0.575**	−0.589*
	(0.0669)	(0.0594)	(0.280)	(0.309)
Inflation	1.44e-05	7.94e-05	8.03e-05	5.66e-05
	(0.000583)	(0.000548)	(0.000713)	(0.000783)
Nat	0.000724	0.0126**	−0.0129	0.0547**
	(0.00213)	(0.00544)	(0.00877)	(0.0240)
Political stability	0.00869	0.0275	0.00277	−0.119
	(0.0331)	(0.0331)	(0.0904)	(0.119)
Law and order	0.532*	0.934***	1.796*	4.521***
	(0.305)	(0.324)	(0.940)	(1.540)
Polity2	0.0203**	0.0152*	0.0518	0.0505
	(0.00965)	(0.00886)	(0.0465)	(0.0491)
Nat*law		−0.0210**		−0.122***
		(0.00969)		(0.0451)
Constant	−0.162	−0.247	−5.844	−6.692
	(0.970)	(0.921)	(4.452)	(5.851)
Observations	895	895	895	895
Number of ID	92	92	92	92
AR(1)-pvalue	5.14e-08	9.02e-08	5.10e-06	1.34e-05
AR(2)-pvalue	0.325	0.336	0.209	0.401
Hansen-pvalue	0.263	0.308	0.666	0.624
Instrument number	43	44	39	42

Note: robust standard errors in parentheses; *** $p < 0.01$, ** $p < 0.05$, * $p < 0.1$; year dummies included but not reported. Dependent variable is the log of FDI as share of GDP. Nat is the share of fuel and oil and ores and metal export to total export. In column 1 and 2 all regressors except the lagged dependent variables are exogenous. In columns 3 and 4 all regressors are endogenous except the year controls.

We are also interested in exploring in greater depth how different levels of export intensity affect the interrelationship between the institutions analysed and natural resources. Table 4.2 reports the effect of 'law and order' on FDI inflow for meaningful levels of fuels and oil and ores and metal export intensity. The calculations show that an increasing level of natural resource export has a substantial effect on the impact of property rights on FDI. For instance, an increase in fuels and oil and ores and metal export intensity from 4 per cent, the level of Thailand, to 36 per cent, the level of South Africa, decreases the impact of 'law and order' from 0.84 to 0.16. The calculations also show that at

DOI: 10.1057/9781137367204.0011

Table 4.2 Effect of 'law and order' on FDI inflow for meaningful levels of fuels and oil, and ores and metal export intensity

Value of oil and metal export intensity	Quantile	Corresponding country	Law and order*
1.651257	10th	Paraguay	0.906357065
4.441002	25th	Thailand	0.847055176
11.29105	50th	Honduras	0.701443021
36.67997	75th	South Africa	0.16174821
74.38813	90th	Russia	−0.639817918

Note: this is the effect of law and order conditional on the value of resources export intensity, which is: $\delta LFDI/\delta Law$ and order $= \hat{\beta}_3 + \hat{\beta}_4 *$ *oil and metal export.*

The calculations are based on the coefficient estimated in Table 4.1 in column 4.

very high levels of natural resource exports the relationship between institutions and natural resource is reversed.

Table 4.3 analyses whether the impact of property rights on FDI is conditional on the type of resources exported. Recent discussion has shown that the impact of resources on economic development depends on the type of resources produced (Boschini et al., 2007). Namely, resources that are highly appropriable (due, e.g., to ease of transportation) may have a negative impact on economic growth, while this may not be the case for other types of resources. As such, minerals and oil tend to be more problematic than agricultural products, as the former are more lootable.[8] Table 4.3 analyses the effect of different types of resources on FDI, so we include three measures of export intensity: one for fuel, one for ores and one for agricultural products.

To save space, Table 4.3 reports estimates for the main parameters of interest from specification (1) (β_2, β_3 and β_4). In column 1, the interaction between the property rights indicator and fuel export is negative and significant, indicating that an increasing intensity in fuel export decreases the positive effect of property rights on FDI. However in column 2, the interaction between 'law and order' and metal export is not significant. The variable is jointly significant with the property rights indicator, although it does not have the expected sign. The results in columns 4 and 5, where we allow the regressors to be endogenous, seem to broadly confirm that only fuel, but not metal export intensity, has a significant influence on the property rights–FDI relationship. Columns 3 and 6 explore the role of agricultural export intensity and show that agricultural exports do not moderate the impact of property rights on FDI.

---

[8] Several theories can explain the negative impact of extractive industry on development. The main explanations are centred on the negative impact of oils and metal on the following: conflict (Collier and Hoeffler, 2004), state institutions (Fearon and Laitin, 2003; Snyder and Bhavnani, 2005) and trade shocks (Humphreys, 2005).

DOI: 10.1057/9781137367204.0011

Table 4.3   The impact of property rights on FDI

Variables	(1)	(2)	(3)	(4)	(5)	(6)
Ores_ex	0.00597**	−0.00971		0.00450	0.0159	
	(0.00263)	(0.0108)		(0.0170)	(0.0633)	
Fuel_ex	−0.00115	0.0130**		−0.0156	0.0526**	
	(0.00266)	(0.00539)		(0.0103)	(0.0230)	
Agri_ex			−0.00472			−0.138
			(0.0290)			(0.0926)
	(0.0324)	(0.0313)	(0.0667)	(0.101)	(0.115)	(0.0780)
Law	0.481	0.649**	1.113	1.970**	4.073**	−0.120
	(0.302)	(0.318)	(0.938)	(0.913)	(1.582)	(0.856)
Ores_ex*law		0.0276			−0.0165	
		(0.0181)			(0.103)	
Fuel_ex*law		−0.0251***			−0.118***	
		(0.00904)			(0.0454)	
Agri_ex*law			−0.0125			0.246
			(0.0574)			(0.156)
Observations	895	895	1,172	895	895	1,172
Number of ID	92	92	113	92	92	113
AR(1)-pvalue	5.12e−08	1.02e−07	2.72e−07	8.35e−06	2.05e−05	2.26e−06
AR(2)-pvalue	0.335	0.318	0.161	0.219	0.383	0.209
Hansen-pvalue	0.291	0.339	0.732	0.695	0.587	0.730
Instrument number	44	46	23	42	48	39

Note: robust standard errors in parentheses; *** $p < 0.01$, ** $p < 0.05$, * $p < 0.1$; year dummies and constant included but not reported. The table reports estimates for the main parameters of interest from specification (1). Dependent variable is the log of FDI/GDP. In columns 1 and 2 all regressors except the lagged dependent variable are exogenous. In columns 4, 5 and 6 all regressors are endogenous except the year controls.

Overall, the results highlight that high resources endowments undermine the positive effect of property rights on FDI. By analysing the interaction terms between different types of natural resource export intensity and property rights, we are able to explore whether the effect of institutions on FDI is conditional on the type of resources produced. We find strong evidence that in oil-rich countries the effects of efficient property rights are undermined. The results also show that the effect of metal export intensity, on its own, is less robust than the impact of oil export intensity. This may be puzzling since scholars have recently discussed that the oil and metal industry may have similar (negative) impact on economic development (Asiedu and Lien, 2011; Sala-i-Martin and Subramanian, 2003). However scholars have pointed out that the measure 'ores and metal export' may be a poor proxy for the importance of extractive industry. In fact, this indicator includes items such as crude fertilizer and scrap metal that are not part of extractive industry (de Soysa and Neumayer, 2007),

DOI: 10.1057/9781137367204.0011

and it fails to include diamonds and other precious gems which can notably have a deleterious effect on economic outcomes (Fearon, 2005). Interestingly, columns 3 and 6 show that agricultural export intensity does not significantly affect the institutions–FDI relationship, confirming recent discussion that the agricultural sector, compared to extractive industries, has a less detrimental effect on economic development (Isham et al., 2005).

Robustness

In order to give some credibility to our results, we carry out a number of robustness checks. First, we use alternative measures of natural resources. Again, we estimate two sets of models. In the first one, only the lagged dependent variable is taken as endogenous; in the second set of specifications, all regressors, except the year dummies, are treated as endogenous. Panel A in Table 4.4 analyses the impact of oil production and oil rent relative to GDP on the interplay between FDI and institutions. When using alternative measures of natural resources, our results confirm that the extraction of oil, but not of minerals, has a significant impact on the interplay between property rights and FDI.

As a second check, we divide the sample into low- and middle-income countries. The results are reported in panel B in Table 4.4. In columns 1 and 2 we measure natural resource endowment with the share of ores and metal and oil and fuel export to total export (nat), while in columns 3 and 4 we measure it with oil production as share of GDP. Our results show that the interactive term between the chosen measure of natural resources and 'law and order' is significant in all except column 1.

As a final check, in Table 4.5, we split the sample into resource-rich and non-resource-rich countries, and we investigate whether this affects the significance of 'law and order'. We use the UNCATD (2011) definition and split countries according to their level of resource export intensity, so resource-rich economies are those whose export intensity is greater than 50 per cent.[9] In Table 4.5 the property rights indicator is positive and significant only in non-resource-rich countries, while it is positive but not significant in resource-rich economies. The last robustness check thus further confirms the hypothesis that resource endowment affects the impact of the quality of institutions, in this instance the legal system, on the inflow of foreign investments.

---

[9] We have also carried out a similar check splitting the sample between countries that exploit resources and those that do not. Following Poelhekke and van der Ploeg (2010), we create a dummy variable equal to 1 when oil rents are positive. This measure allows capturing the effect of a resource discovery by assuming that when rents are zero resources are not extractable (for instance, if there is a civil war). The results are in line with what is reported in Table 4.6, hence they are not reported but are available on request.

DOI: 10.1057/9781137367204.0011

Table 4.4 The impact of oil production and oil rent relative to GDP on the interplay between FDI and institutions

Panel A				
Variables	(1)	(2)	(3)	(4)
Law	0.670***	2.388**	0.585**	2.388**
	(0.242)	(0.938)	(0.252)	(0.938)
Oil production	19.79***	37.82***		
	(5.137)	(13.52)		
Oil production*law	−28.17***	−59.65**		
	(9.763)	(25.35)		
Oil rent			3.169***	37.82***
			(0.887)	(13.52)
Oil rent*law			−4.582***	−59.65**
			(1.377)	(25.35)
Observations	881	881	881	881
Number of ID	88	88	88	88
AR(1)-pvalue	2.13e-07	3.59e-06	2.99e-07	3.59e-06
AR(2)-pvalue	0.459	0.423	0.489	0.423
Hansen-pvalue	0.165	0.458	0.167	0.458
Instrument number	43	42	44	42

Panel B				
	(1)	(2)	(3)	(4)
Variables	Low–income countries	Middle–income countries	Low–income countries	Middle–income countries
Law	2.044**	0.544*	0.985	0.493*
	(0.928)	(0.311)	(0.785)	(0.264)
Nat*law	0.0123	−0.0173*		
	(0.0101)	(0.00960)		
Oil production			33.58***	17.97***
			(10.97)	(5.336)
Oil production*law			−38.65*	−25.33**
			(20.43)	(10.17)
Observations	195	700	154	727
Number of ID	21	77	16	78
AR(1)-pvalue	0.00965	2.99e-06	0.00421	5.74e-06
AR(2)-pvalue	0.397	0.131	0.133	0.159
Hansen-pvalue	1	0.256	1	0.219
Instrument number	44	44	45	45

Note: robust standard errors in parentheses; *** $p < 0.01$, ** $p < 0.05$, * $p < 0.1$; year dummies and constant included but not reported. The table reports estimates for the main parameters of interest from specification (1). Dependent variable is the log of FDI/GDP. Law is the law and order indicator from ICRG, normalized between 0 and 1. Panel A: in columns 1 and 2 all regressors except the lag dependent variable are exogenous; in columns 3 and 4 all regressors are endogenous except the year controls.

DOI: 10.1057/9781137367204.0011

Table 4.5 Analysis of resource-rich and non-resource-rich countries' impact on 'law and order'

Variables	(1) Resource-rich countries	(2) Non-resource-rich countries	(3) Resource-rich countries	(4) Non-resource-rich countries	(5) Resource-rich countries	(6) Non-resource-rich countries
Nat	−0.00245	0.00904**				
	(0.00481)	(0.00429)				
Law	1.179	0.761**	0.464	0.731**	0.739	0.694**
	(0.613)	(0.336)	(0.413)	(0.340)	(0.478)	(0.345)
Oil production			6.036***	21.92***		
			(2.089)	(7.954)		
Oil rent					1.391**	3.987**
					(0.659)	(1.850)
Observations	166	729	244	637	244	637
Number of ID	25	80	38	71	38	71
AR(1)-pvalue	0.0637	2.09e-06	0.0566	3.36e-07	0.0578	3.33e-07
AR(2)-pvalue	0.574	0.519	0.426	0.551	0.307	0.551
Hansen-pvalue	1.000	0.657	0.520	0.183	0.637	0.226
Instrument number	43	43	43	43	43	43

Note: robust standard errors in parentheses; *** $p < 0.01$, ** $p < 0.05$, * $p < 0.1$; year dummies and constant included but not reported. Dependent variable is the log of FDI/GDP. The table reports estimates for the main parameters of interest from specification (1).

Conclusion

This chapter investigates whether the presence of natural resources plays a moderating role in the property rights–FDI relationship. The existing theoretical and empirical literature has emphasized that good institutions are important for both foreign and domestic investors. Accordingly, we should expect property rights to be positively correlated with FDI. However there are at least three reasons why this may not be the case for MNCs in natural resources. First, such companies have few linkages with the rest of the economy, which can decrease the sensitivity to the external environment. Second, institutional risk may be avoided by colluding with a local government. Third, high transaction costs can be compensated for by higher returns from participating in the resource rents. Our econometrics results show clearly that institutions do not act in isolation and that their effect on FDI is influenced by natural resources. We find novel evidence that natural resources significantly affect the impact of property rights on FDI. However the type of resources endowment matter, in fact only oil has a significant moderating impact on the FDI–property rights

DOI: 10.1057/9781137367204.0011

relationship. The existing literature on the effect of different types of natural resources on economic outcomes has shown that lootable resources may be more harmful than diffuse ones, such as agricultural products. The economics literature has traditionally considered the effect of oil to be similar to that of minerals; however political scientists have argued that oil-rich countries are different to other resource-rich countries. In particular, recent studies have found that the institutional environment of oil-producing economies does not reflect the country's level of development, as measured by per capita income; they are weaker than expected and this in turn can have a negative impact on political instability and conflict (Fearon, 2005; Fearon and Laitin, 2003). This study therefore shows how the distorted institutional setting of oil-rich countries may have a negative effect on development. Namely, we find that in oil-based economies investors are less sensitive to weak property rights protection. If this is the case, the influence of FDI on the host country institutional environment may be of concern. What explains the different effects of oil as contrasted with that of metal ores may be that the former generates particularly strong economic rents given the current trend in energy prices. Thus, this chapter gives indirect support to a recent body of the literature arguing that it is the amount of rent generated rather than the presence of natural resources that is a key factor in how natural resources affect development (Fearon, 2005).

The findings presented in this chapter have two important policy implications. First, the results demonstrate that in resource-rich economies institutional reforms may not be an effective tool to attract foreign investments. Second, even if these countries were committed to institutional reforms, progress could be hampered by the presence of foreign investors. If MNCs rely on informal and corrupt practices to protect their assets and to avoid the risk of expropriation, it is likely that the government would not receive any external pressure to improve the existing institutional setting.

DOI: 10.1057/9781137367204.0011

Appendix

Table 4A.1   Variables

Variable name	Variable label	Source
LFDI	Log FDI inflow as per cent of GDP	UNCTAD
LGDP	Log GDP in constant $	World Bank (WB) – World Development indicators (WDI)
LGDPP per capita	Log GDP per capita in constant $	WB – WDI
Inflation	Inflation, consumer price annual %	WB – WDI
Ltrade	Log trade (import and export as percentage of GDP)	WB – WDI
Nat	Fuel and metal export as percentage of total export	WB – WDI
Fuelex	Fuel export as percentage of total export	WB – WDI
Oresex	Ores and metal export as percentage of total export	
Agriex	Agricultural export as percentage of total export	WB – WDI
Political stability	Political stability (principal component of internal/external conflict, government stability and ethnic tension). Normalized between 0 and 1	International country risk guide (ICRG)
Law	Law and order normalized between 0 and 1	ICRG
Polity2	Democracy indicator	PolityIV
Oilprod	Oil production/GDP	WB
Oilrent	Oil rent/GDP	WB
Minrent	Mineral rent/GDP	WB

References

Alfaro, L., Kalemli-Ozcan, S. and Sayek, S. (2009) FDI, productivity and financial development. *The World Economy*, 32: 111–35.

Ali, F.A., Fiess, N. and MacDonald, R. (2010) Do institutions matter for foreign direct investment? *Open Economies Review*, 21(2): 201–19.

Agarwal, S. and Ramaswami, S. (1992) Choice of foreign market entry mode: impact of ownership, location and internalization factors. *Journal of International Business Studies*, 23(1): 1–27.

Asiedu, E. (2002) On the determinants of foreign direct investment in developing countries: is Africa different? *World Development*, 30(1): 107–19.

Asiedu, E. and Lien, D. (2011) Democracy, foreign direct investment and natural resources. *Journal of International Economics*, 84(1): 99–111.

DOI: 10.1057/9781137367204.0011

Ballentine, K. and Nitzschke, H. (2004) Business in armed conflict: an assessment of issues and options. *Journal of International Peace and Security*, 79(1–2): 35–56.

Bayulgen, O. (2010) *Foreign Investment and Political Regimes*. Cambridge: Cambridge University Press.

Bénassy-Quéré, A., Coupet, M. and Mayer, T. (2007) Institutional determinant of foreign direct investment. *The World Economy*, 30(5): 764–82.

Blomström, M. and Kokko, A. (2003) The economics of foreign direct investment incentives. NBER working paper no. 9489.

Blundell, R. and Bond, S. (2000) GMM estimation with persistent panel data: an application to production functions. *Econometric Reviews*, 19(3): 321–40.

Boschini, A.D., Pettersson, J. and Roine, J. (2007) Resource curse or not: a question of appropriability. *Scandinavian Journal of Economics*, 109(3): 593–617.

Brewer, T. (1993) Foreign direct investment in emerging market countries, in L. Oxelheim (ed.) *The Global Race for Foreign Direct Investment*. New York: Springer-Verlag.

Carstensen, K. and Toubal, F. (2004) Foreign direct investment in Central and Eastern European countries: a dynamic panel analysis. *Journal of Comparative Economics*, 32(1): 3–22.

Caves, R. (1996) *Multinational Enterprise and Economic Analysis*. Cambridge: Cambridge University Press.

Chakrabarti, A. (2001) The determinants of foreign direct investment: sensitivity analyses of cross-country regressions. *Kyklos*, 54: 89–113.

Cheng, L.K. and Kwan, Y.K. (2000) What are the determinants of the location of foreign direct investments? The Chinese experience. *Journal of International Economics*, 51(2): 379–400.

Collier, P. and Hoeffler, A. (2004) Greed and grievance in civil war. *Oxford Economic Paper*, 56: 663–95.

Crenshaw, E. (1991) Foreign direct investment as a dependent variable. *Social Forces*, 69: 1169–82.

Daude, C. and Stein, E. (2007) The quality of institutions and foreign direct investment. *Economics and Politics*, 19(3): 317–44.

de Mello, L. (1999) Foreign direct investment-led growth: evidence from time series and panel data. *Oxford Economic Papers*, 51(1): 133–51.

Demsetz, H. (1967) Towards a theory of property rights. *American Economic Review*, 57(2): 347–59.

de Soysa, I. and Neumayer, E. (2007) Natural resources and civil war: another look with new data. *Conflict Management and Peace Science*, 24(3): 201–18.

Dunning, J.H. (1993) *Multinational Enterprise and Global Economy*. Wokingham, UK and Reading, Mass: Addison Wesley.

Eden, L., Lenway, S. and Schuler, D.A. (2004) From the obsolescing bargain to the political bargaining model. Bush School working paper no. 403, Texas A&M University, January.

Fearon, J.D. (2005) Primary commodity exports and civil war. *Journal of Conflict Resolution*, 49(4): 483–507.

Fearon, J.D. and Laitin, D.D. (2003) Ethnicity, insurgency, and civil war. *American Political Science Review*, 97: 75–90.

Fatehi-Sadeth, K. and Safizadeh, H. (1989) The association between political instability and flow of foreign direct investment. *Management International Review*, 29: 4–13.

Gani, A. (2007) Governance and foreign direct investment links: evidence from panel data estimations. *Applied Economics Letters*, 14(10): 753–56.

DOI: 10.1057/9781137367204.0011

Globerman, S. and Shapiro, D. (2002) Global foreign direct investment flows: the role of governance infrastructure. *World Development*, 30(11): 1899–919.

Grosse, R. (1997) Foreign direct investment in Latin America, in R. Grosse (ed.) *Generating Savings for Latin American Development*. Coral Gables, FL: North–South Center Press, University of Miami.

Hayakawa, K. (2007) Small sample bias properties of the system GMM estimator in dynamic panel data models. *Economics Letters*, 95(1): 32–8.

Henisz, W.J. (2000) The institutional environment for multinational investment. *The Journal of Law, Economics and Organizations*, 16(2): 334–64.

Hodler, R. (2005) The curse of natural resources in fractionalized countries. *European Economic Review*, 50(6): 1367–86.

Jenkins, B. (1986) Reexamining the 'obsolescing bargaining': A study of Canada's national energy program. *International Organization*, 40: 139–65.

Isham, J., Pritchett, L., Woolcock, M. and Busby, G. (2005) The varieties of resource experience: natural resource export structures and the political economy of economic growth. *World Bank Economic Review*, 19: 141–74.

Le Billon, P. (2005) *Fuelling War: Natural Resources and Armed Conflict*. Abingdon and New York: Routledge.

Li, S. and Filer, L. (2007) The effect of the governance environment on the choice of investment mode and the strategic implications. *Journal of World Business*, 42: 80–98.

Libecap, G. (1989) *Contracting for Property Rights*. New York: Cambridge University Press.

Lipsey, R.E. (1999) The location and characteristics of US affiliates in Asia, NBER working paper no. 6876.

Liu, X., Wang, C. and Wei, Y. (2001) Causal links between foreign direct investment and trade in China. *China Economic Review*, 12(2): 190–202.

Luo, Y. (2001) Toward a cooperative view of MNC–host government relations: building blocks and performance implications. *Journal of International Business Studies*, 32: 104–419.

Noorbakhsh, F., Paloni, A. and Youssef, A. (2001) Human capital and FDI inflows to developing countries: new empirical evidence. *World Development*, 29: 1593–610.

North, D. (1990) *Institution, Institutional Change and Economic Performances*. New York: Cambridge University Press.

Nunnenkamp, P. and Spatz, J. (2003) Intellectual Property rights and foreign direct investment: the role of industry and host-country characteristics. Kiel working paper no. 1167, Kiel Institute for the World Economy.

Poelhekke, S. and van der Ploeg, R. (2010) Do natural resources attract non-resource FDI? Oxford Centre for the Analysis of Resource Rich Economies, OxCarre working paper no. 051, University of Oxford.

Renner, M. (2002) The anatomy of resource wars. Worldwatch paper no. 162, Worldwatch Institute.

Roodman, D. (2006) How to do xtabond2: an introduction to 'difference' and 'system' GMM in stata, working paper no. 103, Center for Global Development.

Ross, M.L. (1999) The political economy of the resource curse. *World Politics*, 51(1): 297–322.

Sachs, J.D. and Warner, A.M. (1995) Natural resource abundance and economic growth, working paper no. 5398, Cambridge, National Bureau of Economic Research.

Sachs, J.D. and Warner, A.M. (2001) The curse of natural resources. *European Economic Review*, 45(4–6): 827–38.

DOI: 10.1057/9781137367204.0011

Sala-i-Martin, X. and Subramanian, A. (2003) Addressing the natural resource curse: an illustration from Nigeria, NBER working paper no. 9804.

Satyanath, S. and Subramanian, A. (2004) What determines long-run macroeconomic stability? Democratic institution, working paper no. 215, IMF.

Schulz, H. (2007) Political institutions and foreign direct investment in developing countries: does the sector matter? Working paper, University of Pennsylvania.

Stone, B. and Jeon, S. (2000) Foreign direct investment and trade in the Asia-Pacific region: complementarity, distance and regional economic integration. *Journal of Economic Integration*, 15(3): 460–85.

Spar, D. (1999) Foreign investment and human rights. *Challenge*, 42: 55–80.

Tugwell, F. (1975) *The Politics of Oil in Venezuela*. Stanford: Stanford University Press.

Vernon, R. (1971) *Sovereignty at Bay: The Multinational Spread of US Enterprise*. New York: Basic Books.

UNCTAD (2011) Classification Update, Economic Grouping available from: http://www.unctad.org/fdistatistics.

Williamson, O.E. (1987) *The Economic Institutions of Capitalism: Firms, Markets, Relational Contracting*. New York: Free Press.

World Resource Institute (2007) Annual Report 2006/2007. Washington, DC: World Resource Institute.

DOI: 10.1057/9781137367204.0011

5
The Impact of the Financial Crisis on the Performance of European Acquisitions

Rekha Rao Nicholson and Julie Salaber

Introduction

Shareholder wealth accretion is difficult to predict under most circumstances (Doukas and Kan, 2006; Cartwright and Schoenberg, 2006) and it can become a herculean task when cast under the shadows of a financial crisis (Mody and Negishi, 2000). In this chapter, we examine the role of a supranational institution like the Economic and Monetary Union (EMU) on the value creation ability of mergers and acquisitions (M&As) for investors during the financial turmoil. We look at European acquisitions undertaken before and after the 2007–8 financial crisis to ascertain short-term shareholder returns. The majority of earlier studies either look at domestic versus international aspects of M&A deals without paying attention to the regional and supranational arrangements integrating different countries, or they have examined the performance of M&A deals during 'normal' times, which leaves out the effects of financial instability or economic recession within and across a political or economic union as a question yet to be answered.

In this study, we look at acquisitions across 22 European Union (EU) countries (both EMU and non-EMU) and expect countries within the EMU to experience similar institutional constraints from the economic slowdown (Rose and Spiegel, 2012).

As this chapter concentrates on the impact of the recent financial crisis on the short-term performance of European acquisitions, we hypothesize and test the following research questions:

Did the financial crisis impact shareholder returns of European acquisitions? Does the EMU have an influence over the deals undertaken after the financial crisis?

DOI: 10.1057/9781137367204.0012

73

We use institutional theory and transaction cost economic theory to study whether bidders derive lower or higher returns from acquisitions announced after 2008. We investigate shareholders' stock price reaction to 2245 deals which occurred during 2004–12 across 22 EU countries.

By investigating the performance of European cross-border M&As before and after the financial crisis, our study fills a gap in the literature and links two interesting and equally important topics: cross-border M&A activity and performance within an economic union (Cartwright and Schoenberg, 2006) and the impact of a crisis on business performance (Chau et al., 2012). Our study extends the argument on how a crisis will impact short-term returns on companies' inorganic growth strategies through M&As.

Background and hypotheses

The European region has had a single European market since 1992 (the EU and its 28 member countries); and in 1999, the third stage of the EMU began. The EMU integrates 17 countries with a common monetary policy supervised by the European Central Bank. The theoretical arguments, which support links between trade liberalization, regional trade agreements and acquisitions, have been discussed in Coeurdacier et al. (2009). In times of economic growth, a monetary union will foster easy access to goods across national borders and help low-cost firms to buy high-cost firms effortlessly. Also, the integration of financial systems brought about by a monetary union will sustain the flow of equity capital between different countries. Such European integration should drive down the cost of conducting transactions within its borders; and, due to the elimination of financial barriers within the Eurozone and the implementation of a single currency, home bias has greatly decreased within the euro area (Issing, 2006). The EMU has helped the manufacturing sector restructure its capital (Coeurdacier et al., 2009). It also reduces business stealing effects (Bjorvatn, 2004), thus making it attractive for companies to engage in cross-border deals within the EMU. European economic integration reduces the reservation price of the target (Bjorvatn, 2004). Since the run up to 1992, the EMU element of foreign direct investment (FDI) in Europe, including acquisitions, has grown considerably (Chesnais and Simonetti, 2000). European firms have used M&As as a tool to build and develop intra-European networks (Ietto-Gillies et al., 2000). Over the last few decades, there has been a consolidation of stock exchanges, which undeniably helped ease M&A transactions within the EU and beyond.

Hence, looking at this natural setting where both domestic and cross-border deals within the EMU are likely to achieve equal returns to acquirers is an appealing area of research. Extant research on the short-term performance of bidders shows that, on average, acquirers earn negative abnormal returns (Kim

DOI: 10.1057/9781137367204.0012

et al., 2011; Klossek et al., 2012; Kobrin, 1979). The short-term performance outcomes of cross-border acquisitions are mixed. US bidders acquiring in foreign locales can experience positive (Doukas and Travlos, 1988; Kostova et al., 2008) or negative (Ghemawat, 2001) returns. A study on UK cross-border bidders shows that they do not earn any significant abnormal return around the announcement date (Gregory and McCorriston, 2005).

The US began to experience the effects of the financial crisis from December 2007 (Reinhart and Rogoff, 2009) which was followed by the Eurozone debt crisis (Arezki et al., 2011). Global M&A activity peaked in 2007 (UNCTAD, 2011); however when the effects of the crisis began to be realized, FDI, including acquisitions, fell from $1979 billion to $1697 billion in 2008 and the trend continued to decline in 2009 (UNCTAD, 2009). Reduced profits and shrinking operational overheads have compelled businesses to focus their resources on their main business and not diverge into other industries or countries. Also, stock markets have lost much of their value (Te Velde et al., 2009), thus limiting the value of transactions (UNCTAD, 2009). Yet we observe many firms undertaking acquisitions. This is consistent with neoclassical theory suggesting that the occurrence of M&As is a consequence of economic shocks (Harford, 2005; Mitchell and Mulherin, 1996). Hence it is pertinent to scrutinize how these domestic and cross-border deals have fared after the global financial crisis.

The phenomenon of acquisitions and associated shareholder wealth accrual has been extensively researched (Cartwright and Schoenberg, 2006; Schoenberg, 2006). Studies have ranged from country (Eckert et al., 2010) and regional studies (Campa and Hernando, 2006) to those that address outcomes of these activities globally (Doukas and Kan, 2006). Comparative studies have looked at the returns of domestic versus cross-border acquisitions (Anand et al., 2005; Gubbi et al., 2010). Though studies have looked at acquisitions during other crises (Mody and Negishi, 2000; Williams and Nguyen, 2005), there is limited research on acquisitions during the recent financial crisis and the following economic recession. Similarly, there are limited studies on supranational institutions and their influence on regional M&As.

We argue that our understanding of outcomes of acquisitions during a crisis can be enhanced by using multiple theoretical lenses to decipher the influence of the recent crisis on intra-European acquisitions.

Differential value accrual in acquisitions before and after the financial crisis

During an economic slowdown, resource redeployment for firm survival is imperative. Acquisitions provide this opportunity to reconfigure the product-mix (Krishnan et al., 2004). Similarly, resources are scarce during recessionary times, and acquisitions undergone after the financial crisis can be seen as a way to change a firm's resources and capabilities (Wan and Yiu,

DOI: 10.1057/9781137367204.0012

2009; Karim and Mitchell, 2000). Acquisitions may help companies to better adjust to the dynamic nature of the business environment in the post-crisis period. To understand the value generated in acquisitions during the post-crisis period, it might be fruitful to look at the effect of the crisis on transaction costs between the acquiring and target firms. The use of transaction cost economics to explain costs involved in acquisitions derives its intellectual roots from the work of Williamson (1975). The argument developed from this theory centres around numerous imperfections that may be present in markets for intangible resources, including immobility, information asymmetries and related moral hazards, causal ambiguity and monopoly. Williamson's seminal work also looks at the cost of conducting exchanges under various institutional circumstances that allow for protection of relationship-specific investments at the lowest total cost. Transaction cost economics also relates to secondary costs of negotiation and enforcement.

Before the crisis shareholder returns to European M&As, both EMU and non-EMU, were likely to be similar to returns widely discussed in extant literature. Indeed, during the pre-crisis period, monetary union lowers the cost of transactions across borders and facilitates high-cost firms to be bought by low-cost firms. Financial integration within Europe helps reduce the cost of capital, removes exchange rate risk, creates shared common trading platforms and the integration of post-trading market infrastructure (Coeurdacier et al., 2009).

In the post-crisis period, both EMU and non-EMU targets may face a further deterioration in their immediate business environment (Pangarkar and Lie, 2004) and might experience erosion of firm value due to crisis-related economic distress (Wruck, 1990; Acharya and Schnabl, 2010; Mitton, 2002). During the financial crisis, companies are looking to quickly restructure and realign their assets (Campello et al., 2010) reducing the time spent on negotiations prior to acquisitions. Similarly, it can be argued that after the crisis, due to firm devaluation and stock market crash, overpayment for acquisitions is highly unlikely (Wan and Yiu, 2009), thus reducing the cost of individual transactions. Also, transaction costs are reduced by the leveraging of internal capital markets by slack-rich firms who can acquire slack-poor firms with extraordinary growth opportunities (Goergen and Renneboog, 2004). Companies can generate synergies during turbulent economic times by adopting new resources and using new opportunities through acquisitions at low costs (Chattopadhyay et al., 2001; Meyer, 1982). We argue that in Europe the 2007–8 financial crisis will have a significant impact on firm transactions and in determining value to be gained by shareholders. We expect European companies to benefit from the global recession when undertaking acquisitions activites, that is, shareholders give more value to acquisitions announced after the financial crisis due to the higher risks involved and returns associated with undertaking acquisitions during bad economic times.

DOI: 10.1057/9781137367204.0012

Hypothesis 1: European companies that announce acquisitions in the post-crisis period will achieve higher returns as compared to companies that announce acquisitions in the pre-crisis period.

Returns to EMU vis-à-vis non-EMU transactions

Institutional theorists like North (1990) have explored the role and effect of institutions on certainty in business transactions. Both formal and informal institutions introduce constraints that businesses need to understand to engage in their day-to-day activities. Most of these institutions, formal and informal, are nation specific and it is pertinent for companies to comprehend these rules of the game to engage in economic activity across national borders. Similarly, countries that have comparable institutions, including financial ones, are likely to have companies with similar corporate structures and provide a business environment that fosters international acquisitions (Gubbi et al., 2010).

Thus, in terms of internationalization within Europe, non-Eurozone countries will encounter greater institutional dissimilarities. The environmental complexity is minimized when companies engage with host countries that have institutions comparable to their home country (Dikova et al., 2009). Acquirers are able to understand and adjust easily to business environments that are similar to their own (Kostova and Zaheer, 1999). Thus, in good economic times, being part of this exclusive club might prove to be an advantage for some companies internationalizing within Europe. Hence, in the pre-crisis period, transactions occurring within the EMU are likely to derive higher returns than non-EMU transactions.

The economic recession spreading across Europe as a result of the 2007–8 financial crisis adds fresh dynamics to this story. The new financial and corporate assets made accessible through international acquisitions can be particularly useful following a systemic crisis that affects a large number of firms (Mody and Negishi, 2000). Too much similarity, as evidenced within EMU countries, might leave little space to harness cross-border differences and nuances that help businesses leverage their competitive advantages, especially in a recessionary economic landscape (Wan and Yiu, 2009; Gubbi et al., 2010). Indeed some European countries have different currencies and financial institutions as they are outside the EMU. Authors have indicated that differential tax systems can help cross-border deals (Goergen and Renneboog, 2004). Thus we argue that, within Europe, the distinction between EMU and non-EMU transactions is more relevant than the usual distinction between domestic and cross-border transactions. This non-EMU effect is likely to be amplified during bad economic times as firms are looking to find suitable partners to leverage their synergies (Mody and Negishi, 2000; Wan and Yiu, 2009). In this turbulent business climate therefore shareholder's returns are driven by

DOI: 10.1057/9781137367204.0012

what the market perceives as optimal coupling during acquisitions. In the years after 2008, the acquirer and target face differences in terms of financial institutions and implied differences in institutional stability and access to finance can create a new mix of competencies and resources, which can be suitable for adapting to new market conditions. Authors have looked at other high turbulent business environments, such as privatizations in transition economies, and argued that understanding country risk is essential to foreign acquisitions as it can fundamentally alter the basis upon which acquisition decisions are made (Uhlenbruck and De Castro, 2000). During the post-crisis period, we argue that financial contagion and associated economic, political and financial risk will have a much larger impact on a firm's strategic decision to acquire within the EMU or outside. We argue there are several dynamics within this region, which could drive acquisitions and returns to transactions. For example, countries outside the EMU might be shielded from the immediate impact of emergent financial and economic turbulence from, say, the collapse of the common currency. Hence, for countries within the EMU, buying outside the Eurozone might signify risk diversification. Indeed, companies that choose to transact outside the EMU are creating a valuable service for investors by permitting them to diversify their portfolio risk indirectly by purchasing shares in multinationals outside the immediate impact region. Also, a non-EMU company buying an EMU firm could also indicate risk diversification. Thus we argue that stock markets will accordingly reward these non-EMU transactions as compared to intra-EMU deals.

Hypothesis 2: in the post-crisis period, European companies that engage in non-EMU deals derive better returns as compared to firms that engage in EMU deals.

Methodology and data

Event study methodology

We use an event study methodology to assess the effect of the financial crisis and recession on the short-term performance of European acquirers. This event study method measures and tests for the significance of abnormal stock returns around the acquisition's announcement date (MacKinlay, 1997). Abnormal returns are calculated as the difference between actual ex-post and expected normal returns:

$$AR_{it} = R_{it} - E(R_{it} \mid X_t) \tag{1}$$

where AR_{it}, R_{it}, and $E(R_{it} \mid X_t)$ are the abnormal, actual and expected returns respectively at time t and X_t is the conditioning set of information in the

DOI: 10.1057/9781137367204.0012

normal return model. The abnormal return thus measures the stock market response to the announcement of an acquisition as visible in the movement of the share price of the acquiring firm. This method is similar to the extant literature focusing on the short-term performance of M&As (Cartwright and Schoenberg, 2006; Moeller and Schlingemann, 2005; Gubbi et al., 2010; Doukas and Kan, 2006). Also, this ex-ante performance measure prior to the actual integration of the target has been demonstrated to link well with ex-post firm-level outcomes (Kale et al., 2002; Pangarkar and Lie, 2004).

We then calculate the cumulative abnormal return (CAR) for each deal by summing daily abnormal returns over the event window [–5;0]:

$$CAR_i = \sum_{t=-5}^{0} AR_{it} \qquad (2)$$

Multivariate methodology

In order to test our hypotheses, we run a cross-sectional analysis whereby we try to explain the CAR with alternative independent variables.

For our first hypothesis, we construct a post-crisis dummy (POST-CRISIS) equal to one for all deals announced after the 2007–8 financial crisis; zero otherwise.

During the months from late 2007 to early 2009, all stock markets across Europe crashed as a result of the credit crunch initiated in the USA. Moreover economic indicators reacted to the financial crisis with a lag and it was only during the first quarter of 2009 that all European countries were officially in an economic recession (Claessens et al., 2010). Thus we start our POST-CRISIS dummy in March 2009, which coincides with the end of stock market crashes across Europe.

In order to test our second hypothesis, we create a NON-EMU dummy, which equals one when the transaction happens across the EMU border, that is, either the bidder or the target is located in a country outside the Eurozone. The idea is that these non-EMU acquisitions should provide greater diversification effects (along with potential foreign exchange risk) than acquisitions within the Eurozone, especially since the financial crisis and economic slowdown (Wan and Yiu, 2009). Thus we expect these non-EMU deals to earn significantly higher returns over the post-crisis period, and we test this hypothesis by creating an interaction variable NON-EMU*POST-CRISIS.

In order to assess the true impact of the variables mentioned, we need to control deal-specific and firm-specific characteristics. Deal-specific variables commonly used in the M&A literature (Capron and Shen, 2007; Denis et al., 2002; Dos Santos et al., 2008; Gubbi et al., 2010; Moeller and Schlingemann, 2005; Shleifer and Vishny, 2003; von Eije and Wiegerinck, 2010; Blackburn

DOI: 10.1057/9781137367204.0012

et al., 1997; Brown and Ryngaert, 1991; Faccio and Masulis, 2005; Martynova and Renneboog, 2008; Sudarsanam and Mahate, 2006) are: the status of the target, that is, whether it is privately held (PRIVATE=1) or not; the industry relatedness, that is, whether the bidder and the target belong to the same industry (SAMEIND=1); the mode of payment (CASH=1); the relative size of the target (RELATIVESIZE=deal value/market value of the acquirer); and the percentage of the target company acquired during the transaction (PERCACQ). Firm-specific characteristics such as the acquirer's size (MV) and price-to-book ratio (PTB) are also known to impact the short-term returns of the company and so are included (Lang et al., 1991; Moeller and Schlingemann, 2005; Rau and Vermaelen, 1998; Sudarsanam and Mahate, 2006).

Data

Data on European acquisitions come from Thomson One. We collected all deals fulfilling the following criteria:

(a) the acquisition was completed between 2004 and 2012;
(b) the bidder owned a majority stake in the target company after the transaction;
(c) the country of both bidder and target companies is an EU member at the beginning of the sample and at least one counterparty is located in a Eurozone country;
(d) the acquirer is publicly traded; and
(e) the value of the transaction is available.

From this initial sample, we deleted some deals (deal value equals zero, announcement date and effective date are more than three years apart) and matched the data with the list of stocks from Thomson DataStream (each stock must be actively traded around the announcement date).

Our final sample consists of 2245 deals from 1088 bidders located in 20 different EU countries: Austria, Belgium, Cyprus, Denmark, Estonia, Finland, France, Germany, Greece, Republic of Ireland, Italy, Lithuania, Luxembourg, Netherlands, Poland, Portugal, Slovenia, Spain, Sweden and the UK. Table 5.1 shows the distribution of deals used in this study, by acquirer and target country. Note that the Czech Republic and Hungary appear only as target countries as there are no bidders from these countries present in our sample. The top five acquirer nations are France, the UK, Italy, Germany and Spain; and these countries are also the most targeted by European acquirers. Note that acquisitions from non-EMU to non-EMU countries are not included in our sample.

DOI: 10.1057/9781137367204.0012

Table 5.1 Number of deals by acquirer and target country

Acquirer country		AU	BE	CY	CZ	DK	ES	FI	FR	DE	GR	HU	IR	IT	LI	LU	NL	PL	PO	SL	SP	SW	UK	Total
AU	Austria	20							1	14			2	3			2	2		2	1	2	4	54
BE	Belgium		57						29	3			1	5		4	5		1		4		9	118
CY	Cyprus			9							1												1	11
CZ	Czech Republic																							0
DK	Denmark						1	2		5			3				4				3			18
ES	Estonia					1		1	1															3
FI	Finland	1	13					64	2	9				2			4	3			1	22	5	123
FR	France	1		1	2	4	3	2	271	35	6		1	24	1	1	14	6	2		22	4	25	435
DE	Germany	7	1	2	2	4	1	3	15	168	1	1	1	6		2	15	1			3	1	22	254
GR	Greece	1		7			1		1	1	65		1	2							1			79
HU	Hungary																							0
IR	Ireland	1				2	1		1	3		1	24				6				2	2	28	68
IT	Italy	1	3						8	12			1	209		2	5	2			9	1	14	267
LI	Lithuania										1				7			1						9
LU	Luxembourg										1												1	2
NL	Netherlands	4	7		1			2	17	8	1	1	1	4	1	1	56	1			5	10	21	140
PL	Poland	1							1	1			1	2		1					5			13
PO	Portugal									1				1					29	4	4			35
SL	Slovenia										1								4					5
SP	Spain	2	2		2		2		10	6	2		14	1			3	3		1	131	1	13	194
SW	Sweden	4	1				1	29	9	23			3	3	5		13		1	1	7			99
UK	United Kingdom	2	11	1				6	48	96	3		38	35		3	37	4	4	3	31			318
	Total	45	95	18	9	15	10	109	414	385	80	4	73	313	16	13	161	20	41	11	227	43	143	2245

DOI: 10.1057/9781137367204.0012

The deal characteristics we collected from Thomson One are: the deal value, the acquirer/target SIC code, the target status, the method of payment and the percentage acquired during the transaction. Daily financial data on stock return, market value and price-to-book ratio of the acquirer are collected from Thomson DataStream. We also collected from DataStream daily market index returns and daily exchange rates of each EU currency with the US dollar. Table 5.2 presents the characteristics of stock markets in each country, that is, the number of stocks for which we collected daily returns, the stock market index used as a benchmark, and the currency of the returns. All returns and financial data were converted to US dollars.

Figure 5.1 presents various deal characteristics for the pre- and post-crisis periods across different categories of deals: domestic deals within the EMU, cross-border deals within the EMU and cross-border deals between EMU and non-EMU countries.

Table 5.3 reports the correlation coefficients across all of our variables. Overall, most variables are not significantly correlated, the highest coefficient being 25 per cent correlation between PRIVATE and PERCACQ.

Table 5.2   Acquirer's country and stock market characterisics

Bidder nation	EU year of entry	Number of bidders	Market index	Currency
Austria	1995	25	ATX	EUR
Belgium	1952	45	BEL20	EUR
Cyprus	2004	10	FTSE Cyprus SE2O	EUR
Denmark	1973	11	OMX Copenhagen 20	DKK
Estonia	2004	3	OMX Tallinn	EUR
Finland	1995	59	OMX Helsinki 25	EUR
France	1952	187	CAC40	EUR
Germany	1952	136	DAX30	EUR
Greece	1981	51	ATHEX Composite	EUR
Ireland Rep.	1973	24	ISEQ	EUR
Italy	1952	110	FTSE MIB	EUR
Lithuania	2004	6	OMX Vilnius	EUR
Luxembourg	1952	1	Luxembourg SE General	EUR
Netherlands	1952	58	AEX	EUR
Poland	2004	10	TOTMKPO*	PLN
Portugal	1986	21	PSI20	EUR
Slovenia	2004	3	TOTMKSJ*	EUR
Spain	1986	69	IBEX35	EUR
Sweden	1995	59	OMX Stockholm 30	SEK
UK	1973	200	FTSE 100	GBP

Note: * this is an index created by Thomson DataStream covering the total stock market.

DOI: 10.1057/9781137367204.0012

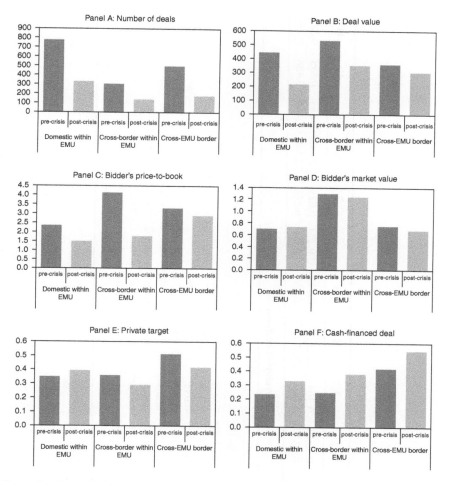

Figure 5.1 Deal characteristics across two sub-periods (pre- and post-crisis) and for different categories of deals

Results

Univariate analysis of CAR

Table 5.4 presents the results of the univariate analysis for CAR[−5;0]. CARs are averaged over two sub-periods, pre- and post-crisis, and student tests are performed in order to compare the difference of CAR between the two periods. Across all deals (left side of Table 5.4), abnormal returns earned in the post-crisis period are significantly higher than abnormal returns earned before 2009. Deals announced after the crisis earned on average an extra 0.69 per

DOI: 10.1057/9781137367204.0012

Table 5.3 Correlation matrix

	CAR[-5;0]	1	2	3	4	5	6	7	8	9	10	11
MEAN	0.011	0.293	0.504	0.304	387.1	0.830	0.273	0.825	2.692	0.685	0.395	0.324
STD	0.059	0.455	0.500	0.460	2022.1	1.986	2.698	0.293	13.540	0.464	0.488	0.466
					Correlation coefficients							
1 POST-CRISIS	0.053**	1.000										
2 CROSS-BORDER	-0.005	-0.019	1.000									
3 NON-EMU	0.041*	-0.040*	0.656***	1.000								
4 DEALVALUE	-0.037*	-0.036*	0.006	-0.013	1.000							
5 MV	-0.074***	0.000	0.059***	-0.033	0.228***	1.000						
6 RELATIVESIZE	0.063***	-0.024	-0.001	0.022	0.024	-0.035*	1.000					
7 PERCACQ	0.057***	-0.011	0.182***	0.213***	-0.011	-0.162***	0.035*	1.000				
8 PTB	0.005	-0.035*	0.044**	0.025	-0.006	-0.007	-0.002	0.001	1.000			
9 SAMEIND	-0.013	-0.056***	0.052*	0.046**	0.069***	0.045**	0.011	-0.020	0.005	1.000		
10 PRIVATE	0.000	-0.021	0.069***	0.126***	-0.122***	-0.204***	0.003	0.253***	-0.002	-0.016	1.000	
11 CASH	-0.009	0.104***	0.134***	0.180***	0.006	0.013	0.008	-0.034	0.007	-0.022	-0.043**	1.000

DOI: 10.1057/9781137367204.0012

Table 5.4 Univariate analysis

	All deals	Domestic	Cross-Border	Difference	EMU	Non-EMU	Difference
Pre-crisis	0.91%	0.98%	0.84%	−0.14%	0.85%	1.03%	0.18%
	1587	*778*	*809*		*1086*	*501*	
Post-crisis	1.60%	1.52%	1.68%	0.16%	1.18%	2.68%	1.50% **
	658	*336*	*322*		*477*	*181*	
Difference	0.69%**	0.54%	0.84%*		0.33%	1.65%**	

cent return (equivalent to 2.5 per cent a month). This is a preliminary indication of a significant difference in the performance of acquisitions announced before versus after the financial crisis, which we sought to test in the first hypothesis.

On the right side of the table, CARs are averaged across EMU and non-EMU transactions in order to further investigate these abnormal returns. We perform additional student tests to compare abnormal returns between EMU and non-EMU deals. On the one hand, the significant difference we found for all deals between the two periods is entirely due to significantly higher abnormal returns for non-EMU acquisitions in the second period. Indeed non-EMU transactions earn an extra 6 per cent monthly return when announced after the crisis; whereas there is no statistical difference between pre- and post-crisis EMU deals. On the other hand, testing for the statistical difference in CARs between EMU and non-EMU acquisitions reveals that non-EMU deals earn significantly higher returns (+5.4 per cent per month) than EMU deals, but only in the post-crisis period.

In the middle part of Table 5.4, we also provide average CARs between domestic and cross-border deals in order to highlight a potential cross-border effect previously emphasized in the literature (Gubbi et al., 2010; Moeller and Schlingemann, 2005). Again we test for the statistical difference in CARs both between the pre- and post-crisis periods and between cross-border and domestic acquisitions. Student tests of these differences are not all statistically significant. When comparing domestic and cross-border deals, we do not find any statistical difference in their CARs, both before and after the crisis. Thus European acquisitions are not subject to the so-called cross-border effect. These results corroborate our hypothesis that, within the EU, the distinction between EMU and non-EMU transactions is more relevant than the usual distinction between domestic and cross-border acquisitions, especially in the post-crisis period.

DOI: 10.1057/9781137367204.0012

Cross-sectional analysis

Table 5.5 shows the results of OLS regressions with White robust standard errors. In Table 5.5 model 1, we include only the control variables in the regression. Throughout the multivariate analysis, three of the control variables significantly impact the short-term abnormal return of the acquirer. MV has a negative impact, which is consistent with the managerial hubris hypothesis (Roll, 1986; Moeller et al., 2004; Faccio et al., 2006) whereas PERCACQ and RELATIVESIZE have a positive effect on CAR. Moreover cash-financed acquisitions are usually associated with higher returns (Faccio and Masulis, 2005; Martynova and Renneboog, 2008) as stock-financed transactions might signal to the investors that the stock is overvalued (Myers and Majluf, 1984). However our sample covers a long period of financial crisis and economic recession and thus is more concerned by undervalued than overvalued stocks.

Our first hypothesis finds strong support in Table 5.5 model 2. Our POST-CRISIS dummy records a positive and significant coefficient (5 per cent statistical significance). The coefficient is 0.0072 indicating returns of 2.6 per cent per month, which shows evidence that acquisitions announced during the economic recession earned higher abnormal returns compared to transactions announced over the period 2004–8. This result is consistent with the univariate analysis, that is, European acquirers on average generate greater returns for their shareholders when undertaking M&A activities during the recessionary period, even after controlling for firm-specific and deal-specific characteristics.

Table 5.5 model 3 presents the regression results with only the first dummy (NON-EMU). This variable alone doesn't have much impact on the short-term return of the acquirer. However the analysis over the post-crisis period shows a different picture. Indeed the interaction term NON-EMU*POST-CRISIS clearly emphasizes a significantly higher return for non-EMU deals after the crisis. We present several models with the inclusion of different explanatory variables. The extra monthly return relative to pre-crisis non-EMU deals is 4.5–6 per cent. It also means that during the economic recession in Europe, acquisitions across Eurozone borders were better received by investors than intra-euro acquisitions. Overall, the cross-sectional analysis is consistent with the univariate results in supporting our theoretical hypotheses. First, due to firm devaluation and low transaction costs as a consequence of the financial crisis, European acquirers benefited from the economic recession in their M&A activities and shareholders recognized these acquisitions as more value generating, on average, than those announced before the crisis. Second, due to the existence of a monetary union in Europe, acquirers seeking to achieve higher returns through institutional and financial diversification need to target companies located in a country with a different currency regime.

DOI: 10.1057/9781137367204.0012

Table 5.5 Cross-sectional regressions

	(1)	(2)	(3)	(4)	(5)	(6)	(7)
POST-CRISIS		0.00724**			0.00350		0.00392
		(0.00281)			(0.00316)		(0.00332)
NON-EMU			0.00450			0.000147	0.00139
			(0.00291)			(0.00322)	(0.00339)
NON-EMU*POST-CRISIS				0.0165***	0.0138***	0.0164***	0.0125**
				(0.00472)	(0.00530)	(0.00524)	(0.00618)
CASH	-0.00121	-0.00188	-0.00207	-0.00255	-0.00265	-0.00256	-0.00285
	(0.00274)	(0.00275)	(0.00279)	(0.00276)	(0.00276)	(0.00279)	(0.00280)
MV	-0.00204***	-0.00204***	-0.00206***	-0.00202***	-0.00202***	-0.00202***	-0.00203***
	(0.000657)	(0.000656)	(0.000657)	(0.000655)	(0.000655)	(0.000656)	(0.000656)
PERCACQ	0.0101**	0.0101**	0.00864*	0.00853*	0.00878*	0.00850*	0.00846*
	(0.00452)	(0.00451)	(0.00461)	(0.00453)	(0.00453)	(0.00460)	(0.00460)
PRIVATE	-0.00347	-0.00332	-0.00378	-0.00335	-0.00330	-0.00336	-0.00339
	(0.00275)	(0.00274)	(0.00275)	(0.00274)	(0.00274)	(0.00275)	(0.00275)
PTB	0.00181	0.00267	0.00145	0.00167	0.00211	0.0166	0.00206
	(0.00922)	(0.00922)	(0.00922)	(0.00920)	(0.00921)	(0.00920)	(0.00921)
RELATIVESIZE	0.00127***	0.00130***	0.00126***	0.00129***	0.00130***	0.00129***	0.00130***
	(0.000463)	(0.000463)	(0.000463)	(0.000462)	(0.000462)	(0.000462)	(0.000462)
SAMEIND	-0.00139	-0.000981	-0.00161	-0.00136	-0.00116	-0.00136	-0.00121
	(0.00275)	(0.00275)	(0.00275)	(0.00274)	(0.00275)	(0.00275)	(0.00275)
Constant	0.00683	0.00455	0.00722	0.00710	0.00595	0.00711	0.00592
	(0.00453)	(0.00461)	(0.00454)	(0.00452)	(0.00464)	(0.00453)	(0.00464)
Observations	2,151	2,151	2,151	2,151	2,151	2,151	2,151
R-squared	0.012	0.015	0.013	0.017	0.018	0.017	0.018
Adj. R-sq	0.009	0.011	0.009	0.014	0.014	0.013	0.013

Note: standard errors in parentheses, *** $p < 0.01$, ** $p < 0.05$, * $p < 0.1$, Dependent variable = CAR[-5;0], White heteroskedasticity-consistent standard errors and covariance.

DOI: 10.1057/9781137367204.0012

Conclusion

This study investigates the impact of the recent financial crisis on the short-term performance of European acquisitions. First, we question whether the financial crisis has had any impact on the announcement returns of bidding companies. We find that the acquirer's short-term performance, measured by its abnormal stock return around the announcement date, is significantly higher in the post-crisis period than in the pre-crisis period. Second, we ask whether membership of the Eurozone has been detrimental towards shareholder gains from European acquisitions during the recessionary period. Our results show that transactions involving non-EMU countries fare better than transactions within the EMU. One reason for this could be that, after the crisis, for EMU deals, the synergies existing between the target and acquirer are unlikely to materialize due to uncertainty in the EMU region. Also, countries in the EMU have experienced tremendous monetary contractions as compared to other European countries like the UK. Membership of the same monetary union brings with it certain rules, regulations and inflexibility, and countries outside this union are unlikely to carry this baggage; hence the market could potentially reward the inherent flexibility and financial certainty of the non-Eurozone currencies. Overall, we show that, within the EU, the distinction between EMU and non-EMU transactions is more relevant than the commonly used classification of domestic and cross-border deals, especially in the post-crisis period.

Theoretical implications

So far, most studies have focused on cross-border acquisitions (Campa and Hernando, 2006) without looking at how the membership of monetary, political and economic alliances might impact returns materialized for acquirers and targets. Though regionalism has its advantages, as our study shows, in the short term and in the recessionary, post-crisis period, this could be a disabling factor for companies choosing to invest in countries that are part of regional alliances; thus limiting the returns they can accrue for their investment activities. Most of the theory is built on regional alliances in stable economic and financial times (Hernando et al., 2009) and/or does not consider the impact of a financial crisis (Charumilind et al., 2006). This chapter shows that there is a great need to extend the current theory in terms of regional scope as well as engage with the temporal aspect of financial instability. Finally, our study highlights the importance of supranational institutions in Europe like the EMU, which can shape the possible outcomes for cross-border investment activities. We argue that institutional theory needs to take into account how these supranational institutions might adapt and limit the target's economic viability and acquirer's strategic activities and possible financial returns from investments in M&As due to the company's membership in certain monetary union.

DOI: 10.1057/9781137367204.0012

Managerial implications

Managers involved in acquisitions during the global economic recession are likely to derive higher returns from their investment than those acquisitions announced before the financial crisis. Though theory implies that acquirers can generate higher returns from acquisitions of low-priced high-value targets in foreign countries during recessionary times, our study presents a cautionary note. Managers need to take into account the regional monetary impact of the financial crisis, which might prevent European companies from maximizing their returns from acquisitions.

References

Acharya, V.V. and Schnabl, P. (2010) Do global banks spread global imbalances? Asset-backed commercial paper during the financial crisis of 2007–09. *IMF Economic Review*, 58: 37–73.

Anand, J., Capron, L. and Mitchell, W. (2005) Using acquisitions to access multinational diversity: thinking beyond the domestic versus cross–border M&A comparison. *Industrial and Corporate Change*, 14: 191–224.

Arezki, R., Candelon, B. and Sy, A. (2011) Sovereign rating news and financial markets spillovers: evidence from the European debt crisis. IMF working papers nos. 1–27.

Bjorvatn, K. (2004) Economic integration and the profitability of cross-border mergers and acquisitions. *European Economic Review*, 48: 1211–26.

Blackburn, V.L., Dark, F.H. and Hanson, R.C. (1997) Mergers, method of payment and returns to manager- and owner-controlled firms. *Financial Review*, 32: 569–89.

Brown, D.T. and Ryngaert, M.D. (1991) The mode of acquisition in takeovers: taxes and asymmetric information. *Journal of Finance*, 46: 653–69.

Campa, J.M. and Hernando, I. (2006) M&As performance in the European financial industry. *Journal of Banking and Finance*, 30: 3367–92.

Campello, M., Graham, J.R. and Harvey, C.R. (2010) The real effects of financial constraints: evidence from a financial crisis. *Journal of Financial Economics*, 97: 470–87.

Capron, L. and Shen, J.C. (2007) Acquisitions of private vs. public firms: private information, target selection, and acquirer returns. *Strategic Management Journal*, 28: 891–911.

Cartwright, S. and Schoenberg, R. (2006) Thirty years of mergers and acquisitions research: recent advances and future opportunities. *British Journal of Management*, 17: S1–S5.

Charumilind, C., Kali, R. and Wiwattanakantang, Y. (2006) Connected lending: Thailand before the financial crisis. *The Journal of Business*, 79: 181–218.

Chattopadhyay, P., Glick, W.H. and Huber, G.P. (2001) Organizational actions in response to threats and opportunities. *Academy of Management Journal*, 44: 937–55.

Chau, V.S., Thomas, H., Clegg, S. and Leung, A.S.M. (2012) Managing performance in global crisis. *British Journal of Management*, 23: S1–S5.

Chesnais, F. and Simonetti, R. (2000) Globalization, foreign direct investment and innovation: a European perspective, in I.-G. Chesnais and R. Simonetti (eds) *European Integration and Global Corporate Strategies*. London: Routledge.

Claessens, S., Dell'Ariccia, G., Igan, D. and Laeven, L. (2010) Cross-country experiences and policy implications from the global financial crisis. *Economic Policy*, 25: 267–93.

DOI: 10.1057/9781137367204.0012

Coeurdacier, N., De Santis, R.A. and Aviat, A. (2009) Cross-border mergers and acquisitions and European integration. *Economic Policy*, 24: 55–106.

Denis, D., Denis, D. and Yost, K. (2002) Global diversification, industrial diversification, and firm value. *Journal of Finance*, 57: 1951–79.

Dikova, D., Sahib, P.R. and Van Witteloostuijn, A. (2009) Cross-border acquisition abandonment and completion: the effect of institutional differences and organizational learning in the international business service industry, 1981–2001. *Journal of International Business Studies*, 41: 223–45.

Dos Santos, M.B., Errunza, V.R. and Miller, D.P. (2008) Does corporate international diversification destroy value? Evidence from cross-border mergers and acquisitions. *Journal of Banking and Finance*, 32: 2716–24.

Doukas, J. and Kan, O.B. (2006) Does global diversification destroy firm value? *Journal of International Business Studies*, 37: 352–71.

Doukas, J. and Travlos, N.G. (1988) The effect of corporate multinationalism on shareholders' wealth: evidence from international acquisitions. *Journal of Finance*, 43: 1161–75.

Eckert, S., Dittfeld, M., Muche, T. and Rässler, S. (2010) Does multinationality lead to value enhancement? An empirical examination of publicly listed corporations from Germany. *International Business Review*, 19: 562–74.

Faccio, M. and Masulis, R.W. (2005) The choice of payment method in European mergers and acquisitions. *Journal of Finance*, 60: 1345–88.

Faccio, M., McConnell, J.J. and Stolin, D. (2006) Returns to acquirers of listed and unlisted targets. *Journal of Financial and Quantitative Analysis*, 41: 197–220.

Ghemawat, P. (2001) Distance still matters. *Harvard Business Review*, 79: 137–47.

Goergen, M. and Renneboog, L. (2004) Shareholder wealth effects of European domestic and cross-border takeover bids. *European Financial Management*, 10: 9–45.

Gregory, A. and McCorriston, S. (2005) Foreign acquisitions by UK limited companies: short- and long-run performance. *Journal of Empirical Finance*, 12: 99–125.

Gubbi, S., Aulakh, P., Ray, S., Sarkar, M. and Chittoor, R. (2010) Do international acquisitions by emerging-economy firms create shareholder value? The case of Indian firms. *Journal of International Business Studies*, 41: 397–418.

Harford, J. (2005) What drives merger waves? *Journal of Financial Economics*, 77: 529–60.

Hernando, I., Nieto, M.J. and Wall, L.D. (2009) Determinants of domestic and cross-border bank acquisitions in the European Union. *Journal of Banking & Finance*, 33: 1022–32.

Ietto-Gillies, G., Meschi, M. and Simonetti, R. (2000) Cross-border mergers and acquisitions, in F. Chesnais, G. Ietto-Gillies and R. Simonetti (eds) *European Integration and Global Corporate Strategies*. London: Routledge.

Issing, O. (2006) *Globalization: Opportunities and Challenges for the World, Europe and Austria*. Brussels: European Central Bank.

Kale, P., Dyer, J.H. and Singh, H. (2002) Alliance capability, stock market response, and long-term alliance success: the role of the alliance function. *Strategic Management Journal*, 23: 747–67.

Karim, S. and Mitchell, W. (2000) Path-dependent and path-breaking change: reconfiguring business resources following acquisitions in the US medical sector, 1978–1995. *Strategic management journal*, 21: 1061–81.

Kim, J.Y., Haleblian, J. and Finkelstein, S. (2011) When firms are desperate to grow via acquisition: the effect of growth patterns and acquisition experience on acquisition premiums. *Administrative Science Quarterly*, 56: 26–60.

DOI: 10.1057/9781137367204.0012

Klossek, A., Linke, B.M. and Nippa, M. (2012) Chinese enterprises in Germany: establishment modes and strategies to mitigate the liability of foreignness. *Journal of World Business*, 47: 35–44.

Kobrin, S.J. (1979) Political risk: a review and reconsideration. *Journal of International Business Studies*, 10: 67–80.

Kostova, T., Roth, K. and Dacin, M.T. (2008) Note: institutional theory in the study of multinational corporations: a critique and new directions. *Academy of Management Review*, 33: 994–1006.

Kostova, T. and Zaheer, S. (1999) Organizational legitimacy under conditions of complexity: the case of the multinational enterprise. *Academy of Management Review*, 24: 64–81.

Krishnan, R.A., Joshi, S. and Krishnan, H. (2004) The influence of mergers on firms' product–mix strategies. *Strategic Management Journal*, 25: 587–611.

Lang, L.H.P., Stulz, R.M. and Walkling, R.A. (1991) A test of the free cash flow hypothesis: the case of bidder returns. *Journal of Financial Economics*, 29: 315–35.

MacKinlay, A. (1997) Event studies in economics and finance. *Journal of Economic Literature*, 35: 13–39.

Martynova, M. and Renneboog, L. (2008) A century of corporate takeovers: what have we learned and where do we stand? *Journal of Banking and Finance*, 32: 2148–77.

Meyer, A.D. (1982) Adapting to environmental jolts. *Administrative Science Quarterly*, 27(4): 515–37.

Mitchell, M.L. and Mulherin, J.H. (1996) The impact of industry shocks on takeover and restructuring activity. *Journal of Financial Economics*, 41: 193–229.

Mitton, T. (2002) A cross-firm analysis of the impact of corporate governance on the East Asian financial crisis. *Journal of Financial Economics*, 64: 215–41.

Mody, A. and Negishi, S. (2000) *The Role of Cross-Border Mergers and Acquisitions in Asian Restructuring*. Washington, DC: World Bank, July.

Moeller, S.B. and Schlingemann, F.P. (2005) Global diversification and bidder gains: a comparison between cross-border and domestic acquisitions. *Journal of Banking and Finance*, 29: 533–64.

Moeller, S.B., Schlingemann, F.P. and Stulz, R.M. (2004) Firm size and the gains from acquisitions. *Journal of Financial Economics*, 73: 201–228.

Myers, S.C. and Majluf, N.S. (1984) Corporate financing and investment decisions when firms have information that investors do not have. *Journal of Financial Economics*, 13: 187–221.

North, D.C. (1990) *Institutions, Institutional Change and Economic Performance*. Cambridge: Cambridge University Press.

Pangarkar, N. and Lie, J.R. (2004) The impact of market cycle on the performance of Singapore acquirers. *Strategic Management Journal*, 25: 1209–16.

Rau, P.R. and Vermaelen, T. (1998) Glamour, value and the post-acquisition performance of acquiring firms. *Journal of Financial Economics*, 49: 223–53.

Reinhart, C.M. and Rogoff, K.S. (2009) The aftermath of financial crises. *American Economic Review: Papers and Proceedings*, 99: 466–72.

Roll, R. (1986) The hubris hypothesis of corporate takeovers. *Journal of Business*: 197–216.

Rose, A.K. and Spiegel, M.M. (2012) Cross-country causes and consequences of the 2008 crisis: early warning. *Japan and the World Economy*, 24: 1–16.

Schoenberg, R. (2006) Measuring the performance of corporate acquisitions: an empirical comparison of alternative metrics. *British Journal of Management*, 17: 361–70.

DOI: 10.1057/9781137367204.0012

Shleifer, A. and Vishny, R.W. (2003) Stock market driven acquisitions. *Journal of Financial Economics*, 70: 295–311.

Sudarsanam, S. and Mahate, A.A. (2006) Are friendly acquisitions too bad for shareholders and managers? Long-term value creation and top management turnover in hostile and friendly acquirers. *British Journal of Management*, 17: S7–S30.

Te Velde, D.W., Ackah, C., Ajakaiye, O., Aryeetey, E., Bhattacharya, D., Calì, M., Fakiyesi, T., Fulbert, A.G., Jalilian, H. and Jemio, L.C. (2009) *The Global Financial Crisis and Developing Countries*. London: Overseas Development Institute.

Uhlenbruck, K. and De Castro, J.O. (2000) Foreign aquisitions in Central and Eastern Europe: outcomes of privatization in transitional economies. *Academy of Management Journal*, 43: 381–402.

UNCTAD (2009) *World Investment Report: Transnational Corporations, Agricultural Production and Development*. New York and Geneva: UNCTAD.

UNCTAD (2011) *World Investment Report 2011: Non-Equity Modes of Production and Development*. Geneva: UNCTAD.

von Eije, H. and Wiegerinck, H. (2010) Shareholders' reactions to announcements of acquisitions of private firms: do target and bidder markets make a difference? *International Business Review*, 19: 360–77.

Wan, W.P. and Yiu, D.W. (2009) From crisis to opportunity: environmental jolt, corporate acquisitions, and firm performance. *Strategic Management Journal*, 30: 791–801.

Williams, J. and Nguyen, N. (2005) Financial liberalization, crisis, and restructuring: a comparative study of bank performance and bank governance in South East Asia. *Journal of Banking & Finance*, 29: 2119–54.

Williamson, O.E. (1975) *Markets and Hierarchies: Antitrust Analysis and Implications*. New York: The Free Press.

Wruck, K.H. (1990) Financial distress, reorganization, and organizational efficiency. *Journal of Financial Economics*, 27: 419–44.

DOI: 10.1057/9781137367204.0012

6
Internal Capital Markets and outward Foreign Investment from India and China*

Abubakr Saeed and Suma Athreye

Introduction

There is growing evidence that the ability to raise finance has been an important characteristic of Indian and Chinese firms that invested abroad. Athreye and Kapur (2009) focus on the role of liberalization, and conclude that the relaxation of policy restrictions on capital outflows has contributed largely to the surge of foreign investment from India and China. Gupta and Yuan (2009) show that stock market liberalization has promoted overall investment from emerging economies by lowering the cost of external finance. For Indian firms, Bhaduri (2005) finds that deregulation of interest rates, a reduction of directed credit and the development of financial markets has alleviated credit constraints and ultimately led to an increase in firm investment. Guariglia et al. (2011) show that the Chinese growth miracle was driven by privatized firms, which hoard large cash stocks.

The existing literature emphasizes the positive role played by group affiliation in reducing financial constraints to investment (Bertrand et al., 2002; Khanna and Palepu, 2000). Group affiliated firms have better access to external finance because of the group's long-term relationships with lenders. In financial markets rendered imperfect by information asymmetry problems, group affiliation can act as a signal of relative financial stability (Becker and Sivadasan, 2010). In addition, through their internal capital markets, groups alleviate financial constraints of distressed subsidiaries, which may lead to economic benefits especially when external financing is scarce and uncertain.

Similar views are held about state-owned firms, although the mechanisms might be different. The positive impact of state ownership in alleviating

---

* This work is drawn from the MPhil dissertation of the first author, Abubakr Saeed.

DOI: 10.1057/9781137367204.0013

financial constraints stems from the privileged treatment to them in the credit market, encouraged by the government mainly to protect their social objectives (Poncet et al., 2010; Chow and Fung, 1998).[1]

The extent of financial constraints also depends on the nature of the investment. The degree of financial constraints on domestic investment is often lower than that of foreign investment mainly because of higher uncertainty and greater monitoring costs. Previous studies, such as Poncet et al. (2010) and Ratti et al. (2008), have only considered the overall level of investment and so may not have accurately gauged the severity of financial constraints due to firm heterogeneity. Therefore disentangling the impact of financial constraints on domestic and foreign investments is necessary in order to understand the role that internal financial markets play in encouraging foreign investments.

In this study, we focus on two ownership characteristics, namely, business group affiliation and state ownership, as a proxy for internal capital markets and study their influence on a firm's domestic and foreign investment. Using data on Chinese and Indian listed companies for the period 2000–9, we employ a simultaneous equations approach to estimate the role of financial constraints on the joint determination of domestic and foreign investment decisions. By adopting this novel empirical approach, we find that standalone (non-group affiliates) Indian and Chinese firms are still credit constrained in relation to domestic and foreign investments. However organizational forms such as business groups (in India) and state-owned enterprises (in China) are able to mitigate credit constraints in both domestic and foreign investments.

The rest of the chapter is organized in the following way. The second section reviews the literature on the impact of business group affiliation and state ownership on financial constraints and develops related hypotheses. We then present the empirical model and estimation technique. We go on to discuss our data and present descriptive statistics before presenting the formal regression results ending with a conclusion.

Literature review and hypotheses development

The impact of business group affiliation on financial constraints

The fundamental explanation for the prevalence of business groups in emerging economies conceptualizes them as a response to financial market imperfections. In such an environment where institutions are weak and

---

[1] There are also a number of studies that argue that the efficiency of investment carried out in this way may be poor (Claessens et al., 2006). Similarly, although soft budget constraints mitigate financial constraints, they also allow government interference in business decisions (mainly investment and employment) which impact negatively on corporate investment efficiency (Chen et al., 2011). However the efficiency of investment is not the focus of our study.

DOI: 10.1057/9781137367204.0013

hindering arms-length contracting, group affiliation facilitates firms in terms of reducing transaction costs by easing information flows between member firms or otherwise by aligning the interests of firms and striving collectively towards mutual benefits.

Earlier research work on the outcome of business group affiliation has primarily investigated how group membership affects various financial outcomes of firms by comparing a cohort of group affiliated firms with a cohort of independent firms. Within this stream, research predominantly has explored how group affiliation affects firm performance in terms of accounting returns and stock market valuation (Caves and Uekusa, 1976; Khanna and Palepu, 2000; Khanna and Yafeh, 2005). Other research in this area has examined the financing structure of group affiliates while concentrating on their lending relationships to banks (Shin and Park, 1999). Meanwhile, there has been a nascent literature looking at the fund allocation amongst affiliated firms. More specifically, this domain focuses on whether business groups facilitate member firms at assessing funds from external capital markets, which ultimately reduces financial constraints to their investment. There are some studies along this line. Hoshi et al. (1991) were amongst the first to examine the effect of business group affiliation on the investment pattern of Japanese keiretsu (group affiliated) firms. They find evidence that keiretsu organizations maintain strong relationships with banks; they therefore face less financial constraints to their investment. Similar evidence is reported by Shin and Park (1999) for the Korean Chaebols. They compare the investment behaviour of Koran Chaebols with standalone firms and observe that investment decisions of non-Chaebol firms are highly sensitive to internal funds indicating the presence of financial constraints to their investment decisions. Further, they also find evidence for the existence of internal capital markets in Chaebols, which explicates why their investment is independent of internal capital. Consistent with these findings, Hermes and Lensink (2003) report the positive effect of business group affiliation amongst Chilean firms. Chilean groups facilitate member firms in providing funds for their investments.

In contrast, Khanna and Palepu (2000) find contradictory evidence for Indian business group affiliates in that they find no difference between the financial constraints of group member and standalone firms. However the performance of group affiliates is found to be higher than standalone firms above a certain degree of diversification. Below that threshold, standalone firms perform better than their group member counterparts. Lins and Servaes (1999) find that the investment efficiency of group-affiliated firms in Japan is inferior to that of independent firms.

Following these arguments, owing to the inconclusive impact of business group affiliation on financing constraints on investment, it is difficult to predict the definitive direction of this relationship. Nevertheless, considering

DOI: 10.1057/9781137367204.0013

the growing significance of groups in emerging economies, Hypothesis 1 predicts a positive relationship for politically connected firms.

Hypothesis 1: business group affiliation reduces the financial constraints on firm investments (both domestic and foreign).

The impact of state ownership on financial constraints

In pursuit of the factors determining the degree of financial constraints on firm investment, there are also studies examining how state ownership may impact on corporate financing behaviour. Fundamentally, when the firm is state owned it has easy access to cheap credit and if projects fail the government may provide bailouts. These soft budget constraints reduce the credit multiplier faced by state-owned firms and thus decrease the financial constraints on investment (Chow et al., 2010).

Prior research on the investment financing of state-owned firms' documents that government facilitation makes them less prone to financial constraints compared to private owned firms (Poncet et al., 2010; Mickiewicz et al., 2004). This view is centred on the privileged access of these firms in credit markets where the state still intervenes in the allocation of capital. In developing countries banks still remain largely state influenced if not state owned and experience government pressure concerning social and political objectives, such as lending and extending loans to state-owned firms based on government ties rather than on the basis of collateral and future cash flow. In this vein, Chow and Fung (1998) argue that since access to stock markets is generally restricted to large and medium-sized state-owned firms and Chinese banks are mostly state controlled, there is a clear bias toward state-owned firms in contrast to other firms present in credit markets.

In contrast there are a number of studies that find conflicting results based on the fact that state intervention brings with it political objectives to corporate decision-making (Shleifer and Vishny, 1994; Bertrand et al., 2007). Such objectives generally appear in the demand for excessive employment and inefficient investment. In this vein, Lin and Bo (2011) report that state ownership does not necessarily help in reducing the firm's financial constraints on investment. In addition, China's corporatization movement has been effective in that the soft budget constraints previously enjoyed by state-owned firms have now been removed.

Once again therefore the empirical evidence is inconclusive. Nevertheless, despite such contradictory evidence, the weight of available empirical evidence suggests that the relationship between state ownership and the degree of financial constraints is negatively correlated. Hypothesis 2 takes this into consideration.

DOI: 10.1057/9781137367204.0013

Hypothesis 2: state ownership reduces the financial constraints on firm investments (both domestic and foreign).

Estimation model and methodology

We follow the Euler model approach of Love (2003) to estimate the effect of financial constraints on domestic and foreign investments. As this study accounts for the effects of financial constraints at domestic and foreign investment separately, two equations are used for each investment type. Specifically, we employ the following regression equations:

$$\frac{I_{i,t}^{d}}{K_{i,t}} = \alpha + \beta_{1}^{d}\frac{I_{i,t-1}^{d}}{K_{i,t-1}} + \beta_{2}^{d}\frac{CF_{i,t-1}}{K_{i,t-1}} + \beta_{3}^{d}\frac{S_{i,t-1}}{K_{i,t-1}} + \beta_{4}^{d}\frac{D_{i,t-1}}{K_{i,t-1}} + f_{i} + d_{s} + \varepsilon_{it} \tag{1}$$

And

$$\frac{I_{i,t}^{f}}{K_{i,t}} = \alpha + \gamma_{1}\frac{I_{i,t-1}^{f}}{K_{i,t-1}} + \gamma_{2}\frac{CF_{i,t-1}}{K_{i,t-1}} + \gamma_{3}\frac{FS_{i,t-1}}{K_{i,t-1}} + \gamma_{4}\frac{FD_{i,t-1}}{K_{i,t-1}} +$$
$$\gamma_{5}NRS_{i} + \gamma_{6}DList_{i} + f_{i} + d_{s} + \varepsilon_{it} \tag{2}$$

where I^{d} is the domestic investment, K is the capital stock, CF is cash flow, S is total sales, D is total debt, I^{f} is foreign investment, FS is foreign sales and FD is foreign debt. The variables NRS and $DList$ are non-reporting subsidiaries and dummy listing respectively, which control for over-estimation measurement bias in domestic investment. The subscripts i and t denote the firm and time period. The variables fi and d_{s} capture firm fixed and industry fixed effects whilst ε_{it} is the error term.

Empirically we follow the investment literature pioneered by Fazzari et al. (1988) that in the presence of financial constraints firms will use their own cash reserves for investment. We compare the investment level of business group affiliates with that of standalone firms and examine the effect of group affiliation on corporate investment spending. Similarly, we distinguish between state-owned and private firms and observe the severity of financial constraints across these groups by looking at their dependence on cash flows for investment. The central thrust of our analysis is that faced with financial constraints, investment will be sensitive to cash flow (CF) and by comparing the investment-cash flow sensitivity of different firm groups (β_{2}) will enable us to determine which groups are more financially constrained for both types of investment (domestic or foreign). From equations (1) and (2), the hypotheses

DOI: 10.1057/9781137367204.0013

for business group affiliation and state ownership are tested as $\beta_2 < 0$ while firms facing financial constraints will show $\beta_2 > 0$.

Unlike previous models such as Jorgenson (1963), the Euler model incorporates the dynamic elements and expectation parameters that appear explicitly in the optimization problem. In addition, the Euler model captures future uncertainty by incorporating the ad-hoc lags in the specification that are missing from the Jorgenson model. Considering that domestic and foreign investment decisions share almost the same determining factors and firms often make domestic and foreign investment decisions at the same time, it is possible that the residuals of both equations are correlated with each other. Under such circumstances, ordinary least squares (OLS) estimation of equations (1) and (2) may yield unsatisfactory results. To account for this, Zellner (1972) indicates that the specification should be modelled as a system of simultaneous equations to control for such estimation bias.

A simultaneous equation system based on Generalized Method of Moments (GMM) is more appropriate in the context of the current study since both of the firm's investment decisions, domestic and foreign, are occurring simultaneously and the factors that determine these investment decisions are related. Such estimation conditions create possible contemporaneous correlation among firms and correlate the error terms across the equations. Therefore to allow for the possibility that the error terms in domestic and foreign investment equations may contain the same unspecified factors, both equations are estimated jointly using the GMM simultaneous equation model. The lagged independent variables of respective domestic and foreign investment model are used as instruments in the estimation.

Data

We utilize firm-level data originating from the ORBIS database, which covers all listed firms around the globe. ORBIS provides globally standardized financial accounts of over 70,000 listed firms from all over the world with approximately ten years of data available. It was deemed necessary to select a long period (2000–9) in order to draw sound statistical conclusions from the relationships tested.

The sample includes non-financial listed firms having foreign subsidiaries from India and China for the period 2000–9. The decision to restrict the sample only to non-financial firms (with SIC less than 6000) is due to the accounting treatment of revenue and profits for financial firms (banks, insurance and investment firms) being significantly different to that of non-financial firms. In addition, a criterion to include firms with foreign subsidiaries is adopted to measure the level of foreign investment. It is necessary for each firm to report a minimum of five consecutive years of data in order to attain the lag values

DOI: 10.1057/9781137367204.0013

required for GMM estimation and also to assess the changes in the financing structure of the firms. Following Ratti et al. (2008) we exclude observations with I/K above 2.5, CF/K above 0.7, S/K above 20 and D/K above 10. We also eliminate firm years with negative values for the capital stock and sales. After applying the aforementioned selection criteria, an unbalanced panel of 2689 firm year observations on 501 firms with foreign subsidiaries is used for the empirical analysis. Amongst them, Indian firms (287) represent 57 per cent of the total sample and Chinese firms (214) account for the remaining 43 per cent. Information on business group affiliation and state ownership is also taken from the relevant firms' financial statements. Business group affiliates in our sample refer to any firm that is associated with business groups in the country. State-owned enterprise refers to a firm that has a presence of government ownership of any fraction. By dividing the sample into group affiliated, standalone, state-owned and private firms, 255 organizations are identified as business group affiliated, whilst 246 firms are considered as not affiliated to any business group. The size of state-owned firms in our sample is 201.

Variable measurement

Our dependent variables are domestic and foreign investments. In the spirit of Ratti et al. (2008), investment of any firm is measured as the change in capital stock at the end of the accounting year, net of depreciation, *that is,* $I_t = K_t - K_{t-1} + Depreciation$, where net depreciation is calculated as the difference between the accumulated depreciation in the current year and the depreciation in the previous year. Importantly, ORBIS does not distinguish between domestic and foreign investment in the reported balance sheet, therefore we have to revert to the financial statements of the foreign subsidiaries and examine the change in their capital stock from the previous year plus depreciation, as the firm's foreign investment (I^f). Regarding domestic investment (I^d), we used the difference between the firm's total investment, which is given in the parent firm's balance sheet, and its foreign investment.

The capital stock (K) is calculated as the balance sheet item 'tangible fixed assets', which include accumulated depreciation. More specifically, capital stock is the sum of machinery, plant, equipment, buildings, land, property, other tangible assets and construction-in-progress. Inventories are reported separately and not included in the calculations. The variable of interest (CF) is operating cash flow at time t, which is calculated as operating income in a given period t plus depreciation. A firm is considered financially constrained if it does not have access to external finance to undertake investment and is forced to rely mostly on internal capital. Therefore we use investment cash flow sensitivity as a measure of financial constraint. A significant and positive coefficient of cash flow would indicate financial constraint. Alternatively, a negative sign on this coefficient would indicate elimination or reduction of financial

DOI: 10.1057/9781137367204.0013

constraints to firms' investments. Firm debt (D) is measured as the firm's total long-term and short-term debt. Sales (S) are measured as the firm's total sales in a specific period. The foreign debt (FD) of each firm is considered as the sum of the total debt of all the foreign subsidiaries. Finally, foreign sale (FS) of each firm is measured as the sum of total sales of all the foreign subsidiaries.

The variable definitions taken from the information provided in the financial statements of foreign subsidiaries, such as foreign investment, foreign debt and foreign sale, are likely to be sensitive to the number of non-reporting subsidiaries (NRS). In order to control for this potential bias we include a variable (NRS), which measures the ratio of the number of reporting subsidiaries to the total number of each firm's subsidiaries.

It is common for large firms with foreign subsidiaries to list their shares in foreign markets; however it is unusual for such firms to list exclusively in one adjacent integrated foreign market. In the case of the emerging economies that are the focus of this chapter, integration is common between Chinese and Hong Kong markets, and Indian and Mauritius markets. Although such listings may occur for tax purposes, Guo et al. (2010) argue that firms list abroad often for publicity reasons and to generate a favourable view among investors. Their argument is supported empirically by Saudagaran (1988), who reports that investors are often overly optimistic about the prospects of foreign listed firms. Considering such motives of foreign listing there is a possibility that such listings may bias the estimation. Therefore we use adjacent market listing for our Indian and Chinese firms as a control variable because it is not aimed solely at securing the cheapest credit. To control for this effect in the estimation, we introduce a dummy variable that distinguishes between 'dummy' listed firms and others. We include a dummy variable ($DList$), which takes the value 1 if a Chinese (Indian) firm is listed exclusively on a Hong Kong (Mauritius) market. To summarize, a list of variables with their definitions is provided in Table 6.1.

Sample characteristics

Table 6.2 presents the sample characteristics and distribution of firms across both economies. The distribution of firm total investment to capital stock ratio varies widely between Indian and Chinese firms. This can be thought of as a measure of the intensity of the firm's investment. Based on this measure, Chinese firms are investing more (almost 86 per cent of their capital stock) compared to Indian firms (53 per cent of their capital stock). The pattern is similar for ratios of foreign and domestic investment (as proportion of capital stock). Other significant differences are: the cash flow ratio is higher for Indian firms at around 23 per cent, compared to 18.6 per cent for Chinese firms. We can attribute this higher cash flow ratio for India to the fact that the sampled firms retain large cash stocks to buffer against adverse cash flow shocks. Of

DOI: 10.1057/9781137367204.0013

Table 6.1   Definition of variables used

Variables	Acronym	Definition
Foreign investment	I^f	Change in net capital stock from period t–1 to t, plus accumulated depreciation of foreign subsidiaries
Domestic investment	I^d	Difference between total investment and foreign investment, where total investment is the change in net capital stock from period t–1 to t, plus accumulated depreciation of parent firm
Capital stock	K	Tangible assets of period t
Cash flow	CF	Firm operating net income at the end of period t plus the accumulated depreciation
Net sale	S	Total sale at the end of period t
Total Debt	D	Book value of total debt at the end of period t
Foreign sale	FS	Total sale at the end of period t of all foreign subsidiaries of a firm
Foreign Debt	FD	Total book value of debt at the end of period t of all foreign subsidiaries of a firm
Non-reporting subsidiaries	NRS	Ratio of number of reporting subsidiaries to total number of subsidiaries of each firm
Dummy Listing	$DList$	A dummy variable taking value 1 if a Chinese or Indian firm is listed exclusively in Hong Kong or Mauritius market, respectively.

these, 66 per cent of Indian firms are affiliated to a business group compared to 31 per cent of Chinese firms. On the other hand, more than 58 per cent of Chinese firms have some fraction of state ownership compared to only 27 per cent of Indian firms.

The level of foreign and domestic investments of Chinese firms is higher compared to Indian firms. The fraction of sales to capital stock, which measures the firm's operational performance, is not significantly different across Indian and Chinese sample (3.095 for Indian and 3.009 for Chinese firms). There is no significant difference between Indian and Chinese firms with regard to debt utilization. The Indian firms in our sample have a leverage ratio of 1.912, compared to 1.905 for Chinese firms. Levels of foreign debt are also not significantly different for Chinese and Indian companies.

We further decompose the Indian and Chinese sample into group affiliated and standalone (non-group affiliated) firms, and state-owned and private firms. Indian group affiliated firms have higher domestic and foreign investment as compared with their standalone counterparts. This difference is statistically significant at 1 per cent level. On the other hand, we do not find such difference amongst Chinese group affiliates. Group firms tend to have relatively more cash flow than the standalone firms. This difference is strongly significant at the 1 per cent level. Moreover Indian group affiliates utilize less external debt,

DOI: 10.1057/9781137367204.0013

Table 6.2 Mean values of variables across countries

| | Indian firms | | | | | | | Chinese firms | | | | | | |
	Full sample	Group affiliates	Standalone	t-stat	State owned	Private	t-stat	Full sample	Group affiliates	Standalone	t-stat	State owned	Private	t-stat
I^a/K	0.427	0.441	0.419	2.38***	0.421	0.429	−0.65	0.713	0.707	0.719	−1.13	0.931	0.670	5.16***
I/K	0.102	0.106	0.099	1.57***	0.101	0.103	−1.79	0.145	0.140	0.145	0.46	0.250	0.139	3.92***
CF/K	0.230	0.254	0.214	4.22***	0.234	0.226	2.53	0.186	0.168	0.192	−1.04**	0.235	0.180	4.06***
S/K	3.095	3.094	3.096	−0.26	3.002	3.310	−4.01***	3.009	3.005	3.011	−0.22	3.021	3.000	0.84
D/K	1.912	1.914	1.987	−2.48***	2.204	1.715	5.08***	1.905	1.894	1.926	1.00**	2.028	1.901	1.15*
FS/K	1.435	1.433	1.436	−0.76	1.432	1.429	0.92	1.074	1.070	1.077	−0.35	1.115	1.060	1.49**
FD/K	0.881	0.929	0.865	3.50**	0.880	0.887	−1.10	0.893	0.812	0.930	−3.40***	1.002	0.852	6.02***
NRS	0.431	0.431	0.430	0.20	0.432	0.430	0.61	0.419	0.419	0.420	−0.22	0.422	0.418	0.70
DList	0.038	0.037	0.038	−0.64	0.036	0.038	0.39	0.088	0.087	0.088	−0.51	0.085	0.089	−0.70

Note: ***, ** and * are significant at 1 per cent, 5 per cent and 10 per cent, respectively.

DOI: 10.1057/9781137367204.0013

showing that there is a significant transfer of financial resources across group firms through internal capital market.

In addition, we also compare the firm characteristics between state-owned and private firms. In India, there are no statistically significant differences in domestic and foreign investments. However higher debt and low sales are observed for state-owned firms, which are found to be statistically significant. The Chinese state-owned firms show statistically significant differences from private firms in domestic investment, foreign investment, cash flow and foreign debt.

Taken together, the overall lower usage of external debt for financing their investment amongst Indian group affiliates indicates the existence of an internal capital market, where business groups typically use subordinated intra-group loans as a means of intra-group transfers (i.e. Khanna and Palepu, 2000). In contrast, the higher usage of debt and borrowing amongst Chinese state-owned firms indicates the presence of soft financial constraints, as observed by other studies (i.e. Poncet et al., 2010).

Regression results

We perform a multiple regression analysis to examine whether and how group affiliation and state ownership might affect the level of firms' financial constraints on investment. Table 6.3 reports the results for the Indian sample. To capture the valuation effects associated with group affiliation and state ownership, we divide the sample into group affiliated firms, standalone firms, state-owned firms and private firms. All coefficients of the lagged investment variable are positive and statistically significant at the 1 per cent level. Next, the coefficient on our main variable of interest (*CF*) is negative and statistically significant for group affiliated firms (columns 1 and 2 in Table 6.3); whereas it is found positive and statistically significant for standalone firms (columns 3 and 4 in Table 6.3). The positive sign for standalone firms indicates that these firms rely on their cash flows to finance both domestic and foreign investment, which suggests evidence of financial constraints, while group affiliates do not. The results support Hypothesis 1, which asserts that business group affiliation reduces financial constraints on firms' domestic and foreign investment.

Regarding control variables, total debt is important for the domestic investment decisions of standalone firms. Further, net sale is a significant determinant for domestic investment for both types of firms. The estimated coefficients for foreign debt appear to be negative and statistically significant only for affiliated firms. It implies that foreign investment of member firms is driven by external finance raised in foreign markets. The coefficients on foreign sales turnout to be positive and significant for both types of firms, confirming that superior performances have played an important role in spurring outward

DOI: 10.1057/9781137367204.0013

Table 6.3   Effects of group affiliation and state ownership on financial constraints of Indian firms

	Group affiliates firms		Standalone firms		State-owned firms		Private firms	
	1	2	3	4	5	6	7	8
	Domestic investment	Foreign investment	Domestic investment	Foreign investment	Domestic investment	Foreign investment	Domestic investment	Foreign investment
I^d_{it-1}/K_{it-1}	0.791*** (0.201)		0.577*** (0.135)		0.525*** (0.101)		0.481*** (0.116)	
I^f_{it-1}/K_{it-1}		0.403*** (0.098)		0.517*** (0.149)		0.396*** (0.075)		0.570*** (0.130)
CF_{it-1}/K_{it-1}	-0.149*** (0.031)	-0.028*** (0.07)	0.036** (0.011)	0.090*** (0.031)	-0.012*** (0.002)	0.008*** (0.001)	0.054** (0.017)	0.116** (0.041)
D_{it-1}/K_{it-1}	-0.012 (0.008)		0.067* (0.029)		0.136** (0.052)		0.014 (0.005)	
S_{it-1}/K_{it-1}	0.104*** (0.018)		0.073*** (0.012)		0.021** (0.008)		0.115* (0.053)	
FD_{it-1}/K_{it-1}		0.037** (0.012)		0.068 (0.044)		0.106 (0.059)		0.019 (0.011)
FS_{it-1}/K_{it-1}		0.152*** (0.024)		0.078*** (0.010)		0.033** (0.012)		0.021*** (0.003)
NRS_t		0.051 (0.018)		0.020 (0.008)		0.044 (0.025)		0.086 (0.051)
$DList_{it}$		0.006 (0.004)		0.018 (0.010)		0.003 (0.002)		0.010 (0.006)
Constant	0.360*** (0.058)	0.279*** (0.040)	0.191*** (0.056)	0.452*** (0.114)	0.105*** (0.019)	0.225*** (0.038)	0.293*** (0.041)	0.405*** (0.102)
No. of Obs.	968	968	495	495	408	408	1056	1056
No. of firms	189	189	98	98	77	77	210	210
Hansen J-stat	0.14	0.22	0.20	0.16	0.11	0.26	0.32	0.19

Note: this table reports the GMM simultaneous equation regressions. I^d/K is domestic investment, I^f/K is foreign investment, CF/K is cash flow, D/K is total debt, S/K is total sales, FD/K is foreign debt, FS/K is foreign sales and NRS is the ratio of the number of reporting subsidiaries to the total number of subsidiaries of each firm. DList is a dummy variable that takes the value 1 if the Indian or Chinese firm is listed only in Mauritius or Hong Kong respectively. All estimations include firm and country fixed effects. Standard errors are presented in parentheses. ***, ** and * are significant at 1 per cent, 5 per cent and 10 per cent, respectively.

DOI: 10.1057/9781137367204.0013

investment by Indian firms. The other control variables (NRS) and dummy listing (DList) are positive, but statistically insignificant.

Next, we investigate whether state ownership has any effect on the firms' financial constraints. In Table 6.3 columns 5 and 6 report the estimated results for state-owned firms and results for private firms are shown in columns 7 and 8. The coefficients on our variable of interest indicate that state ownership is beneficial in reducing financial constraints on only domestic investment, partially supporting our Hypothesis 2. On the other hand, private firms are found to be financially constrained for both types of investments. We find positive effects of net sale and foreign sale on domestic and foreign investment, respectively for state-owned and private firms. The estimates on foreign debt clearly are not likely to be an important determinant of foreign investment.

Overall, our findings for the Indian sample show that group affiliation helps in reducing financial constraints on domestic and foreign investment, whereas state ownership is effective in mitigating such constraints only for domestic investment. The magnitudes of coefficients on cash flow indicate that the mitigating effect of group membership is stronger than the mitigating effect of state ownership. These results are broadly consistent with the principal benefits of group membership, which is providing support to member firms in poorer financial condition (Khanna and Palepu, 2000; Hoshi et al., 1991). We also find that foreign investment appears to be demand led, as it follows foreign sales for all firms. Similarly domestic investment responds to domestic sales.

Next we investigate the effect of group affiliation and state ownership on domestic and foreign investment in the Chinese sample of firms. The results of our estimation are reported in Table 6.4. Domestic and foreign investments have an autoregressive character, indicating the dependence of current investment decision on investments made over a year.

With regard to the effect of group affiliation, (in columns 1 and 2 of Table 6.4) the estimated coefficients on firms associated with business groups are positive and significant at the 5 per cent level, suggesting the presence of financial constraints for both Chinese business groups and standalone firms. However we see that state ownership alleviates financial constraints on firm investment. The coefficients on the cash flow variable are negative and significant for both domestic and foreign investment of state-owned firms. This result suggests evidence in support of soft budget constraints (Poncet et al., 2010; Konings and Vandenbussche, 2004). In contrast, columns 7 and 8 of Table 6.4 show that private firms are financially constrained in their domestic and foreign investment.

Furthermore debt is an important means of financing domestic and foreign investments for state-owned firms. However all firms resort to foreign debt in

DOI: 10.1057/9781137367204.0013

Table 6.4 Effects of group affiliation and state ownership on financial constraints of Chinese firms

| | Group affiliates firms | | Standalone firms | | State-owned firms | | Private firms | |
	1	2	3	4	5	6	7	8
	Domestic investment	Foreign investment	Domestic investment	Foreign investment	Domestic investment	Foreign investment	Domestic investment	Foreign investment
I^d_{It-1}/K_{It-1}	0.485***		0.371***		0.362***		0.557***	
	(0.101)		(0.082)		(0.077)		(0.146)	
I^f_{It-1}/K_{It-1}		0.539**		0.312**		0.404***		0.612***
		(0.125)		(0.068)		(0.090)		(0.158)
CF_{It-1}/K_{It-1}	0.013**	0.041**	0.021***	0.069***	-0.082***	-1.153***	0.090**	0.104**
	(0.004)	(0.015)	(0.004)	(0.010)	(0.014)	(0.300)	(0.042)	(0.047)
D_{It-1}/K_{It-1}	0.009		0.025		0.040**		0.017*	
	(0.005)		(0.016)		(0.013)		(0.008)	
S_{It-1}/K_{It-1}	0.012		0.036		0.022		0.031	
	(0.008)		(0.019)		(0.014)		(0.022)	
FD_{It-1}/K_{It-1}		0.078**		0.051**		0.226***		0.090**
		(0.032)		(0.022)		(0.050)		(0.041)
FS_{It-1}/K_{It-1}		0.014		0.005		0.020		0.038
		(0.008)		(0.004)		(0.011)		(0.026)
NRS_i		0.001		0.006		0.014		0.002
		(0.000)		(0.004)		(0.010)		(0.002)
$DList_{it}$		0.018		0.025		0.029		0.033
		(0.010)		(0.014)		(0.018)		(0.021)
Constant	0.360***	0.279***	0.191***	0.452***	0.105***	0.221***	0.293***	0.409***
	(0.050)	(0.035)	(0.040)	(0.094)	(0.023)	(0.042)	(0.017)	(0.088)
No. of Obs.	337	337	889	889	744	744	482	482
No. of firms	66	66	148	148	124	124	90	90
Hansen J–stat	0.26	0.11	0.14	0.20	0.17	0.15	0.10	0.13

Note: this table reports the GMM simultaneous equation regressions. I^d/K is domestic investment, I^f/K is foreign investment, CF/K is cash flow, D/K is total debt, S/K is total sales, FD/K is foreign debt, FS/K is foreign sales and NRS is the ratio of the number of reporting subsidiaries to the total number of subsidiaries of each firm. DList is a dummy variable that takes the value 1 if the Indian or Chinese firm is listed only in Mauritius or Hong Kong respectively. All estimations include firm and country fixed effects. Standard errors are presented in parentheses. ***, ** and * are significant at 1 per cent, 5 per cent and 10 per cent, respectively.

DOI: 10.1057/9781137367204.0013

order to finance their overseas investments. In contrast to the results for India, neither domestic nor foreign investment is strongly led by sales.

To summarize, the results suggest that firms from both countries do face financial constraints – their investments are sensitive to internal capital irrespective of their investment type. However business group affiliation in India and state ownership in China mitigate financial constraints.

Conclusion

This chapter investigates the role of group affiliation and state ownership in mitigating financial constraints on domestic and foreign investments for both Indian and Chinese firms. To identify financial constraints we follow the investment literature pioneered by Fazzari et al. (1988) by investigating the extent to which Indian and Chinese firms' investment (both domestic and foreign) is affected by the availability of internal capital. Using a panel of 501 Indian and Chinese non-financial firms over the period 2000–9 we find that firms in both countries display high sensitivities of investment to cash flow, suggesting the existence of financial constraints. As we expected, belonging to a business group in India and being state owned in China mitigates the financial constraints on domestic and foreign investment. This mitigating effect is stronger for foreign investment when compared to domestic investment. Our results also show that foreign and domestic investments in India are demand-led (they respond to net sales and foreign sales) while foreign borrowing (proxied by foreign debt) has played an important role in financing the foreign investment by Chinese firms over the last decade.

References

Athreye, S. and Kapur, S. (2009) The internationalization of Chinese and Indian firms – trends, motivations and strategy. *Industrial and Corporate Change,* 18: 209–21.

Becker, B. and Sivadasan, J. (2010) The effect of financial development on the investment-cash flow relationship: cross-country evidence from Europe. European Central Bank working paper no. 689.

Bertrand, M., Kramaraz F., Schoar, A. and Thesmar, D. (2007) Politicians, firms and the political business cycle: evidence from France. Working paper, University of Chicago.

Bertrand, M., Mehta, P. and Mullainathan, S. (2002) Ferreting out tunnelling: an application to Indian business groups. *Quarterly Journal of Economics,* 117: 121–48.

Bhaduri, S.N. (2005) Investment, financial constraints and financial liberalization: some stylized facts from a developing economy, India. *Journal of Asian Economics* 16: 704–718.

Caves, R. and Uekusa, M. (1976) *Industrial Organization in Japan.* Washington: The Brookings Institution.

Chen, S., Sun, Z., Tang, S. and Wu, D. (2011) Government intervention and investment efficiency: evidence from China. *Journal of Corporate Finance,* 17: 259–71.

DOI: 10.1057/9781137367204.0013

Chow, C.K. and Fung, M.K.Y. (1998) Ownership structure, lending bias, and liquidity constraints: evidence from Shanghai's manufacturing sector. *Journal of Comparative Economics*, 26: 301–316.

Chow, C. K., Frank, S. and Kit, W.P. (2010) Investment and the soft budget constraint in China. *International Review of Economics and Finance*, 19: 219–227.

Claessens, S. Fan, J. and Lang, L. (2006) The benefits and costs of group affiliation: evidence from East Asia. *Emerging Markets Review*, 7: 1–26.

Fazzari, S., Hubbard, G. and Petersen, B. (1988) Financing constraints and corporate investment. *Brookings Papers on Economic Activity*, 19: 141–95.

Guariglia, A., Liu, X., and Song, L. (2011) Internal finance and growth: microeconometric evidence on Chinese firms, *Journal of Development Economics*, 96: 79–94.

Guo, L., Zhenzhen, S. and Tong, Y. (2010) Why do Chinese companies dual-list their stocks? Working paper.

Gupta, N. and Yuan, K. (2009) On the growth effect of stock market liberalization. *Review of Financial Studies*, 22: 4715–52.

Hermes, N. and Lensink, R. (2003) FDI, financial development and economic growth. *Journal of Development Studies*, 40: 142–63.

Hoshi, T., Kashyap, A. and Scharfstein, D. (1991) Corporate structure, liquidity and investment: evidence from Japanese industrial groups. *Quarterly Journal of Economics*, 106: 33–60.

Jorgenson, D.W. (1963) Capital theory and investment behaviour. *The American Economic Review*, 53: 247–59.

Khanna, T. and Palepu, K. (2000) The future of business groups: long-run evidence from Chile. *Academy of Management Journal*, 43: 268–285.

Khanna, T. and Yafeh, Y. (2005) Business groups and risk sharing around the world. *Journal of Business*, 78: 301–40.

Konings, J. and Vandenbusssche, H. (2004) Antidumping protection and mark-ups of domestic firms. LICOS discussion paper no. 141, Catholic University of Leuven, available at: http://www.econ.kuleuven.ac.be/licos/DP/DP2004/ DP141.pdf), p. 42.

Lin, H-C.M. and Bo, H. (2011) State ownership and financial constraints on investment of Chinese listed firms: new evidence. *European Journal of Finance*, 18: 497–513.

Lins, K. and Servaes, H. (1999) International evidence on the value of corporate diversification. *Journal of Finance*, 54: 2215–39.

Love, I. (2003) Financial development and financing constraints: international evidence from the structural investment model. *Review of Financial Studies*, 16: 765–91.

Mickiewicz, T., Bishop, K. and Varblane, U. (2004) Financial constraints in investment: panel data results from Estonia, 1995–1999. *Acta Oeconomica*, 54: 425–49.

Poncet, S., Steingress, W. and Vandenbussche, H. (2010) Financial constraints in China: firm-level evidence. *China Economic Review*, 21: 411–22.

Ratti, R., Lee, S. and Seol, Y. (2008) Bank concentration and financial constraints on firm-level investment in Europe. *Journal of Banking & Finance*, 32: 2684–94.

Saudagaran, S.M. (1988) An empirical study of selected factors influencing the decision to list on foreign stock exchanges. *Journal of International Business Studies*, 19: 101–27.

Shin, H.H. and Park, Y. (1999) Financing constraints and internal capital markets: evidence from Korean Chaebols. *Journal of Corporate Finance*, 5: 169–91.

Shleifer, A. and Vishny, R. (1994) Politicians and firms. *Quarterly Journal of Economics*, 109: 995–1025.

Zellner A. (1972) Corrigenda. *Journal of the American Statistical Association*, 67: 255.

DOI: 10.1057/9781137367204.0013

7
The Investment Development Path in the Context of Poland's Accession to the European Union and the Global Financial and Economic Crisis*

Ewa Kaliszuk and Agata Wancio

Introduction

The investment development path (IDP) was provided by Dunning (1981, 1986) as a framework for understanding the dynamic interaction between foreign direct investment (FDI) and the level of economic development of a given country (Dunning and Narula, 1996). It has been used in a range of theoretical and empirical studies across the world (see reviews by Boudier-Bensebaa, 2008; Narula and Dunning, 2010; Narula and Guimón, 2010). Basically, it assumes that the conditions for domestic and foreign companies change along with the change in the level of country development, thereby affecting the flows of inward and outward FDI. Inward flows interact with the upgrading of the country's location advantages, while outward flows do so with the development of domestic firms' ownership advantages. The difference between outward and inward FDI stocks constitutes the country's net outward investment position (NOIP). The concept suggests that, as countries develop, they go through five distinct stages (Dunning, 1986; Dunning and Lundan, 2008). The most important stages from the point of view of this study are the third and fourth stages representing an innovation-driven economy and a knowledge-based economy, respectively.

Although there has been much research looking at the IDP in the context of Poland, there is still ambiguity as to which stage of the IDP model the country should be assigned; besides, little has been said so far about factors determining

* This research was financed by the Polish National Science Centre within the HARMONIA funding scheme (grant No. 2011/01/M/HS4/03715).

DOI: 10.1057/9781137367204.0014

Poland's transition from earlier to further stages of the IDP. In particular, little attention has been paid to external political and economic events that could provide momentum or hamper the country's further progress along its IDP.

Given the aforementioned, we set two aims in this study. First, to test whether Poland's FDI follows a path similar to that provided by the IDP paradigm and to which stage the country should be assigned taking into account features typical of this stage described by the IDP concept. Second, to verify the hypothesis that the Polish IDP has been significantly influenced by the country's accession to the European Union (EU) and afterwards by the global financial and economic crisis. In regards to the EU factor, we pay particular attention to its conse-quences for Poland's transition to the third stage and onwards, as its positive impact on transition towards the second stage of the IDP and changes within the second stage are not disputable. While analysing the crisis's impact on the IDP, we focus on long-term consequences rather than short-lived effects, as the former are more vital for the country's transition to the fourth stage, namely towards the knowledge-based economy.

The chapter starts with a brief review of earlier studies on the Polish IDP followed by a discussion on the interaction between the country's economic development and its investment. To verify the hypothesis that Poland has entered the third stage we use the 'broad version' of the IDP. In the following two sections we focus on Poland's accession to the EU and the recent global financial crisis, trying to assess their influence on the country's further movements along its IDP. Although most of the research has been conducted at the macro level, we could not discuss issues such as motives or investment strategies of Polish multi-nationals (MNEs) without applying the microeconomic approach. Therefore apart from macroeconomic data drawn from national and international sources we use information on Polish MNEs collected through surveys – both by us and other researchers. The chapter ends with a number of conclusions.

Review of earlier research on the Polish IDP

There is an abundance of research on the IDP of the European countries in transition. However only a fraction of it has been dedicated exclusively to Poland's IDP trajectory. In a paper published a decade ago (Durán and Ubeda, 2001), Poland was placed at the third stage of its IDP. Despite the fact that its economic structure characterized that of countries at the second stage and the fact that Polish outward FDI remained very modest, the authors identified Poland as a country at the third stage due to its highly skilled labour force. This factor has not been explored more deeply in subsequent studies, most of which place Poland at the second stage of the IDP path. In research conducted by Kottaridi, Filippaios and Papanastassiou (2004), Poland – along with other new member states that joined the EU in 2004 – was identified as an economy going

DOI: 10.1057/9781137367204.0014

through the second stage of the IDP. As the main characteristics of this stage, the authors pointed out Poland's location advantages, such as market size, quality of labour and rising demand for mature products, and consequently predominance of market and efficiency-seeking investments.

Gorynia, Nowak and Wolniak (2007) find that Poland was close to the borderline between the second and the third stage of its IDP in 2003 due to the rising growth rate of its outward FDI stock. Their further studies based mainly on the net changes in the NOIP per capita growth rates confirmed that the country had made progress in its gradual movement towards the third stage of the IDP (Gorynia, Nowak and Wolniak, 2010a). However the data on FDI published shortly thereafter made authors revisit their previous expectations (Gorynia, Nowak and Wolniak, 2009) as in the light of their new observations they could not see any clear signs of Poland moving towards the third stage. The authors supplemented their previous research on the IDP with an analysis of changes in geographic and sectoral/industrial composition of FDI. While the industry analysis enables important conclusions regarding the country's movement along the IDP path to be drawn, the proposed geographical approach does not allow such deduction. The value of NOIP per se has low explanatory power in the context of the IDP as it informs only about the balance of bilateral investment, revealing almost nothing about its relation to the country's development, the core of the IDP concept.

Relying on the newly proposed ROIP index (Relative Outward Investment Position), Chilimoniuk and Radło (2008) place Poland at the second stage of its IDP. According to their observations, many countries, prior to entering the third stage, had reached values of ROIP close to 0.3 or 0.4, whereas at the end of 2006 Poland did not even surpass the value of 0.1. The authors also indicate significant differences between various Polish sectors; the infant sectors such as business services seemed to only enter the second stage, while other sectors such as manufacturing or trade and repairs were approaching the end of this stage, attracting substantial inflows of FDI for several years and getting ready for cross-border expansion.

Many signs of the transition to the third stage were also pointed out by Kola and Kuzel (2007). A change in motives and a growing role of non-cost factors were mentioned among other location advantages that attract FDI inflows to Poland. Perhaps the most daring thesis was put forward by Gorynia, Nowak and Wolniak (2010b) in a paper expanding their previous studies, which placed Poland at the third stage of its IDP, along with four other new EU member states. However this assessment was based mainly on the country's NOIP value, which has rather low explanatory power. The opposite view was taken by Radło and Sass (2012), who argued that no country within the so-called Visegrad Group (the Czech Republic, Hungary, Poland and Slovakia, hereinafter referred to as the V4) entered the third stage of the IDP.

DOI: 10.1057/9781137367204.0014

Different approaches to the IDP concept

Although Dunning, while describing the relationship between foreign investment and economic development, drew attention to many factors that determine a country's transition from one stage of the IDP path to another, many researchers limit their studies on the IDP to analysis of the 'NOIP–GDP' relation. This approach allows researchers to apply econometric methods and make comparisons between IDPs of different countries, but it also has a number of drawbacks, hence their results should be treated with caution.

Since the NOIP value only reflects the balance between outward and inward FDI and does not capture changes in FDI trends in the case of similar inward–outward growth rates, the interaction between gross domestic product (GDP) and the investment position might be difficult to interpret. Therefore Narula and Guimón (2010) recommend enriching the so-called 'narrow perspective' with a broader framework that allows researchers to explore the interactive relationship between the ownership advantages of firms and the locational advantages of countries. The broad version of the IDP places more emphasis on the idiosyncratic economic structures of countries and to the heterogeneity of FDI as it takes into account historical, social and political conditions of a given country.

In some countries the investment position lags behind the country's economic development (e.g. Austria, see Bellak, 2001), while in others, the investment position changes faster than the indicators of development of the national economy suggest (e.g. Russia, see Kalotay, 2008). Many peculiarities are responsible for those idiosyncratic IDPs. Some of them could be attributed to specific internal factors such as strong support from the state that enabled national champions to invest heavily abroad despite the lack of ownership advantages; others could derive from external conditions. The latter may happen as a result of the country's decision (e.g. accession to the EU) or may remain beyond the country's influence (e.g. global or regional crises). Poland, along with other European post-communist countries, is also recognized as an 'atypical case' since its economic development was disrupted by the adverse political and economic circumstances before 1989. Therefore some authors include the so-called economies in transition in the IDP research area as a separate group (Jaklic and Svetličič, 2001; Gorynia, Nowak and Wolniak, 2010a; Narula and Guimón, 2010). The fact that their general economic development is in some ways distinct could significantly change the role played by inward FDI in those countries. Similarly, outward FDI of companies anchored in the economies of transition could differ from FDI of transnational corporations described in Dunning's concept of the IDP.

The issue that additionally makes an econometric analysis of country IDP awkward is FDI statistics that include transactions involving Special Purpose

DOI: 10.1057/9781137367204.0014

Entities (SPEs). As they are of a purely financial nature (usually no production, no employees and the lack of non-financial assets), they seriously distort the real picture of FDI activities (particularly geographical allocation) and thus make economic interpretation difficult (for details see VCC-IBRKK, 2013).

Poland's track to the third stage

If we treat changes in the NOIP value as the chief criterion determining the moment of a country switching between different stages, we could conclude that Poland entered the third stage of the IDP path in 2011 when the NOIP growth rate had reached a value close to zero. However given the frequent updates of FDI statistics the possibility of a continuing NOIP downward trend and other reasons discussed in the previous section, the IDP can be misleading and thus an in-depth analysis of the different IDP's stages is necessary. Trying to satisfy this need, we have analysed numerous features that are characteristic for a country being at the third stage and tested them one by one for Poland. We outline the most important characteristics for FDI–development interaction at this stage in Table 7.1.

EU factor

Poland has seen a substantial growth in inward and outward FDI since joining the EU in 2004 (Table 7.2). The EU member states remain major investors in Poland and recipients of Polish outward FDI. Although the geographical structure of FDI based on FDI flows should be analysed with caution (see the previous section for more details), the dominant role of the EU countries in Poland's FDI flows is undisputable. Nonetheless, it is difficult to determine precisely the extent to which the significant growth of FDI and other FDI-related economic changes may be attributed to EU integration. Non-EU specific factors such as the business cycle or fluctuations in the exchange rate of the Polish zloty also might affect FDI projects. Moreover it is also highly probable that a significant number of investors from the EU-15 would have taken similar decisions even without the prospects of accession or with a long-term prospect.

The EU dominance, visible primarily in inward investment, has recently also strengthened in outward investment. However our findings suggest that at the end of 2010 the dominance in the number of foreign affiliates (60 per cent) and the number of employees (42 per cent) was much weaker than in terms of the value of assets (75 per cent). This may be partly explained by the character of Polish investment outside the EU (efficiency seeking in countries with cheaper labour).

There have been several studies on the relationship between EU integration and direct investment. The impact of integration processes on the investment

DOI: 10.1057/9781137367204.0014

Table 7.1 The third stage of the IDP – the shift from investment- to innovation-driven economy

Feature	IDP concept		Poland
Inward FDI	Increasing but at a slower pace	+	Although inward FDI stock showed an upward trend, its growth rate was declining (the average annual rate of 12% in 2008–11). This cannot be attributed entirely to the crisis as the decreasing rate was observed in the pre-crisis era.
	Focus on activities supplying more sophisticated products for the domestic market or requiring more skilled labour, thus help the host country to boost innovation-intensive sectors	+	See the section on the global crisis.
Outward FDI	Start of a dynamic increase	+	The FDI stock value started to increase dynamically in 2004, but the base was low. By 2011 outward FDI stock reached 25% of the total amount of inward FDI stock.
	All kinds of investment including efficiency- and asset-seeking investment	+	Research on motives of foreign investors investing in Poland and Polish companies expanding abroad (VCC-IBRKK, 2011; Jaworek, 2012; Wilinski, 2012) suggests that both groups of investors undertake all kinds of investment described by Dunning, including efficiency and asset-seeking investment considered to be more advanced strategies compared to resource- and market-seeking FDI. However, market- and efficiency-related motives dominate in both inward and outward FDI.
	Increasing investment in services	+	The share of the service sector in OFDI reached 60% at the end of 2011 (the NBP data); although a large part of this share is related to the SPEs (in the items of *activities of holding companies and financial intermediation* particularly). Polish MNEs started to take a strong position in IT services (e.g. Asseco Poland).
	Mostly greenfield but some M&As	–	The predominance of greenfield investment has not been confirmed by recent studies on Polish MNEs. One of them found that nearly 52% of Polish MNEs invested abroad purchasing majority or minority stakes in foreign companies abroad (Jaworek, 2012). Data on M&As deals show that Polish outward investors use this mode of entry regardless of the level of the host country development (Zimny, 2012).
	Foreign operations still geographically concentrated, MNEs mostly regional (not global) investors	+	A strong geographical concentration is characteristic of Polish OFDI – the majority of M&A transactions in 2009–11 were concluded in Europe, particularly in the EU member states (49 out of 68 deals; Zimny, 2012). At the end of 2010, the vast majority of affiliates held abroad by Polish MNEs were established in Europe (60% in the EU and further 30% in other European countries) (CSO, 2012b).
Balance of IFDI and OFDI	NOIP negative most of the time but approaches the 'zero' value, reaching it at the final part of the stage	?	The negative NOIP value is still increasing, although its growth rate approached 'zero' in 2011. However the data for 2011 can be updated, so the value of NOIP may change.

Trade	Exports increasingly consist of mostly medium-technology goods and services. Imports mainly consist of higher-income consumer goods and technology-intensive intermediate products	+ Due to large inward FDI, Poland has transformed from a net importer to a net exporter in the automotive industry, electronics and white goods. In all these groups Poland has served as the export-platform for multinationals. In 2002–10 the cumulated share of computers, electronic and optical products, and electrical equipment in sold production increased from 7% to 10% (CSO data). Nevertheless, Polish exports have still been dominated by vehicles and parts thereof.
	Intra-industry trade beginning to become significant	+ In 1995–2008, the intensity of the intra-industry trade in Poland increased by nearly 16 percentage points (Ambroziak, 2012). As a result, in 2008, almost one-third of Polish trade turnover was of an IIT character. The growth rate was especially high in the pre-accession period (1996–2004). FDI in Poland has stimulated both vertical and horizontal intra-industry trade. In the automotive sector, the IIT indices were generally higher than in total trade.
Ownership advantage of firms investing abroad	Many domestic firms shift from export to outward direct investment since their foreign sales increased significantly and the costs of production at home rose	+ Almost 90% of the surveyed Polish companies were present on the foreign market through exports (KPMG, 2010). Only 23% of them established their own sales affiliates and 18% have their own production affiliate abroad. However, expansion through FDI is rising. Many Polish MNEs seek off-shore locations due to falling competitiveness on the domestic market or the need to improve corporate efficiency. Lower energy and material prices were a valid motive for investment in CIS countries, while in emerging Asian countries – lower labour costs (VCC-IBRKK, 2012).
	Ability to differentiate products and adapt to local tastes; some limited product and process innovation	+ The largest part of market-oriented Polish OFDI (most sensitive to local tastes) was conducted in the EU, where consumer needs and customs are similar to those in Poland. However, in the case of affiliates processing and selling food adaptations to local needs are required. Such a type of FDI is also carried out outside the EU and in various sectors (e.g. cosmetics shops in the Middle East).
Location advantages of the home country	Entrepreneurship, larger and more sophisticated markets, government efforts to enforce competitive markets, increasing importance of informal institutions	+ An increasingly sophisticated IT sector: e-government and e-health large-scale projects (Frost and Sullivan and PAIIZ); actions enforcing competition: the reform of the system of grants in higher education (six acts) or the government proposal of limiting state aid in SEZs. A growing number of think tanks (e.g. 'Poland, go global' of KGHM and ICAN Institute, the independent analysis centre THINKTHANK POLSKA) testify of increasing importance of informal institutions.
	Surge in expenditure on innovation activities and substantial increase in government expenditure on tertiary education and ICT facilities	+ Public expenditure on tertiary education increased more than fivefold in 1995–2010 (CSO data). The vast majority of young Poles graduate from public or private universities. Government spending on R&D has also been growing but the GERD is still very low compared to the EU-27 average. The country's innovative potential has been rising, partly due to the funds under the cohesion policy (see more in the section titled EU factor).

Table 7.2   EU-27 countries as a source of FDI in Poland and recipients of Polish outward investment before and after Poland's accession to the EU, in %

	Inward FDI in Poland											
	2000	2001	2002	2003	2004	2005	2006	2007	2008	2009	2010	2011
EU-27	77.0	82.8	82.9	83.8	85.4	85.1	84.9	92.6	85.8	07.7	84.3	87.1
non-EU	23.0	17.2	17.1	16.2	14.6	14.9	15.1	7.4	14.2	29.3	15.7	12.9
Total	100.0	100.0	100.0	100.0	100.0	100.0	100.0	100.0	100.0	100.0	100.0	100.0

	Outward FDI from Poland											
	2000	2001	2002	2003	2004	2005	2006	2007	2008	2009	2010	2011
EU-27	48.4	41.8	55.8	57.3	58.1	48.4	67.7	40.9	59.8	44.8	60.4	59.8
non-EU	51.6	58.2	44.2	42.7	41.9	51.6	32.3	40.2	39.6	40.2	24.7	22.3
Total	100.0	100.0	100.0	100.0	100.0	100.0	100.0	100.0	100.0	100.0	100.0	100.0

Source: authors' own calculations based on data from the NBP. Available at: http://nbp.pl/home.aspx?f=/publikacje/raporty_I_analizy.html.

flows of Poland and other Central and Eastern European countries (CEEC) that joined the EU in 2004 and 2007 has been assessed predominantly on the basis of the theory of integration and the theory of investment creation/diversion/restructuring developed by Yannopoulos (1990), Baldwin, Forslid and Haaland (1995) and Dunning and Robson (1998) as an extension of Viner's (1950) trade theory. The effect of EU membership on CEEC's IDP has received less attention in the literature. We were able to identify only a few studies that devote more than cursory attention to these issues (Gorynia, Nowak and Wolniak, 2010b; Kalotay, 2005, 2006, 2007; Narula and Bellak, 2009; Svetličič and Jaklič, 2006; Witkowska, 2011). Gorynia, Nowak and Wolniak (2010b: 73), while analysing the effects of CEEC membership of the EU on their IDP trajectories, rank EU accession as the most significant external factor to have affected the evolution of the NOIPs of the Czech Republic, Hungary, Poland and Slovakia. A similar conclusion was drawn by Witkowska (2011: 113–14). She emphasizes however that while the FDI has played an important role in the modernization of Hungarian industry, its impact on industrial restructuring for the rest of the country has been modest. Some studies note that 'the role of transition-specific factors is gradually evaporating while EU integration-specific factors will be gradually enhancing its impact' (Svetličič and Jaklič, 2006: 12–13), and that EU membership per se does not necessarily lead to an increase in the quality or the quantity of FDI received by a country, giving Greece as an example (Narula and Bellak, 2009: 76–8).

DOI: 10.1057/9781137367204.0014

We attempt to assess the influence of Poland's membership of the EU on the country's transition to the third stage as follows: first, we identify and categorize key internal and external factors affecting FDI flows to/from Poland in the post-accession period (see Table 7.3); then we discuss the selected 'EU factors' in more detail.

Table 7.3 Internal and external factors affecting FDI flows to/from Poland after joining the EU

Location advantages			Ownership advantages		
Internal factors	External factors		Internal factors	External factors	
	EU accession	Others		EU accession	Others
Geographical location	Membership of the customs union	Global trend of intensive use of outsourcing and offshoring	Development of local financial and capital markets	Structural and cohesion funds	Technological progress in transport and ICT
Size and growth of the domestic market	Full access to the single market guaranteeing four freedoms and a unique set of rules	International fragmentation of production and global supply chains	Government support for export and outward investment	Strengthening competition on the domestic market, thereby inducing local firms to innovate and improve productivity	An improved business climate with major trading partners due to China's and Russia's WTO accession
Relatively cheap and skilled workforce	Reduced perception of investment risks	Economic and financial crisis	Entrepreneurship enhanced by special programs	Knowledge and technology transfer to local firms	Economic and financial crisis
Privatization and other reforms	Labour costs pressures		Growth of the domestic market enabling firms to increase profits	Funds for innovation projects	
Dynamic increase in local human resources for science and technology	EU structural and cohesion funds (impact on GDP and incentives for foreign companies)			Strengthening managerial (and technical) skills through employees' movement between firms	
Government FDI incentives (not subject to EU rules)	Significant productivity growth				

DOI: 10.1057/9781137367204.0014

Membership of the customs union

The adoption of EU external tariffs caused a general lowering of the average level of tariff protection in trade with non-EU countries (according to our calculations, the weighted average customs duty declined from 3.8 per cent in 2003 to 1.3 per cent in 2006), thereby weakening the tariff-jumping motive for FDI. However, customs duties on certain goods increased (from 12 per cent to 14 per cent on TV sets). High tariff protection encouraged several Asian MNEs to invest in TV manufacturing centres in Poland in 2005–7 (Kaliszuk, 2009).

Full access to the single market

The EU internal market, with almost free movement of persons, capital, goods and services, and the regulatory convergence, created advantageous conditions for market-seeking investment. Poland is one of the most competitive countries within the EU in terms of labour costs and has become an attractive destination for the so-called export-platform FDI (Ekholm et al., 2003), not only for the EU-15 MNEs but also for investors from third countries. As a result, in the initial years of EU membership Poland recorded rapid growth in inward FDI flows. A substantial contribution to this amount, with the exception of 2008, was made by reinvested earnings at a 35–53 per cent share of FDI value between 2004 and 2011, while in the pre-accession period their input had been negative. A high export orientation of large companies with foreign capital has been visible up to now, although since 2007 their share in Polish merchandise exports has been declining (Chojna, 2011).

The adoption of EU restrictive state aid rules seemed especially controversial. On the one hand, EU rules have created a level playing field and limited discretionary government policy in granting tax relief and subsidies, in what could be perceived as a positive change for both EU and non-EU investors. On the other hand, restrictions on grants and other bonuses might encourage potential investors to choose locations outside the EU, where no state aid rules exist. However as a result of the tough stance of the Polish authorities oriented at involving foreign investment in rescuing ailing industries, the European Commission granted Poland temporary derogations and special settlements on existing and new aid, beneficial for both domestic and foreign investors (e.g. Mittal, Toyota and Daewoo). An important role in the Polish system of attracting investors is played by special economic zones (SEZs), offering pro-investment tax relief. Although they are available to domestic and foreign companies, so far the contribution of the latter has been dominant. No wonder that the restrictions recently proposed by the government (prohibition of cumulating support, that is, linking of EU funds and governmental grants or tax exemptions in SEZs, or eliminating SEZs by 2020) have aroused objections from foreign investors enjoying generous benefits. This could lead to a reduction in the level of reinvestment by entities currently operating in the SEZs, which, in

DOI: 10.1057/9781137367204.0014

turn, could affect Poland's leading position in CEEC in the area of investment attractiveness (Ernst & Young, 2012).

Structural funds and the cohesion fund

Poland has been the largest beneficiary of the EU Cohesion Policy, receiving €22.5 billion in the years 2004–7 and above €67 billion for the period 2007–13 (European Commission, 2009). This financial 'injection' strengthened Poland's location advantages on several fronts. The most important seems to be its impact on the country's socio-economic development as the funds were spent for purposes such as an extension and upgrading of basic infrastructure (particularly transport infrastructure that is by far the least rated element of the investment climate in Poland), environmental protection and education. The effect on economic growth was also significant, particularly in the period 2009–11. The utilization of cohesion funds increased the GDP annual growth rate by 2.5 percentage points in 2009 in comparison with the 'no funds' scenario (IBS, 2011). However the IBS estimates found a limited impact of EU funds on the GDP structure, particularly in terms of increasing the role of services in the national economy; a change that is typical of a country at the third stage of the IDP. Moreover the funds strengthened (moderately) the relative position of industry in terms of employment structure (Table 7.4) and this trend is expected to continue in the coming years, mainly at the expense of employment in the service sector and to a lesser extent in agriculture.

Since a part of the EU funds are granted to support the development of enterprises, especially their innovation capacity, these funds could become a financial incentive to attract foreign investors. Current experience shows that the foreign entities operating in Poland are less inclined to finance investment

Table 7.4 Change in the employment structure in the national economy by sector

Sector	2005		2011		2005/2011
	Share, in %	EU funds' impact, in pp	Share, in %	EU funds' impact, in pp	Change, in pp
Agriculture	17.3	−0.1	11.9	−0.6	−5.4
Industry	29.3	0.1	30.2	1.7	0.9
Market services	29.0	0.1	31.7	0.1	2.7
Non-market services*	24.4	−0.1	26.1	−1.3	1.7

Note: *Non-market services consist of the following activities: public administration, defence, education, human health and social work (O-Q activities, NACE rev. 2), while the rest are market services.

Source: adapted from IBS (2011) *Wpływ realizacji polityki spójności na kształtowanie się głównych wskaźników dokumentów strategicznych*, annual report.

DOI: 10.1057/9781137367204.0014

from EU funds than their domestic counterparts. In regards to investment in innovation activities, they received only 17 per cent of all the funds from this source in 2011, while their share in the total expenditure on innovation in the business sector reached 37 per cent (CSO data).

The impact of EU grants for development investment is more visible in the case of strengthening the ownership advantages of Polish companies, mostly small or medium-sized enterprises. Their importance to increasing the innovation potential of large companies, which constitute the majority of Polish MNEs, is rather limited (in 2011 less than 1 per cent of their innovation expenditure was financed from the EU resources, according to CSO data). Small businesses, however, experience problems with the utilization of granted aid due to numerous obstacles to its acquisition (mainly the high cost and complexity of application procedures) (Lisowska and Stanisławski, 2012). At the same time though, the requirements connected with EU co-financing have strengthened their management skills that are crucial for planning international expansion. Finally, it is worth mentioning that EU funds also have negative aspects, such as distortions in market competition resulting from grants (e.g. in the energy sector or education and consulting services) and disparities in regional development (induced by the EU funds absorption).

The crisis and its impact on Poland's movement along the IDP

The impact of the global financial and economic crisis on Poland's economy has been widely discussed. Although the majority of studies have adopted a macroeconomic perspective, a number of them have been devoted to the impact of the crisis on FDI inflows (e.g. Chojna, 2010; Marczewski, 2010; Witkowska, 2011; Filippov and Kalotay, 2011), as well as Polish investments abroad (Obłój and Wąsowska, 2012), with strong predominance of the former. However to our knowledge only one academic study has examined the influence of global financial crisis on the Polish IDP. Gorynia, Nowak, and Wolniak (2010b) identify the crisis as one of the factors that has influenced the positioning of the ten new EU members states (without Cyprus and Malta) on their respective IDPs. On the basis of the countries' individual NOIPs per capita the authors conclude that the recent global recession has pushed a few of them (including Poland) well into the third stage. Thus they propose that exogenous macroeconomic factors, such as a downturn in the business cycle, should be included in the general IDP concept.

Polish IDP during the crisis – the narrow perspective

A comparison of the FDI data reported in three currencies, which are the Polish zloty, the euro and the US dollar, shows that the growth of inward FDI stock

DOI: 10.1057/9781137367204.0014

in 2008 was positive when measured in local currency, whereas it was negative when expressed in the two other currencies (Figure 7.1). This stems from the sudden depreciation of the zloty against the US dollar and the euro at the end of 2008, and poorly reflects the activity of foreign investors in Poland at that time. A similar situation occurred in 2008 for outward FDI. The growth rate of FDI reported in local currency was higher (37 per cent) than those of two other currencies (18 per cent and 13 per cent, respectively).

This obviously does not mean that the crisis has had no impact on FDI to/from Poland. The growth rate of the inward and outward FDI stock was slightly lower in 2008 than in the pre-crisis period, as the balance of payments recorded a drop in FDI inflows and outflows (45 and 29 per cent respectively in PLN). In 2009, despite the fact that the global crisis deepened, FDI in both directions increased modestly, exceeding the pre-crisis value in 2010 only in the case of outward FDI. The recovery in inward FDI was slower as foreign-owned companies in Poland were hit by the crisis more severely than domestic companies, mainly through weak demand for exports (Marczewski, 2011). All in all, the value of inward FDI stock in Poland increased by 47 per cent at the time of crisis (2010/2008), while assets located abroad by Polish direct investors more than doubled in the same period. This upward trend in Polish outward FDI is also confirmed by data on Polish MNEs' affiliates established abroad and the number of employees in their foreign entities. The respective figures rose by 18 per cent and 23 per cent within two years, that is from 2008 to 2010 (CSO, 2010, 2011, 2012a).

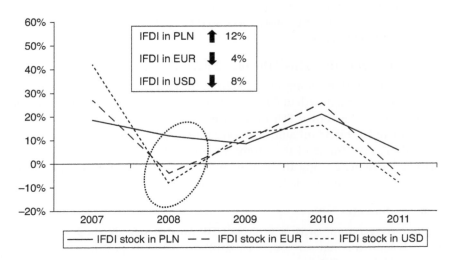

Figure 7.1   The growth rate of inward FDI in Poland in different currencies, 2007–11 (year-on-year)

Source: authors' own calculations based on data from the NBP.

DOI: 10.1057/9781137367204.0014

As the exchange rate of the Polish zloty to the US dollar (as well as to the euro) was subject to large fluctuations at the time of the crisis, the use of FDI data in different currencies for calculation of the NOIP may affect the obtained results and lead to quite different conclusions on the crisis's impact on the IDP. Exchange rate volatility explains why the findings of Gorynia, Nowak and Wolniak (2010b) based on FDI data reported in US dollars differs from our conclusion drawn upon analysis conducted in local currency. Our finding does not confirm any deviations in the NOIP's shape during the recent crisis and thereby Poland's movement to the third stage that time. Although we agree that unexpected events in the global economy could affect the IDP trajectories of countries expediting their movement to the next stage or otherwise, the impact of the global crisis on the Polish IDP is not unambiguous.

The other side of the IDP model, that is, GDP growth, slowed down in 2009, but remained positive (1.6 per cent) in contrast to the other V4 countries that experienced a recession at that time (European Commission, 2012: 148). Leaving aside the set of factors that allowed Poland to 'keep its head above water' in 2009, one point is worth mentioning in the light of the discussion in the preceding section. The estimations assessing the impact of EU funds on Poland's GDP suggest that without using these resources the national economy would have recorded a modest (1 per cent) decrease in GDP that year (IBS, 2011). Nonetheless, the rest of the V4 countries achieved worse results despite the fact that they had also benefited from the cohesion fund. All in all, only Poland avoided a specific downturn-related 'step back' on its IDP path (Figure 7.2). Until 2011, the country followed the path set by Dunning without any apparent deviations.

Polish IDP during the crisis – the broad perspective

Although the Polish economy emerged from the first crisis almost unscathed in terms of short-term growth of GDP, the deterioration of the economic situation in the EU may slow down FDI flows in both directions and affect economic development in Poland inhabiting important structural changes. However due to the short time frame of this study we will only focus on those critical for Poland's movement along the IDP path, that is, its transition to the fourth stage of the IDP (the knowledge-based economy).

Location advantages

As the only economy with a positive GDP growth rate in 2009 within the EU-27, Poland was named 'a green island' or 'a bright spot' in a number of reports and media. This fact was also used by the government as a part of its PR strategy when attracting investors to the country. As such, the crisis improved Poland's image and thus positively influenced the country's perception among

DOI: 10.1057/9781137367204.0014

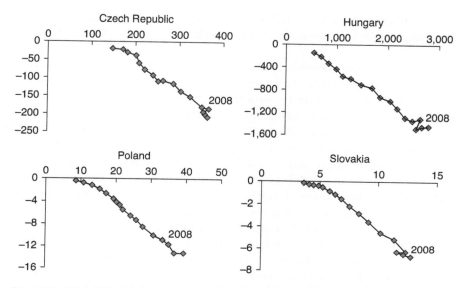

Figure 7.2 The IDP of selected new EU member states from 1995 to 2011 (GDP per capita – the horizontal axis, NOIP per capita – the vertical axis)*

Note: *data are provided in thousand units of national currencies, which are as follows: the Czech crown, the forint, the Polish zloty and the euro ('fixed' series for Slovakia, which joined the Eurozone in 2009).

Source: authors' own calculation based on Eurostat data.

potential investors. This is a very important factor as the size and growth of the Polish market is still one of the major location advantages attracting FDI to Poland (PAIiiZ, 2011). However the slowdown in the Eurozone may result in a further decrease in the importance of the country as the destination for export-platform FDI, at least in the short term. The share of foreign enterprises in Polish merchandise exports has been declining since 2008; although this could be attributed not only to the economic slowdown (it hit foreign investors more than domestic investors), but also to the on-going process of de-industrialization of Poland's economy (Chojna, 2011).

Owing to the crisis, the importance of domestic human resources as a location determinant for FDI in Poland has increased. What is even more crucial in the context of the country's movement along third and next stages of the IDP, investors have rated the availability of skilled labour higher than that of labour cost. Poland has been steadily losing its comparative advantage in terms of cheap labour since the Asian countries, the CIS and the Balkan countries have appeared to become a better alternative for such types of investment. Increased remuneration is a natural consequence of the economic development of countries and thus the decreasing role of this factor is a typical feature of a third-stage country (Dunning and Lundan, 2008). However despite wage growth

DOI: 10.1057/9781137367204.0014

in the pre-crisis period, the relation of labour cost to output (productivity) in Poland is still very attractive and competitive as compared with other EU countries.

As a result of the aforementioned changes, the country has started to attract projects requiring highly skilled employees and this tendency is expected to continue. The important features worth mentioning are: growing human resources for science and technology, the highest percentage of graduates in the EU among those aged 20 to 29 years and a growing number of engineers and technical specialists (CSO, 2012b). The latter plays a crucial role in conducting technology- and knowledge-intensive projects and helps enable the change in the industrial pattern of FDI along with the structure of the GDP. The combined share of medium-high and high-technology industries and the knowledge-intensive services sector in the total FDI stock reached 40 per cent at the end of 2011 (authors' own calculation based on the NBP data). A rising interest from foreign investors has been recently observed particularly in the sector of business services. At least two facts may serve as evidence: an increase in the number of international business centres in Poland offering such services (from 202 in 2007 to 337 in 2011, according to ABSL, 2012) and the 2010 promotion of Cracow as the regional leader in terms of attractiveness for outsourcing (Tholons's ranking). Although those centres provide services of different knowledge intensity, there is a visible trend to locate more specialized centres in Poland, including those engaged in R&D (Wancio, 2012).

The recent economic crisis shows however that at the time of an economic downturn foreign companies are, on average, more likely to reduce spending on both R&D and other innovation activities compared to domestic companies. In 2009, their share in the total business sector expenditure on innovation and R&D declined by seven percentage points and 20 percentage points respectively compared to the previous year (Table 7.5). Admittedly the foreign entities' spending on R&D and their share in the total R&D expenditure increased in the service sector in 2011, but the overall amount was still very low when compared internationally.

Ownership advantages

The development of the domestic financial market, especially the capital market, allowed Polish companies to raise the capital needed to make investments abroad. About 30 per cent of Polish MNEs listed on the Warsaw Stock Exchange (WSE) obtained funds for international projects by issuing shares or bonds (Wilinski, 2012). This way of obtaining funds for foreign acquisitions was difficult during the crisis due to the change in the financial market sentiment, resulting, among other things, in the withdrawal of foreign portfolio investors from Poland. Admittedly the WSE ranked first in Europe in terms of

DOI: 10.1057/9781137367204.0014

Table 7.5 Total expenditure on innovation activity and expenditure on R&D in industrial and service sector enterprises, 2006–11, in PLN billion

Specification	Expenditure on innovation activities									
	In industrial enterprises					In the service sector				
	2007	2008	2009	2010	2011	2006*	2008	2009	2010	2011
Total expenditure	20.2	25.4	22.7	23.8	20.8	7.2	12.6	8.3	10.8	11.0
Foreign enterprises	7.3	7.9	6.4	8.0	7.8	1.2	5.1	1.8	2.0	2.7

	Expenditure on R&D									
	In industrial enterprises					In the service sector				
	2007	2008	2009	2010	2011	2006*	2008	2009	2010	2011
Total expenditure	1.6	2.1	2.2	3.4	2.8	0.8	0.9	0.8	1.4	1.5
Foreign enterprises	0.6	0.9	1.1	2.0	1.3	0.2	0.3	0.2	0.4	0.7

Note: * in the case of the service sector, data for 2006 are provided as no survey was conducted in 2007.

Source: authors' own calculation based on CSO data.

the number of IPOs for two years in a row (2011 and 2012); however due to the weak demand for shares many Polish companies withdrew from their planned IPOs.

The difficult situation in the markets hosting Polish investors affected them in two ways. On the one hand, the companies from industries heavily hit by the crisis (such as the metal or furniture industries) were forced to focus primarily on introducing restructuring plans and on survival rather than on business development. Some of them were pressured to reduce their activities abroad, either through selling individual assets (e.g. warehouses), liquidating an affiliate or selling the whole group. On the other hand, Polish MNEs being in a relatively good financial shape benefited from the opportunities created by the crisis, first of all through acquiring valuable assets of collapsing companies or entities at risk of losing liquidity and thus looking for a strategic investor. In this way, they followed the global trend of a rising number of strategic asset-seeking projects carried out by MNEs from emerging markets (e.g. Pradhan, 2010).

However the crisis has not encouraged Polish enterprises to improve their competitiveness through so-called creative destruction at home. Their

DOI: 10.1057/9781137367204.0014

propensity to innovate has been hampered, which may have long-term implications for building and strengthening their technological advantage.

Conclusions

Analysing the Polish IDP from a narrow perspective, we can conclude that Poland entered the third stage in 2011 when the NOIP growth rate reached a value close to zero. Moreover the broader analysis indicates that Poland has a number of characteristics of a third-stage country in regards to both FDI and the country's economic development; just to mention a few: a dynamic increase in outward FDI; the growing importance of medium and medium-high technology exports as well as of intra-industry trade; progress in changing the economy's structure towards a greater share of the service sector (visible also in FDI industrial composition); and the rising role of the government in improving the country's innovation capacity.

EU membership has had a strong impact on Poland's inward and outward FDI. Although it is difficult to conclude precisely on its effect on Poland's NOIP, there is no doubt that EU membership has been a kind of catalyst for the country's transition to the third stage, mainly through structural funds, which improved the country's investment potential. As the Polish economy avoided recession in 2009 and FDI in both directions increased in that period, the global financial crisis has not affected the Polish IDP in the narrow sense. Its implications for Poland's ability to move forward along the IDP path may be particularly discernible in innovation activity as the business sector (foreign enterprises to a larger extent) reduced this type of investment at that time and spending on innovation has been recovering modestly until 2011. A further deterioration of the situation in the Eurozone may also affect the financial ability of Polish MNEs to expand in to foreign markets, mainly through the stock exchange.

References

ABSL (2012) *Business Services Sector in Poland*. Warsaw: Association of Business Service Leaders in Poland.

Ambroziak, Ł. (2012) FDI and intra-industry trade: theory and empirical evidence from the Visegrad Countries. *International Journal of Economics and Business Research*, 4(1–2): 180–198.

Baldwin, R.E., Forslid, R. and Haaland, J. (1995) Investment creation and investment diversion: simulation analysis of the single market programme. NBER working paper no. 5364.

Bellak, C. (2001) The Austrian investment development path. *Transnational Corporations*, 10(2): 106–34.

Boudier-Bensebaa, F. (2008) FDI-assisted development in the light of the investment development path paradigm: evidence from Central and Eastern European countries. *Transnational Corporations*, 17(1): 37–63.

DOI: 10.1057/9781137367204.0014

Chilimoniuk, E. and Radło, M.J. (2008) Service offshoring and location factors: evidence from Poland. Paper delivered at the conference of ETSG 2008. Warsaw, 10th Annual Conference, 11–13 September.

Chojna, J. (2010) Role of entities with foreign capital in the Polish foreign trade, in J. Chojna (ed.) *Foreign investment in Poland 2008–2010*. Warsaw: IBRKK, pp. 217–64.

Chojna, J. (2011) Role of entities with foreign capital in the Polish foreign trade, in J. Chojna (ed.) *Foreign investment in Poland 2009–2011*. Warsaw: IBRKK, pp. 51–89.

CSO (2010, 2011, 2012a) *Działalność podmiotów posiadających udziały w podmiotach z siedzibą za granicą w 2008, 2009 i 2010 roku*. Warsaw: Central Statistical Office.

CSO (2012b) *Science and Technology in 2010*. Warsaw: Central Statistical Office.

Dunning, J.H. (1981) Explaining outward direct investment of developing countries: in support of the eclectic theory of international production, in K. Kumar and M. McLeod (eds) *Multinationals from Developing Countries*. San Francisco: Lexington Press, pp. 1–22.

Dunning, J.H. (1986) The investment development cycle revisited. *Weltwirtschaftliches Archiv*, 122: 667–77.

Dunning, J.H. and Lundan, S.M. (2008) *Multinational Enterprises and the Global Economy*, 2nd edn. Basingstoke: Edward Elgar.

Dunning, J.H. and Narula, R. (1996) The investment development path revisited: some emerging issues, in J.H. Dunning and R. Narula (eds) *Foreign Direct Investment and Governments*. London: Routledge, pp. 1–41.

Dunning, J.H. and Robson, P. (eds) (1988) *Multinationals and the European Community*. Oxford: Basil Blackwell.

Durán, J.J. and Ubeda, F. (2001) The investment development path: a new empirical approach and some theoretical issues. *Transnational Corporations*, 10(2): 1–34.

Ekholm, K., Forslid, R. and Markusen, J.R. (2003) Export-platform foreign direct investment. National Bureau of Economic Research, working paper no. 9517.

Ernst & Young (2012) *Special Economic Zones Beyond 2020: Analysis of Current Activities and an Outlook for their Existence*.

European Commission (2009) *European Cohesion Policy in Poland*, available at: http://ec.europa.eu/regional_policy/sources/docgener/informat/country2009/pl_en.pdf.

European Commission (2012) *European Economic Forecast: Autumn 2012. European Economy*. Brussels: European Commission.

Filippov, S. and Kalotay, K. (2011) Global crisis and activities of multinational enterprises in new EU member states. *International Journal of Emerging Markets*, 6(4): 304–28.

Gorynia, M., Nowak, J. and Wolniak, R. (2007) Poland and its investment development path. *Eastern European Economics*, 45(2): 52–74.

Gorynia, M., Nowak, J. and Wolniak, R. (2009) Poland's investment development path: in search of a synthesis. *International Journal of Economic Policy in Emerging Economies*, 2(2): 153–74.

Gorynia, M., Nowak, J. and Wolniak, R. (2010a) Investment development paths of Central European countries: a comparative analysis. *Argumenta Oeconomica*, 1(24).

Gorynia, M., Nowak, J. and Wolniak, R. (2010b) Foreign direct investment of Central and Eastern European countries, and the investment development path revisited. *Eastern Journal of European Studies*, 1(2).

IBS (2011) *Wpływ realizacji polityki spójności na kształtowanie się głównych wskaźników dokumentów strategicznych*. Warsaw: Institute for Structural Research, available at: http://www.mrr.gov.pl/rozwoj_regionalny/Ewaluacja_i_analizy/Oddzialywanie_makroekonomiczne/Documents/Raport_Hermin_12072012.pdf.

DOI: 10.1057/9781137367204.0014

Jaklič, A. and Svetličič, M. (2001) Does transition matter? Outward foreign direct investment by the Czech Republic, Hungary and Slovenia. *Transnational Corporations*, 10(2): 67–106.

Jaworek, M. (2012) Oczekiwania polskich przedsiębiorstw związane z bezpośrednimi inwestycjami zagranicznymi i stopień ich spełnienia. Unpublished data presented at the Polskie inwestycje za granicą – stan i wyzwania conference, Warsaw.

Kaliszuk, E. (2009) Trade policy and regulation: lessons from Poland's accession to the European Union. *International Journal of Public Policy*, 4(1/2): 135–58.

Kalotay, K. (2005) The late riser TNC: outward FDI from Central and Eastern Europe, in K. Liuhto and Z. Vincze (eds) *WIDER EUROPE*. Lahti and Tampere: Esa Print Oy, pp. 199–223.

Kalotay, K. (2006) The impact of EU enlargement on FDI flows. *International Finance Review*, 6: 473–99.

Kalotay, K. (2007) Investment creation and diversion in an integrating Europe, in P. Vahtra and E. Pelto (eds) *The Future Competitiveness of the EU and Its Eastern Neighbours: Proceeding of the Conference*. Turku: Pan-European Institute, pp. 49–65.

Kalotay, K. (2008) Russian transnationals and international investment paradigms. *Research in International Business and Finance*, 22(2): 85–107.

Kola, M. and Kuzel, M. (2007) Bezpośrednie inwestycje zagraniczne polskich przedsiębiorstw na gruncie teorii ścieżki inwestycyjno-rozwojowej, in W. Karaszewski (ed.), *Bezpośrednie inwestycje zagraniczne w budowaniu potencjału konkurencyjności przedsiębiorstw i regionów*. Toruń: Wydawnictwo Uniwersytetu Mikołaja Kopernika, pp. 171–202.

Kottaridi, C., Filippaios, F. and Papanastassiou, M. (2004) The investment development path and the product cycle – and integrated approach: empirical evidence from the new EU member states of CEE. *Economics & Management Discussion Papers*, em-dp2004–03, Henley Business School, Reading University.

KPMG Poland (2010) *Ekspansja międzynarodowa polskich przedsiębiorstw produkcyjnych*. Warsaw: KGHM Sp. z o.o., available at: http://www.atlas.com.pl/pdf/Raport%201.pdf.

Lisowska, R. and Stanisławski, R. (2012) *Impact of EU Funds on Building the Innovation Potential of Poland's Small and Medium Enterprises from the Metal and Machine-Building Industries*. Brno: Metall.

Marczewski, K. (2010) Reactions of companies with foreign capital to symptoms of the economic crisis, in J. Chojna (ed.) *Foreign Investment in Poland 2008–2010*. Warsaw: IBRKK, pp. 120–37.

Marczewski, K. (2011) Business situation and the barriers to activities of companies with foreign capital share, in J. Chojna (ed.) *Foreign Investment in Poland 2009–2011*. Warsaw: IBRKK, pp. 264–79.

Narula, R. and Bellak, C. (2009) EU enlargement and consequences for FDI assisted industrial development. *Transnational Corporations*, UNCTAD, 18(2).

Narula, R. and Dunning, J.H. (2010) Multinational enterprises, development and globalisation: some clarifications and a research agenda. *Oxford Development Studies*, 38(3): 263–87.

Narula, R. and Guimón, J. (2010) The investment development path in a globalised world: implications for Eastern Europe. *Eastern Journal of European Studies*, 1(2): 5–19.

Obłój, K. and Wąsowska, A. (2012) Location determinants of Polish outward FDI and the impact of the Global Crisis, in M.A. Marinov and S. Marinova (eds), *Emerging Economies and Firms in the Global Crisis*. Basingstoke: Palgrave Macmillan, pp. 240–58.

PAIiIZ (2011) *Klimat inwestycyjny w Polsce: Raport z badania zrealizowanego przez TNS Pentor*. Warsaw: Polish Information and Foreign Investment Agency.

DOI: 10.1057/9781137367204.0014

Pradhan, J.P. (2010) Strategic asset-seeking activities of emerging multinationals. *Organizations and Markets in Emerging Economies*, 1(2): 9–31.

Radło, M.J. and Sass, M. (2012) Outward foreign direct investments and emerging multinational companies from Central and Eastern Europe: the case of Visegrád countries. *Eastern European Economics*, 50(2): 5–21.

Svetličič, M. and Jaklič, A. (2006) Outward FDI from new European Union member states (first draft). Ljubljana: Faculty of Social Sciences, University of Ljubljana.

VCC-IBRKK (2012) *Polish Multinationals Go Beyond Europe*. Warsaw and New York: VCC and IBRKK.

VCC-IBRKK (2013) *Polish Multinationals: Expanding and Seeking Innovation Abroad*. Warsaw and New York: VCC and IBRKK.

Viner, J. (1950) *The Customs Union Issue*. New York: Carnegie Endowment for International Peace.

Wancio, A. (2012) W drodze ku innowacyjnej gospodarce – rozwój wiedzochłonnych usług biznesowych w Polsce na tle pozostałych krajów UE-10. *Unia Europejska.pl*, 2(213): 25–37.

Wilinski, W. (2012) Internationalization through the Warsaw Stock Exchange – an empirical analysis. *Post-Communist Economies*, 24(1): 145–54.

Witkowska, J. (2011) The role of foreign capital in the modernization of the economy of the new member countries of the European Union. *Zeszyty Naukowe*. Krakow: Polskie Towarzystwo Ekonomiczne, p. 9.

Yannopoulos, G.N. (1990) Foreign direct investment and European integration: the evidence from formative years of the European Community. *Journal of Common Market Studies*, 28(3): 247–57.

Zimny, Z. (2012) Outward FDI from Poland and its policy context. *Columbia FDI Profiles*. New York: VCC, available at: http://academiccommons.columbia.edu/catalog/ac%3A148493.

DOI: 10.1057/9781137367204.0014

8
Adoption of the Global Reporting Initiative by FT500 firms: Overcoming the Liability of Foreignness

Stephen Chen and Petra Bouvain

Introduction

The Global Reporting Initiative (GRI) is the most widely accepted global framework for voluntary corporate reporting of environmental and social performance and has been adopted by thousands of businesses across 72 countries (GRI, 2013). It is considered the 'leading template for voluntary sustainability reporting' (Brown et al., 2009) and the 'most relevant institution in the sustainability context' (Moneva et al., 2006). However GRI reporting has fallen far short of attaining a status equivalent to financial reporting standards, which are mandatory in most countries. Sustainability reporting standards such as the GRI have not yet achieved the same status and are only mandatory in a few countries. Despite its name, implementation of the GRI has been highly uneven geographically. Indeed, in some countries such as the USA and the UK, an analysis of companies in the GRI database (http://database.globalreporting. org/) shows that the uptake and diffusion of the GRI to new organizations appears to be slowing down (Levy et al., 2010).

What explains the wide variation in the adoption of the GRI between countries? Various industry and country level factors have been suggested to be important in influencing the adoption of the GRI by firms. Adoption of the GRI has been shown to be influenced by industry sector and found to be higher for firms that operate in high risk industries such as petroleum, chemical, forest and paper, automobile, airline, oil industries, agriculture, liquor and tobacco, and media and communications (Legendre and Coderre, 2012). According to Nikolaeva and Bicho (2011: 142) 'Companies may also believe that they will gain a competitive edge and enhanced legitimacy if they follow the adoption of practices that are spreading across different industries'.

DOI: 10.1057/9781137367204.0015

It has also been shown that both the nature and extent of disclosure are influenced by a firm's country of origin (Kolk, 2008; Kolk and Perego, 2010; Wanderley et al., 2008). Some contextual factors that have been examined previously in the literature include political, social, cultural and economic factors (Adams, 2002). In this chapter we focus specifically on two sets of country factors: the national institutional environment and the influence of foreign customers and investors.

Firstly, we focus specifically on the national institutional factors that influence adoption of the GRI. Previous studies (Chapple and Moon, 2005; Chen and Bouvain, 2009; Jackson and Apostolakou, 2010; Matten and Moon, 2008; Simnett et al., 2009) have been instrumental in highlighting the role played by different features of the national institutional environment in promoting and/or inhibiting the adoption of global standards. Guler et al. (2000), among others, have argued that generally widespread sustainability practices in the national environment encourage sound sustainability practices by companies in the country. It has also been suggested that companies from developing countries may also adopt global standards such as the GRI in order to increase their 'legitimacy' with business partners from developed countries (Eccles and Krzus, 2010).

The second set of factors that influence firms' sustainability practices investigated here arise from foreign customers and investors. International business in many industries now involves sophisticated global supply chains and firms competing globally face pressures to conform to international standards from customers and investors. One argument is that this increased globalization of business might lead to the increased adoption of global sustainability reporting (Stolz, 2010). Another argument is that some firms may adopt global standards as a signal of quality in order to overcome a 'liability of foreignness' (Zaheer, 1995) in competing in foreign markets with domestic firms or else in order to attract foreign investment (Goyal, 2006). However these competing arguments have not been tested against others in the same study and previous studies have been based on aggregate data at the country level. In this study, we test the predictions of these two arguments using firm-level data from a sample of firms in the FT500 index

The rest of the chapter is organized as follows. First, we provide a brief introduction to the GRI. Then we review previous studies that have sought to explain the cross-country variations in the take up of global voluntary standards. Based on these previous studies we develop a number of hypotheses firstly about the effects of the country institutional environment and then about the effects of country exports and FDI on adoption of the GRI by firms. We then describe the data and methods used, followed by the results and a broader discussion of the implications of our research.

DOI: 10.1057/9781137367204.0015

The Global Reporting Initiative

The Global Reporting Initiative (GRI) is the most widely accepted framework for voluntary corporate reporting of environmental and social performance worldwide (Brown et al., 2009) and since its launch in 1999 the GRI has attracted thousands of businesses across 72 countries. It has become the de-facto standard with 80 per cent of the 250 largest companies worldwide reporting their sustainability using the GRI guidelines (GRI Annual Report 2011/12: 20). The vision of the Global Reporting Initiative is that 'disclosure on economic, environmental and social performance become as commonplace and comparable as financial reporting and as important to organizational success' (http://www.globalreporting.org/AboutGRI). Unlike other corporate social responsibility (CSR) standards, such as the ISO9000 quality management standard developed by the International Standards Organization (ISO), the GRI was deliberately designed to mobilize a wide range of actors and to encourage a dialogue between them (Levy et al., 2010). The GRI was launched in 1997 by Ceres, a network of investors, environmental organizations and other public interest groups to address sustainability changes. The 1997 draft paper stated:

> The GRI vision is to improve corporate accountability by ensuring that all stakeholders – communities, environmentalists, labour, religious groups, shareholders, investment managers – have access to standardized, comparable and consistent environmental information akin to corporate financial reporting. Only in this fashion will we be able to (1) use the capital markets to promote and ensure sustainable business practices; (2) measure companies' adherence to standards set from Ceres principles; and (3) empower NGOs around the globe with the information they need to hold corporations accountable. (Ceres, 1997)

In 1998 the UN Environment Program (UNEP) formally joined GRI as a partnering institution and between 1999 and 2002 the GRI's founders succeeded in obtaining more than $7 million from several foundations as well as additional support from various participating organizations, including the World Bank. By the early 2000s, the GRI was widely regarded as the best developed international framework for sustainability reporting (Brown et al., 2009). A 2002 survey of 107 MNCs showed that the GRI was second only to the ISO 14001 standard in having the greatest influence on their practices with regard to social responsibility (Berman et al., 2003). Major organizations such as the OECD Committee on International Investment and Multinational Enterprises continue to promote the use of GRI.

Although the GRI has been adopted across a number of countries, a closer examination suggests a greater concentration in some countries compared to

DOI: 10.1057/9781137367204.0015

others. Perego and Kolk (2012) show that of the 212 firms from the Fortune 500 who adopted the GRI in the period 1999–2008, 33 per cent were from the USA, 22.6 per cent were from Japan and 9.9 per cent were from Germany. In addition, at the end of April 2012, 53 per cent of companies in the SP 500 produced CSR reports of which 63 per cent reported using the guidelines of the GRI (2012).

Possible effects of the institutional environment

The growing literature on the diffusion of global standards indicates that a complex interplay of institutional, country-specific, industry-specific and firm-specific factors influences the international spread of voluntary standards such as the GRI.

Institutional theorists have found that organizations are more likely to imitate the behaviour of similar organizations (mimetic behaviour) (Di Maggio and Powell, 1983; Tolbert and Zucker, 1983; Zucker, 1987). As Prakash and Potoski (2007) have demonstrated, voluntary standards can be perceived as 'clubs' where firms receive specific benefits because they belong to a specific community. Competitive 'bandwagon' pressures may arise from a threat of lost competitive advantage. Firms may also adopt the same practices because not doing so would place them at a disadvantage relative to the competition and erode their edge in the market place.

Studies of the adoption of managerial practices (Kostova, 1999) and studies of other global standards such as the ISO9000 quality management standard (Guler, Guillen and MacPherson, 2000) have shown how such institutional pressures from competitors can influence firms to adopt a voluntary standard. The question of why firms display such 'mimetic' behaviour (Di Maggio and Powell, 1983) can be explored from both information-based theories and rivalry-based theories. Managers may be inclined in situations that can be considered uncertain to seek information from other firms to guide their own actions (Liebermann and Asaba, 2006). A more cynical view has been taken by Lutz, Lyon and Maxwell (2000) who describe how leading companies may agree to minor environmental improvements on a voluntary basis in order to avoid harsher regulation. The pre-emptive move towards sustainability can be seen as a way to avoid the imposition of stricter regulations by governments (Lyon and Maxwell, 2008). A study of German, UK and Canadian companies (Bondy et al., 2004) found that among the reasons for adopting company codes of conduct were in order to meet legal requirements as well as to protect or enhance reputation and to promote business principles.

CSR approaches have been shown to become institutionalized both within and across industry sectors. According to Bertels and Peloza (2008) norms

DOI: 10.1057/9781137367204.0015

for CSR are first established in elite firms within specific geographic locations, owing to their higher visibility, and then trickle down the industry as industry rules, norms, beliefs and perceptions influence the evolution of industry-specific practices and standards. This would suggest that the nature of the country environment, particularly the reaction of leading firms, has a significant effect on the subsequent adoption of CSR practices by firms in that location. Hellman, Jones and Kaufmann (2000) show that besides country differences, purely domestic firms operating in emerging economies behave differently compared to firms headquartered in the country but operating internationally, and also differ from firms with FDI in the country but headquartered abroad. They find that the propensity to engage in 'state capture' (where firms significantly influence a state's decision-making processes to their own advantage) was highest in firms that had FDI and domestic headquarters, while lowest for firms with FDI but headquartered abroad. However when bribes for public procurement are taken into account, firms headquartered abroad had the highest propensity.

Since one of the aims of the GRI was to improve the reporting of social and environmental performance by companies (Mohrhardt et al., 2002), one would expect the adoption of the GRI to be strongly related to the general level of corporate social and environmental responsibility in home and host countries. One factor which has been extensively examined in previous studies is the level of corruption in a country. As discussed by Rodriguez et al. (2006), the issues of politics, corruption and CSR are linked. The level of corruption in a country may also have an indirect effect by affecting the level of FDI. Research by Egger and Winner (2006) has shown that the level of corruption has an influence on foreign direct investment (FDI). Both Lambsdorff (2003) and Cuervo-Cazurra (2006) show that the level of corruption in a country is negatively related to inward FDI in that country. Given that one of the Society Performance Indicators required to be reported in the GRI concerns actions taken against corruption, we might expect that adoption of the GRI would be greater in countries with a greater control of corruption. Therefore we propose Hypothesis 1A.

Hypothesis 1A: the greater the level of control of corruption in a country the greater the number of firms that adopt the GRI.

However an alternative argument is that adoption of a global sustainability standard serves as a signal about the trustworthiness of the firm. Signalling theory in economics (Spence, 1973) argues that, where there are asymmetries in access to information in the market, buyers and sellers can get around the problem of market coordination through signals that reveal some piece of relevant information to the other party. Spence (1973) provides an example in the recruitment market where all applicants may appear suitable but educational

DOI: 10.1057/9781137367204.0015

qualifications are used as signals of unobservable quality to employers. An educational qualification is not only a signal of knowledge and skills attained but, because education requires investment of money and time as well as commitment by the applicant, an educational qualification might also be a signal that the applicant will be a trustworthy and reliable worker. Similarly, joining the GRI can be seen as a 'signal' that the firm is honest and reliable since it has taken the trouble to join and abide by an internationally recognized standard. It can also contribute to product differentiation (Siegel and Vitaliano, 2007). Robinson et al. (2011: 504) found that 'applying for a "best in class" index such as the DJSI (Dow Jones Sustainability Index) may be an effective way to signal sustainability leadership in a credible manner'. However signals may not only be directed to consumers but may also be directed to investors. For example, environmental responsibility can be interpreted as a 'signal' to investors about the trustworthiness of the company (Hussainey and Salama, 2010). This is supported by findings from the financial industry by Wright and Rwabizambuga (2006) who observe higher rates of adoption of environmental standards among North American and western European organizations compared to organizations in other regions.

The global reach of the GRI provides firms with the added advantage that the signal is amplified and endorsed. The association with the GRI increases the strength of the signal and provides credibility to the receiver who is likely to interpret the information more favourably as it is conveyed by a third party. If membership of the GRI fulfils a signalling role in the market, we would expect there to be a greater number of adoptions in countries where producers face higher uncertainty about their quality in the global marketplace and there is greater asymmetry of information. Therefore an alternative hypothesis is Hypothesis 1B.

Hypothesis 1B: the lower the level of control of corruption in a country the greater the number of firms that adopt the GRI.

Stakeholder engagement is another principle in the GRI, so we expect this to be related to the level of 'voice and accountability' in the country as measured by the World Bank. As defined by the World Bank, voice and accountability captures 'perceptions of the extent to which a country's citizens are able to participate in selecting their government as well as freedom of expression, freedom of association; and a free media' (http://info.worldbank.org/governance/wgi/index.asp). We hypothesize that citizens of countries with greater voice and accountability of government institutions would expect a similar degree of voice and accountability in their business corporations and hence there would be a greater number of adoptions of the GRI by businesses in such countries: Hypothesis 2A.

DOI: 10.1057/9781137367204.0015

Hypothesis 2A: the higher the level of voice and accountability in a country the greater the number of firms that adopt the GRI.

On the other hand, if, as some people have argued, firms are just using the GRI to compensate for poor perceptions of the country then we would expect the opposite effect: Hypothesis 2B.

Hypothesis 2B: the lower the level of voice and accountability in a country the greater the number of firms that adopt the GRI.

Another indicator included in the GRI guidelines is that companies must report on their environmental performance, including use and impact of materials, energy, water, biodiversity, emissions, effluents, products and compliance to environmental regulations. Environmental legislation and sanctions tend to be weaker in developing countries (Dasgupta et al., 2001). If this weakness in national institutions results in firms being less environmentally responsible then we expect this to be reflected in a fewer number of firms that adopt the GRI reporting framework, which requires them to report on their environmental sustainability. This seems to be supported in a study by Perego and Kolk (2012), which found an increase in third party assurances by Fortune 250 companies and that most companies were from developed countries, with US and Japanese companies making up over 50 per cent of the sample. Therefore if there is a positive relationship between environmental responsibility and GRI adoption we would expect Hypothesis 3A.

Hypothesis 3A: the higher the level of environmental responsibility in a country the greater the number of firms that adopt the GRI.

However as in the previous hypotheses concerning corruption and voice and accountability, if firms are using the GRI to compensate for actual or perceived weaknesses in the general level of environmental responsibility in the country then we would expect the opposite effect: Hypothesis 3B.

Hypothesis 3B: the lower the level of environmental responsibility in a country the greater the number of firms that adopt the GRI.

Foreign influences

The second set of factors influencing firms' sustainability practices that we investigate arises from foreign customers and buyers. Firms competing globally face pressures to conform to international standards from customers and other stakeholders. A meta-analysis of 41 research studies on sustainability by

DOI: 10.1057/9781137367204.0015

Stolz (2010: 13) suggests that 'internationalization and globalization might lead to the incorporation of regulatory frameworks for corporate citizenship (CC) or CSR in contexts that actively initiate global trade'. Indeed, global trade now involves sophisticated global supply chains, in which Logistics Social Responsibility (LSR) (Carter and Jennings, 2002), or what could be termed sustainability of all parties in the supply chain, has become an important issue for consumers (Maloni and Brown, 2006).

Foreign firms may also suffer from a 'liability of foreignness', which Zaheer (1995: 342–3) defines as 'all additional costs a firm operating in a market overseas incurs that a local firm would not incur'. These include social costs as well as economic costs that arise from 'the unfamiliarity, relational and discriminatory hazards that foreign firms face and domestic firms do not' (Eden and Miller, 2004). These social and economic costs are likely to be greater in markets where there is more uncertainty about the other party, such as in export markets where firms may be less well known by customers. These arguments suggest that, in order to reduce the uncertainty of foreign buyers, firms in countries with a greater reliance on exports should be more likely to adopt sustainability standards compared with firms in countries with less reliance on exports. Perkins and Neumayer (2010) found that transnational economic linkages are significant in explaining the diffusion of two corporate voluntary standards – ISO14001 and the Global Compact. We suggest that they may also be significant in the case of the GRI and we propose Hypothesis 4.

Hypothesis 4: the higher the contribution of exports to GDP of a country the greater the number of firms that adopt the GRI.

A country's sustainability record may also serve to attract foreign investors, particularly ethical investors. Dowell, Hart and Yeung (2000) found that firms in developing countries that adopt stringent environmental policies attract better foreign investments than those that do not. In their study of 89 extractive and manufacturing companies from the SP 500, they found that companies that adopted higher global environmental standards rather than minimum country standards had an individual market value of $10.4 billion higher than those that adopted the less rigid US standard. Goyal (2006) found that the increase in adoption of CSR practices has accompanied a rise in FDI to developing countries in the 1990s and suggested that this could be explained as a signalling device about the quality of firms that adopt CSR practices. These studies would suggest that inward FDI should be positively related to the adoption of sustainability by companies in the country: Hypothesis 5.

Hypothesis 5: the higher the inward FDI to GDP ratio of a country the greater the number of firms that adopt the GRI.

DOI: 10.1057/9781137367204.0015

Sample

We tested our hypotheses on a sample consisting of the 500 firms in the FT500. These are the world's largest firms by market capitalization. Table 8.1 shows the breakdown of the sample by country.

Table 8.1　Composition of Fortune 500

Country	Non-GRI reporter	GRI reporter	Total
AUSTRALIA	5	9	14
BELGIUM	1	0	1
BRAZIL	6	6	12
CANADA	15	10	25
CHILE	2	0	2
CHINA	10	12	22
CZECH REPUBLIC	1	0	1
DENMARK	1	1	2
FINLAND	1	1	2
FRANCE	8	15	23
GERMANY	3	16	19
HONG KONG	11	6	17
INDIA	6	6	12
INDONESIA	2	1	3
ISRAEL	1	0	1
ITALY	3	5	8
JAPAN	17	19	36
KOREA	2	6	8
MALAYSIA	3	0	3
MEXICO	4	2	6
NETHERLANDS	2	5	7
NORWAY	3	0	3
QATAR	2	0	2
RUSSIA	5	5	10
SAUDI ARABIA	3	0	3
SINGAPORE	5	1	6
SOUTH AFRICA	1	6	7
SPAIN	1	5	6
SWEDEN	1	8	9
SWITZERLAND	5	10	15
TAIWAN	3	2	5
THAILAND	1	2	3
UAE	1	0	1
UK	11	22	33
US	96	77	173
Totals	242	258	500

Source: compiled by authors from FT500 and GRI lists of companies.

DOI: 10.1057/9781137367204.0015

Variables

Dependent variable

The dependent variable (GRI) is a binary variable indicating whether the firm has adopted the GRI (1) or not (0).

Independent variables

The independent variables were measured as follows:

Control of corruption (corruption) and *voice and accountability* (voice) in the country were measured using the ratings from the World Bank Governance Indicators (http://info.worldbank.org/governance/wgi/sc_country.asp). These indicators measure the effectiveness of Governance in a country using 30 individual data sources produced by a variety of survey institutes, think tanks, non-governmental organizations, international organizations and private sector firms.

Environmental performance (EP) of the country was measured using the Environmental Performance Index measure from Yale University (http://epi.yale.edu/). This measures the environmental performance of a country by measuring its achievement towards a number of environmental policy targets. For simplicity we used the overall score.

Country exports (exports) was measured as the percentage exports/GDP sourced from the World Bank database (http://data.worldbank.org).

Inwards FDI of the country (FDI) was measured as the percentage inwards FDI stock/GDP sourced from the World Bank database (http://data.worldbank.org).

Control variables

We controlled for the effect of firm size, which has been identified by Legendre and Coderre (2012) as a significant factor, by including total firm assets and we used the logarithmic value to make the distribution of the values a closer fit to normality. The number of firms reporting per country will also depend on the number of firms in that country so we also included as a control variable the country GDP (World Bank). We controlled for the effect of industry by including a random effect for industry sector (INDUSTRY) using the sectors listed in the FT500. Some studies have shown a significant relationship between financial performance and CSP (e.g. Barnett and Solomon, 2012) so in order to control for the effect of firm profitability we also included the firm's reported return on assets (ROA). To control for the effect of the company's overall sustainability record, we also included the corporate sustainability performance (CSP), measured using the overall score for sustainability for the company provided by CSR Hub (http://www.csrhub.com). (CSRHub rates companies according to 12 performance indicators in the areas of employee, environment, community and governance based on data from more than 230 sources.)

DOI: 10.1057/9781137367204.0015

Analysis

We tested our hypotheses using a multilevel logistic regression model (Luke, 2004) with firms (level 1) nested within industry (level 2). Multilevel models (also known as hierarchical linear models, mixed models or random effects models) are statistical models of parameters that vary at more than one level. Multilevel models are particularly appropriate for research designs where the data are nested, for example, firms within industries as in this study. An advantage over standard linear regression is that multilevel models allow the slopes and/or intercepts to vary according to the group (industry sector in this study) and thus avoids the need to make the possibly unrealistic assumption that the same regression slopes and intercepts apply across all groups.

In a two level regression model, two sets of equations are derived. The level 1 regression equation is as follows:

$$Y_{ij} = \beta_{0j} + \beta_{1j}(X_{1ij}) + \beta_{2j}(X_{2ij}) + \beta_{3j}(X_{2ij}) \ldots + e_{ij} \tag{1}$$

where Y_{ij} is the score on the dependent variable for an individual observation at level 1 – GRI adoption in this study (subscript i refers to individual case, subscript j refers to the group); $X_{1ij}, X_{2ij}, X_{3ij}\ldots$ are the Level 1 predictors; β_{0j} is the intercept of the dependent variable in group j (level 2 – industry sector in this study); $\beta_{1j}, \beta_{2j}, \beta_{3j}\ldots$ are the slopes for the relationship in group j (level 2) between the level 1 predictor and the dependent variable; and e_{ij} is the random error of prediction for the level 1 equation.

In the level 2 regression equation, the dependent variables are the intercepts and the slopes for the independent variables at level 1 (firm level) in the groups of level 2 (industry level).

$$\beta_{0j} = \gamma_{00} + \gamma_{01}W_j + u_{0j} \tag{2}$$
$$\beta_{1j} = \gamma_{10} + u_{1j}$$
$$\beta_{2j} = \gamma_{20} + u_{2j}$$
$$\beta_{3j} = \gamma_{30} + u_{3j}$$

where γ_{00} is the overall intercept (or the grand mean of the scores on the dependent variable across all the groups when all the predictors are equal to 0); W_j is the Level 2 predictor; γ_{01} is the overall regression coefficient, or the slope, between the dependent variable and the Level 2 predictor; u_{0j} is the random error component for the deviation of the intercept of a group from the overall intercept; γ_{10} is the overall slope, between the dependent variable and the Level 1 predictor X_{1ij}; and u_{1j} is the error component for the slope (equivalent to the deviation of the group slopes from the overall slope) and so on.

DOI: 10.1057/9781137367204.0015

Results

Descriptive statistics

The correlation matrix shows no significant multicollinearity problems between the variables in the models tested (see Table 8.2). (Prior tests indicated that there was a strong relationship between control of corruption, voice and environmental performance so in order to avoid multicollinearity problems each of these variables was tested in separate models.)

Regression results

Tables 8.3 and 8.4 show the results of our multilevel logistic regressions (* indicates $p < 0.05$, ** indicates $p < 0.005$, *** indicates $p < 0.0005$).

Firstly, we tested models with only the control variables to test their effects alone. Models 1 and 2 with the control variables show significant effects of firm size, profitability and corporate social performance (CSP) but no significant effect of GDP.

Then we added the institutional variables to test the effect of the country's institutional environment on GRI adoption. Model 3 including the control of

Table 8.2   Correlation table

	ROA	Lnassets	GDP	CSP	CCorruption	Voice	EP
ROA	1.0000						
Lnassets	−0.6049	1.0000					
GDP	0.0853	−0.1384	1.0000				
CSP	−0.0207	0.1476	−0.1300	1.0000			
CCorruption	−0.0790	−0.0136	0.1874	0.3990	1.0000		
Voice	0.0143	−0.1337	0.3882	0.4003	0.8275	1.0000	
EP	−0.1648	0.0804	−0.1020	0.4149	0.6443	0.5407	1.0000

Table 8.3   Effect of corruption control

	Model 1			Model 2			Model 3	
	Coef.	Sig.		Coef.	Sig.		Coef.	Sig.
Lnassets	.370172	**	Lnassets	.3716182	**	Lnassets	.3462727	**
ROA	7.212121	**	ROA	7.211878	**	ROA	6.610271	**
CSP	.1674989	***	CSP	.1633823	***	CSP	.1830522	***
Constant	−13.37741	***	GDP	−3.75e-14		GDP	−2.37e-14	
			Constant	−13.02046	***	CCorruption	−.3004853	*
						Constant	−13.4002	***
Random effects	Estimate	s.e.	Random effects	Estimate	s.e.	Random effects	Estimate	s.e.
Industry	.3355174	.1656593	Industry	.3355174	.1656593	Industry	.3394228	.1639263

DOI: 10.1057/9781137367204.0015

Table 8.4   Effect of voice and accountability

	Model 4	
	Coef.	Sig.
ROA	6.590337	**
Lnassets	.3361914	**
GDP	−2.90e-15	
CSP	.1893401	***
Voice	−.3956746	*
Constant	−13.72498	
Random effects	Estimate	s.e.
Industry	.3608857	.1635428

corruption variable shows a significant negative relationship between control of corruption and GRI adoption, thus supporting Hypothesis 1B and rejecting Hypothesis 1A. Model 4 shows a significant negative effect of voice and accountability supporting Hypothesis 2B and rejecting Hypothesis 2A.

Next we tested for the effect of the country's environmental performance on adoption of GRI by firms in the country. Environmental performance of the country is only significant when the corporate sustainability performance measure was removed, in which case Environmental Performance has a positive effect on GRI adoption (Table 8.5), supporting Hypothesis 3A.

Finally, we tested the effects of foreign firms on GRI adoption in the country. Tables 8.6 and 8.7 show the effects of exports and inwards FDI respectively.

Exports are not significant when all the control variables are included (model 7) and are only significant when the corporate sustainability performance measure was removed (model 8), in which case the level of country exports has a negative effect (Table 8.6), contrary to Hypothesis 4. Inwards FDI is not significant in either case (models 9 and 10), contrary to Hypothesis 5 (Table 8.7).

Discussion and conclusion

The findings confirm that, after controlling for firm size, GDP, industry, firm financial performance and CSP, GRI adoption is greater in countries that have a lower rating for control of corruption and voice and accountability. This is consistent with arguments that the GRI may serve as a type of signal to external parties about the trustworthiness of firms in countries which suffer from a poor country perception abroad (Goyal, 2006).

The finding of no significant relationship with the measure of environmental responsibility in the country in the presence of CSP but a significant

DOI: 10.1057/9781137367204.0015

Table 8.5 Effect of environmental performance

Model 5			Model 6		
	Coef.	Sig.		Coef.	Sig.
ROA	6.872182	**	ROA	7.810721	***
Lnassets	.380033	**	Lnassets	.5633727	***
GDP	−4.12e-14		GDP	−5.06e-14	+
CSP	.1748441	***	EP	.0322368	*
EP	−.0243642		Constant	−8.147333	***
Constant	−12.31757	***			
Random effects	Estimate	s.e.	Random effects	Estimate	s.e.
Industry	.3655596	.1689787	Industry	.4843214	.1663959

Table 8.6 Effect of country exports

Model 7			Model 8		
	Coef.	Sig.		Coef.	Sig.
Lnassets	.3604532	**	Lnassets	.5452302	***
ROA	7.091156	**	ROA	6.28175	**
CSP	.1604517	***	GDP	−8.99e-14	**
GDP	−5.75e-14		Exports	−.0092441	*
Exports	−.0049927		Constant	−5.644227	***
Constant	−12.51979	***			
Random effects	Estimate	s.e.	Random effects	Estimate	s.e.
Industry	.3306452	.1687382	Industry	.5265198	.1612103

Table 8.7 Effect of country inwards FDI

Model 9			Model 10		
	Coef.	Sig.		Coef.	Sig.
Lnassets	.3652755	**	Lnassets	.5648901	***
ROA	7.283256	**	ROA	6.615922	**
CSP	.163045	***	GDP	−6.17e-14	*
GDP	−4.83e-14		FDI	−.041794	
FDI	−.0500921		Constant	−6.132645	***
Constant	−12.7598	***			
Random effects	Estimate	s.e.	Random effects	Estimate	s.e.
Industry	.3139225	.1678807	Industry	.5284196	.1611268

DOI: 10.1057/9781137367204.0015

positive effect when CSP is removed suggests that environmental responsibility in the country is not significant in comparing firms of similar CSP and is only significant in comparing firms with different CSP. This was unexpected but might indicate either that country environmental responsibility is a less important factor in GRI adoption when firms have similar corporate social responsibility ratings or else that more environmentally-focused standards such as ISO9000 fulfil this need for firms. Unfortunately our dataset does not contain this information but if data are available further research could examine the effect of competing standards.

The findings also show a strong and statistically significant effect of country exports on adoption of the GRI. However the effect was negative, contrary to our expectations, and the fact that the effect is only significant in the absence of CSP suggests that the relationship is not straightforward. The relationships between country exports, CSP and GRI require further investigation. One possible explanation is that firms in countries with a high level of exports have less need to adopt the GRI. This would be consistent with the findings for the effect of the institutional variables we tested and might suggest that the GRI only serves as a signal for firms in countries with low exports, which are seeking to improve their international perception.

The finding of no significant effect of inwards FDI on adoption of the GRI was also unexpected but might be explained by the fact that most of the companies in the FT500 are from developed countries where companies are less reliant on attracting foreign investors. We suspect that a stronger effect might be observed in a sample of firms from less-developed countries.

In conclusion, our results confirm the importance of the institutional environment of the home country on the adoption of the GRI by companies in the FT500. This is consistent with the findings of previous studies on corporate responsibility reporting, which have examined the content of company CSR reports (e.g. Chen and Bouvain, 2009). Secondly, our results showed a significant negative effect of country-level exports on adoption of the GRI by firms in the country. This was unexpected but might indicate that the GRI plays a role as a signal of quality of firms from countries that suffer from a liability of foreignness and are seeking to improve export performance.

Nevertheless we urge some caution in interpreting the results and encourage further research. Firstly, we only tested some institutional measures of society, overall scores for environmental responsibility and aggregate measures of exports and FDI. Further research could examine other features of the institutional environment, different aspects of environmental responsibility or different types of exports and FDI. Secondly, as demonstrated by the recent delisting of some companies from the Global Compact for failure to report (UN, 2010), membership of the GRI does not necessarily guarantee compliance with their principles. Firms may have signed up to the GRI without any real

DOI: 10.1057/9781137367204.0015

commitment to the aims. Further research is required to determine if the deeds match the words.

References

Adams, C.A. (2002) Internal organisational factors influencing corporate social and ethical reporting: beyond current theorising. *Accounting, Auditing and Accountability Journal*, 15(2): 223–50.

Barnett, M.L. and Salomon, R.M. (2012) Does it pay to be *really* good? Addressing the shape of the relationship between social and financial performance. *Strategic Management Journal*, 33: 1304–20.

Bertels, S. and Peloza, J. (2008) Running just to stand still? Managing CSR reputation in an era of ratcheting expectations. *Corporate Reputation Review*, 11(1): 56–72.

Berman, J.E., Webb, T., Fraser, D.J., Harvey, P.J., Barsky, J. and Haider, A. (2003) Race to the top: attracting and enabling global sustainable business. *Business Survey Report*. Washington, DC: World Bank Group.

Bondy, K., Matten, D. and Moon, J. (2004) The adoption of voluntary codes of conduct in MNCs: a three-country comparative study. *Business and Society Review*, 109(4): 449–77.

Brown, H.S., de Jong, M. and Lessidrenska, T. (2009) The rise of the global reporting initiative: a case of institutional entrepreneurship. *Environmental Politics*, 18(2): 182–200.

Carter, C.R. and Jennings, M.M. (2002) Transportation research. *Logistics and Transportation Review*, 38(1): 37–52.

Chapple, W. and Moon, J. (2005) Corporate social responsibility (CSR) in Asia: a seven-country study of CSR web site reporting. *Business Society*, 44(4): 415–41.

Chen, S. and Bouvain, P. (2009) Is corporate responsibility converging? A comparison of corporate responsibility reporting in the USA, UK, Australia and Germany. *Journal of Business Ethics*, 87: 299–317.

Cuervo-Cazurra, A. (2006) Who cares about corruption? *Journal of International Business Studies*, 37(6): 803–22.

Dasgupta, S., Laplante, B. and Mamingi, N. (2001) Pollution and capital markets in developing countries. *Journal of Environmental Economics and Management*, 42(3): 310–35.

Di Maggio, P.J. and Powell, W.W. (1983) The iron cage revisited: institutional isomorphism and collective rationality in organizational fields. *American Sociological Review*, 48(2): 47–160.

Dowell, G., Hart, S. and Yeung, B. (2000). Do corporate global environmental standards create or destroy market value? *Management Science*, 46(8): 1059–74.

Eccles, R.G. and Krzus, M.P. (2010) *One Report: Integrated Reporting for a Sustainable Strategy*. New York: John Wiley & Sons Inc.

Eden, L. and Miller, S.R. (2004) Distance matters: liability of foreignness, institutional distance and ownership strategy. *Advances in International Management*, 16: 187–221.

Egger, P. and Winner, H. (2006) How corruption influences foreign direct investment: a panel data study. *Economic Development and Cultural Change*, 54(2): 459–86.

Goyal, A. (2006) Corporate social responsibility as a signalling device for foreign direct investment. *International Journal of the Economics of Business*, 13(1): 145–63.

Guler, I., Guillen, M.F. and MacPherson, J.M. (2000) Global competition, institutions and the diffusion of organizational practices: the international spread of the ISO 9000 quality standard. *Administrative Science Quarterly*, 47(2): 207–32.

DOI: 10.1057/9781137367204.0015

Hellman, J.S., Jones, G. and Kaufmann, D. (2000) Are foreign investors and multinationals engaging in corrupt practices in transition economies? *Transition*, 11(3–4): 4–7.

Hussainey, K. and Salama, A. (2010) The importance of corporate environmental reputation to investors. *Journal of Applied Accounting Research*, 11(3): 229–41.

Jackson, G. and Apostolakou, A. (2010) Corporate social responsibility in Western Europe: an institutional mirror or substitute? *Journal of Business Ethics*, 94(3): 371–394.

Kolk, A. (2008) Sustainability, accountability and corporate governance: exploring multinationals' reporting practices. *Business Strategy and the Environment*, 17(1): 1–15.

Kolk, A. and Perego, P. (2010) Determinants of the adoption of sustainability assurance statements: an international investigation. *Business Strategy and the Environment*, 19(3): 182–198.

Kostova, T. (1999) Transnational transfer of strategic organizational practices: a contextual perspective. *Academy of Management Review*, 24 (2): 308–24.

Lambsdorff, J. (2003) How corruption affects persistent capital flows. *Economics of Governance*, 4(3): 229–43.

Legendre, S. and Coderre, F. (2012) Determinants of GRI G3 application levels: the case of the Fortune Global 500. *Corporate Social Responsibility and Environmental Management*, 20: 182–92.

Levy, D.L., Brown, H.S. and de Jong, M. (2010) The contested politics of corporate governance: the case of the global reporting initiative. *Business and Society*, 49(1): 88–115.

Lieberman, M. and Asaba, S. (2006) Why do firms imitate each other? *Academy of Management Review*, 31(2): 366–85.

Luke, D.A. (2004) *Multilevel Modeling*. Thousand Oaks, CA: Sage.

Lutz, S., Lyon, T.P. and Maxwell, J.W. (2000) Quality leadership when regulatory standards are forthcoming. *The Journal of Industrial Economics*, 48(3): 331–48.

Lyon, T.P. and Maxwell, J.W. (2008) Corporate social responsibility and the environment: a theoretical perspective. *Review of Environmental Economics and Policy*, 2(2): 240–60.

Maloni, M.J. and Brown, M.E. (2006) Corporate social responsibility in the supply chain: an application in the food industry. *Journal of Business Ethics*, 68(1): 35–52.

Matten, D. and Moon, J. (2008) 'Implicit' and 'explicit' CSR: a conceptual framework for a comparative understanding of corporate social responsibility. *The Academy of Management Review*, 33(2): 404–24.

Morhardt, J.E., Baird, S. and Freeman, K. (2002) Scoring corporate environmental and sustainability reports using GRI 2000, ISO 14031 and other criteria. *Corporate Social Responsibility and Environmental Management*, 9(4): 215–33.

Moneva, J.M., Archel, P. and Correa, C. (2006) GRI and the camouflaging of corporate unsustainability. *Accounting Forum*, 30(2): 121–37.

Nikolaeva, R. and Bicho, M. (2011) The role of institutional and reputational factors in the voluntary adoption of corporate social responsibility reporting standards. *Journal of the Academy of Marketing Science*, 39(1): 136–57.

Perego, P. and Kolk, A. (2012) Multinationals' accountability on sustainability: the evolution of third-party assurance of sustainability reports. *Journal of Business Ethics*, 110(2): 173–90.

Perkins, R. and Neumayer, E. (2010) Geographic variations in the early diffusion of corporate voluntary standards: comparing ISO 14001 and the Global Compact. *Environment and Planning A*, 42(2): 347–65.

Prakash, A. and Potoski, M. (2007) Collective action through voluntary environmental programs: a club theory perspective. *Policy Studies Journal*, 35(4): 773–92.

DOI: 10.1057/9781137367204.0015

Robinson, M., Kleffner, A. and Bertels S. (2011) Signaling sustainability leadership: empirical evidence of the value of DJSI membership. *Journal of Business Ethics*, 101(3): 493–505.

Rodriguez, P., Siegel, D.S., Hillmann, A. and Eden, L. (2006) Three lenses on the multinational enterprise: politics, corruption and corporate social responsibility. *Journal of International Business Studies*, 37: 733–46.

Siegel, D.S. and Vitaliano, D.F. (2007) An empirical analysis of the strategic use of corporate social responsibility. *Journal of Economics and Management Strategy*, 16(3): 773–92.

Simnet, R., Vanstraelen, A. and Chua, W.F. (2009) Assurance on sustainability reports: an international comparison. *Accounting Review*, 84(3): 937–67.

Spence, M. (1973) Job market signaling. *Quarterly Journal of Economics*, 87(3): 355–74.

Stolz, I. (2010) International and intercultural perspectives on corporate citizenship: a meta-synthesis. Working paper SGOCI, 4, available at: http://www.sgoci.com.

Tolbert, P. and Zucker, L. (1983) Institutional sources of change in the formal structure of organizations: the diffusion of civil service reform, 1880–1935. *Administrative Science Quarterly*, 28(1): 22–39.

UN (2010) *859 Companies Delisted for Failure to Communicate on Progress*. UN Media Release, 1 February.

Wanderley, L.S.O., Lucian, R., Farache, F. and de Sousa Filho, J.M. (2008) CSR information disclosure on the web: a context-based approach analysing the influence of country of origin and industry sector. *Journal of Business Ethics*, 82(2): 369–78.

Wright, C. and Rwabizambuga, A. (2006) Institutional pressures, corporate reputation and voluntary codes of conduct: an examination of the equator principles. *Business and Society Review*, 111(1): 89–117.

Zaheer, S. (1995) Overcoming the liability of foreignness. *Academy of Management Journal*, 38(2): 341–63.

Zucker, L. (1987) Institutional theories of organizations. *Annual Review of Sociology*, 1: 443–64.

DOI: 10.1057/9781137367204.0015

Part III

Knowledge Flows and Firm Performance

DOI: 10.1057/9781137367204.0016

9
Inward Investment, Technology Transfer and Innovation: Direct Evidence from China

Meng Song, Nigel Driffield and Jun Du*

Introduction

This chapter contributes to the understanding of technology transfer between inward investors and the host country economy at the micro level. The focus here is on the innovation of host country firms directly, rather than through the indirect lens of productivity.

The theoretical basis of believing that foreign direct investment (FDI) contributes to technological development and productivity growth in host countries is based on Dunning's (1979) analysis of firm specific advantages, and the extent to which these are embodied in FDI flows. These arguments then spawn a large and growing 'spillovers' literature (see e.g. Driffield and Love, 2007), concerned with the extent to which the technology is transferred, either formally or informally, to domestically-owned sectors in host countries.

The theoretical literature of economics and international business has identified several channels through which technology transfer from inward investors can take place, including demonstration and competition effects, vertical linkages with multinational enterprises (MNEs) and labour turnover. Empirical studies have found rather mixed results. Whether or not domestic firms benefit from horizontal technology transfer from inward investors varies greatly between nations. Some find positive effects (see e.g. Gorg and Greenaway, 2004) while others observe no such benefits (see e.g. Aitken and Harrison, 1999). As for technology transfer via value chains,

* Contact details: Meng Song: Aston Business School, Aston University Birmingham, B4 7ET, United Kingdom. E-mail: songm1@aston.ac.uk. Nigel Driffield: Aston Business School. E-mail: n.l.driffield@aston.ac.uk. Jun Du: Aston Business School. E-mail: j.du@aston.ac.uk.

DOI: 10.1057/9781137367204.0016

recent meta-analysis suggests that technology transfer is more prominent via backward linkages and forward linkages with MNEs. The magnitude tends to be larger from backward than forward linkages (Havranek and Irsova, 2011; Irsova and Havranek, 2013).

We argue that the mixed findings are partly due to the indirect methodologies adopted in the literature linking economic performance with FDI. Typically the literature seeks to link FDI flows to productivity growth, but is unable to distinguish between direct and indirect technology transfer, and only infers the impact on the individual drivers of productivity, such as innovation, as part of an overall net effect. It is typically unable to distinguish technology transfer from the greater innovation rates in local firms as a response to investment by more technologically advanced competitors. Garcia, Jin and Salomon (2013) argue, for example, that the response to such inward investment is at least as important as the indirect technology transfer effects. The rationale is that firms produce innovation after searching for knowledge externally and combining it with internal knowledge. Such innovation, especially that which has been codified into products or processes, will eventually result in improved firm performance (Roper, Du and Love, 2008). However we understand little about the role of FDI in this particular process. In addition, innovation is essential for sustainable economic growth and to overcome growth bottleneck (Grossman and Helpman, 1994). External knowledge obtained through the channels related to FDI plays an important role in upgrading firms' capabilities to produce innovation output (Love, Roper and Bryson, 2011). Therefore it is important to understand the impact of FDI on firm innovativeness, in addition to what we already know about that of the overall firm productivity, and on other drivers of productivity that are not directly related to innovation (e.g. through labour and wage effects). Such an understanding is undoubtedly crucial when evaluating the cost and benefit of attracting foreign investment. For an emerging economy such as China, it is particularly important to learn from MNEs in order to upgrade its position in the global production value chain from a manufacturing centre to an innovation-driven economy. From a practitioner's perspective, understanding the role played by FDI in domestic firms' innovation production is important in order to make strategic business plans, such as predicting future technology, market change as well as competitors' behaviour in order to make early business decisions (Ernst, 2001). The research described here investigates this question by linking FDI with the direct technology transfer output.

Inward FDI and domestic innovation

How can FDI improve innovativeness?

Firms that can combine external and internal learning are found to achieve high levels of innovative capabilities, such as implementing innovative activities,

DOI: 10.1057/9781137367204.0016

developing competitive advantages based on innovation and catching up with global leaders in introducing innovative products (Figueiredo, Cohen and Gomes, 2013). Hence it is reasonable to expect that higher innovativeness is associated with FDI, which is an important knowledge source for local firms.

Technologies can be transferred by communication with MNEs in downstream sectors and this can improve the innovation performance of domestic suppliers. For example, MNEs may provide information that is complementary to suppliers' knowledge pools. Suppliers can have a better understanding of customers' needs and refine products to generate innovation (Shaw, 1994). When Proctor & Gamble launches a new detergent, local chemical firms are encouraged to develop new inputs. Moreover MNEs could engage small-scale local suppliers to become more efficient and innovative (Javorcik, Keller and Tybout, 2008). Additionally interactions with foreign customers in downstream sectors can create new marketing practices and provide product details that are important for building firms' abilities to generate innovation (Figueiredo, Cohen and Gomes, 2013).

MNEs in supplying sectors also act as a conduit for technology transfer and generate innovation by domestic firms in downstream sectors. Especially in developing countries where firms often lack economies of scale and incentives to invest in R&D, manufacturers tend to produce products with incremental improvement. In this case, knowledge and technologies from foreign suppliers could be important for local firms to access innovation and upgrade final products (Javorcik, Keller and Tybout, 2008). Training with foreign suppliers can enhance firms' learning capabilities and their ability to innovate, such as training to introduce technical and organizational innovations, product design and development (Figueiredo, Cohen and Gomes, 2013).

Employee movement is an important channel of knowledge flowing from MNEs to local firms and it is usually associated with more tacit and embedded knowledge diffusion (Spencer, 2008). Human capital is an important factor to address customer needs and introduce technological solutions (Marvel and Lumpkin, 2007). It is reasonable to argue that apart from productivity augmentation, tacit knowledge embedded in employees is intrinsically important for technology transfer and to generate innovation output. This is supported by empirical evidence from Liu et al. (2010). Their study shows that inter-firm employee movement contributes to domestic firms' innovation production.

Furthermore innovations of MNEs could stimulate innovation of local competitors (Javorcik, Keller and Tybout, 2008). Frequent introduction of new technologies by MNEs creates competition that encourages domestic and foreign firms to adopt innovations at higher pace. This is because domestic firms will use innovation to defend their market share, or they are more motivated to do reverse engineering (Blomström, Globerman and Kokko, 1999; Blomström

DOI: 10.1057/9781137367204.0016

and Kokko, 1998). Empirical evidence by Hallin and Lind (2012) shows that competitive pressure from MNEs encourages domestic firms to generate new products and processes. However Yueh (2009) observes that foreign firms could dominate sectors, in which case domestic firms are forced to operate in less innovative parts of the value chain.

Studies linking FDI with host country innovation

Empirical evidence linking FDI with host country innovation is mixed and positive technology transfer tends to take place under certain conditions. Innovation is usually measured by research and development (R&D) input, patent counts or new product sales. Hu and Jefferson (2009) find that local firms' R&D expenditure can only explain a fraction of patent applications in China. In contrast, MNEs play a significant role in boosting indigenous firms' patent applications. Wang and Kafouros (2009) report that the potential for technology transfer by MNEs is greatest when there is a modest level of foreign presence in the industry. However when foreign penetration is very high, there is no sign of technological benefits. Li, Chen and Shapiro (2010) show that innovation output of MNEs contributes to the innovation production of domestic firms only within clusters, because technology transfer tends to be confined within a certain distance. Liu and Zou (2008) find that R&D activities of greenfield FDI within and across sectors can improve domestic industries' new product sales. In contrast, Filatotchev et al. (2011) argue that the R&D activities of MNEs do not singularly affect the innovation of domestic firms. Only those that have skilled employees can benefit from technology transfer. A related study by Li (2011) shows that the share of foreign sales in industries does not necessarily lead to higher patent production, because the strong competition of MNEs could make it difficult for domestic firms to launch patents.

FDI could also negatively affect domestic firms' innovation production. For example, Yueh (2009) reports that FDI reduces the number of patents that have been granted to provinces in China. Garcia, Jin and Salomon (2013) find that Spanish firms do not receive technology transfer from inward FDI to produce patents. They argue that foreign firms in Spain still mainly focus on innovative activities in home countries and are reluctant to transfer technology to Spain. Therefore domestic firms have few opportunities to learn. Liu and Zou (2008) find that competing directly with greenfield FDI in the labour market will crowd out the innovation output of domestic firms.

An important limitation of these studies is that it remains unclear how domestic firms benefit from technology transfer via vertical linkages, despite the fact that empirical evidence using the indirect methodology finds this channel of knowledge flows to be important (Gorg and Greenaway, 2004).

DOI: 10.1057/9781137367204.0016

Competition effect

Competition is a double-edged sword. Competitive pressure may give firms incentives to alter their innovative behaviour, yet how exactly competition affects firms' innovativeness is still debatable. On the one hand, competition pressure is often the main driver of research, development and innovation (Arrow, 1962) and competition from MNEs may encourage local firms to innovate. MNEs tend to invest in industries with relatively high entry barriers and the existing competition between local firms is limited. The entry of MNEs could reduce monopoly inefficiency and improve the efficiency with which resources are allocated (Caves, 1974). Competing with MNEs encourages local firms to adopt similar production methods in order to stay competitive in the market (Jenkins, 1990). Competition could increase X-efficiency of local firms such as management and capacity ulilization (Page, 1980). Local firms have incentives to update production technologies and to adopt more advanced management and marketing methods. Technologies transferred seem to be more evident in less developed countries where the local firms are more inefficient than MNEs (Blomström and Kokko, 1998). Competition from MNEs could lead to price decrease in one sector and benefit all firms, both local and foreign, in downstream sectors (Markusen and Venables, 1999).

On the other hand, the Schumpeterian School believes that competition discourages innovation (Shumpeter, 1943), in that monopolies favour innovation because they face less market uncertainty and have larger and stable cash flows to fund innovative activities (Levin, Cohen and Mowery, 1985). This view is largely supported by the endogenous growth model (e.g. Aghion and Howitt, 1992; Grossman and Helpman, 1991), where an increase in product market competition, or in the rate of imitation (as indicated by horizontal product innovation) has a negative effect on productivity growth by reducing the monopoly rents that reward new innovation. Recent studies show that there is a U-shaped relationship between competition and innovation (Aghion et al., 2005; Tishler and Milstein, 2009). In the context of MNEs where foreign firms steal market shares from local companies, the latter will experience decreasing returns of scale and even be crowded out (Konings, 2001). In addition, foreign firms tend to pay higher wages to the most qualified employees than domestic firms and bid the resources away (Spencer, 2008). With regard to vertical linkages, although local suppliers could benefit from economies of scale when the demand from downstream sectors increases due to foreign entry, factor supplies could be limited in the short term. If factor prices grow substantially and quickly, local firms could experience lower profitability (Garcia, Jin and Salomon, 2013). Local firms may be relegated to less profitable and less innovative segments of the market (Hanson, 2001). The inflow of FDI can decrease the entry of domestic entrepreneurs because of lower prices in

DOI: 10.1057/9781137367204.0016

product markets and higher wages paid to labour, leading potential entrepreneurs to earn wages instead of launching their own businesses (De Backer and Sleuwaegen, 2003). Under these circumstances, competition pressure induced by MNEs may discourage local firms from innovation.

Finally, the literature on FDI and innovation cannot be totally divorced from the literature on FDI and technology transfer more generally. The literature in this area typically focuses on the extent to which inward investors generate technology transfer effects to the domestic sectors. However as much of the literature contends, this is strongly linked to both the level of innovation by the inward investors and to the absorptive capacity of the domestic firms. Typically the transfer mechanisms are defined as follows.

Demonstration effect

On average, MNEs tend to use advanced technologies more intensively than domestic firms (Driffield and Taylor, 2005), though there is some evidence that once one corrects for firm size and internationalization, some of the differences disappear (Temouri, Driffield and Higon, 2008). However what is clear is that potential users of knowledge in a particular location have an incentive to source the technology and other advantages that accompany FDI. Being exposed to the advanced technologies employed by MNEs, local firms can update production methods (Barrios and Strobl, 2002), imitate and reverse engineer products produced by MNEs (Saggi, 2002) and apply better management practices and organizational innovations. The scope of demonstration effects depends on the complexity of the products and production processes. The simpler the manufacturing processes are, the easier it is for local firms to imitate (Gorg and Greenaway, 2004). However MNEs have incentive to prevent knowledge leaking to local competitors by means of intellectual property protection, and offering higher wages to employees to prevent labour turnover (Javorcik, 2004).

Backward linkages

Many existing productivity-based analyses argue that one reason for the mixed results is that researchers have been looking in the wrong place by putting emphasis on horizontal (within industry) effects rather than vertical (supply chain) effects (Javorcik, 2004). Rodriguez-Clare (1996) demonstrates this by providing a model that depicts how MNEs create linkages with domestic firms in host countries. The model assumes that MNEs produce more complex products than domestic firms do and all firms prefer a variety of inputs. The higher the communication costs between MNEs' headquarters and their subsidiaries, the stronger the linkages will be between those subsidiaries and domestic firms in host countries. Such linkages will also be stronger if MNEs use locally purchased intermediate goods more intensively. Driffield, Munday and Roberts

DOI: 10.1057/9781137367204.0016

(2002) argue that technology transfer is more likely through vertical linkages in order to improve an inward investors' supply base. In addition, the degree of local purchase of MNEs depends on their local market or export market orientation. Locally-oriented MNEs tend to purchase more locally than export-oriented MNEs do, but the latter will increasingly buy from local suppliers over time (Lim and Fong, 1982).

MNEs have incentives to transfer technology to local suppliers in order to reduce input costs and increase product quality. Rather than transferring knowledge to a single supplier, diffusing to multiple suppliers can create diverse supply sources of improved inputs at lower prices for MNEs (Blalock and Gertler, 2008). Such knowledge could take a variety of forms such as training employees, quality control, delivery and process technologies (Blalock and Simon, 2009). Lall (1980) identifies that local suppliers of MNEs can receive transferred knowledge such as technical assistance, training, management and operations. Suppliers may be forced to meet higher standards set by MNEs such as quality control and reliable delivery (Javorcik, Keller and Tybout, 2008). In addition, the demand for intermediate inputs from downstream sectors increases due to the entry of foreign firms. Local suppliers could reap the benefits of economies of scale and product prices will be lower. Local firms competing with MNEs in the same downstream industry can also benefit from lower input costs (Rodriguez-Clare, 1996).

Forward linkages

Technology transfer also takes place where, following the entry of MNEs, local firms have access to a variety of inputs with technical complexity (Markusen and Venables, 1999). In addition, better complementary services by MNEs could also be available so that the qualities of final products are improved (Javorcik, 2004). Forward linkages may also promote the adoption of new technologies and solve contract implementation problems (Gow and Swinnen, 1998). Manufacturers in less developed countries tend to lack the ability to achieve economies of scale and therefore lack the motivation to invest heavily in R&D. Purchasing more innovative inputs from MNEs is a way to make their products more advanced in technological terms (Javorcik, Keller and Tybout, 2008).

Labour mobility

Another channel of technology transfer takes place via labour mobility. MNEs generally have superior technologies to the domestic firms in host countries. They provide employees with more intensive training and work experience than indigenous firms do (Smeets, 2008; Sousa, 2001). Fosfuri, Motta and Ronde (2001) model how technologies can be transferred when workers who have been trained by MNEs are employed by local firms later. The model shows

DOI: 10.1057/9781137367204.0016

that technologies are expected to be transferred if the labour turnover rate is high and local firms are not in fierce competition with MNEs. Additionally such benefits will be larger if the training is general, because the local firms may not gain much if the knowledge is quite specific and the costs of MNEs' training are high. When workers are hired by indigenous firms or set up their own business after leaving MNEs, they take the knowledge with them and improve domestic firms' performance (Gorg and Strobl, 2005). Empirical evidence shows that the transferred knowledge and technologies could be confined to the local firms operating in the same industry as the MNEs (Gorg and Strobl, 2005).

Patent trends and patterns of FDI in China

In this section, we describe the trends of patents and FDI in China during the period of 2000–8, based on matched firm-level data from two sources. One is the Annual Report of Industrial Enterprise Statistics collected from the National Bureau of Statistics of China (NBS). The other is the State Intellectual Property Office of People's Republic of China (SIPO). We focus on domestic firms' patenting behaviour in our analyses. The firms in the matched data cover about 85 per cent of industrial output in China. We consider all manufacturing sectors in all the provinces in China. According to the definition from the SIPO, there are three types of patents granted in China, namely invention, utility model (UM) and external design with a descending level of novelty and practicality. We consider the first two types to capture the most innovative output.[1]

Figure 9.1 shows the annual statistics of capital share of foreign firms to total firms and granted patent counts to domestically owned firms during the period 2000–8. Although there is a slight drop of foreign capital share[2] in 2008, it has been increasing steadily reaching approximately 38 per cent of total capital investment by the end of 2007. The growth of both types of patents is dramatic, from less than 5000 to around 38,000. Utility model (UM) patent counts are larger than invention patent counts before 2005, but they grow simultaneously afterwards.

Figures 9.2 and 9.3 present the distributions of invention and UM patents by sectors over the years. The major trend is that both types of patents appear to increase faster after 2005 (especially in sectors such as food and beverages, textiles and clothing, wood and furniture, petroleum and plastic, metal and non-metal products, machinery and pharmaceutical).

---

[1] Definition of different types of patents can be found in Notes.
[2] Foreign capital share is measured by the share of foreign capital to total capital in a given year.

DOI: 10.1057/9781137367204.0016

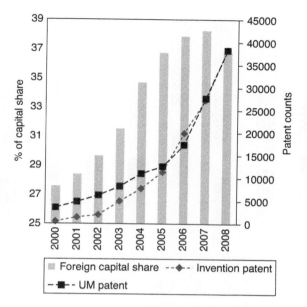

Figure 9.1   Foreign capital share and patent counts

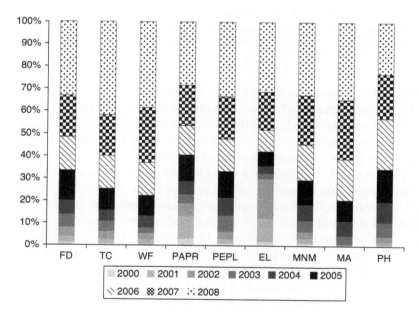

Figure 9.2   Granted invention patent counts by sector

Note: FD (food and beverages); TC (textiles and clothing); WF (wood and furniture); PAPR (paper and printing); PEPL (petroleum and plastic); EL (electronics); MNM (metal and non-metal); MA (machinery); PH (pharmaceutical).

DOI: 10.1057/9781137367204.0016

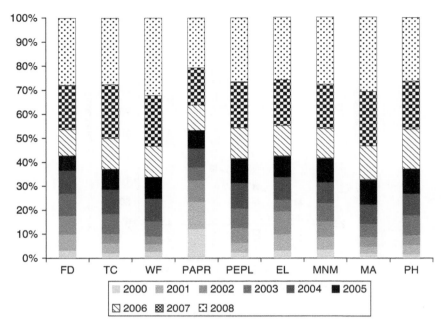

Figure 9.3   Granted UM patent counts by sector

Note: FD (food and beverages); TC (textiles and clothing); WF (wood and furniture); PAPR (paper and printing); PEPL (petroleum and plastic); EL (electronics); MNM (metal and non-metal); MA (machinery); PH (pharmaceutical).

Figure 9.4 shows the share of foreign capital across sectors. The electronics sector has the highest level of foreign capital share (above 45 per cent) while the metal and non-metal sector has the least (around 22 per cent). The machinery sector has experienced the highest growth of foreign capital from less than 25 per cent in 2000 to above 45 per cent in 2008.

Figures 9.5 and 9.6 display the distributions of invention and UM patents across regions. The general trend is that both types of patents grow steadily over the years. In the coastal region, invention patents grow faster than UM patents in the most recent years. Central and western regions are still at the early stage of innovation, compared with the coastal region. This could be due to the fact that the coastal region is the first to benefit from the trade opening and attracting FDI policies in China. However for central and western regions in China, UM patents expand more quickly than invention patents do and the UM patent counts exceed invention patent counts.

Interestingly Figure 9.7 illustrates a stable accumulation of foreign capital in the central and western regions, with the share of foreign capital being higher in the former region. This corresponds to the UM patents expansion in

DOI: 10.1057/9781137367204.0016

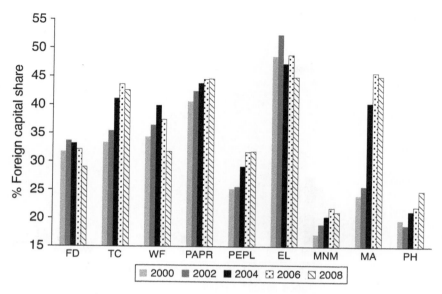

Figure 9.4 Foreign capital share by sector

Note: FD (food and beverages); TC (textiles and clothing); WF (wood and furniture); PAPR (paper and printing); PEPL (petroleum and plastic); EL (electronics); MNM (metal and non-metal); MA (machinery); PH (pharmaceutical).

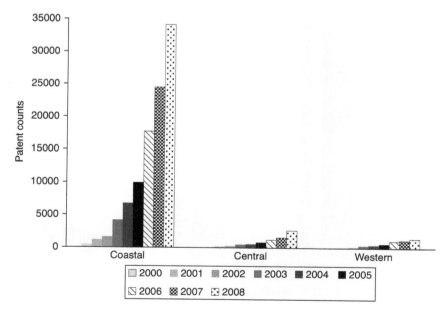

Figure 9.5 Invention patent counts by region

DOI: 10.1057/9781137367204.0016

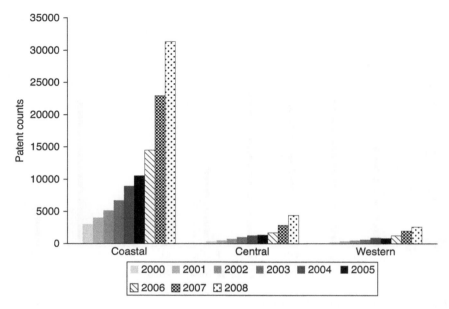

Figure 9.6   UM patent counts by region

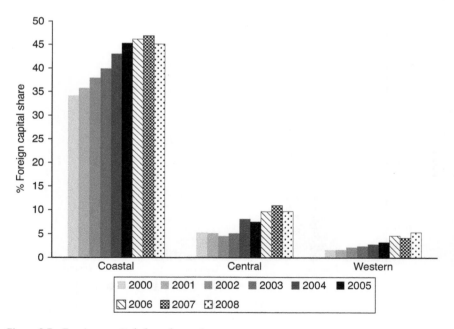

Figure 9.7   Foreign capital share by region

DOI: 10.1057/9781137367204.0016

these areas. In other words, the augmentation of foreign capital in central and western regions seems to contribute more to the growth of UM patents than to the growth of invention patents.

Figures 9.8 to 9.16 show the share of foreign capital and patent counts in different sectors during 2000–8. Figure 9.8 shows that the foreign capital share in the food and beverages sector constantly decreases but the magnitude is small. There is still around 29 per cent foreign capital share at the end of 2008. Invention patents grow faster after 2004 reaching around 900 in 2008. However UM patent counts are around one third of invention and grow slower than invention patents.

It can be seen from Figure 9.9 that foreign capital share in the textiles and clothing sector rises by around 10 per cent over the period. This trend is consistent with the expansion of both types of patents. For example, the growth of foreign capital share nearly stops from 2004 to 2005, and UM patents have dropped during this time. When the foreign capital share picks up in 2006, UM patents subsequently start increasing again.

Figure 9.10 illustrates that the foreign capital share in the wood and furniture sector increases by around 5 per cent during 2000–4, then drops to less than 32 per cent in 2008. However the grant invention and UM patents keep growing reaching 200 and 700 at the end of 2008, respectively. The number of UM patents increases faster after 2006 and it is about three times the number of invention patents in 2008.

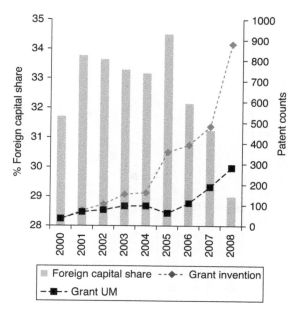

Figure 9.8 Food and beverages

DOI: 10.1057/9781137367204.0016

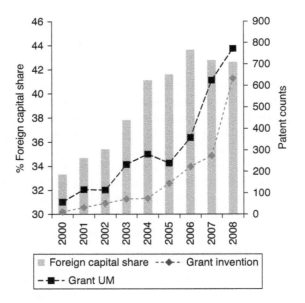

Figure 9.9   Textiles and clothing

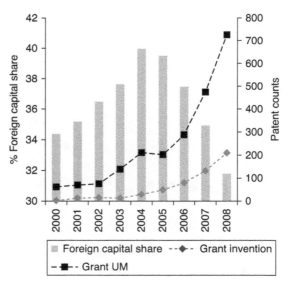

Figure 9.10   Wood and furniture

DOI: 10.1057/9781137367204.0016

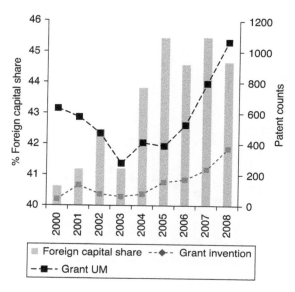

Figure 9.11   Paper and printing

Figure 9.11 illustrates that the share of foreign capital increases about 5 per cent during 2000 and 2008 in the paper and printing sector. The fall of UM patents from 2002 to 2003 seems to be correlated with fall of foreign capital share during this period. After the rise of foreign capital share in 2004, the invention and UM patent counts also increase.

Figure 9.12 clearly indicates that the growth of patents is correlated with the accumulation of foreign capital share in the petroleum and plastic sector. As the percentage of foreign capital increases, the invention and UM patent counts expand from less than 500 to around 4200 and 2000 at the end of 2008, respectively. The growth rates of patents and foreign capital share are slower before 2003, and become faster afterwards.

Figure 9.13 shows a similar correlation in the electronics sector as that in the petroleum and plastic sector. Foreign capital share increases steadily before 2002, but decreases by about 5 per cent in 2003. It then grows slowly afterwards until 2006. As for both types of patents, they accumulate quickly from 2000 to 2002, but drop in 2003 as the foreign capital share decreases, bouncing back in 2004.

Figure 9.14 demonstrates that in the metal and non-metal sector, foreign capital share has increased by around 8 per cent during 2000–8. This is accompanied by a steady expansion of both types of patents. At the beginning of 2000, there were about 100 and 500 invention and UM patents. At the end of 2008, the numbers reached approximately 2500 and 4300, respectively.

DOI: 10.1057/9781137367204.0016

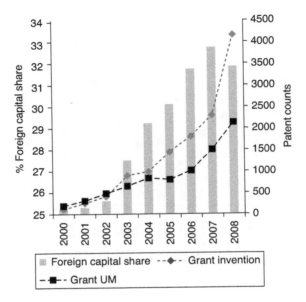

Figure 9.12   Petroleum and plastic

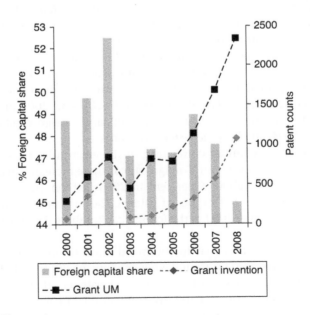

Figure 9.13   Electronics

DOI: 10.1057/9781137367204.0016

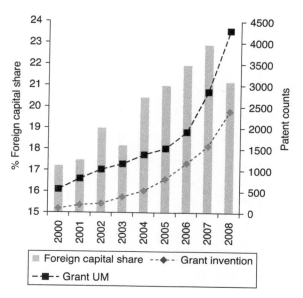

Figure 9.14   Metal and non-metal

Figure 9.15 shows that the machinery sector has experienced the largest growth of foreign capital share (by around 25 per cent). The growth is slow before 2003, and expands quickly afterwards reaching 45 per cent in 2008. Meanwhile the growth of patents is slow before 2003, becoming faster during 2003 and 2005 and then expanding at an even higher rate thereafter. The growth of both types of patents is in line with the growth of foreign capital share. They increase more slowly before 2005 and faster from 2006 to 2008.

Figure 9.16 illustrates that the number of invention patents is much higher than that of UM patents in the pharmaceutical sector. While invention patent counts increase dramatically during the sample period, the UM patent counts stay almost the same. This could be due to the fact that in pharmaceutical sectors innovations are likely to be more novel and innovative than in other sectors. Again the trend of foreign capital share is increasing together with patent counts. Note that in 2006 we see a small drop in foreign capital share, with invention patent counts experiencing a big drop in 2007.

Based on the graphs in Figures 9.8 to 9.16, we find that the FDI in China has increased steadily over 2000 to 2007, although the figure dropped slightly in 2008 due to the worldwide economic crisis. Domestically-owned patent counts have also grown dramatically, from less than 5000 in year 2000 to around 40,000 by the end of 2008. The growth of patents seems to be accompanied by the accumulation of foreign capital in the majority of manufacturing sectors.

DOI: 10.1057/9781137367204.0016

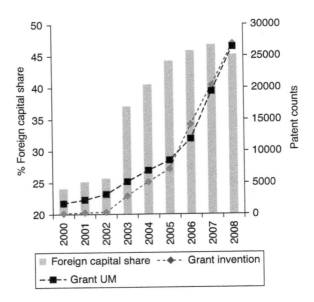

Figure 9.15   Machinery

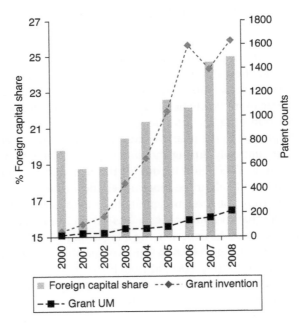

Figure 9.16   Pharmaceutical

DOI: 10.1057/9781137367204.0016

Our sector analysis shows that this association is heterogeneous among different sectors. The positive correlation between FDI and patents owned by domestic firms appears to be more pronounced in technology intensive sectors (such as pharmaceutical) than labour intensive sectors (such as food and beverages). This may indicate that domestic firms in technology intensive sectors are keen to seek and adopt new technologies from FDI and they are more likely to transfer new knowledge into innovation output such as patents.

Conclusions

This chapter investigates the technology transfer of inward FDI to domestic firms. We use the direct evidence of technological benefits of FDI to study how domestic firms can learn from FDI to produce patents. We first review the main channels of technology transfer, followed by statistical analyses of the trend of FDI penetration and domestic firms' patent production in China during 2000–8. We find that in general patent production of indigenous firms accompanies the changes of FDI in different sectors. Such correlation is more apparent in technology-intensive sectors than labour-intensive sectors. We therefore hypothesize that FDI is an important driver of technology transfer and innovation production of domestic firms.

Patent production is an important indicator of receiving technology transfer from inward FDI. Conceptually the channels through which domestic firms can learn from foreign firms include imitation, competition, labour turnover and learning via vertical linkages with foreign firms. Current empirical studies on how FDI affects innovation performance in domestically-owned sectors in host countries generally stress the technology transfer within sectors. However given that the traditional FDI literature shows the knowledge flows through vertical linkages with MNEs are crucial for technology transfer, it is important to study how indigenous firms can receive technological benefits from communications with foreign customers and suppliers in future studies.

Note

There are three types of patents in China: invention, utility model (UM) and external design. An invention patent is a technical scheme for products or methods which have high novelty, creativity and practicality. A UM patent is defined as a new technical proposal regarding a product's shape and/or structure in order to improve its practicality. External design patents are not included in this study as they are of minor innovativeness and technical complexity. It is the design in shape, pattern, colour or the combination of them in a product (Eberhardt, Helmers and Yu, 2012). We employ invention and

DOI: 10.1057/9781137367204.0016

UM patents as the indicator of firms' innovativeness because external design patents are the least technological sophisticated type of patents.

References

Aghion, P., Bloom, N., Blundell, R., Griffith, R. and Howitt, P. (2005) Competition and innovation: an inverted-u relationship. *The Quarterly Journal of Economics*, 120(2): 701–28.

Aghion, P. and Howitt, P. (1992) A model of growth through creative destruction. *Econometrica*, 60(2): 323–51.

Aitken, B.J. and Harrison, A.E. (1999) Do domestic firms benefit from direct foreign investment? Evidence from Venezuela. *The American Economic Review*, 89(3): 605–18.

Arrow, K.J. (1962) Economic welfare and the allocation of resources for invention, in R.R. Nelson (ed.) *The Rate and Direction of Inventive Activity*. Princeton, NJ: Princeton University Press.

Barrios, S. and Strobl, E. (2002) Foreign direct investment and productivity spillovers: evidence from the Spanish experience. *Weltwirtschaftliches Archiv*, 138(3): 459–81.

Blalock, G. and Gertler, P.J. (2008) Welfare gains from foreign direct investment through technology transfer to local suppliers. *Journal of International Economics*, 74(2): 402–21.

Blalock, G. and Simon, D.H. (2009) Do all firms benefit equally from downstream FDI? The moderating effect of local suppliers' capabilities on productivity gains. *Journal of International Business Studies*, 40(7): 1095–112.

Blomström, M., Globerman, S. and Kokko, A. (1999) The determinants of host country spillovers from foreign direct investment: a review and synthesis of the literature. Working paper no. 76, September, The European Institute of Japanese Studies.

Blomström, M. and Kokko, A. (1998) Multinational corporations and spillovers. *Journal of Economic Surveys*, 12(2): 1–31.

Caves, R.E. (1974) Multinational Firms, competition, and productivity in host-country markets. *Economica*, New Series, 41(162): 176–93.

De Backer, K. and Sleuwaegen, L. (2003) Does foreign direct investment crowd out domestic entrepreneurship? *Review of Industrial Organization*, 22(1): 67–84.

Driffield, N. and Love, J.H. (2007) Linking FDI motivation and host economy productivity effects: conceptual and empirical analysis. *Journal of International Business Studies*, 38(7): 460–73.

Driffield, N., Munday, M. and Roberts, A. (2002) Foreign direct investment, transactions linkages, and the performance of the domestic sector. *International Journal of the Economics of Business*, 9(3): 335–51.

Driffield, N. and Taylor, K. (2005) Are foreign firms more technologically intensive? UK establishment evidence from the ARD. *Scottish Journal of Political Economy*, 52(1): 38–53.

Dunning, J.H. (1979) Explaining changing patterns of international production: in defence of the eclectic theory. *Oxford Bulletin of Economics and Statistics*, 41(1): 269–95.

Eberhardt, M., Helmers, C. and Yu, Z. (2012) Is the dragon learning to fly? The Chinese patent explosion at home and abroad. Available at: http://www.chelmers.com/projects/dragon.pdf [accessed 1/5/2013].

DOI: 10.1057/9781137367204.0016

Ernst, H. (2001) Patent applications and subsequent changes of performance: evidence from time-series cross-section analyses on the firm level. *Research Policy*, 30(1): 143–57.

Figueiredo, P.N., Cohen, M. and Gomes, S. (2013) Firms' innovation capability-building paths and the nature of changes in learning mechanisms: multiple case-study evidence from an emerging economy. No. 007 United Nations University, Maastricht Economic and Social Research and Training Centre on Innovation and Technology.

Filatotchev, I., Liu, X., Lu, J. and Wright, M. (2011) Knowledge spillovers through human mobility across national borders: evidence from Zhongguancun Science Park in China. *Research Policy*, 40(3): 453–62.

Fosfuri, A., Motta, M. and Ronde, T. (2001) Foreign direct investment and spillovers through workers' mobility. *Journal of International Economics*, 53(1): 205–22.

Garcia, F., Jin, B. and Salomon, R. (2013) Does inward foreign direct investment improve the innovative performance of local firms? *Research Policy*, 42(1): 231–44.

Gorg, H. and Greenaway, D. (2004) Much ado about nothing? Do domestic firms really benefit from foreign direct investment? *The World Bank Research Observer*, 19(2): 171–97.

Gorg, H. and Strobl, E. (2005) Spillovers from foreign firms through worker mobility: an empirical investigation. *The Scandinavian Journal of Economics*, 107(4): 693–709.

Gow, H.R. and Swinnen, J.F.M. (1998) Up- and downstream restructuring, foreign direct investment, and hold-up problems in agricultural transition. *European Review of Agricultural Economics*, 25(3): 331–50.

Grossman, G.M. and Helpman, E. (1991) Trade, knowledge spillovers, and growth. *European Economic Review*, 35(2–3): 517–26.

Grossman, G.M. and Helpman, E. (1994) Endogenous innovation in the theory of growth. *The Journal of Economic Perspectives*, 8(1): 23–44.

Hallin, C. and Lind, C.H. (2012) Revisiting the external impact of MNCs: an empirical study of the mechanisms behind knowledge spillovers from MNC subsidiaries. *International Business Review*, 21(2): 167–79.

Hanson, G.H. (2001) Should countries promote foreign direct investment? G-24 Discussion Paper Series, United Nations Conference on Trade and Development.

Havranek, T. and Irsova, Z. (2011) Estimating vertical spillovers from FDI: why results vary and what the true effect is. *Journal of International Economics*, 85(2): 234–44.

Hu, A.G. and Jefferson, G.H. (2009) A great wall of patents: what is behind China's recent patent explosion? *Journal of Development Economics*, 90(1): 57–68.

Irsova, Z. and Havranek, T. (2013) Determinants of horizontal spillovers from FDI: evidence from a large meta-analysis. *World Development*, 42: 1–15.

Javorcik, B.S. (2004) Does foreign direct investment increase the productivity of domestic firms? In search of spillovers through backward linkages. *The American Economic Review*, 94(3): 605–27.

Javorcik, B., Keller, W. and Tybout, J. (2008) Openness and industrial response in a Wal-Mart world: a case study of Mexican soaps, detergents and surfactant producers. *The World Economy*, 31(12): 1558–80.

Jenkins, R. (1990) Comparing foreign subsidiaries and local firms in LDCs: theoretical issues and empirical evidence. *The Journal of Development Studies*, 26: 205–28.

Konings, J. (2001) The effects of foreign direct investment on domestic firms evidence from firm-level panel data in emerging economies. *Economics of Transaction*, 9(3): 619–33.

Lall, S. (1980) Vertical inter-firm linkages in LDCs: an empirical study. *Oxford Bulletin of Economics and Statistics*, 42(3): 203–26.

DOI: 10.1057/9781137367204.0016

Levin, R.C., Cohen, W.M. and Mowery, D.C. (1985) R&D appropriability, opportunity, and market structure: new evidence on some Schumpeterian hypotheses. *The American Economic Review*, 75(2): 20–4.

Li, J., Chen, D. and Shapiro, D.M. (2010) Product innovations in emerging economies: the role of foreign knowledge access channels and internal efforts in Chinese firms. *Management and Organization Review*, 6(2): 243–66.

Li, X. (2011) Sources of external technology, absorptive capacity, and innovation capability in Chinese state-owned high-tech enterprises. *World Development*, 39(7): 1240–8.

Lim, L.Y.C. and Fong, P.E. (1982) Vertical linkages and multinational enterprises in developing countries. *World Development*, 10(7): 585–95.

Liu, X., Lu, J., Filatotchev, I., Buck, T. and Wright, M. (2010) Returnee entrepreneurs, knowledge spillovers and innovation in high-tech firms in emerging economies. *Journal of International Business Studies*, 41(7): 1183–97.

Liu, X. and Zou, H. (2008) The impact of greenfield FDI and mergers and acquisitions on innovation in Chinese high-tech industries. *Journal of World Business*, 43(3): 352–64.

Love, J.H., Roper, S. and Bryson, J.R. (2011) Openness, knowledge, innovation and growth in UK business services. *Research Policy*, 40(10): 1438–52.

Markusen, J.R. and Venables, A.J. (1999) Foreign direct investment as a catalyst for industrial development. *European Economic Review*, 43(2): 335–56.

Marvel, M.R. and Lumpkin, G.T. (2007) Technology entrepreneurs human capital and its effects on innovation radicalness. *Entrepreneurship Theory and Practice*, 31(6): 807–28.

Page, J.M. (1980) Technical efficiency and economic performance: some evidence from Ghana. *Oxford Economic Papers*, New Series, 32(2): 319–39.

Rodriguez-Clare, A. (1996) Multinationals, linkages, and economic development. *The American Economic Review*, 86(4): 852–73.

Roper, S., Du, J. and Love, J.H. (2008) Modelling the innovation value chain. *Research Policy*, 37(6–7): 961–977.

Saggi, K. (2002) Trade, foreign direct investment, and international technology transfer: a survey. *The World Bank Research Observer*, 17(2): 191–235.

Schumpeter, J.A. (1943) Capitalism in the postwar world, in S.E. Harris (ed.) *Postwar Economic Problems*. New York: McGraw-Hill.

Shaw, B. (1994) User–supplier links and innovation, in M. Dodgson and R. Rothwell (eds) *The Handbook of Industrial Innovation*. Cheltenham: Edward Elgar.

Smeets, R. (2008) Collecting the pieces of the FDI knowledge spillovers puzzle. *The World Bank Research Observer*, 23(2): 107–38.

Sousa, N. (2001) Multinationals and technology transfer through labour training. Paper presented at CEPR Workshop on Labour Market Effects of European Foreign Investments, Dublin, July.

Spencer, J.W. (2008) The impact of multinational enterprise strategy on indigenous enterprises: horizontal spillovers and crowding out in developing countries. *Academy of Management Review*, 33(2): 341–61.

Temouri, Y., Driffield, Y.L. and Higon, D.A. (2008) Analysis of productivity differences among foreign and domestic firms: evidence from Germany. *Review of World Economics*, 144(1): 32–54.

Tishler, A. and Milstein, I. (2009) R&D wars and the effects of innovation on the success and survivability of firms in oligopoly markets. *International Journal of Industrial Organization*, 27(4): 519–31.

DOI: 10.1057/9781137367204.0016

Wang, C. and Kafouros, M.I. (2009) What factors determine innovation performance in emerging economies? Evidence from China. *International Business Review*, 18(6): 606–16.

Yueh, L. (2009) Patent laws and innovation in China. *International Review of Law and Economics*, 29(4): 304–13.

DOI: 10.1057/9781137367204.0016

10
Knowledge Sources of Persistent Exporters: Effects on the Growth and Productivity of Firms

Hans Lööf, Pardis Nabavi, Gary Cook and Börje Joansson

Introduction

The idea that firm-specific advantages might be developed in strong clusters has been a mainstay of Michael Porter's work and that such advantages developed in home markets can be leveraged into overseas markets has a long tradition in theories of the MNE (Dunning, 2001). It is well recognized in the literature that higher rates of innovation are associated with geographic clusters and there is a decay with distance which affects the extent of knowledge spillovers potentially available (Audretsch and Feldman, 1996; Jaffe et al., 1993). It has long been recognized that MNE activity, and more generally the ability to succeed in overseas markets, is particularly associated with firms in knowledge-intensive and research and development (R&D)-intensive activities (Buckley and Casson, 1976). The resource-based view has become influential in international business as an explanation for why some firms are more successful in internationalization than others, with innovation again being a prime example (e.g. Oviatt and MacDougall, 1994). All firms may, in principle, draw on three sources of input to their innovation process: any specific advantages of their location; their own internal R&D effort and capabilities; and benefits based on external linkages, which may range from local to global. This chapter examines the linkages between access to different types of knowledge input and success in exporting and the influence of exporting, innovation and access to knowledge on firm performance. The chapter contributes to the literature in two key respects. It brings together exporting, innovation and access to knowledge as sources of firm performance in a way seldom seen. It also takes a more sophisticated look at accessibility to knowledge, combining the central ideas that access diminishes with distance, but that the ability to benefit from knowledge spillovers varies with firm-specific absorptive capacity,

DOI: 10.1057/9781137367204.0017

which is influenced by its own innovation effort. In so doing, it poses a challenge to received wisdom regarding cluster promotion policies, which tends to assume, naively, that knowledge spillovers are equally available to all firms in a cluster and that only local linkages matter.

Innovation and exporting

A growing empirical literature using firm- or plant-level data documents that exporters are found to be more productive than other firms due to factors such as the direct effect of exporting on future productivity, self-selection of the more productive firms into the export market, and possibly also due to a simultaneity bias in the regressions (see, for instance, Aw, Roberts and Xu, 2011; Bernhard and Wagner, 1997; Greenaway, Gullstrand and Kneller, 2005). Because R&D and innovation are closely related to productivity, firms' patenting activity or R&D engagement might be a major self-selection mechanism, increasing the likelihood of more productive firms entering export markets. There may also be a positive feedback loop in as much as exporting may be a means of accessing innovation inputs overseas. Branstetter (2001) found that, whilst knowledge can be transmitted internationally through trade, knowledge spillovers were predominantly *intranational*. MacGarvie (2006) likewise suggests that trade flows may be a way in which knowledge diffuses internationally, although the empirical literature on this subject is ambiguous. As she points out, one reason for this is that, whilst exporters do learn about technological development overseas by monitoring their overseas competitors and through interactions with buyers, such learning is not well captured in the measure of knowledge flows that is typically used: patent citations. This partly explains Branstetter's result.

In order to address the issues given here, the subsequent analysis divides all firms into persistent exporters and other firms. In turn, exporters are divided into innovators (innovation active) and non-innovators (innovation inactive). This distinction is used as a way to capture the idea that innovation-active firms will learn through making innovation efforts and thereby accumulate internal knowledge. At the same time the analysis recognizes that R&D and other renewal activities can benefit from a firm's access to external knowledge. Thus we may ask: do innovation-active firms benefit more than other firms from being located in a knowledge-rich environment? In other words, to what extent is internal knowledge a pre-requisite for a firm's capacity to absorb and utilize external knowledge.

Observing that the focus group consists of persistent exporters, we recall that for such firms innovation may be aimed towards introducing new product varieties, which could be directed to either existing or new markets. In the case of process R&D, innovation may enable firms to compete more effectively and/ or to raise profitability. However a substantial fraction of the exporting firms

DOI: 10.1057/9781137367204.0017

are not engaging in innovation at all, or they are only occasional innovators (Harris and Moffat, 2011). It has been suggested that these firms may access strategic knowledge from external sources (Baum, Caglayan and Talverna, 2009). Almeda and Phene (2012), Andersson et al. (2012), Cantwell and Zhang (2012) and Wolff (2012) argue that non-innovative firms can receive strategic knowledge from the local milieu where they are located or through their company group, while Blind and Jungmittag (2004) claim that exporting allows non-innovative firms to improve their innovative capabilities, among other things.

In this chapter, we mainly consider how the combination of internal and external knowledge can improve the firm's export performance, and how these factors affect the productivity of exporters. In order to do that, we classify exporters into six broad categories of firm depending on their innovation activities and location, where the latter is characterized in terms of its knowledge accessibility. In addition, we also investigate whether there is any learning impact from exporting among non-innovators.

Innovation and learning

In their seminal paper on innovation and learning, Cohen and Levinthal (1989) suggest a dual role of firms' R&D investments. The most obvious output is new knowledge, for example, a product innovation, and the other is accumulation of more general knowledge within each innovating firm. The latter output is generated in a learning process, which augments a firm's capacity to make additional innovations. Following Cohen and Levinthal (1989), this chapter assumes that firms with recurrent innovation activities get a larger stock of knowledge, which improves their capacity to combine internal and external knowledge. This learning aspect includes insights with regard to procedures for how to organize innovation efforts and how to access relevant external knowledge.

Being innovation active has thus two consequences. First, R&D activities and other innovation efforts bring about new product varieties, contacts with new customer groups and markets and new firm routines. Second, it increases the firm's capability to access external knowledge and to combine it with the firm's own competence (Almeida and Phene, 2012).

We use two alternative ways of identifying if a firm is innovation active or not. The first makes use of patent data, and the second collects information on firms' recorded R&D efforts. In both cases the ambition is to find out how persistent a firm's R&D activities are. In the first case we count the patent applications during a time interval and observe that such a measure can be obtained for all firms for a long time. The disadvantage of this approach is that most innovation-related activities do not result in any patent applications. The second approach uses the Community Innovation Surveys (CISs), which survey firms from EU member states on a regular and harmonized basis.

DOI: 10.1057/9781137367204.0017

The attractiveness of the CISs data is that they include information about the sustainability of both intra-mural and extra-mural R&D such as purchase of machinery, equipment and consultancy services.

External knowledge sources

Many studies have examined how aggregate knowledge sources and R&D activities inside an urban region generate spillovers, which can affect innovation activities and innovation outcomes of firms located in the region. Other studies have focused on technology spillovers. Recent economic research estimates the importance of various sources of knowledge spillovers to be of about the same size as the return from the firms' own investments (Keller, 2009; Wolff, 2012). These studies emphasize the importance of spillovers from external knowledge sources.

However 'knowledge spillovers' is somewhat misleading terminology, since an important share of knowledge flows through the economy in the form of purchased knowledge, often embodied in equipment and systems or specialized consultancy services. The analysis may be more accurate if one considers the two main components of knowledge flows: (a) spillover corresponding to transfer that occurs without intention, and sometimes contrary to what players want, and (b) intentional flows that are based on market transactions (Lööf, Nabavi and Johansson, 2012).

In this chapter we describe the knowledge milieu as a potential source by calculating for each firm its accessibility with regard to the supply of knowledge-intensive producer services. This access to external knowledge is subject to decay with distance. It is also viewed as being a potential source of knowledge, on which firms may capitalize to differing degrees. This measure captures both intentional knowledge transactions and pure knowledge externalities. Both knowledge-intensive services and other producer services represent a growing share of all jobs in the economy. This growth is stimulated by outsourcing processes in which companies externalize both standard routine services and specialized knowledge services. Producer services include agency and wholesale distribution, repair and maintenance services, transportation and consulting services, but also a large number of other market-related services. Producer service sectors with a high share of university educated employees are classified as knowledge intensive and some of these undertake scientific research or provide services that directly support scientific research.

Producer services can affect the performance of other firms in two ways. First, a higher proportion of producer services may facilitate the development of a more efficient resource allocation, which is then reflected in higher productivity of the firms concerned. Second, the interaction with knowledge-intensive services improves the firm's capacity to develop new technology and introduce new products and processes. In addition, the pertinent knowledge

DOI: 10.1057/9781137367204.0017

providers have an incentive to serve as many customers as possible and hence stimulate knowledge diffusion. There is an important role played by various 'go-betweens', which would be classified as producer services, in networks. Venture capitalists, consultants and legal advisers may all play an important role in linking up firms with complementary resources, including knowledge (Whittington et al., 2009). The important role played by such go-betweens, who can solve important information asymmetries, particularly for SMEs, by putting them in contact with both reliable and capable partners, has been seriously neglected in the clusters literature (Kirkels and Duysters, 2010). Go-betweens can also act as valuable 'honest-brokers' who will hold the proprietary knowledge of potential partners secret until a suitable match has been made, reducing the risk of opportunistic exploitation by either side (Lee et al., 2010; Tether, 2002).

The structure of the chapter is as follows. The second section introduces a composite variable, which describes six different combinations of internal and external knowledge, labelled the conjunction variable. The section explores the theoretical basis for assumptions about how the conjunction variable influences exporting firms' economic performance with regard to product innovation and export as well as growth in value added, labour productivity and employment. The section also presents the data sources.

We then present empirical results in the form of regressions showing the association of a firm's conjunction variable and economic-performance indicators before reflecting on our findings in the chapter and concluding.

Theoretical basis and data

Conjunction of internal and external knowledge

A standard representation is that a firm generates innovations in a process of R&D and other innovation activities which bring about new knowledge, while at the same time using inputs from the conjunction of internal and external knowledge sources. The combination of internal and external knowledge is cumulated into knowledge embedded in firm routines regarding product variety attributes, markets and customers' willingness to pay for product attributes. In addition, some knowledge will be relevant to routines for how to organize and perform innovation activities.

A major hypothesis in the subsequent analysis is that a firm's knowledge cumulates as a consequence of continuing innovation efforts in distinction to occasional efforts. Thus firms displaying persistent innovation engagement are expected to outperform other firms in several performance dimensions. In addition, innovation and adoption activities are interlinked processes, both requiring absorption capacity and internal knowledge that can be combined with external knowledge sources.

DOI: 10.1057/9781137367204.0017

Table 10.1 presents a view of knowledge sources that are relevant for an innovating firm. The right hand column points at mechanisms that firms engaged in R&D must be able to manage, and this in turn explains why recurrent R&D effort is a route via which firms obtain innovation skills. Indirectly these mechanisms also have location implications. In particular, knowledge flows reduce in volume and intensity as the distance between origin and destination grows. This form of spatial discounting implies that localized knowledge is a fundamental characteristic of an innovation-active firm's environment.

This chapter suggests that the right hand column of Table 10.1 presents knowledge creation, transfer and exchange activities that are carried out, supported and facilitated by the local supply of knowledge-intensive producer services. Thus we construct a measure that proxies the knowledge-flow potential available to firms in a given location. Our measure captures the widely accepted view that there is typically decay with distance for innovation-related knowledge. To do this, Sweden is divided into 290 local economies, referred to as locations. The car-travel time distance between location i and j is denoted by t_{ij}. For a

Table 10.1 Sources, accession and generation of knowledge inputs to innovation activities

Origin or source of knowledge flows	Mechanisms of knowledge generation and accession
Knowledge interaction	Collaboration with customers, suppliers, universities and other knowledge providers
Purchase of knowledge (e.g. from knowledge-intensive producer services suppliers)	Knowledge transactions may require links of trust between buyer and seller
Spillovers from normal transactions between a firm and its customers and suppliers	The firm's interplay with customers, suppliers and other actors open up for unintended knowledge flows
Job mobility bringing the firm new labour embodying knowledge achieved in previous job(s)	Recruitment inflow to a firm may be the basic source for unintended spillovers. Such flows decline with increasing distance
Scanning and searching for knowledge accession opportunities	Renewal in the form of innovation and adoption is fuelled by the conjunction of internal and external knowledge
Internal knowledge flows between units of a company group, especially multinationals	The internal networks of a multinational company group can overcome long distance and protect knowledge from leakage
Investment in R&D collaboration networks locally and globally	These networks include strategic alliances as well local links based on trust

DOI: 10.1057/9781137367204.0017

firm located in i, the discounted access to the supply of knowledge-intensive producer services in location j, G_j, is given by $\exp\{-\lambda t_{ij}\}G_j$ (Weibull, 1976; Fujita and Thisse, 2002). The total knowledge accessibility, A_i, of the same firm then becomes $A_i = \sum_j \exp\{\lambda t_{ij}\} G_j$, where we observe that t_{ii} signifies the average time distance between places inside location i.

Firms can be divided into three groups, where LAC refers to a low-, MAC to a medium- and HAC to a high-accessibility value (A-value). If our earlier assumption about the role of knowledge accessibility is correct, we should expect innovation-active firms to benefit more from a high A-value than other firms. In order to empirically test this we make use of the conjunction variable C_k, which sorts firms in the following way:

$$C_1 = (LAC, NI), \quad C_2 = (MAC, NI), \quad C_3 = (HAC, NI)$$
$$C_4 = (LAC, I), \quad C_5 = (MAC, I), \quad C_6 = (HAC, I)$$

where NI denotes that a firm is not innovation active (non-innovator) and I denotes that a firm is innovation active (innovator). Observe also that the classification of firms into the I-category and NI-category is made in two alternative ways, one based on patenting activities, and the other based on R&D engagement.

A spectrum of firm performance indicators

In a sense the conjunction category C_6 represents the highest knowledge stock a firm can access both using internal and external resources, whereas category C_1 represents the lowest stock, and we should expect C_6 to positively affect firm performance more than C_1. But the construction has also the capacity to reveal if it is possible that high knowledge accessibility can sufficiently compensate for a lack of internal R&D activity for innovation-inactive firms as represented by C_3. By the same token, it is important to consider if a poor environment with small knowledge accessibility (LAC) can be compensated by internal knowledge (I) as represented by C_4.

Our analysis is focused on a subset of all firms, namely those that are persistent exporters during the entire period 1997–2008. For this group, we first examine the size of exports, exports per employee and exports as a proportion of total sales for each of the six C-categories. This comparison of the six categories of firms is made for all export products and for the sub-group of new export products. In the econometric models we analyse each firm's export performance over three different dimensions: (a) export value per employee, (b) number of export products and (c) number of destination countries. Explanatory factors in the regressions are ordinary firm characteristics and the conjunction variable classifies firms as six groups. Again, observe that the

DOI: 10.1057/9781137367204.0017

separation of innovators and non-innovators is done in two different, alternative ways, patents measuring outputs and internal R&D activity measuring inputs, albeit that both measures have well-known limitations. Moreover we argue that the number of export products reflects product innovation, while the number of destination countries of a firm reflects 'market innovation'. What is more, superior products and processes may help firms overcome the 'liability of foreignness' in overseas markets (Zaheer, 1995).

In another group of regression equations, the study examines how the conjunction phenomenon influences growth properties of firms. Three growth processes are considered. The first is growth in value added, the second is growth in labour productivity and the third is growth in employment. Employing firm characteristics as control variables, the models explore how the conjunction of internal and external knowledge influences a firm's growth performance.

Data and methods

The basic data used in this research are provided by Statistics Sweden and cover all registered firms in Sweden, both in manufacturing and service sectors, over the period 1997–2008. The database contains information on a rich set of firm and employment statistics including physical capital, sales, value added, corporate ownership, geographical location of the firm and human capital measured as employees with at least three years of university education. In order to calculate exports per employee and labour productivity, we have restricted the data to firms with at least one employee. The monetary terms in the data are deflated by the Swedish Consumer Price Index.

We then match the basic data with the European Patent Office worldwide patent statistical database (PATSTAT) in order to add patent applications of firms. As a second innovation measure, this study considers observations from three consecutive CISs for years 2004, 2006 and 2008. In order to be classified as innovative in this survey, a firm must have been engaged in some kind of internal or insourced R&D during at least two surveys.

Our basic data set includes all the 3993 Swedish manufacturing firms that exported every year between 1997 and 2008. The data shows that 78 per cent of the persistent exporters did not apply for a single national or international patent during the 12 year period we consider. The second data set is restricted to firms that were included in at least two CISs between 2004 and 2008 and therefore had the possibility of reporting innovation activity in two different periods. This set includes 1611 unique firms that were persistent exporters, and one third belongs to the non-innovative group, as although they were surveyed they did not record sufficient R&D activity.

The initial analysis starts from a sample consisting of 400,000 observations from all Swedish manufacturing firms with at least one employee and around 70,000 patent applications. Applying a selection model, we then investigate

DOI: 10.1057/9781137367204.0017

influences on exports per employee for persistently exporting firms. The key interest is on the conjunction variable, which classifies firms with regard to three types of locations and two types of innovation engagement. The locations are local economies with low, medium and high accessibility to knowledge-intensive producer services, and we distinguish between firms with at least one patent application in 1997–2008 and other firms. Since the firms in the CIS-survey consist of a selected sample in itself, we start from about 40,000 observations of CIS-firms.

In the second part of the analysis, we apply Poisson and negative binomial models for estimating the correlations between number of products and number of export destinations for non-innovative and innovative firms in different local milieus. The next step consists of a random effects regression on the growth rate of value added, productivity and employment.

Empirical results

We estimate three different categories of models for two different samples, where the basic issue is the interaction between the local milieu and long-run innovation activity and, ultimately, firm performance variously measured. The controls are key firm characteristics such as human capital, physical capital, size, ownership and industry classification at the four-digit level.

Export value and intensity across categories of firms

Tables 10.2 to 10.5, which provide summary statistics on firm characteristics and exports for innovative and non-innovative persistent exporters, are our first set of evidence on the two faces of persistent exporters. The vast majority of exporters are not engaged in patent activities, and one third of the firms that recurrently export can be classified as non-innovative firms according to our definitions. Regarding patent activities, we require that the firms should have applied for at least one patent during the 12 years we observe, in order to be classified as innovative. The corresponding requirement for R&D is that the firm must have self-reported themselves as being engaged in R&D occasionally or persistently in at least two of the three CIS-surveys for 2004, 2006 and 2008. Interestingly, the tables indicate no disadvantage of being located in low-accessibility areas among non-innovative firms. In contrast, innovative firms seem to benefit from being located in places with high access to external knowledge.

Tables 10.4 and 10.5 present information about export intensity, measured as export value per employee. For this measure, there is a clear difference between innovators and non-innovators, whereas the influence from external knowledge is obvious primarily for innovators. Using both approaches to identify innovators, the category $C_6 = (HAC, I)$ has a much higher export value per employee than all other categories.

DOI: 10.1057/9781137367204.0017

Table 10.2 Descriptive statistics manufacturing firms exporting all years 1997–2008. Innovative activity based on patent applications and location classified by accessibility to knowledge producer services

	All products					Only new products				
	Share of firms	Share of exports	Emp. mean	Std. dev.	Emp median	Share of firms	Share of exports	Emp. mean	Std. dev.	Emp median
Innovative										
HAC	7.6 %	49.9%	434	1,673	51	12.4%	54%	943	2,470	128
MAC	8.2 %	21.2%	246	715	56	11.7%	16%	427	1,074	82
LAC	6.1 %	6.1%	147	236	66	8.3%	6%	220	306	98
Total	**22%**	**77%**	**284**	**1,091**	**58**	**32%**	**76%**	**571**	**1,844**	**101**
Non-innovative										
HAC	24.8 %	4.3%	60	221	13	22.4%	4%	97	322	23
MAC	27.1 %	7.4%	54	117	17	23%	11%	77	147	33
LAC	26.9 %	8.9%	53	108	21	22.3%	9%	80	152	29
Total	**78%**	**21%**	**56**	**156**	**19**	**68%**	**24%**	**85**	**222**	**28**

Note: LAC is low access to external knowledge, MAC is medium access and HAC is high access.

Table 10.3 Descriptive statistics manufacturing firms exporting all years 1997–2008. Innovative activity based on R&D engagement applications and location classified by accessibility to knowledge producer services

	All products					Only new products				
	Share of firms	Share of exports	Emp. mean	Std. dev.	Emp median	Share of firms	Share of exports	Emp. mean	Std. dev.	Emp median
Innovative										
HAC	22.3%	57%	411	1,525	60	28.2%	60%	861	2,536	992
MAC	21.5%	26%	263	689	65	24.4%	24%	432	1,037	856
LAC	20.3%	11%	157	244	57	20.7%	12%	238	313	726
Total	**64.1%**	**94%**	**281**	**999**	**61**	**73.3%**	**96%**	**542**	**1,713**	**111**
Non-innovative										
HAC	11.1%	2%	103	317	28	8.4%	1%	131	387	295
MAC	12.0%	1%	54	76	30	9.5%	2%	66	80	333
LAC	12.8%	2%	66	103	31	8.8%	2%	87	128	311
Total	**35.9%**	**5 %**	**73**	**193**	**30**	**26.7%**	**13%**	**93**	**235**	**39**

Note: LAC is low access to external knowledge, MAC is medium access and HAC is high access.

Exports per employee

Table 10.6 presents our results for log exports per employee when an augmented Heckman selection equation is used. The model is augmented with a predicted

DOI: 10.1057/9781137367204.0017

Table 10.4   Summary statistics over exports 1997–2008. Innovative activity based on patent applications and accessibility to knowledge intense producer services

Panel A: all products											
	Exports/emp			Exports/sales			Number of destination			Number of products		
	Mean	Std. dev.	Median	Mean	Std. dev.	Median	Mean	Std. dev.	Median	Mean	Std. dev.	Median
Innovative												
HAC	1,125	1,359	858	0.505	0.315	0.536	30.0	25.7	23	40.5	75.7	18
MAC	879	948	622	0.451	0.308	0.440	24.5	21.9	20	26.6	48.7	14
LAC	752	1,242	566	0.420	0.280	0.389	23.7	20.2	19	22.1	28.1	13
Non-innovative												
HAC	513	1,168	158	0.238	0.275	0.114	9.9	12.6	5	11.5	16.2	6
MAC	530	1,437	144	0.253	0.261	0.156	8.9	10.4	5	10.8	18.1	6
LAC	545	1,419	141	0.268	0.261	0.177	8.7	11.0	5	8.7	12.7	5

Panel B: only new products											
	Exports/emp			Exports/total sales			Number of destination			Number of products		
	Mean	Std. dev.	Median	Mean	Std. dev.	Median	Mean	Std. dev.	Median	Mean	Std. dev.	Median
Innovative												
HAC	44	245	0	0.020	0. 099	0	12.7	18.8	5	5.9	14.3	2
MAC	25	143	0	0.013	0.075	0	10.0	15.5	3	4.3	8.1	2
LAC	27	176	0	0.013	0.077	0	8.9	14.0	3	3.6	4.7	2
Non-innovative												
HAC	17	159	0	0.008	0.061	0	4.4	7.7	1	2.6	4.0	1
MAC	18	164	0	0.008	0.062	0	4.6	7.9	1	2.6	3.2	1
LAC	18	336	0	0.008	0.058	0	4.1	7.5	1	2.3	2.6	1

Note: LAC is low access to external knowledge, MAC is medium access and HAC is high access.

Mills ratio estimated in a panel probit model. The patent sample includes all manufacturing firms in the first step of the equation, and the selection criterion is exporting all 12 years between 1997 and 2008. The first step of the Heckman model for CIS-observations includes firms that participated in at least two of the CIS surveys 2004, 2006 and 2008, and the selection criterion is the same as in the patent sample.

We see a large similarity across the four regressions: innovative firms have significantly larger coefficient estimates than non-innovative firms on the knowledge conjunction variable. Moreover among the non-innovative firms, exports per employee is a decreasing function of the proximity to external knowledge, which is systematically larger in large urban regions. Comparing

DOI: 10.1057/9781137367204.0017

Table 10.5 Summary statistics over exports 1997–2008. Innovative activity based on R&D and accessibility to knowledge intense producer services

	Panel A: all products											
	Exports/emp			Exports/sales			Number of destination			Number of products		
	Mean	Std. dev.	Median	Mean	Std. dev.	Median	Mean	Std. dev.	Median	Mean	Std. dev.	Median
Innovative												
HAC	999	1,423	675	0.437	0.319	0.418	27.6	25.0	20	36.4	68.9	17
MAC	825	909	523	0.415	0.314	0.385	22.4	21.3	16	27.01	49.8	13
LAC	758	1,273	483	0.378	0.285	0.337	19.0	19.4	13	20.1	28.9	10
Non-innovative												
HAC	393	767	118	0.187	0.232	0.086	9.6	11.2	6	13.0	20.5	7
MAC	503	1,007	235	0.253	0.238	0.187	9.8	10.5	6	12.2	17.2	7
LAC	577	9,078	252	0.278	0.258	0.211	10.4	13.1	6	9.7	12.0	6

	Panel B: only new products											
	Exports/emp			Exports/total sales			Number of destination			Number of products		
	Mean	Std. dev.	Median	Mean	Std. dev.	Median	Mean	Std. dev.	Median	Mean	Std. dev.	Median
Innovative												
HAC	35	204	0	0.017	0.091	0	11.5	18.2	3	5.4	13.2	2
MAC	30	196	0	0.015	0.085	0	9.8	15.4	3	4.4	8.1	2
LAC	24	165	0	0.012	0.073	0	8.0	13.4	2	3.4	4.7	2
Non-innovative												
HAC	14	134	0	0.006	0.050	0	4.1	6.2	2	3.0	6.5	1
MAC	17	142	0	0.009	0.055	0	4.3	6.5	2	2.6	3.4	1
LAC	16	143	0	0.009	0.062	0	4.5	8.5	1	2.3	2.3	1

Note: LAC is low access to external knowledge, MAC is medium access and HAC is high access.

the two samples, there is some weak evidence that patenting firms in high accessibility areas have higher export productivity than patenting firms in other areas, while the case is the opposite for R&D firms in the CIS-based sample.

The control variables show expected results: exports per employee are an increasing function of both human capital and physical capital, and multi-national firms are more export intense than purely domestic firms.

Scope of export varieties and scope of markets

Tables 10.7 and 10.8 present our estimates for persistent exporters when exporting is measured in terms of number of export products and number

DOI: 10.1057/9781137367204.0017

Table 10.6 Dependent variable: log exports per employee. Heckman selection model, patenting and non-patenting firms

	Patent	R&D
Selection criteria on export	12 year	12 year
LAC_	Reference	Reference
MAC_	−0.156***	−0.295***
	(0.020)	(0.052)
HAC_	−0.350***	−0.775***
	(0.020)	(0.054)
LAC_ INNO	0.777***	0.500***
	(0.042)	(0.049)
MAC_ INNO	0.814***	0.475***
	(0.040)	(0.050)
HAC_INNO	0.873***	0.395***
	(0.040)	(0.052)
Log human capital	0.551***	0.807***
	(0.054)	(0.076)
Log physical capital	0.018***	0.018***
	(0.002)	(0.003)
Domestic multinational[a]	0.939***	0.523***
	(0.025)	(0.030)
Foreign owned multinational[a]	1.316***	0.742***
	(0.028)	(0.034)
Non-affiliate firms[a]	0.079***	−0.054***
	(0.019)	(0.019)
Industry dummies	Incl	Incl
Year dummies	Incl	Incl
Observations	402,771	41,143

Note: LAC is low access to external knowledge, MAC is medium access and HAC is high access.
* significant at 10 per cent; ** significant at 5 per cent; *** significant at 1 per cent. Year and sector dummies included.
(a) Reference is domestic uninational firms.

of destination countries. Two different non-linear estimators are applied on the two samples of panel data. Considering first the Poisson estimates, we once again find that firms with patent applications are different from firms without applications. The innovating firms have a significantly larger number of export products, *ceteris paribus*, but no location effect can be found for innovators. That is, the degree of accessibility to external knowledge does not seem to matter. However a non-innovative firm in a high-accessibility place has a significantly larger number of export products than an identical firm in a place with low knowledge accessibility. This indicates that external knowledge spillovers can be significant for at least some firms.

DOI: 10.1057/9781137367204.0017

Table 10.7 Dependent variable: number of export products. Innovative and non-innovative firms

Innovation variable	Patent		R&D	
	Xtpoisson	Xtnbreg	Xtpoisson	Xtnbreg
LAC_	Reference	Reference	Reference	Reference
MAC_	0.171***	0.074**	0.009	−0.084
	(0.045)	(0.033)	(0.112)	(0.076)
HAC_	0.282***	0.122***	0.165	−0.106
	(0.057)	(0.038)	(0.136)	(0.110)
LAC_ INNO	0.593***	0.337***	0.307**	0.207***
	(0.078)	(0.056)	(0.141)	(0.058)
MAC_ INNO	0.461***	0.124**	0.298**	0.146**
	(0.066)	(0.062)	(0.127)	(0.062)
HAC_INNO	0.514***	0.314***	0.423***	0.314***
	(0.063)	(0.063)	(0.128)	(0.086)
Log human capital	0.174	−0.010	0.414*	−0.108
	(0.110)	(0.082)	(0.213)	(0.165)
Log physical capital	0.004*	0.005***	0.000	0.000
	(0.002)	(0.002)	(0.004)	(0.003)
Log firm size	0.360***	0.240***	0.397***	0.255***
	(0.015)	(0.013)	(0.027)	(0.023)
Domestic multinational[a]	0.121***	0.089***	0.138***	0.092***
	(0.023)	(0.019)	(0.031)	(0.023)
Foreign owned multinational[a]	0.068***	0.045**	0.071***	0.030
	(0.022)	(0.022)	(0.023)	(0.022)
Non-affiliate firms[a]	−0.018	−0.030**	0.006	−0.031
	(0.024)	(0.015)	(0.027)	(0.026)
Observations	42,873	42,873	18,091	18,091
Number of unique firms	3,993	3,993	1,611	1,611

Note: LAC is low access to external knowledge, MAC is medium access and HAC is high access.
* significant at 10 per cent; ** significant at 5 per cent; *** significant at 1 per cent. Year and sector dummies included.
(a) Reference is domestic uninational firms.

Column 2 reports negative binomial (NB) estimates for the sample based on patent information. The results are almost the same as in the Poisson model with one exception: the coefficient estimates are almost identical for non-innovative firms in high accessibility areas and innovative firms in medium accessibility areas. The main message however from the CIS sample and R&D as innovation indicator is that innovative firms have a larger number of products and the magnitude of the estimate is largest for firms in high-accessibility areas.

DOI: 10.1057/9781137367204.0017

Table 10.8   Dependent variable: number of destination countries. Innovative and non-innovative firms

Innovation variable	Patent		R&D	
	Xtpoisson	Xtnbreg	Xtpoisson	Xtnbreg
LAC_	Reference	Reference	Reference	Reference
MAC_	0.064*	0.054	0.069	0.052
	(0.036)	(0.033)	(0.062)	(0.067)
HAC_	0.070*	0.047	−0.026	−0.089
	(0.043)	(0.032)	(0.081)	(0.096)
LAC_ INNO	0.603***	0.594***	0.504***	0.508***
	(0.053)	(0.044)	(0.073)	(0.083)
MAC_ INNO	0.635***	0.637***	0.512***	0.514***
	(0.053)	(0.046)	(0.064)	(0.070)
HAC_INNO	0.663***	0.634***	0.578***	0.557***
	(0.051)	(0.048)	(0.071)	(0.079)
Log human capital	0.181***	0.175***	0.349***	0.330**
	(0.064)	(0.057)	(0.130)	(0.140)
Log physical capital	0.007***	0.007***	0.004*	0.005*
	(0.002)	(0.002)	(0.002)	(0.002)
Log firm size	0.322***	0.329***	0.310***	0.317***
	(0.012)	(0.012)	(0.018)	(0.020)
Domestic multinational[a]	0.048***	0.053***	0.044**	0.048***
	(0.014)	(0.014)	(0.021)	(0.019)
Foreign owned multinational[a]	0.032*	0.037**	0.026	0.030
	(0.019)	(0.016)	(0.020)	(0.020)
Non-affiliate firms[a]	−0.027	−0.025	−0.024	−0.023
	(0.017)	(0.016)	(0.022)	(0.023)
Industries dummies	Incl	Incl	Incl	Incl
Year dummies	Incl	Incl	Incl	Incl
Observations	42,873	42,873	18,091	18,091
Number of unique firms	3,993	3,993	1,611	1,611

Note: LAC is low access to external knowledge, MAC is medium access and HAC is high access.
* significant at 10 per cent; ** significant at 5 per cent; *** significant at 1 per cent. Year and sector dummies included.
(a) Reference is domestic uninational firms

Table 10.8 reports the association between the number of export destinations and the conjunction variable that classifies a firm's external and internal knowledge. The results provide an even clearer picture than Table 10.7, showing a significant difference between innovative and non-innovative exporters. Our conclusion from Tables 10.7 and 10.8 is that irrespective of whether we use

DOI: 10.1057/9781137367204.0017

patents or R&D inputs to classify firms as innovative they have a much greater variety of products and export markets than non-innovative exporters.

Growth of value added, labour productivity and employment

The next sets of results are given in Table 10.9, and consider the growth rate of value added, labour productivity and employment. A large literature on so called exporter premiums has focused on the productivity differences between (a) exporters and non-exporters, (b) persistent and occasional exporters and (c) high-intensity and low-intensity exporters. Our study adds to the literature by comparing persistent exporters with different locations and different innovation engagement. Similar to the analysis given already, we consider one sample classifying firms as innovative based on observed patent applications and a second sample classifying them based on self-reported R&D.

Starting with the patent-sample, columns 1–3 in Table 10.9 report three interesting results. First, within the categories non-innovative and innovative firms respectively, productivity is an increasing function of accessibility to external knowledge. We compare two alternative productivity measures: value added controlling for firm size and value added per employee not controlling for firm size. This indicates that all exporting firms benefit from various forms of knowledge flow in knowledge-intense areas. Second, innovative firms in medium- and high-accessibility areas have a significantly greater productivity growth than the four other types of exporters. Third, innovative exporters have notably higher growth rates than other firms. Looking then at the CIS sample, the table shows exactly the same pattern as the patent sample. The only difference is that the size of the estimates is somewhat lower. This makes sense in as much as R&D measures effort and patents measure achievement.

So what conclusions can be drawn from Table 10.9? We can establish that innovative exporters grow faster than other exporters, and that innovative firms in regions with a high accessibility to producer services grow fastest. But we cannot say that they are growing faster due to their presence on the export market, since we have not accounted for possible self-selection bias. One method that could be applied to solving this problem is to compare their performance with persistent innovators that do not export. However, since this control group is very small in relation to the 'target group' this would create statistical problems in the matching approach. However our data (results not reported in full) allow some insight into this question based on a matching analysis using observations on non-innovative firms in the patenting sample. Non-innovative firms that export persistently have significantly higher productivity growth than non-innovative firms that do not export, but significantly lower employment growth. The non-innovative non-exporters do not appear to gain from access to external knowledge.

DOI: 10.1057/9781137367204.0017

Table 10.9 Dependent variable: growth in value added, labour productivity and employment. Innovative and non-innovative firms

	Patent	Patent	Patent	R&D	R&D	R&D
Dep.var	ΔLNVA	ΔLN LP	ΔLN EMP	ΔLN LP	ΔLN EMP	ΔLN EMP
LAC_	Reference	Reference	Reference	Reference	Reference	Reference
MAC_	0.015**	0.009*	0.004	−0.005	−0.002	0.002
	(0.008)	(0.005)	(0.004)	(0.013)	(0.010)	(0.007)
HAC_	0.031***	0.023***	0.004	0.003	0.001	0.009
	(0.008)	(0.006)	(0.004)	(0.016)	(0.012)	(0.007)
LAC_ INNO	0.022*	0.011	0.032***	−0.004	−0.008	0.028***
	(0.012)	(0.008)	(0.006)	(0.013)	(0.009)	(0.006)
MAC_ INNO	0.052***	0.036***	0.030***	0.034***	0.019*	0.034***
	(0.011)	(0.008)	(0.006)	(0.013)	(0.010)	(0.007)
HAC_INNO	0.093***	0.061***	0.040***	0.038***	0.023**	0.029***
	(0.013)	(0.009)	(0.006)	(0.014)	(0.010)	(0.007)
Log human capital	0.165***	0.140***	−0.006	0.405***	0.314***	0.051
	(0.035)	(0.027)	(0.016)	(0.052)	(0.040)	(0.031)
Log physical capital	0.024***	0.019***	0.019***	0.025***	0.019***	0.022***
	(0.002)	(0.002)	(0.002)	(0.003)	(0.003)	(0.003)
Log emp	0.447***	–	–	0.441***	–	–
	(0.015)			(0.024)		
Log value added t–1	−0.466***	−0.346***	−0.057***	0.012	−0.347***	−0.063***
	(0.015)	(0.010)	(0.003)	(0.010)	(0.014)	(0.006)
Domestic MNE[a]	0.013*	0.019***	0.023***	0.017	0.019***	0.022***
	(0.007)	(0.005)	(0.004)	(0.011)	(0.007)	(0.006)
Foreign MNE	0.013	0.024***	0.021***	−0.010	0.028***	0.018***
	(0.009)	(0.006)	(0.005)	(0.008)	(0.008)	(0.007)
Non-affiliate firms[a]	−0.038***	−0.029***	−0.022***	−0.462***	−0.007	−0.008
	(0.006)	(0.005)	(0.003)	(0.023)	(0.006)	(0.022***)
Industries dummies	Incl	Incl	Incl	Incl	Incl	Incl
Year dummies	Incl	Incl	Incl	Incl	Incl	Incl
Observations	38,628	38,628	38,628	16,400	16,400	16,400
Number of unique firms	3,919	3,919	3,919	1,595	1,595	1,595

Note: LAC is low access to external knowledge, MAC is medium access and HAC is high access.
* significant at 10 per cent; ** significant at 5 per cent; *** significant at 1 per cent. Year and sector dummies included.
(a) Reference is domestic uninational firms

Conclusion

In this chapter, we estimate nonlinear and linear panel data models, on the links between internal knowledge accumulation, captured by recurrent R&D

DOI: 10.1057/9781137367204.0017

and innovation activities, and external knowledge, captured by access to knowledge intensive producer services.

We first explore the correlation between exports and the key indicator variable that groups firms into six distinct classes depending on innovation engagement and access to knowledge-rich milieu. Using recurrent exporting over a 12 year period as the selection criteria in an augmented Heckman selection model, and including all manufacturing firms in Sweden with at least one employee in the regression, we find that innovative exporters have higher export productivity than other firms, and that their export productivity increases with accessibility to external knowledge. Considering non-innovative exporters, our results suggest that firms in regions with high accessibility to knowledge (mainly larger cities) have lower export value per employee than firms located in low-accessibility areas. This finding requires further investigation.

In the second part of the analysis, we explore influences on the number of export products and export destinations for both innovative and non-innovative firms that are consistent exporters and consider the impact of knowledge transmission from the nearby local milieu. The results suggest that non-patenting firms in more dense environments with higher access to knowledge produce more export products than other non-patenting exporters, when we control for size, physical capital, human capital and four-digit industry. In the R&D sample with CIS firms there is no significant difference in the number of products among non-innovators, based on access to external knowledge. All count-data regressions show that innovative firms are both shipping more products and serving more markets than non-innovative exporters. Our last results concern productivity and employment growth. The estimates indicate that firms that apply for patents have faster growth in both labour productivity and employment. We also find that location in dense environments gives an extra boost to the growth rate.

The superior performance of innovative firms is consistent with the evidence presented by Geroski and Gregg (1997). Importantly, they found that innovative firms typically weathered the recession much better than non-innovative firms. A final important characteristic of our findings is that, in general, improvements in accessibility to knowledge seem to be of greater benefit to innovative firms than to non-innovative firms, which is consistent with the idea that innovative firms have greater absorptive capacity and this partly explains why some firms gain greater advantage from a given location than others.

References

Almeda, P. and Phene, A. (2012) Managing knowledge within and outside the multinational corporation, in M. Andersson, B. Johansson, C. Karlsson and H. Lööf

DOI: 10.1057/9781137367204.0017

(eds) *Innovation and Growth: From R&D Strategies of Innovating Firms to Economy-wide Technological Change*. Oxford: Oxford University Press, pp. 21–37.

Andersson, M., Johansson, B., Karlsson, C. and Lööf, H. (2012) Introduction, in M. Andersson, B. Johansson, C. Karlsson and H. Lööf (eds) *Innovation and Growth: From R&D Strategies of Innovating Firms to Economy-wide Technological Change*, Oxford: Oxford University Press, pp 1–20.

Audretsch, D.B. and M.P. Feldman (1996) R&D spillovers and the geography of innovation and production. *American Economic Review*, 86: 630–40.

Aw, B.Y., Roberts, M.J. and Xu, D.Y. (2011) R&D investment, exporting, and productivity dynamics. *American Economic Review*, 101: 1312–44.

Baum, C.F., Caglayan, M. and Talavera, O. (2012) R&D expenditures and the global diversification on export sales. Working paper no. 794, Boston College.

Blind, K. and Jungmittag, A. (2004) Foreign direct investment, imports and innovations in the service industry. *Review of Industrial Organization*, 25: 205–27.

Bernhard, A.B. and Wagner, J. (2001) Export entry and exit by German firms. *Weltwirtschaftliches Archiv/Review of World Economics*, 137: 105–23.

Branstetter, L. (2001) Are knowledge spillovers international or intranational in scope? Microeconometric evidence from the US and Japan. *Journal of International Economics*, 53: 53–79.

Buckley, P.J. and Casson, M. (1976) *The Future of the Multinational Enterprise*. London: Macmillan.

Cantwell, J. and Zhang, F. (2012) Knowledge accession strategies and spatial organization of R&D, in M. Andersson, B. Johansson, C. Karlsson and H. Lööf (eds) *Innovation and Growth: From R&D Strategies of Innovating Firms to Economy-wide Technological Change*. Oxford: Oxford University Press, pp. 88–114.

Cohen, W.M. and Levinthal, D.A. (1989) Innovation and learning: the two faces of R&D. *The Economic Journal*, 99: 569–96.

Dunning, J.H. (2001) The key literature on IB activities: 1960–2000, in A.M. Rugman and T.L. Brewer (eds) *The Oxford Handbook of International Business*. Oxford: Oxford University Press, pp. 36–68.

Fujita, M. and Thisse, J-F. (2002) *Economics of Agglomeration*. Cambridge: Cambridge University Press.

Geroski, P.A. and Clegg, P. (1997) *Coping with Recession: UK Company Performance in Adversity*. Cambridge: Cambridge University Press.

Harris, R. and Moffat, J. (2011) R&D, innovation and exporting. SERC Discussion Papers 0073, Spatial Economics Research Centre, LSE.

Greenaway, D., Gullstrand, J. and Kneller, R. (2005) Exporting may not always boost firm level productivity. *Review of World Economics*, 141: 561–82.

Jaffe, A.B., Trajtenberg, M. and Henderson, R. (1993) Geographic localisation of knowledge spillovers as evidenced by patent citations. *Quarterly Journal of Economics*, 108: 577–98.

Keller, W. (2009) international trade, foreign direct investment, and technology spillovers. NBER working paper no. 15442, National Bureau of Economic Research, Inc.

Kirkels, Y. and Duysters, G. (2010) Brokerage in SME networks. *Research Policy*, 39: 375–85.

Lee, S., Park, G., Yoon, B. and Park, J. (2010) Open innovation in SMEs – an intermediated network model. *Research Policy*, 39: 290–300.

Lööf, H., Nabavi, P., and Johansson, B. (2012) How can firms benefit from access to knowledge intense producer services? CESIS WP Series 282.

DOI: 10.1057/9781137367204.0017

MacGarvie, M. (2006) Do firms learn from international trade? *The Review of Economics and Statistics*, 88: 46–60.

Oviatt, B.M. and McDougall, P.P. (1994) Toward a theory of international new ventures. *Journal of International Business Studies*, 25; 45–64.

Tether, B.S. (2002) Who cooperates for innovation, and why? An empirical analysis. *Research Policy*, 31: 947–67.

Weibull, J. (1976) An axiomatic approach to the measurement of accessibility. *Regional Science and Urban Economics*, 6: 357–79

Whittington, K.B., Owen-Smith, J. and Powell, W.W. (2009) Networks, propinquity and innovation in knowledge-intensive industries. *Administrative Science Quarterly*, 54: 90–122.

Wolff, E. (2012) Spillover, linkages, and productivity growth in the US economy 1958 to 2007, in M. Andersson, B. Johansson, C. Karlsson and H. Lööf (eds) *Innovation and Growth: From R&D Strategies of Innovating Firms to Economy-wide Technological Change.* Oxford: Oxford University Press, pp. 235–67.

Zaheer, S. (1995) Overcoming the liability of foreignness. *Academy of Management Journal*, 38: 341–63.

DOI: 10.1057/9781137367204.0017

11
Financing Patterns, Multinationals and Performance: Firm-level Evidence from 47 Countries*

Sushanta Mallick and Yong Yang

Introduction

The recent financial instability of 2007–9 has been the result of less tight financial regulation enabling securitization that allowed and encouraged reckless credit expansion, leading to excessive leverage, supported in part by lax monetary policy (see Carmassi et al., 2009; Acharya et al., 2009). A higher aggregate leverage, that is, the ratio of debt to equity, indicates in general a lower capacity to absorb losses and hence greater fragility. This chapter addresses two key questions:

(1) Which sources of financing contribute more in improving firm-performance, distinguishing multinational corporations (MNCs) from domestic firms covering 47 countries?
(2) Do multinationals transmit their performance to their affiliates across borders?

In other words, do financial constraints or financial access (sources of financing) affect domestic firms' performance disproportionately more than multinational firms' performance? These questions can be related to how the effects of financial constraint varies across firms with access to only the local capital market (domestic firms) compared to firms that have access to both

* The authors acknowledge financial support from the School of Business and Management, Queen Mary University of London, UK. We gratefully acknowledge the comments and suggestions by participants at the European Economics and Finance Society (9th Annual Meeting, Athens, Greece, 3–6 June 2010), and the 40th Annual Conference of Academy of International Business – UK and Ireland Chapter in Birmingham, 21–23 March 2013. We are solely responsible for any error that might yet remain.

DOI: 10.1057/9781137367204.0018

the local and foreign capital markets via subsidiaries (multinationals). This suggests that firm performance of a multinational in one country can affect performance of firms in other countries via the MNC-subsidiary channel. We aim to provide evidence in this chapter that financing sources affect domestic firms differently than MNCs and that the productivity and leverage of a parent MNC is related to its subsidiaries' performance.

In a broader perspective, it has been widely accepted that financial development is associated with higher growth, but how a country's financial structure affects economic growth at a macro level would depend on its impact on how corporations raise and manage funds at the firm level. The empirical literature at a macro level goes back to King and Levine (1993), showing that a country's financial development matters for firm performance and aggregate growth. While much of the research in this line of literature has focused on macroeconomic issues across countries (see Levine and Zervos, 1998; Arestis et al., 2001), there is limited research looking at firm-level access to different sources of external financing and their impact on performance by using firm-level data for a large set of developed and emerging countries.

It is generally understood that increasing financial leverage lowers firm performance (Myers, 2001). But the theory of capital structure does not yield a unique and unambiguous prediction on the equilibrium relationship between financial structure and firm performance. If we look at the degree of a firm's innovation as one important dimension of performance, there are several classes of theories with diverging predictions on the sign of the equilibrium relationship between financial structure and performance. For example, the bankruptcy cost theory (Jensen and Meckling, 1976), the theory of conflicts of interest between equity holders and debt holders (Jensen and Meckling, 1976; Myers, 1977) and the theory of control rights (Aghion and Bolton, 1992; Hart, 1995) all predict a negative link between the degree of innovation (and thereby performance) and leverage. On the contrary, the theory of conflicts of interest between managers and shareholders (Harris and Raviv, 1990; Stulz 1990) and between insiders and outsiders (Myers and Majluf, 1984) predict that the equilibrium relationship between the degree of a firm's innovation and the level of leverage is positive. These different theoretical predictions suggest that the sign of the equilibrium relationship is not unique in the literature, which primarily motivates our empirical investigation in the context of multinationals, for which there is limited research in this line of literature.

The chapter draws on firm-level annual data covering over 10,000 firms from 47 countries. We provide evidence that while retained earnings and equities have a positive effect on productivity, bank and non-bank loans tend to have a negative impact on productivity. Further, the parent multinationals' performance significantly influences the overseas subsidiaries' performance.

DOI: 10.1057/9781137367204.0018

Finally, we also find that higher debt ratios of parents do not have any impact on the productivity of overseas subsidiaries.

The remainder of our chapter is organized as follows. The next section develops our hypotheses before we move on to describe the data sources and present descriptive statistics. Then our empirical methodology is discussed and we present the results and robustness checks. And, finally, we conclude.

Hypotheses development

The first hypothesis is to examine the extent to which financing sources matter for firm-level performance. We investigate how best one could relate the total factor productivity (TFP) improvements to different sources of financing. Using a comprehensive firm-level dataset from 47 countries spanning the period 1996–2007, this chapter investigates the relationship between TFP (as a forward looking indicator of performance) and sources of financing. The chapter therefore departs from the existing empirical studies in the literature and focuses on the effect of sources of financing on performance for domestic versus multinational firms, along with separating the multinational firms in terms of parents and affiliates by including a large enough firm-level dataset with firms having different levels of financial leverage (see summary statistics in Table 11.1).

Firms with a higher proportion of internal funds will have better performance, because firms using more internal funds relative to external equity will experience a decline in their cost of equity capital. Further, we investigate whether firms using higher debt financing do experience lower performance than those financed by alternative channels, along with a distinction between domestic and multinational firms (separating domestic subsidiaries from overseas counterparts). Agency theory dominates research on equity holdings and firm performance relationships, but extant studies provide no consensus about the direction and magnitude of such relationships. Conducting a series of meta-analyses of relevant empirical ownership-performance studies, Dalton et al. (2003) provide few examples of systematic relationships, lending little support for agency theory. While the expected signs for retained earnings and equity could be positive, bank loans and non-bank loans can have a negative impact on performance: Hypothesis 1.

> *Hypothesis 1*: retained earnings and equity can have positive impact on performance, while bank loans and non-bank loans could have a negative impact on performance.

Earlier theories of foreign direct investment (Vernon, 1966) leading to internationalization (Buckley and Casson, 1976; Dunning and Lundan, 2008) offered

DOI: 10.1057/9781137367204.0018

Table 11.1 Descriptive statistics

	Variable	Obs	Mean	Std. dev.
All firms	TFP	39829	8.27	0.81
	Sales	39829	1774.80	5499.03
	Capital	39829	670.06	2710.86
	Employment	39829	9596.11	29668.34
	Retained earning	39829	450.84	1828.60
	Equity	39829	750.18	2535.89
	Bank loan	39829	281.81	1073.48
	Non-bank loan	39829	393.90	2064.33
	Debt-to-equity ratio	39829	0.69	0.59
	Time period	39829	2002.9	2.77
Domestic firms	TFP	16945	8.14	0.92
	Sales	16945	691.48	3400.64
	Capital	16945	268.38	1684.04
	Employment	16945	4144.91	19187.51
	Retained earning	16945	153.74	1050.57
	Equity	16945	291.43	1686.04
	Bank loan	16945	116.34	686.87
	Non-bank loan	16945	147.18	1364.23
	Debt-to-equity ratio	16945	0.62	0.57
	Time period	16945	2003.3	2.63
Multinational firms	TFP	22884	8.37	0.70
	Sales	22884	2576.97	6523.51
	Capital	22884	967.50	3237.69
	Employment	22884	13632.58	34944.30
	Retained earning	22884	670.83	2211.08
	Equity	22884	1089.87	2969.27
	Bank loan	22884	404.33	1273.21
	Non-bank loan	22884	576.59	2441.42
	Debt-to-equity ratio	22884	0.74	0.60
	Time period	22884	2002.5	2.84

Note: 'sales', 'capital', 'retained earning', 'equity', 'bank loan' and 'non-bank loan' are denominated in millions of euro. 'Multinational firms' are firms with at least one subsidiary in an overseas market.

a general framework for the extent and pattern of international trade and foreign investment, based in part on the role of transaction costs. According to those views, multinational firms have opportunities to share their core competitive advantages among different markets through the internalization of intangible assets. These theories can explain the emergence and growth of multinational firms. A related approach includes resource-based views, which are based on the concept of ownership advantage (Barney, 1991). These views postulate that resources are the source of competitive advantages if they are

DOI: 10.1057/9781137367204.0018

valuable, rare and difficult to imitate. Resources include all assets, capabilities, organizational processes, information and human competencies controlled by a firm that enable the company to improve its efficiency and effectiveness.

Other theories on foreign direct investment (FDI) include those about learning (Johanson and Vahlne, 1977, 2009), which predict increasing resource commitments to foreign markets over time as a result of the accumulation of organizational experience that can affect the firm's perceived opportunities and risks. Moreover economic theory predicts that the level of engagement with international business is strongly related to the efficiency of the firm. For instance, while the most productive firms will tend to export and/or to invest in foreign plants, their least productive counterparts may only serve the domestic market (Krugman, 1980; Bernard et al., 2003; Melitz, 2003; Helpman et al., 2004; Yang and Mallick, 2010). This is explained in part by the considerable sunk costs that need to be met before a firm can export or produce abroad.[1] Given this rationale for overseas production by multinationals, it becomes important to understand whether the financing sources matter for productivity improvement at the firm level for MNCs.

Both retained earnings and equity could have a positive impact on performance, as they are less costly relative to debt financing. However, compared to the performance of domestic firms, retained earnings and equity could contribute less to the performance of multinational firms. Since multinationals have higher retained earnings relative to domestic firms (see Table 11.1), this could mean lower reinvestment and thereby lower performance. Besides, multinationals have greater exposure to international risks, which could imply higher expected cost of equity capital for multinational firms, thereby suggesting lower performance for MNCs: Hypothesis 2.

Hypothesis 2: retained earnings and equity contribute less to the performance of multinational firms, compared to domestic firms.

Alfaro et al. (2009) found that countries with well-developed financial markets gain significantly from FDI through improvements in TFP rather than factor accumulation in explaining cross-country income differences – a key finding in the growth literature. This macro-level finding in the FDI-growth literature implies that multinationals' TFP improvement can positively influence its subsidiaries (whether domestic or overseas) performance via the channel of alternative available sources of financing for a firm. However one may argue that parent companies' leverage may not affect affiliate TFP. In order to examine this, we propose Hypothesis 3.

---

[1] Also see recent meta paper on exports and productivity (Martins and Yang, 2009).

DOI: 10.1057/9781137367204.0018

Hypothesis 3: multinational parents' TFP can positively influence their subsidiaries, but parents' debt does not influence their subsidiaries.

Key variables

Given the above Hypotheses 1–3, our next step is to describe the definitions of key variables considered in this study, which are given as follows:

(1) *Measurement of firm performance*: productivity refers to the returns achieved by internal stakeholders and increases in productivity represent an increase in discretionary resources potentially available to both the internal stakeholders (the insiders) and the external stakeholders (the shareholders and the tax collectors) (Girma et al., 2006). We employ a standard measure of total factor productivity, addressing any effects in total output that are not caused by capital and labour inputs and generally accepted as a measure of technical efficiency, which is seen as the real driver of long-term growth and a forward-looking firm performance indicator (Olley and Pakes, 1996; Levinsohn and Petrin, 2003).[2]

(2) *Retained earnings*: as internal sources of financing should be less costly than raising funds by issuing common shares or debt, we expect that firms with internal funds will have better performance, because firms using more internal funds relative to external equity will experience a decline in their cost of equity capital and also the rate the market uses to discount expected earnings of such organizations will be lower.

(3) *Equity*: we define equity as the value of total common shareholder's equity as a proxy for the cumulative proceeds from issuing common shares and consider the natural log of the value of equity in our regressions. This can also measure the impact of firm size on performance.

(4) *Bank loan*: these loans include financing from all types of banks and financial institutions. The higher the level of debt, the lower will be the firm's performance. With limited access to capital markets as in bank-based financial systems, the availability of capital to borrowing firms may not lead to higher profitability or growth because banks could discourage firms from investing in risky profitable projects (see Weinstein and Yafeh, 1998).

(5) *Non-bank loan*: these liabilities primarily comprise the outstanding value of total bond issuance of a firm as a long-term source of financing. Debt financing can boost or hurt firm performance. Campello (2006) finds that

---

[2] Given the standard problems with market based (Tobin's Q) and accounting performance measures (such as return on asset (ROA) and return on equity (ROE)) (see e.g. Demsetz and Villalonga, 2001), productivity analysis is used in our study to explore the effects of financing structure on firm performance.

DOI: 10.1057/9781137367204.0018

moderate debt taking is associated with sales gains, whereas high indebtedness leads to product market underperformance.

(6) *Debt-to-equity ratio (leverage)*: we measure leverage as the ratio of long-term debt to common equity, which is expected to capture the degree of financial riskiness of a firm. Financial leverage ratios measure the extent to which a firm is using long-term debt that can indicate the long-term solvency of a firm.

Data

Our analysis draws on the Orbis data, collected by Bureau van Dijk, a firm-level information provider. According to Bureau van Dijk, the information in Orbis is sourced from different providers, all of which are experts in their regions, providing detailed descriptive information, including the company financial statements.[3]

The records of each company include information on whether the company has ownership stake in its subsidiaries (defined as a minimum 25.01 per cent equity control over its overseas subsidiary). Therefore we are able to differentiate between domestic and multinational firms. We consider firms that have information available on sales, capital, employees, retained earnings, equity, bank loans and non-bank loans. Firms without at least one of these variables are excluded from our sample. This criterion leads to the exclusion of several firms in some countries, but we do not believe that this is a serious problem, as we still have a considerable number of firms from most major countries. At the end, 9180 firms are included in our analysis, which include 4412 domestic firms and 4768 multinational firms.

Financial and operational information of firms in our dataset are available for the period 1996–2007 at an annual frequency. Firms are concentrated in some EU countries, most in G-8 countries and some from developing countries, with significant numbers in China, France, Germany, Japan, South Korea, Singapore, Taiwan, Thailand, the UK and the USA.

A Sample of 2280 multinational parents and 8132 subsidiaries

Our dataset includes information on whether the company has an ownership stake in an affiliate and identifies affiliates by name. We are therefore able to find matches between multinational parents and their matched subsidiaries.

---

[3] Orbis also contains further details such as news, market research, ratings and country reports, scanned reports, ownership and M&A data. Orbis has a number of different reports per company. For listed companies, banks and insurance companies plus major private companies, more detailed information is available. See Ribeiro et al. (2010) for more information on the Orbis dataset and Mallick and Yang (2011) who use this dataset.

DOI: 10.1057/9781137367204.0018

The records of each company include the subsidiary location; therefore we are able to differentiate between domestic and overseas subsidiaries. Given the focus of the data on large companies and our limited access to the data, we were not able to obtain information about all subsidiaries of all multinationals. However we were still able to create a large enough dataset. Over the period 1996–2007, we find 2280 multinational parents and their 8132 subsidiaries, 5301 of which are located in the domestic market, while 2831 subsidiaries are located in overseas markets.

Descriptive statistics

Table 11.1 presents summary statistics of our dataset. There is a total of 9180 firms, giving rise to 39,829 observations. The first panel of the table presents descriptive statistics for all firms, while the middle panel contains domestic firms only, and the third panel contains firms with at least one subsidiary in an overseas country (multinational firms). Some of the key variables are TFP, different sources of financing (retained earnings, equity, bank loan and non-bank loan) and debt-to-equity ratio. Unsurprisingly multinational firms appear to have more sales (2576 vs. 691 million), hire more employees (13,632 vs. 4144) and are more capital intensive (967 vs. 268 million) than domestic firms. Multinational firms, on average, are marginally more productive than domestic firms (8.37 vs. 8.14). Monetary values were converted into euros using exchange rates retrieved from the IMF.

We also find on average that multinational firms have higher levels of alternative sources of financing than domestic ones. For instance, the average retained earnings for multinational firms are 670 million, while for domestic firms that figure is 153 million. Moreover multinational firms have more equity financing (1089 vs. 291 million), bank loans (404 vs. 116 million) and non-bank loans (576 vs. 147 million). However multinational firms also have higher debt-to-equity ratio (0.74 vs. 0.62). Tables 11.2 and 11.3 present the country distribution of firms, along with the most important variables used in our analysis. Firms are concentrated in some EU countries, mostly G-8 countries and some developing countries.

Now we turn to our second sample of multinational parents and their subsidiaries. Summary statistics for this sub-sample are presented in Table 11.4, and there are 2280 multinational parents and their 2831 domestic subsidiaries and 5201 overseas subsidiaries, giving rise to 34,046 observations in total. Table 11.4 contains some descriptive statistics on capital and employees of both multinational parents and subsidiaries, which are used to calculate the TFP. Unsurprisingly we find on average multinational parents have more sales (10,055 vs. 638 million), are more capital intensive (3,467 vs. 199 million) and hire more employees (48,823 vs. 2840) than their subsidiaries. We also include

DOI: 10.1057/9781137367204.0018

Table 11.2   Number of firms and key variables per country

Country	N.	TFP	Sales	Cap.	Emp.	Ear.	Eq.	Bank	Non-b.	Lev.
Australia	151	8.26	982	551	5,679	222	573	125	307	0.64
Austria	54	8.2	1,061	565	4,752	264	458	148	298	0.87
Belgium	49	8.59	3,642	1,018	16,922	682	1,462	335	965	0.85
Brazil	13	7.8	950	1,217	6,832	229	908	307	267	0.80
Bulgaria	2	7.06	47.3	22.8	1,532	18.4	58.3	11.2	3.24	0.39
Canada	15	8.11	978	937	5,120	478	871	157	605	0.96
China	1,025	7.29	504	401	6,937	65.1	301	82.6	53.8	0.41
Hong Kong	64	7.79	1,192	1,212	14,028	728	1,391	381	484	0.60
Czech Republic	8	7.65	1,064	1,841	8,248	635	1,362	306	354	0.41
Denmark	60	8.31	725	331	3,654	284	353	127	89.6	0.66
Estonia	19	7.38	105	102	1,630	30.2	62.4	48.6	5.14	0.59
Finland	90	8.32	1,749	724	6,384	474	750	156	336	0.63
France	348	8.53	1,996	597	11,624	172	803	166	637	0.74
Germany	291	8.53	4,149	1,296	18,496	715	1,273	206	1,549	1.07
Greece	75	8.08	675	618	2,714	95.2	383	181	228	0.80
Hungary	11	7.89	1,548	772	6,721	272	671	140	251	0.39
Iceland	10	8.02	253	81.7	1,385	26.8	88.1	86.8	17.2	1.25
Indonesia	96	7.28	226	154	4,635	63.9	111	29.6	70.9	0.77
Ireland	21	8.86	1,724	550	6,940	325	569	231	322	0.74
Italy	125	8.54	2,859	1,699	8,323	585	1,457	493	1,163	0.80
Japan	2,262	8.57	1,509	566	5,345	347	587	145	315	0.63
Korea	400	8.06	83.2	32.5	342	14.3	37.4	5.66	8.4	0.41
Latvia	17	7.07	80.3	62.8	1,451	8.47	79	3.01	11.9	0.30
Lithuania	24	7.06	82.7	112	1,911	23.1	92.3	15.4	11.8	0.49
Luxemburg	15	7.78	663	575	7,797	187	674	143	283	0.75
Malaysia	79	7.17	147	136	3,019	79.6	136	39	42.6	0.55
Malta	1	9.2	93.8	5.89	211	67.2	117	12.8	1.63	0.12
Mexico	58	7.66	1,340	941	14,777	769	749	362	395	0.89
Netherlands	75	8.53	3,234	813	18,489	498	1,184	178	903	0.85
New Zealand	7	7.89	202	89.1	3,540	37.3	85.1	13.9	44.4	0.69
Norway	50	8.24	1,932	1,134	7,678	535	956	199	728	0.99
Philippines	35	7	261	265	3,627	109	211	68.7	124	0.64
Poland	13	7.81	1,578	1,069	10,608	635	983	123	263	0.39
Portugal	26	8.11	1,352	1,472	6,214	207	930	473	705	1.10
Romania	3	7.19	173	220	2,492	17.9	145	74.8	19.6	0.44
Russia	44	7.07	2,281	3,423	46,769	2,577	3,271	674	527	0.57
Singapore	228	7.49	209	109	2,545	65.9	139	29	67	0.43
Slovenia	9	7.76	614	277	5,667	67.9	234	64.2	41.2	0.41
South Africa	10	7.5	260	125	7,863	87.2	124	25.6	61.4	0.52
Spain	80	8.27	2,328	1,678	9,227	267	1,120	557	788	0.83
Sweden	129	8.37	1,025	239	8,424	182	391	105	183	0.79
Switzerland	105	8.22	1,764	462	10,187	791	917	58.7	407	0.63
Taiwan	661	7.72	443	223	4,409	54	266	57.4	61.4	0.37
Thailand	241	7.43	403	169	3,486	67.9	157	65.4	63.7	0.56
Turkey	31	8.3	1,436	427	6,242	198	517	168	166	0.50
UK	391	8.28	1,671	855	11,884	450	773	174	405	0.70
US	1,659	8.47	2,952	966	16,895	903	1,254	706	514	0.87

Note: 'Emp.' – employment. 'Ear.' – retained earnings. 'Non-b.' – non-bank loans. 'Lev.' – leverage. 'Cap.' – capital. 'Eq.' – equity. 'Bank' – Bank loan. 'Sales', 'Cap.', 'Ear.', 'Eq.', 'Bank' and 'Non-b.' are denominated in millions of euro.

DOI: 10.1057/9781137367204.0018

Table 11.3 Sources of financing and total factor productivity

	(1)	(2)	(3)	(4)	(5)
Retained earning* *mul.*		−0.043***			
		(0.011)			
Equity* *mul.*			−0.074***		
			(0.018)		
Bank loan* *mul.*				−0.005	
				(0.008)	
Non-bank loan* *mul.*					0.0007
					(0.012)
Retained earning	0.090***	0.129***			
	(0.006)	(0.009)			
Equity	0.065***		0.162***		
	(0.012)		(0.015)		
Bank loan	−0.036***			−0.027***	
	(0.004)			(0.007)	
Non-bank loan	−0.030***				−0.006
	(0.006)				(0.010)
Obs	39829	39829	39829	39829	39829
No. countries	47	47	47	47	47
No. firms	9180	9180	9180	9180	9180
Firm fixed effect	X	X	X	X	X
Business cycle effect	X	X	X	X	X
R-squared	.949	.949	.948	.948	.948
F statistics	203.299	214.831	201.408	204.931	198

Note: dependant variable is total factor productivity. 'Mul.' is a dummy equal to one if it is a multi-national firm, and zero if it is a domestic firm. 'Retained earning', 'Equity', 'Bank loan' and 'Non-bank loan' are in logarithm. Values in parentheses are standard errors. Significance levels: *: 0.10; **: 0.05; ***: 0.01.

Table 11.4 Descriptive statistics (a sample of 2280 multinational parents and their 8132 subsidiaries)

	Variable	Obs	Mean	Std. dev.
Multinational parents	Total factor productivity	34046	8.48	0.59
	Sales	34046	10055.66	14685.52
	Capital	34046	3467.07	6555.36
	Employment	34046	48823.79	72418.20
	Debt-to-equity ratio	34046	0.89	0.65
	Retained earning	34046	2842.63	5663.54
Subsidiary	Total factor productivity	34046	11.11	0.92
	Sales	34046	638.09	2647.68
	Capital	34046	199.57	1042.43
	Employment	34046	2840.83	13143.01
	Asset	34046	650.48	3316.97

Note: 'Sales', 'Capital' and 'Retained earning' are denominated in millions of euro.

DOI: 10.1057/9781137367204.0018

Table 11.5   List of number of firms and key variables in each country (a sample of 2280 multinational parents and their 8132 subsidiaries)

Country	Affiliates			Parents			
	N.	TFP	Asset	N.	TFP	Leverage	Earning
Australia	39	10.65	725.12	30	8.38	0.58	281.92
Austria	61	11.15	250.24	24	8.27	1.01	504.08
Belgium	229	11.59	617.95	37	8.49	0.87	905.79
Brazil	3	10.76	2244.76	0			
Bulgaria	30	9.54	51.11	1	6.86	0.21	21.29
Canada	4	10.99	495.42	4	8.26	1.17	378.54
China	268	10.35	293.78	41	7.96	0.40	1783.59
Czech Republic	145	10.24	92.84	1	7.22	0.58	2281.11
Denmark	161	10.98	203.16	37	8.33	0.59	1590.40
Estonia	36	9.77	14.17	5	7.21	0.28	16.24
Finland	229	10.95	217.35	59	8.44	0.71	2071.90
France	1,152	11.28	646.78	184	8.53	0.90	965.90
Germany	399	11.54	1372.88	113	8.64	1.23	3534.29
Greece	104	10.91	181.12	35	8.16	0.97	401.46
Hong Kong	13	10.44	1725.29	17	8.16	0.44	3005.21
Hungary	41	10.71	171.01	4	7.92	0.46	646.74
Iceland	3	10.97	361.87	5	8.03	1.17	60.93
India	4	9.46	56.40	0			
Indonesia	16	9.99	258.51	1	7.92	0.58	129.91
Ireland	99	12.30	2153.57	14	8.75	0.95	656.78
Italy	455	11.21	320.83	58	8.60	1.09	4773.98
Japan	881	11.45	778.30	274	8.66	1.02	4446.80
Latvia	26	9.45	19.07	0			
Lithuania	16	10.03	85.24	0			
Luxembourg	11	10.73	591.62	5	8.24	0.44	378.86
Malaysia	35	9.96	367.33	18	7.17	0.70	616.27
Mexico	7	10.40	464.33	8	7.70	1.16	4510.89
Netherlands	199	11.72	1230.22	45	8.62	1.00	2409.04
New Zealand	5	10.87	451.49	0			
Norway	99	10.94	212.95	23	8.33	1.02	1571.96
Philippines	8	9.83	341.30	3	7.40	0.72	425.12
Poland	201	10.43	97.63	10	8.19	0.34	1246.35
Portugal	110	10.82	307.36	12	7.98	1.34	483.56
Romania	82	9.53	111.49	1	7.34	0.45	171.17
Russia	70	9.90	259.00	15	7.21	0.42	23228.14
Singapore	190	10.67	232.15	36	7.78	0.67	993.64
Slovenia	17	10.36	82.00	6	7.57	0.59	100.07
South Africa	26	10.34	831.22	14	8.40	0.55	290.37
South Korea	83	10.98	135.41	3	7.86	0.21	8.17
Spain	290	11.43	617.71	46	8.41	0.88	678.87
Sweden	264	11.12	577.08	74	8.45	0.73	1306.26
Switzerland	31	10.90	1858.61	53	8.54	0.69	6889.86
Taiwan	345	10.24	526.76	212	8.18	0.40	146.08
Thailand	51	9.90	236.73	8	8.18	1.08	795.75
Turkey	12	11.39	751.04	6	9.28	0.93	459.56
UK	1,320	11.13	580.20	237	8.34	0.81	1324.99
US	262	11.14	2229.08	501	8.52	0.92	4047.30

Note: 'Earning' refers to the retained earning. 'Asset' and 'Earning' are denominated in millions of euro.

DOI: 10.1057/9781137367204.0018

some other key variables in Table 11.4, including parents' debt-to-equity ratio and retained earnings.

Table 11.5 presents the country distribution of firms, along with the most important variables used in our analysis. Data cover 47 countries, including many OECD countries and also the largest developing nations. The parents are concentrated in developed markets, with significant number of firms in France, Germany, Japan, Taiwan, the UK and the USA. The majority of subsidiaries are also found in Belgium, China, Finland, France, Germany, Italy, Japan, Poland, Spain, Sweden, Taiwan, the UK and the USA. We also present a distribution of headquarters' productivity and debt-to-equity ratio, along with subsidiaries' productivity (Figures 11.1 and 11.2), in which we find some evidence that subsidiary's productivity is positively associated with headquarters' productivity. However headquarters' debt-to-equity ratio does not lead to poor productivity of their subsidiaries. We will test these relationships by controlling for firm characteristics in the empirical results section.

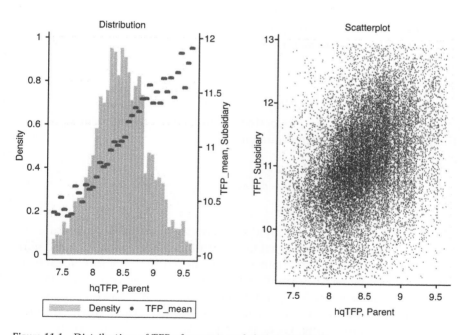

Figure 11.1 Distribution of TFP of parents and their subsidiaries

Note: X-axis presents multinational parent's total factor productivity. Y-axis presents affiliate's total factor productivity.

DOI: 10.1057/9781137367204.0018

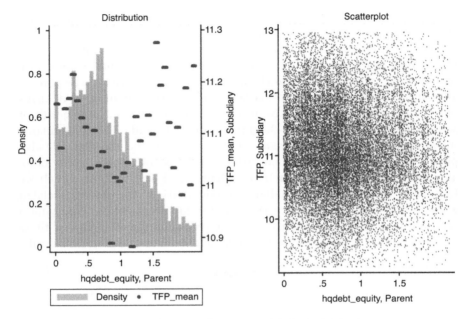

Figure 11.2   Distribution of leverage of parents and TFP of subsidiaries

Note: X-axis presents multinational parent's total factor productivity. Y-axis presents affiliate's total factor productivity.

Empirical results

We analyse whether firm productivity is influenced by different sources of financing from the following equation:

$$Y_{it} = \sum_{k=1}^{k=4} \beta_k Z_{kit} + \sum_{k=1}^{k=4} \lambda_k Z_{kit} * Mul_i + \alpha_i + \gamma_t + e_{it} \tag{1}$$

where Y_{it} is TFP of firm i in period t. Z_{kit} are the variables that measure the sources of financing, including retained earnings, equity, bank loan and non-bank loan. Mul_i is a dummy variable equal to one if firm is a multinational firm, and zero if it is a domestic firm. Equation (1) also includes firm fixed effect α_i and business cycle effect γ_t. Y_{it} and different sources of financing are in logarithms, β_k indicates the average change in firm productivity driven by alternative sources of financing. We consider $Z_{kit} * Mul_i$ as the interaction term.

Table 11.3 reports our main estimates on assessing the role of sources of financing on firm productivity. All columns control for firm and year fixed effects. In order to compare the effects of each 'source of financing' variable

DOI: 10.1057/9781137367204.0018

we standardize them. Specifically we subtract the mean of the variable across all non-missing observations and then divide that difference by the standard deviation of the variable.

As documented in Table 11.3, we find from column 1 that on average different sources of financing have the expected signs and sizes in terms of their impact on our measure of firm productivity. For instance, retained earnings and equity predict higher level of firm productivity. We find that every one percentage point increase in retained earnings leads to a 0.090 percentage point increase in firm productivity, and every one percentage point increase in equity financing suggests a 0.065 percentage point increase in productivity. On the other hand, we find that bank loans and non-bank loans have negative impact on firm productivity. It indicates that every one percentage point increase in bank loans leads to a 0.036 percentage point decrease in firm productivity, and every one percentage increase in non-bank loans suggests a 0.030 percentage point decrease in productivity. All these coefficients are significant at 1 per cent level of significance.

Turning now to the interaction terms (from columns 2–5), two of the four coefficients are significant in Table 11.3. We find that the role of retained earnings and equity financing on performance are smaller if the firm is a multinational firm. Multinational firms are likely to have 4.3 per cent lower firm performance compared to domestic firms when both of them have 1 per cent increase in retained earnings. Similarly, the role of equity financing on firm performance is 7.4 per cent weaker when the organization is the multinational firm, and these are always precisely estimated.

A sample of multinationals and their subsidiaries

As described in the data section, we are able to find matches between multinational parents and their matched foreign subsidiaries. Over the period 1996–2007, we are able to find 2280 parents and their 8132 subsidiaries, of which 2831 are located in the domestic market, while 5301 subsidiaries are located in the overseas markets. In this sub-sample we aim to find the relationship between subsidiaries' productivity and parents' productivity and their leverage. This approach is in many ways more satisfactory than the traditional methods used in the literature, as one can measure with some precision the actual relevance of the effect from headquarters to subsidiaries.

We now test whether multinational firms' performance and leverage affect their subsidiaries' performance, using the following equation:

$$Y_{it} = \beta_1 HQ'TFP_{jt} + \beta_2 HQ'(D/E) + \lambda X + \alpha_j + \gamma_t + e_{it} \tag{2}$$

where Y_{it} is the TFP of subsidiary i in period t. $HQ'TFP_{jt}$ refers to the TFP of the matched multinational enterprise over the same period. $HQ'(D/E)_{jt}$ refers to the

DOI: 10.1057/9781137367204.0018

debt-to-equity ratio of the matched multinational parent. Equation (2) also includes other control variables, which are (log) retained earnings of matched parent j and (log) total asset of subsidiary i in period t. We also include firm parent fixed effect α_j and business cycle effect γ_t in this equation. The key parameters are β_1 and β_2. β_1 indicates the elasticity of headquarters' TFP on subsidiary's TFP. β_2 indicates whether debt-to-equity ratio of multinationals will influence their subsidiaries' productivity.

A related question addressed in our analysis is whether the effect from headquarters to subsidiaries is the same for domestic and overseas subsidiaries. Table 11.6 reports our main estimates. In this table, the first column includes all subsidiaries (both domestic and overseas subsidiaries), and the second column considers only domestic subsidiaries, while the third column considers overseas subsidiaries.

As documented in Table 11.6, we find that the headquarters' productivity has positive effects on their subsidiaries' productivity, and when we separate by estimating the role of parents' productivity on domestic and overseas subsidiaries productivity, they are still positive and significant, although the latter

Table 11.6 Productivity of subsidiaries and financing of headquarters (a sample of 2280 multinational parents and their 5301 overseas subsidiaries and 2831 domestic subsidiaries)

	(All sub.)	(Domestic sub.)	(Overseas sub.)
TFP, parent	0.143***	0.143***	0.137***
	(0.019)	(0.031)	(0.023)
Debt-to-equity, parent	−0.010	0.013	−0.019
	(0.012)	(0.021)	(0.013)
Retained earning, parent	0.010	0.014	0.007
	(0.006)	(0.010)	(0.008)
Firm size, affiliate	0.231***	0.207***	0.241***
	(0.003)	(0.006)	(0.004)
Obs	34046	10339	23707
No. parents	2280	1052	1613
No. subsidiaries	8132	2831	5301
No. parent countries	42	30	38
No. subsidiary countries	47	30	47
Firm fixed effect	X	X	X
Business cycle effect	X	X	X
R-squared	.553	.623	.590
F statistics	452.194	111.417	356.614

Note: dependant variable is the total factor productivity of subsidiaries in each column. 'Retained earning, parent' and 'Firm size, affiliate' are in logarithm. Values in parentheses are standard errors. Significance levels: *: 0.10; **: 0.05; ***: 0.01.

DOI: 10.1057/9781137367204.0018

effect is smaller. Most importantly, the coefficient on debt-to-equity ratio being insignificant across all columns indicates that multinationals' leverage does not get transmitted to their subsidiaries.[4]

Conclusion

Given the lack of consensus in the literature on how financial distress affects corporate performance, employing firm-level data on over 10,000 firms from 47 countries, this chapter investigated the effect of financial leverage on firm performance, distinguishing multinationals from domestic firms after having controlled for a range of factors namely company size and alternative financing sources. Among the alternative sources of financing, we find that, while retained earnings and equity financing boost firm performance, our results are consistent with the theory of capital structure, and they are statistically and economically significant, and robust. We find that the impact of retained earning and equity financing on performance is smaller if the firm is a multinational firm. Given better access to capital markets by multinational firms, these firms tend to rely on higher financial leverage, which in turn can make them riskier with negative consequences for firms. Also firms operating in different countries can have difficulty overcoming the higher information asymmetry and agency costs of debt due to the differences in legal traditions and institutional settings across countries. Therefore leverage effect can dominate relative to the impact of internally generated funds or equity.

We also examined whether the parent firm performance spills over to the performance of subsidiaries, and found evidence that headquarters' productivity has positive effects on their subsidiaries' productivity. However we found that the high debt ratio of parents does not lead to lower productivity of subsidiaries in domestic and overseas markets. This suggests that multinational firms will not contribute to the severity of global economic crisis, as the debt ratio of multinational firms does not affect the productivity of domestic and overseas subsidiaries. We regard these results as supportive of our main finding about the role of different financing patterns on firm productivity. Overall we conclude from this set of results that parents' productivity contributes to subsidiaries' productivity, but parent firm's leverage does not get transmitted to their subsidiaries in overseas markets.

---

[4] In order to avoid possible endogeneity issue of multinationals' TFP and multinationals' debt-to-equity ratio, we also undertake further tests by including either multinationals' TFP or debt-to-equity in the equation. We still find that results remain the same and hence we conclude that our above results are robust. To save space, we have not included these two tables in the chapter, but they are available upon request.

DOI: 10.1057/9781137367204.0018

References

Acharya, V., Philippon, T., Richardson, M. and Roubini, N. (2009) The financial crisis of 2007–2009: causes and remedies. *Financial Markets, Institutions Instruments*, 18(2): 89–137.

Aghion, P. and Bolton, P. (1992) An incomplete contracts approach to financial contracting. *The Review of Economic Studies*, 59(3): 473–94.

Alfaro, L., Kalemli-Ozcan, S. and Sayek, S. (2009) Productivity and financial development. *World Economy*, 32(1): 111–35.

Arestis, P., Demetriades, P. and Luintel, K. (2001) Financial development and economic growth: the role of stock markets. *Journal of Money, Credit and Banking*, 33(1): 16–41.

Barney, J.B. (1991) Firm resources and sustained competitive advantage. *Journal of Management*, 17(1): 99–120.

Bernard, B.A., Eaton, J., Jensen, B. and Kortum, S. (2003) Plants and productivity in international trade. *American Economic Review*, 93(4): 1268–90.

Buckley, P.J. and Casson, M. (1976) *The Future of the Multinational Enterprise*. New York: The McMillan Company.

Campello, M. (2006) Debt financing: does it boost or hurt firm performance in product markets? *Journal of Financial Economics*, 82(1): 135–72.

Carmassi, J., Gros, D. and Micossi, S. (2009) The global financial crisis: causes and cures. *Journal of Common Market Studies*, 47(5): 977–96.

Dalton, D., Daily, C., Certo, S. and Roengpitya, R. (2003) Meta-analyses of financial performance and equity: fusion or confusion? *The Academy of Management Journal*, 46(1): 13–26.

Demsetz, H. and Villalonga, B. (2001) Ownership structure and corporate performance. *Journal of Corporate Finance*, 7(3): 209–33.

Dunning, J.H. and Lundan, M. (2008) *Multinational Enterprises and the Global Economy*. Cheltenham, UK and Northampron, USA: Edward Elgar.

Girma, S., Thompson, S. and Wright, P. (2006) International acquisitions, domestic competition and firm performance. *International Journal of the Economics of Business*, 13(3): 335–49.

Harris, M. and Raviv, A. (1990) Capital structure and the informational role of debt. *Journal of Finance*, 45(2): 321–49.

Hart, O. (1995) *Firms, Contracts, and Financial Structure*. Oxford: Oxford University Press.

Helpman, E., Melitz, M.J. and Yeaple, S.R. (2004) Export versus FDI with heterogeneous firms. *American Economic Review*, 94(1): 300–16.

Jensen, M. and Meckling, W. (1976) Theory of the firm: managerial behavior, agency costs and ownership structure. *Journal of Financial Economics*, 3(4): 305–60.

Johanson, J. and Vahlne, J.E. (1977) The internationalization process of the firm – a model of knowledge development and increasing foreign market commitments. *Journal of International Business Studies*, 8(1): 23–32.

Johanson, J. and Vahlne, J.E. (2009) The Uppsala internationalization process model revisited: from liability of foreignness to liability of outsidership. *Journal of International Business Studies*, 40(9): 1411–31.

King, R. and Levine, R. (1993) Finance and growth: Schumpeter might be right. *Quarterly Journal of Economics*, 108(3): 717–37.

Krugman, P. (1980) Scale economies, product differentiation, and the pattern of trade. *American Economic Review*, 70(5): 950–9.

DOI: 10.1057/9781137367204.0018

Levine, R. and Zervos, S. (1998) Stock markets, banks, and economic growth. *The American Economic Review*, 88(3): 537–58.

Levinsohn, J. and Petrin, A. (2003) Estimating production functions using inputs to control for unobservables. *Review of Economic Studies*, 70(2): 317–41.

Mallick, S. and Yang, Y. (2011) Sources of financing, profitability and productivity: first evidence from matched firms. *Financial Markets, Institutions and Instruments*, 20(5): 221–52.

Martins, P. and Yang, Y. (2009) The effects of exporting on firm productivity: a meta analysis of the learning-by-exporting hypothesis. *Review of World Economics/ Weltwirtschaftliches Archiv*, 145(3): 434–45.

Melitz, J.M. (2003) The impact of trade on intra-industry reallocations and aggregate industry productivity. *Econometrica*, 71(6): 1695–725.

Myers, C. (1977) Determinants of corporate borrowing. *Journal of Financial Economics*, 5(2): 147–75.

Myers, S. (2001) Capital structure. *Journal of Economic Perspectives*, 15(2): 81–102.

Myers, S. and Majluf, N. (1984) Corporate financing and investment decisions when firms have information that investors do not have. *Journal of Financial Economics*, 13(2): 187–221.

Olley, G.S. and Pakes, A. (1996) The dynamics of productivity in the telecommunications equipment industry. *Econometrica* 64(6): 1263–97.

Ribeiro, S.P., Menghinello, S. and Backer, K.D. (2010) The OECD ORBIS database: responding to the need for firm-level micro-data in the OECD, OECD Statistics Working Papers 2010/1.

Stulz, R. (1990) Managerial discretion and optimal financing policies. *Journal of Financial Economics*, 26(1): 3–27.

Vernon, R. (1966) International investment and international trade in the product cycle. *Quarterly Journal of Economics*, 80(2): 190–207.

Weinstein, D.E. and Yafeh, Y. (1998) On the costs of a bank-centered financial system: evidence from the changing main bank relations in Japan. *The Journal of Finance*, 53(2): 635–72.

Yang, Y. and Mallick, S. (2010) Self-selection, export premium and learning-by-exporting: evidence from Chinese matched firms. *The World Economy*, 33(10): 1218–40.

DOI: 10.1057/9781137367204.0018

12
The Role of Language in Bilateral FDI: A Forgotten Factor?

Palitha Konara and Yingqi Wei

Introduction

The rapid development of modern transportation, information and communication technologies has accelerated the pace of globalization. Multinational enterprises (MNEs) have increasingly broadened their use of foreign direct investment (FDI), and as a result they often need to deal with multiple languages and the associated administrative and transactions costs that come with language differences (Luo and Shenkar, 2006; Welch et al., 2001). FDI involves production, organization and management of business activities. The key to the success often lies in effective interactions and communications within MNEs and between MNEs and economic agents in host countries. To this end, language distance (LD) between home and host countries tends to influence FDI location choice.

There exists a sizable literature that explicitly and systematically examines the impact of differences/commonalities in languages on bilateral trade (Egger and Lassmann, 2012). However studies on language and bilateral FDI are few and far between with the exceptions of Goldberg et al. (2005), Hejazi and Ma (2011) and Oh et al. (2011). Most studies of FDI that do recognize the role of language have treated it as a component of cultural, psychic and/or administrative distance (Dow and Karunaratna, 2006; Welch et al., 2001). Due to the dearth of research this field has been described as 'the most neglected field in management' and 'the forgotten factor' (Harzing et al., 2011; Marschan et al., 1997).

To address the research gap, we use bilateral FDI flows between 29 OECD countries and 111 partner countries during the period 1986–2008 to investigate the impact of LD on FDI. The sample coverage is larger than previous studies (Goldberg et al., 2005; Hejazi and Ma, 2011; Oh et al., 2011). The measure of the LD variable used, capturing the incidence of one country's dominant language(s) in another country, represents all major languages and the total

DOI: 10.1057/9781137367204.0019

population of countries (Dow and Karunaratna, 2006) and therefore is more comprehensive than previously employed constructs that often do not take into account the possibility that MNEs and economic agents of host countries can communicate via a non-official language, for example, a lingua franca. Moreover the study includes a relatively extensive set of FDI determinants as control variables.

The remainder of this chapter proceeds as follows. We review the literature and develop a conceptual framework to explain how language matters to FDI location decisions. Then the chapter discusses data and methodology, followed by empirical analysis, before concluding in the final section with implications.

How language matters to FDI?

Liability of foreignness (Hymer, 1976), that is, the difficulties that MNEs must overcome when undertaking FDI in a host country, is a key factor that influences their location decisions. Differences in languages increase the liability of foreignness (Berry et al., 2010; Luo and Shenkar, 2006) and the uncertainties of international transactions (Dow and Karunaratna, 2006). FDI is particularly sensitive to LD because the extent of operational interactions with economic agents in the host country is much higher for FDI than that of other international transactions such as trade and licensing. LD can be associated with high information costs, which make legitimacy building in a host country difficult; it creates complications in transferring core competencies to MNEs' host country subsidiaries and affects the efficiency of global production networks (GPNs). As a result, it hinders bilateral FDI flows between countries.

Zaheer and Mosakowski (1997) contend that liability of foreignness arises 'mainly from the foreign firm not being sufficiently embedded in the information networks in the country of location'. Larger LD gives rise to higher informational disadvantages that imply higher costs. Language difference increases costs of communications/interpretation and the risk of miscommunication/misinterpretation. Human interactions are an important dimension of FDI both in the set up and the management of international ventures. Effective human interactions through language usage enable MNEs to acquire, present and interpret information in order to distinguish between good and bad investments, improve post-investment management and possibly increase subsequent investments (Goldberg et al., 2005). For example, when collecting information and undertaking business negotiations prior to FDI being made, the cost and efficiency may differ across MNEs due to LD, which in turn affects the FDI location decision. When managing employees in the host country and communicating with local suppliers and customers after FDI is made, MNEs incur different levels of costs again due to LD. Language barriers can create

DOI: 10.1057/9781137367204.0019

frustration, conflict, mistrust and resistance among co-workers in the MNE and between the MNE's personnel and those of the suppliers and customers (Vidal-Suárez and López-Duarte, 2013), all of which contribute towards increasing the transaction costs of FDI.

To operate effectively in a host country, MNEs need to gain institutional legitimacy (Xu and Shenkar, 2002). Institutional theory suggests that organizations gain a 'common understanding of what is appropriate and fundamentally meaningful behaviour' as a result of isomorphic pressures embedded in different institutional contexts (Zucker, 1983). MNEs must align their practices with the host country environment when seeking acceptance as legitimate entities (Davis et al., 2000; Kostova and Zaheer, 1999). The locus of efforts must be closely linked to language. The existence of language barriers may complicate communications between the MNE and economic agents in the host country and result in filtration (the partial transmission of messages) and distortion (intended meaning is altered during the transmission of the message) (Vidal-Suárez and López-Duarte, 2013). This therefore could prolong the host country's 'continuing suspicion towards the MNE' (Kostova and Zaheer, 1999) and adversely affects MNE legitimacy building (Luo and Shenkar, 2006). As a result, MNEs are cautious in undertaking FDI in countries where they face large LD.

Language barriers can act as a significant impediment to knowledge transfer and information sharing (Welch and Welch, 2008). It has long been established in international business literature that MNEs need their own ownership advantages to overcome liability of foreignness. Knowledge and information flows across national borders and within the MNE are vital for its success (Kogut and Zander, 1992). The effectiveness of knowledge transfer and information sharing depends on the language ability of both the sender and the receiver. Language 'determines aspects such as who has the information and knowledge, whether and how it is articulated, when and if it is shared, and in what form' (Welch and Welch, 2008). The sender needs to use the language that can be understood by the receiver to accurately encode and articulate a meaningful, complete message. The receiver needs to decode and assimilate the message as it is intended. In the course of this process, personal communication through the language medium, for clarification and interpretation, is essential for both the sender and the receiver to check for transmission accuracy and consistency. Large LD can easily lead to the distortion of the original message, translation errors, codification problems or even the blockage of knowledge and information flows, while a common language gives MNEs confidence to undertake more FDI in the host country.

LD may hinder successful management, coordination and integration of a MNE's GPNs and slow down business processes. In a GPN, leading MNEs potentially disperse all elements of the value added chain and incorporate

DOI: 10.1057/9781137367204.0019

their supply, knowledge and customer base into the network (Ernst and Kim, 2002; Hanson, 2012; Hayakawa and Yamashita, 2011; Kim, 2012). Accordingly, the MNE must focus on internal communication among the corporate headquarter and subsidiaries scattered around the world and external communication with global suppliers and customers. Barner-Rasmussen and Aarnio (2011) demonstrate that there is widespread bilingualism and multilingualism in MNEs. Subsidiaries use several different languages to communicate with other units both within and outside the MNE – often two different languages in parallel. As argued already, LD disturbs international information flows, making administrative/governance activities such as supervision and management of subsidiaries and coordination with suppliers more difficult. Opportunistic behaviour (shirking) is more likely as LD increases. Language differences also contribute to power distortion, which affects communication. For all parties involved in a GPN, a functional language must be selected, that is, the language formally designed for verbal and written use in order to be able to work together (Luo and Shenkar, 2006). However such functional language could become a control mechanism and empowers individuals whose native language is the functional language to be in a stronger position in controlling information and influencing decisions. On the other hand, other parties in the GPN whose native language is different from the functional language may feel that they have relinquished some of the control over the relationship. As a result there could be a loss of credibility and trust, causing the disturbance of information flows and knowledge exchange between the two sides (Harzing and Feely, 2008; Harzing et al., 2011).

On the empirical side, an observation in the FDI literature is the country-bias effect, that is, FDI source countries tend to invest more in host countries that use the same language. For example, much of Chinese FDI inflows originate from East Asian countries with similar ethnic backgrounds and countries that have large Chinese Diaspora (Wei and Wang, 2009); Indian FDI inflows mainly come from English speaking countries (Aggarwal, 2008); and some of the major recipients of Turkish FDI are newly independent Turkish speaking Central Asian Republics (Demirbag et al., 1998). Lundan and Jones (2001) suggest that the widespread use of the English language, along with other similarities within the Commonwealth, have lowered the cost of foreignness, and thereby increased bilateral trade and investment among the Commonwealth members. Adding to these, there is a tendency for MNEs to confine their early expansion to regions within their language groups (Welch et al., 2001). In many MNEs, staff in different countries are often required to operate in a common corporate language (Harzing et al., 2011; Travis Selmier and Oh, 2012; Welch and Welch, 2008), and therefore language skills are an important consideration of MNE strategy.

DOI: 10.1057/9781137367204.0019

There are a limited number of large-scale systematic empirical studies on the LD-FDI link. To the best of our knowledge, only three papers – Goldberg et al. (2005), Hejazi and Ma (2011) and Oh et al. (2011) – give attention to the topic. The findings are mixed. Goldberg et al. (2005) use the language difference between countries to proxy the level of personal contact and investigate how it affects US inward and outward FDI. English as a common language is found to affect US MNEs' investments abroad but not foreign MNEs' investments in the US. Hejazi and Ma (2011) examine the role of six more languages (Dutch, French, German, Italian, Spanish and Swedish) in addition to English in explaining bilateral FDI stocks among 30 OECD countries. By employing one common language dummy and seven language-specific dummies, they reveal that common languages have a positive impact on FDI. Common English language has above-average positive impact and, among all language-specific dummies, English is the only statistically significant one for both outward and inward FDI. An alternative measure of LD constructed by Chiswick and Miller (2005) is based on the difficulties faced by Americans to learn foreign languages. It also shows that having an official language that is linguistically close to English is more likely to enhance inward FDI. Oh et al. (2011) assess FDI from 28 OECD countries to 115 countries (28 OECD countries and 87 non-OECD countries) and use language dummies for English, French, Spanish and Arabic and the direct communication variable from Melitz (2008) to capture language effects. Melitz's (2008) construct is created by working out the percentage of speakers in a country pair who can communicate directly. There is strong evidence that shared language positively affects bilateral FDI.

Among these studies, Goldberg et al. (2005) is the only one with a theoretical model. Despite concerted efforts in the theoretical development, the paper relies on a stringent assumption. If country i accounts for x per cent of total world FDI, it is expected that x per cent of country j's inward FDI should be coming from country i. The discrepancy between the expected FDI and the received FDI, termed as abnormal FDI, is assumed to be due to personal interactions proxied by distance, language and travel. The expected FDI is assumed to take place due to other FDI determinants. This naive assumption brings about fallacies that render empirical testing unreliable.

There are several limitations on the empirical parts of these papers. The first is the use of FDI stocks as the dependent variable instead of FDI flows. As recognized by Goldberg et al. (2005), FDI stocks can be understated or overstated to the extent of differences between market and historical-cost values at different times. Considering FDI stocks instead of flows not only restricts the sample size but also overlooks the important time sensitive dynamics of the relationship between the regressors and the regressand.

Secondly, the language variables used are not comprehensive enough to capture the language distance applicable to FDI; that is, capacity to communicate

DOI: 10.1057/9781137367204.0019

in official languages may not be essential because MNEs can operate in a lingua franca. Moreover the scope of the previous studies is restricted to mainly English language, or a limited number of languages. Goldberg et al. (2005) study only English. Hejazi and Ma (2011) investigate seven languages; however the sample only covers 30 developed countries and for four out of seven languages (Spanish, Dutch, Italian and Swedish) there are only one or two country pairs in the sample, thereby seriously weakening some of the inferences. In Oh et al. (2011), when common language dummies are adopted, only four languages are considered. Using Melitz's (2008) measure, only 29 out of the total of over 5000 languages are taken into account.

Finally, important FDI determinants such as market size and trade openness, which has been shown to be the most robust variables in the empirical literature (Chakrabarti, 2001), need to be controlled for. Most importantly, none of the studies have controlled for human capital, which can be strongly linked to FDI flows (Noorbakhsh et al., 2001) as well as language capabilities. Such omission can bias the results.

Data and methodology

The sample covers bilateral FDI between 29 OECD and 111 partner countries, of which 29 are OECD and 82 non-OECD countries (see Appendix for a full list). Altogether, there are 4820 country pairs. Data source and variable measurements are provided in Table 12.1.

The gravity model is widely used in empirical studies of bilateral trade, and recently in the FDI literature (e.g. Anderson and van Wincoop, 2003; Egger and Lassmann, 2012; Guerin and Manzocchi, 2009; Melitz, 2008; Wang et al., 2007; Wang et al., 2010; Zwinkels and Beugelsdijk, 2010). However statistics for FDI are different from those for trade because there are many more non-positive values for the former than for the latter. Using log transformation excludes non-positive values in the estimations. Given 53 per cent of the observations in our sample are non-positive, leaving these out could lead to selection bias; that is, if linguistically distant countries tend to have zero FDI flows between them, then dismissing them would undermine the whole purpose of our research. In the literature, adding sufficiently large constant values to dependent variables is often adopted to transform non-positive into positive values. Dhanaraj and Beamish (2009) propose an alternative solution – taking the logged absolute value of the variable, incrementing it by one, then multiplying by the sign of the original variable. Given the extent of non-positive values in the sample and the range of FDI spanning from $-48 billion to $172 billion (see Table 12.2), the bias introduced from various forms of transformations could be considerably large. We therefore select a linear model to probe the relationship between LD and FDI.

DOI: 10.1057/9781137367204.0019

Table 12.1   Variable measurement

Variable	Description	Measurement	Data source
FDI	FDI	Bilateral FDI flow from home country *j* to host country *i* at time *t*	OECD's International Direct Investment Database (2012)
LD	Language distance	5-point scale based on the incidence (p) of home country *j*'s dominant language(s) in host country *i* 5 = p < 1 per cent; 4 = 1 per cent p < 5 per cent; 3 = 5 per cent p < 50 per cent; 2 = 50 per cent p < 90 per cent; 1 = p 90 per cent	
RD	Religious distance	5-point scale based on the incidence (p) of home country *j*'s dominant religion(s) in host country *i* 5 = p < 1 per cent; 4 = 1 per cent p < 5 per cent; 3 = 5 per cent p < 50 per cent; 2 = 50 per cent p < 90 per cent; 1 = p 90 per cent	Dow and Karunaratna (2006)
GDP_HOME	Market size of home country *j*	GDP of home country *j*	
GDP_HOST	Market size of host country *i*	GDP of host country *i*	UNCTAD database
OPEN	Trade openness of host country *i*	Represented by trade intensity (X+M/GDP), where X and M are exports and imports, respectively	
MOBILE	Infrastructure of host country *i*	Mobile cellular subscriptions per 100 people	World development indicators
HC	Human capital of host country *i*	Secondary school enrolment (per cent gross)	

We estimate the following model.

$$\text{FDI}_{ijt} = \beta_0 + \beta_1 LD_{ij} + \beta_2 RD_{ij} + \beta_3 GDP_{jt} + \beta_4 GDP_{it} + \beta_5 OPEN_{it} + \beta_6 MOBILE_{it} + \beta_7 HC_{it} + \mu_i + \mu_j + \delta_t + \gamma_{ij} + \varepsilon_{ijt} \tag{1}$$

Where FDI_{ijt} is bilateral FDI flows between host country *i* and home country *j* at time *t*. RD_{ij} is religion distance measured as the incidence of country *j*'s

DOI: 10.1057/9781137367204.0019

dominant religion(s) in country i. GDP_{jt} and GDP_{it} are GDP of country j and i at time t and are used to indicate market size of the home and host countries, respectively. HC is human capital, proxied by secondary education enrolment rate. OPEN is trade openness, represented by trade intensity (total trade as a percentage of GDP). MOBILE is the mobile cellular subscriptions per 100 people in the host country as a proxy for the level of infrastructure. The controls μ_i, μ_j, δ_t and γ_{ij} are host-country-specific, home-country-specific, year-specific and country-pair-specific (dyadic) effects respectively. The term ε_{ijt} is the white noise disturbance term. We expect the coefficients β_3–β_7 to be positive as is consistent with the literature.

LD$_{ij}$ is language distance (our primary focus) and is measured as the incidence of country j's dominant language(s) in country i based on the indicator developed by Dow and Karunaratna (2006). This indicator is a five point scale that measures the proportion of the population (p) in the host country who are able to speak the major language(s) of the home country. The five point scale is coded as follows: five if p is less than 1 per cent, four if p is greater than or equal to 1 per cent but less than 5 per cent, three if p is greater than or equal to 5 per cent but less than 50 per cent, two if p is greater than or equal to 50 per cent but less than 90 per cent and one if p is greater than or equal to 90 per cent. Therefore as LD$_{1j}$ increases, language distance increases. For example, Canada has two major languages (English and French), the UK has one major language (English) and France has one major language (French). Since the percentage of English and French speakers in Canada are approximately 61 per cent and 23 per cent, respectively (Lewis et al., 2013), the value of the indicator variable is equal to 2 for FDI flows from UK to Canada and 3 for FDI flows from France to Canada. We expect β_2 to be negative for the reasons discussed already.

Econometrically, we can treat μ_i, μ_j, δ_t and γ_{ij} as random variables (error component approach) or fixed parameters (fixed effects approach). When unobserved characteristics are correlated with explanatory variables, the random effects estimator leads to biased and inconsistent estimates of the parameters. In such a situation, fixed effects estimation, which uses deviations from individual means to estimate parameters, is preferred over random effects. However time-invariant variables are eliminated in the fixed effects transformation. Therefore we cannot use dyadic-specific fixed effects given our interest in time-invariant bilateral variables (i.e. LD and RD). However we can use fixed effects for home-country, host-country and time-specific effects. This enables us to account for host and home country heterogeneity and business cycle effects (Anderson and van Wincoop, 2003). Many studies have advocated and employed this approach (see e.g. Ku and Zussman, 2010; Oh et al., 2011).

The existing literature has repeatedly emphasized the potential endogeneity between FDI and GDP (Wang et al., 2010), but this issue is unlikely to be critical in our study. Bilateral FDI flows between any pair of countries

DOI: 10.1057/9781137367204.0019

tend to be a fraction of the aggregate (multilateral) FDI flows to or from any country. Therefore the impact of an individual country's bilateral FDI flow on the host/home country's GDP is small. Employing the Durbin–Wu–Hausman (DWH) test for endogeneity, Wang et al. (2010) show that endogeneity between bilateral FDI and partner countries' GDP is insignificant. Therefore we can reasonably expect there is no potential endogeneity issue of GDP that could compromise the validity of our study.

Results

Table 12.2 presents descriptive statistics and correlation coefficients for the variables used in the estimations. Results of three sets of baseline estimations for full sample, sample based on FDI outflows from OECD countries (subsample 1) and that based on FDI inflows to OECD countries (sub-sample 2) are shown in Table 12.3. In all three samples, the variable of our concern, LD is negative and statistically significant as expected. However the coefficients are higher in the sub-sample 1 than those in the sub-sample 2. Therefore the effects of LD appear to be more pronounced for FDI outflows from OECD countries than FDI inflows to OECD countries. This difference may have resulted due to the use of English language as a lingua franca in international business. Most of the developing countries use English as a lingua franca in their local business environment even when English is not spoken widely in the country. Such a country can undertake horizontal FDI in English-speaking developed countries with less hassle compared to horizontal FDI undertaken by latter in the former. For example, since India's businesses operate mostly in English, a MNE from India may comfortably interact with English speaking customers in an English speaking country. But an English speaking MNE from an English speaking country may find it difficult to interact with Indian customers, many of whom do not speak English.

Control variables mostly have the expected signs for their coefficients. GDP of both home and host countries and infrastructure (MOBILE) are of the usual order and are robustly positive and statistically significant. When country-specific fixed effects are not included, RD, trade openness (OPEN) and human capital (HC) are statistically significant. However when a large number of country dummies are introduced, in some estimations, either they lose statistical significance or their signs change. This is not surprising. It is well recognized in the literature that the estimation of the coefficients of slow moving variables performs inefficiently when fixed effects are used (Plümper and Troeger, 2007) and movements of OPEN and HC over time (within variation) are small.

It is noticeable that results for the second sub-sample based on FDI inflows to OECD countries appear weaker than those for the first sub-sample based on FDI outflows from OECD countries. This is acceptable since our model relies heavily on

DOI: 10.1057/9781137367204.0019

Table 12.2 Descriptive statistics and correlation matrix

Variable	Full sample				Correlation coefficients							FDI outflows from OECD sample				FDI inflows to OECD sample			
	Mean	Std. dv.	Min	Max	1	2	3	4	5	6	7	Mean	Std. dv.	Min	Max	Mean	Std. dv.	Min	Max
1 FDI	277.2	2389.3	-48323.2	172210.1								431.4	2980.0	-48323.2	172210.1	329.7	2718.4	-59139.6	108566.0
2 LD	4.8	0.6	1.0	5.0	-0.11							4.8	0.7	1.0	5.0	4.8	0.7	1.0	5.0
3 RD	2.7	1.4	1.0	5.0	-0.04	0.11						2.4	1.3	1.0	5.0	2.7	1.4	1.0	5.0
4 GDP_HOME	745.2	1764.6	0.2	11670.8	0.14	-0.08	0.01					1121.6	2135.7	5.8	11670.8	479.7	1399.4	0.2	11670.8
5 GDP_HOST	677.8	1654.8	0.2	11670.8	0.13	-0.18	0.06	-0.07				474.2	1379.8	0.2	11670.8	999.2	1984.7	5.8	11670.8
6 OPEN	83	57	11	446	0.01	0.06	0.05	0	0			84	60	11	446	80	50	16	320
7 MOBILE	49	45	0	166	0.04	0.04	0.03	-0.1	0	-0.27		40	42	0	166	60	45	0	151
8 HC	90.0	26.7	5.0	162.3	0.04	-0.01	-0.04	-0.13	0.11	-0.01	0.39	81.9	28.9	5.0	162.3	103.5	15.2	43.9	162.3

Table 12.3 The effect of language on bilateral FDI flows

Dependent variable: FDI flows	Full sample		FDI outflows from OECD sample (FDI flows from OECD countries to OECD and non-OECD countries)		FDI inflows to OECD sample (FDI flows from OECD and non-OECD countries to OECD countries)	
LD	−229.3**	−219.3***	−367.5***	−394.9***	−229.2**	−231.0**
	(91.12)	(80.36)	(135.5)	(120.5)	(116.0)	(102.6)
RD	−21.36	−67.99***	−77.66***	−81.20***	16.03	−89.06***
	(15.69)	(11.57)	(27.04)	(19.29)	(23.59)	(16.12)
GDP_HOME	0.390***	0.188***	0.297**	0.157***	0.685***	0.323***
	(0.117)	(0.0346)	(0.124)	(0.0335)	(0.201)	(0.0672)
GDP_HOST	0.196*	0.176***	0.789***	0.474***	0.358***	0.179***
	(0.116)	(0.0471)	(0.288)	(0.114)	(0.128)	(0.0506)
OPEN	1.756**	1.185***	1.112	1.597***	−3.974	2.301**
	(0.891)	(0.410)	(1.195)	(0.567)	(3.003)	(1.013)
MOBILE	2.420***	2.780***	3.619***	4.917***	2.347	−0.419
	(0.769)	(0.688)	(1.055)	(0.989)	(2.799)	(2.117)
HC	−1.646	1.184**	−5.482**	1.456*	−2.049	−1.212
	(1.214)	(0.600)	(2.150)	(0.864)	(1.905)	(1.209)
Constant	−184.0	659.3*	1,201*	1,320**	516.4	791.6
	(448.5)	(374.5)	(647.5)	(549.0)	(537.4)	(519.0)
Year fixed effect	YES	YES	YES	YES	YES	YES
Host country fixed effect	YES	NO	YES	NO	YES	NO
Home country fixed effect	YES	NO	YES	NO	YES	NO
Adjusted-R^2	0.0921	0.0530	0.132	0.0873	0.113	0.0591
N	46,169	46,169	28,436	28,436	28,859	28,859
Country pairs	4,820	4,820	2,773	2,773	2,769	2,769

Note: *t*-statistics are based on robust standard errors and are in parentheses.
*, **, and *** represent significance at the 10 per cent, 5 per cent and 1 per cent level, respectively.
Country-specific fixed effects and year specific fixed effects are not reported for brevity.

host country characteristics to explain FDI flows and the second sample includes only 29 host countries compared to the first sample with 111 host countries.

Dynamic effects of language on bilateral FDI

This section considers an extension of the previous results. The evolution of technological development has facilitated interactions between countries. We therefore expect that the impact of language on bilateral FDI may change with time. First, we divided the full sample into two temporal sub-samples; 1985–96

DOI: 10.1057/9781137367204.0019

and 1997–2008. Estimated results are presented in Table 11.4. LD is negative for both periods but the magnitudes are far greater for the latter period than those for the former period. Moreover for the former period, the estimated coefficient is marginally statistically insignificant when country-specific fixed effects are included. Therefore the results suggest an increasingly more negative impact of language distance on FDI flows over time. We also estimate the full sample with an interaction term between LD and time trend variable (Trend). The term is negative and highly significant; again indicating that the negative impact of LD on FDI flows is increasing over time. The results therefore suggest that FDI

Table 12.4 Dynamic effect of language on bilateral FDI flows

Dependent variable: FDI flows	For the period 1985–96		For the period 1997–2008		For the period 1985–2008 with interaction term between language distance and year	
LD	−97.61*	−77.07	−269.0**	−285.9***	32.12	101.6*
	(59.28)	(54.04)	(108.4)	(102.7)	(80.83)	(60.08)
LD x Trend					−17.81***	−21.38***
					(6.273)	(6.662)
RD	−18.43	−23.92**	−17.95	−77.20***	−18.78	−66.49***
	(24.23)	(12.18)	(16.04)	(11.64)	(16.04)	(11.52)
GDP_HOME	0.822***	0.154***	0.321	0.190***	0.367***	0.187***
	(0.175)	(0.0320)	(0.222)	(0.0367)	(0.116)	(0.0345)
GDP_HOST	0.366**	0.120**	−0.462	0.171***	0.147	0.172***
	(0.178)	(0.0483)	(0.489)	(0.0458)	(0.110)	(0.0469)
OPEN	−0.648	0.453**	2.312*	1.468***	2.030**	1.187***
	(0.453)	(0.203)	(1.362)	(0.488)	(0.893)	(0.410)
MOBILE	1.670	3.710	0.00237	2.095***	2.541***	2.912***
	(3.114)	(3.138)	(0.703)	(0.708)	(0.759)	(0.689)
HC	1.599**	1.428***	−0.151	2.050**	−1.660	1.182**
	(0.753)	(0.527)	(2.414)	(0.811)	(1.212)	(0.599)
Constant	−165.9	37.73	−136.6	1,162**	−1,452***	−848.1***
	(382.8)	(283.4)	(503.0)	(498.7)	(451.4)	(307.5)
Year fixed effect	YES	YES	YES	YES	YES	YES
Host country fixed effect	YES	NO	YES	NO	YES	NO
Home country fixed effect	YES	NO	YES	NO	YES	NO
Adjusted-R²	0.185	0.110	0.0975	0.0511	0.0927	0.0531
N	12,189	12,189	33,980	33,980	46,169	46,169
Country pairs	1,796	1,796	4,747	4,747	4,820	4,820

Note: *t*-statistics are based on robust standard errors and are in parentheses.
*, **, and *** represent significance at the 10 per cent, 5 per cent and 1 per cent level, respectively.
Country-specific fixed effects and year specific fixed effects are not reported for brevity.

DOI: 10.1057/9781137367204.0019

flows are getting increasingly self-selected to bilateral partner countries that speak the same language(s). Likewise, Egger and Lassmann (2012), conducting a meta-analysis based on 81 academic articles that study language-trade links, find evidence for an increasing language effect on trade over time.

Summary and conclusion

In this chapter, we attempt to probe the role of language in FDI. Language is important in every aspect of a firm's FDI operation. It could impose internal challenges affecting interactions between sections, departments and divisions, between headquarters and subsidiaries, and between subsidiaries. It could equally impose external challenges in MNEs' dealing with consumers, suppliers and government agents. We attempt to provide a conceptual framework to demonstrate how language can exert influence on FDI location decision and empirically assess the independent and influential role of language. Understanding language-FDI links is critical for two reasons. Extent research on the determinants of FDI has leaned heavily on economic factors such as GDP and trade openness, the role of language remains understudied. By undertaking this study, we have attempted to address this research gap. Second, the study could potentially validate the prescription of language strategies, which have not been systematically adopted and implemented by countries.

Our findings show a strong negative relationship between language and bilateral FDI flows; countries that have less language distance tend to have higher bilateral FDI flows between them. We also find evidence for a dynamic effect of language on bilateral FDI flows; the negative relationship between language distance and FDI flows appears to be increasing over time. Therefore our results indicate that language is becoming more and more important in determining bilateral FDI flows. Our results are robust. We address the structural deficiencies and misspecifications identified in the previous studies. We include a relatively extensive set of control variables and control for bilateral characteristics that might be correlated with bilateral FDI flows as well as language distance. Our sample is inclusive in terms of both country coverage and language measurement, improving the generalizability of our study.

The findings have important implications for policymakers in both host and home countries. Since language differences seem crucial in deciding bilateral FDI flows, both host and home countries should give more attention to their language strategy and FDI strategy and try to align both to get the maximum benefit. Countries in which only vernacular languages are spoken or countries that are linguistically distant from major FDI source countries are likely to be at a disadvantage in attracting FDI. On the other hand, firms in countries that are linguistically distant from other countries may find it difficult to expand beyond their borders. One possible solution to mitigate this issue could be to

DOI: 10.1057/9781137367204.0019

train the workforce of such a country in the most widely spoken lingua franca in international business. For example, for a country in which English is not spoken, acquisition of English language proficiency could improve the prospects of attracting FDI from English speaking countries as well as improve competitiveness of local firms in the international arena. Our findings can also inform MNEs about the importance of language differences in the distribution of international activities around the globe. MNEs could benefit by improving their own linguistic skills within the firm; MNEs with wider linguistic capabilities can afford to be more flexible when their locational choices are made.

Appendix

Table 12A.1 List of countries used in the study

OECD (29)	Non-OECD (82)		
Australia	Algeria	Jordan	Serbia
Austria	Argentina	Kazakhstan	Sierra Leone
Belgium	Bahrain	Kenya	Singapore
Canada	Bangladesh	Kuwait	Slovenia
Czech Republic	Brazil	Lao People's Dem. Rep.	Solomon Islands
Denmark	Bulgaria	Latvia	South Africa
Finland	Cameroon	Lebanon	Sri Lanka
France	Chile	Libyan Arab Jamahiriya	Sudan
Germany	China	Lithuania	Suriname
Greece	Colombia	Madagascar	Syrian Arab Republic
Hungary	Congo, Dem. Rep. of	Malaysia	Tanzania, United Rep. of
Iceland	Costa Rica	Malta	Thailand
Ireland	Cote d'Ivoire	Mexico	Trinidad and Tobago
Italy	Croatia	Morocco	Uganda
Japan	Ecuador	Mozambique	Ukraine
Korea, Republic of	Egypt	Nepal	United Arab Emirates
Luxembourg	El Salvador	New Caledonia	Uruguay
Netherlands	Estonia	Nigeria	Uzbekistan
New Zealand	Ethiopia	Oman	Vanuatu
Norway	Fiji	Pakistan	Venezuela
Poland	French Polynesia	Panama	Vietnam
Portugal	Ghana	Papua New Guinea	Yemen
Slovakia	Guatemala	Peru	Zambia
Spain	Hong Kong	Philippines	Zimbabwe
Sweden	India	Qatar	
Switzerland	Indonesia	Romania	
Turkey	Iran	Russian Federation	
United Kingdom	Israel	Samoa	
United States of America	Jamaica	Saudi Arabia	

DOI: 10.1057/9781137367204.0019

References

Aggarwal, A. (2008) *Regional Economic Integration and FDI in South Asia: Prospects and Problems*. Indian Council for Research on International Economic Relations.

Anderson, J.E. and van Wincoop, E. (2003) Gravity with gravitas: a solution to the border puzzle. *American Economic Review*, 93(1): 170–92.

Barner-Rasmussen, W. and Aarnio, C. (2011) Shifting the faultlines of language: a quantitative functional-level exploration of language use in MNC subsidiaries. *Journal of World Business*, 46: 288–95.

Berry, H., Guillen, M.F. and Zhou, N. (2010) An institutional approach to cross-national distance. *Journal of International Business Studies*, 41(9): 1460–80.

Chakrabarti, A. (2001) The determinants of foreign direct investment: sensitivity analyses of cross-country regressions. *Kyklos*, 54: 89–113.

Chiswick, B.R. and Miller, P.W. (2005) Linguistic distance: a quantitative measure of the distance between English and other languages. *Journal of Multilingual and Multicultural Development*, 26(1): 1–11.

Davis, P.S., Desai, A.B. and Francis, J.D. (2000) Mode of international entry: an isomorphism perspective. *Journal of International Business Studies*, 31(2): 239–58.

Demirbag, M., Gunes, R. and Mirza, H. (1998) Political risk management: a case study of Turkish companies in Central Asia and Russia, in Mirza, H. (ed.) *Global Competitive Strategies in the New World Economy*. London: Edward Elgar.

Dhanaraj, C. and Beamish, P.W. (2009) Institutional environment and subsidiary survival. *Management International Review*, 49(3): 291–312.

Dow, D. and Karunaratna, A. (2006) Developing a multidimensional instrument to measure psychic distance stimuli. *Journal of International Business Studies*, 37(5): 578–602.

Egger, P.H. and Lassmann, A. (2012) The language effect in international trade: a meta-analysis. *Economics Letters*, 116(2): 221–24.

Ernst, D. and Kim, L. (2002) Global production networks, knowledge diffusion, and local capability formation. *Research Policy*, 31(8/9): 1417–29.

Goldberg, M.A., Heinkel, R.L. and Levi, M.D. (2005) Foreign direct investment: the human dimension. *Journal of International Money and Finance*, 24(6): 913–34.

Guerin, S. and Manzocchi, S. (2009) Political regime and FDI from advanced to emerging countries. *Review of World Economics*, 145(1): 75–91.

Hanson, G.H. (2012) The rise of middle kingdoms: emerging economies in global trade. *Journal of Economic Perspectives*, 26(2): 41–64.

Harzing, A.-W. and Feely, A.J. (2008) The language barrier and its implications for HQ-subsidiary relationships. *Cross Cultural Management: An International Journal*, 15(1): 49–61.

Harzing, A.-W., Köster, K. and Magner, U. (2011) Babel in business: the language barrier and its solutions in the HQ-subsidiary relationship. *Journal of World Business*, 46(3): 279–87.

Hayakawa, K. and Yamashita, N. (2011) The role of preferential trade agreements (PTAs) in facilitating global production networks. *Journal of World Trade*, 45(6): 1181–207.

Hejazi, W. and Ma, J. (2011) Gravity, the English language and international business. *Multinational Business Review*, 19(2): 152–67.

Hymer, S.H. (1976) *The International Operations of National Firms: A Study of Foreign Direct Investment*. Cambridge, MA: MIT Press.

Kim, W.B. (2012) The rise of coastal China and inter-regional relations among core economic regions of East Asia. *Annals of Regional Science*, 48: 283–99.

DOI: 10.1057/9781137367204.0019

Kogut, B. and Zander, U. (1992) Knowledge of the firm, combinative capabilities, and the replication of technology. *Organization Science*, 3(3): 383–97.

Kostova, T. and Zaheer, S. (1999) Organizational legitimacy under conditions of complexity: the case of the multinational enterprise. *Academy of Management Review*, 24(1): 64–81.

Ku, H. and Zussman, A. (2010) Lingua franca: the role of English in international trade. *Journal of Economic Behavior & Organization*, 75(2): 250–60.

Lewis, M.P., Simons, G.F. and Fennig, C.D. (eds) (2013) *Ethnologue: Languages of the World*, 17th edn. Dallas, Texas: SIL International.

Lundan, S.M. and Jones, G. (2001) The 'Commonwealth Effect' and the process of internationalisation. *World Economy*, 24(1): 99–118.

Luo, Y. and Shenkar, O. (2006) The multinational corporation as a multilingual community: language and organization in a global context. *Journal of International Business Studies*, 37(3): 321–39.

Marschan, R., Welch, D. and Welch, L. (1997) Language: the forgotten factor in multinational management. *European Management Journal*, 15(5): 591–8.

Melitz, J. (2008) Language and foreign trade. *European Economic Review*, 52(4): 667–99.

Noorbakhsh, F., Paloni, A. and Youssef, A. (2001) Human capital and FDI inflows to developing countries: new empirical evidence. *World Development*, 29(9): 1593–610.

Oh, C.H., Travis Selmier, W. and Lien, D. (2011) International trade, foreign direct investment, and transaction costs in languages. *The Journal of Socio-Economics*, 40(6): 732–5.

Plümper, T. and Troeger, V.E. (2007) Efficient estimation of time-invariant and rarely changing variables in finite sample panel analyses with unit fixed effects. *Political Analysis*, 15(2): 124–39.

Travis Selmier, W. and Oh, C.H. (2012) International business complexity and the internationalization of languages. *Business Horizons*, 55: 189–200.

Vidal-Suárez, M. and López-Duarte, C. (2013) Language distance and international acquisitions: a transaction cost approach. *International Journal of Cross Cultural Management*, 13(1): 47–63.

Wang, C., Liu, X. and Wei, Y. (2007) Does China rival its neighbouring economies for inward FDI? *Transnational Corporations*, 16(3): 61–82.

Wang, C., Wei, Y. and Liu, X. (2010) Determinants of bilateral trade flows in OECD countries: evidence from gravity panel data models. *World Economy*, 33(7): 894–915.

Wei, Y. and Wang, C. (2009) Understanding China's international economic integration. *Journal of Chinese Economic and Business Studies*, 7(4): 401–08.

Welch, D. and Welch, L. (2008) The importance of language in international knowledge transfer. *Management International Review*, 48(3): 339–60.

Welch, D.E., Welch, L.S. and Marschan-Piekkari, R. (2001) The persistent impact of language on global operations. *Prometheus*, 19(3): 193–209.

Xu, D. and Shenkar, O. (2002) Institutional distance and the multinational enterprise. *Academy of Management Review*, 27(4): 608–18.

Zaheer, S. and Mosakowski, E. (1997) The dynamics of the liability of foreignness: a global study of survivial in financial services. *Strategic Management Journal*, 18: 439–64.

Zucker, L. (1983) Organizations as institutions, in S.B. Backarack (ed.) *Research in the Sociology of Organizations*. Grenwish, CN: Jai Press.

Zwinkels, R.C.J. and Beugelsdijk, S. (2010) Gravity equations: workhorse or trojan horse in explaining trade and FDI patterns across time and space? *International Business Review*, 19(1): 102–15.

DOI: 10.1057/9781137367204.0019

13
The Impact of Foreign Direct Investment on Economic Performance in the Enlarged Europe: A Meta-Regression Analysis

Randolph Luca Bruno and Maria Cipollina

Introduction

Foreign direct investment (FDI) inflows in 2011 increased in all major economic groups, developed, developing and transition economies (UNCTAD, 2012). Developing countries accounted for 45 per cent of global FDI inflows in 2011, of which East and South-East Asia accounted for almost half. Inflows to the transition economies of south-east Europe, the Commonwealth of Independent States (CIS) and Georgia accounted for 6 per cent. In fact, the overall increase was driven by East, South-East Asia and Latin America. In 2011 FDI outflows to developed countries also grew strongly, reaching $748 billion, up 21 per cent from 2010. FDI flows to Europe increased by 19 per cent, mainly owing to large cross-border mergers and acquisitions (M&As) by foreign multinational corporations (MNCs).

There is a vast literature on the relationship between FDI and economic performance and a quite substantial number of empirical studies on European countries, both for the old and new member states (Meyer and Sinani, 2009; Havrenek and Irsova, 2010, 2011). Some theoretical models on FDI effects[1] predict the existence of a favourable impact, direct or indirect, on the host country: in the former case MNCs bring new capital to the economy and therefore enhance the increase of inputs in the production function; in the latter FDI might produce positive externalities towards domestic firms, by enhancing their productivity and ultimately economic growth. This chapter will focus on the indirect impact, by recognizing the importance of the wider

---

[1] These are mainly focused on advanced economies though; see Bruno and Falk (2012).

DOI: 10.1057/9781137367204.0020

effect of FDI on domestic companies' performance. In fact, in recent years policymakers in many countries have decided to liberalize their policies in order to attract investments from foreign MNCs and therefore to stimulate growth on a wider scale, that is, for foreign as well as domestic owned companies. As a consequence of this renewed interest towards FDI by scholars, policymakers, practitioners and businessmen, there seems to have been a strong effort by governments to lower entry barriers and to offer incentive schemes (tax breaks, subsidies, co-investments and so on) in order to attract FDI. In other words, governments increasingly recognize the importance of cultivating FDI because they have witnessed how knowledge brought by foreign investors could *spillover* to indigenous firms, upgrade their technological capabilities, bolster skills in the local workforce and consequently increase the overall competitiveness of their economies (World Bank Group, 2010). As a result, new regulatory and industry-targeted measures have been introduced (UNCTAD, 2012).

Despite the theoretical rationale for these positive FDI spillovers[2] on host country productivity and economic growth, empirical analyses have provided inconclusive or at least inconsistent evidence on the growth or productivity enhancing effect of FDI. In other words different studies show different relationships (positive, negative or not significant). This is explicit evidence that the impact is ambiguous. From a policy perspective, the lack of robust empirical evidence is particularly delicate and it is probably due to the relevant differences among studies in datasets, sample sizes, models specification and so on.

This chapter provides a survey for evaluating and combining the empirical results from a group of studies on the Enlarged Europe and tries to measure the strength of the FDI–performance relationship. There is a vast literature on the economic impacts of FDI in the EU at the firm, industry and country level. Given the considerable amount of empirical studies dealing with this subject matter, we will limit our review as follows. On the one hand, we focus on the *indirect* impact of FDI on host countries and therefore we do not consider all other possible *direct* impacts on the host country's productivity and growth, that is, the direct accumulation of more capital in the receiving countries. On the other hand, we take into account studies based on firm-level data only: while rapid growth and high ratios of inward FDI to GDP tend to be witnessed together, causality mechanisms are not easily discernible through aggregate analysis because FDI is often associated with other growth-promoting factors, for example, the ratio of investment to GDP and the degree of openness of the economy, among other determinants.[3] Finally we focus on the EU, given the recent surge in FDI, and the political and economic resources devoted by

---

[2] For a comprehensive survey of literature see De Mello (1997).
[3] This leads to omitted variables biases.

DOI: 10.1057/9781137367204.0020

EU governments to remove the still large explicit and implicit restrictions to foreign investment (World Bank Group, 2010). We believe that our research will shed some light on the economic impact of FDI in Europe, which remains one of the main recipients of FDI in the advanced economy world.

Using a Meta-regression Analysis (MRA) approach this chapter provides pooled estimates, obtained from fixed and random effects models,[4] of FDI's effect on growth in the EU. The MRA methodology reviews the literature and tries to explain why there is variation in the empirical results reported in the economic studies, which supposedly investigate the very same phenomenon. *Regression analysis of the existing regression analyses* represents a methodology for quantitatively combining all these estimates (commonly referred to as the 'effect size'), investigating the sensitivity to variations in the underlying assumptions, identifying and filtering out possible biases and explaining the diversity in the studies' results in terms of heterogeneity of their features (Rose and Stanley, 2005).

The rest of the chapter is organized as follows. The next section briefly reviews the empirical literature and some of the existing MRA studies on FDI. The chapter then presents key methodological points regarding the MRA approach before giving some motivation for the so-called 'publication bias' analysis. The fifth section discusses the econometric results. Conclusions and policy implications are drawn in the final section.

Literature review: effects of FDI on productivity and performance

FDI can provide direct financing for the acquisition of new plants and equipment, and be an important catalyst of economic restructuring. It can also directly transfer technology to foreign affiliates, as well as indirectly diffuse or 'spillover' into local economies. The impact can be direct (on the foreign subsidiary) or indirect (on fully domestic firms). In the latter case, the indirect effect can be horizontal (intra-industry effect) or vertical (inter-industry). Finally, the vertical effect can be divided into forward linkages (downstream domestic customers) and backward linkages (upstream domestic suppliers).

Although FDI is potentially capable of producing all the aforementioned effects this does not mean it necessarily does, that is, having the potential does not guarantee that these positive externalities (indirect effect) will be actually present. Whatever the direct or indirect impact FDI has on a given host economy, the effect produced will be conditional upon the nature of FDI and the reasons why MNCs make such investments (distinguishing among market, resource, efficiency and strategic assets seeking FDI); the nature and

---

[4] RobuMeta command in STATA.

DOI: 10.1057/9781137367204.0020

capacity of the host country (broadly speaking, absorptive capacity); and the mode of entry, for example, greenfield; takeover, merger and acquisition; size of entry majority/minority shares in domestic firms (Magai, 2012).

As far as the FDI *direct* effect is concerned (FDI brings capital to the host country) there is widespread consensus on the positive effect on the host countries' firms and the empirical literature provides quite robust findings (Blomström and Kokko, 1998; Eichengreen and Kohl, 1998; Holland et al, 2000; Navaretti and Venables, 2004).

On the other hand, the unintended *indirect* impact (spillovers or externalities) on host countries has been characterized by less conclusive findings, for example, depending on the level of development of a hosting country, whose employment/working conditions, environmental standards and technology transfer potential towards domestic firms are idiosyncratic. In fact, the indirect effect of FDI on host countries has been largely studied from the perspective of economic growth and development, for example in low income countries (Bruno and Campos, 2013), employment/working conditions (labour mobility), the business environment and technology transfer from foreign to domestic firms and so on. It is widely documented that FDI inflows have the potential to upgrade the technological capabilities, skills and competitiveness of established domestic firms in the host countries generating positive externalities. We will also focus on this latter stream of the literature and point our attention towards indirect effects, where the debate is much more open.

The channels through which FDI may spillover from foreign affiliates to other firms in an economy have been analysed in detail in a number of papers (Markusen and Venables, 1999; Kokko, 1992; Javorcik, 2004; Blomström and Kokko, 1998). The main channels identified by the literature are through imitation or demonstration, the movement of workers and via competition. We now analyse each in order:

(1) Through *imitation* (or eventually through collaboration), domestic firms can learn how to export and reach foreign markets. Their proximity to foreign firms facilitates their learning process.

(2) Movement of *labour* entails *movement* of skills *via* acquisition since a MNC has to train the employees in the host country to transfer practices or technology to affiliates (inter-firms mobility and intra-firm training). In fact, a number of empirical studies suggest that the movement of workers within and between firms is one of the most important mechanisms for technology and knowledge spillovers (Barry, Görg and Strobl, 2004 for Ireland; Pesola, 2011 for Finland; Martins, 2011 for Portugal).

(3) Another channel is the *competition effect*. It is argued that the entrance of a MNC (owning better technology and managerial practices) will force the host country's firms in similar sectors to use existing technology and

DOI: 10.1057/9781137367204.0020

resources more efficiently and/or upgrade to more efficient technologies. If they fail, the externality will be negative, that is, they will not cope with the MNC competition. Indeed, not all of the associated effects are positive: competitive pressure can force domestic firms to exit the industry due to crowding-out or business-stealing effects (Dunning, 1994).

The closer the economy is to the world technology frontier, the more important innovation is with regard to imitation. Keller and Yeaple (2008) show that the complexity of technology makes knowledge costly to transfer, and the problem is exacerbated if the affiliate does not have the absorptive capacity to adapt the new technical knowledge. In the context of the EU-27, these concepts can be considered particularly relevant for new member states, which implemented very serious and rapid economic reforms in order to catch up with their neighbouring old members.

While FDI flows may go hand-in-hand with economic success, they do not tend to exert an *independent* effect on growth (Choe, 2003; Carkovic and Levine, 2005; Alfaro et al., 2009).[5] For example, the macro/industry-level literature focuses on human capital (Borensztein et al., 1998), on financial markets (Alfaro et al., 2004), on the difference in the variety of intermediate goods, on the impact of communication distance between headquarters and production plants and more in general on the *absorption capacity* (Rodriguez-Clare, 1996). Using a meta-regression analysis, Meyer and Sinani (2009) study the simultaneous effect produced by the level of development, institutional frameworks and human capital in the context of countries hosting FDI. Recent studies have explored more specific externality transmission channels: the level and rate effect of spillovers (Liu, 2008), meditating factors and FDI heterogeneity (Smeets, 2008) and multiple simultaneous channels (Javorcik, 2004), to name just a few. Furthermore recent systematic meta-regression analyses of the updated evidence (Havrenek and Irsova, 2010, 2011; Bruno and Campos, 2013; Bruno and Falk, 2012) further dissect the differential impact of horizontal, backward and forward spillovers. Meta-analyses suggest that spillovers are mainly created through backward linkages to affiliates' suppliers and not forward linkages to their customers. These backward linkages to suppliers suggest that global production networks play an important role in facilitating knowledge transfer.

---

[5] Using a panel VAR model to explore the interaction between FDI and economic growth in 80 countries in the period 1971–95, Choe (2003) finds evidence that FDI Granger cause economic growth, but the opposite is also true and it is economically and statistically stronger. Carkovic and Levine (2005) use GMM to study a large sample of countries between 1960 and 1995, and find no robust causal effect between foreign investment inflows and economic growth. Similarly Alfaro et al. (2009) find no significant evidence of a positive impact of FDI on growth, except for some financially developed countries.

DOI: 10.1057/9781137367204.0020

Empirical strategy

With reference to the distinction between the direct and indirect effect of FDI, we consider only papers focusing on the estimation of the *indirect impact*. The heterogeneity of approaches and specifications of academic papers studying the host country effects of FDI at the firm level is impressive, but it is also possible to consider the 'representative' FDI spillover regression as follows (z, j and t subscripts stand for firm sector and time, respectively):

$$\ln\left(productivity_{zjt}\right) = \beta_{jt}^{h}horizontal_{jt} + \beta_{jt}^{b}backward_{jt} + \beta_{jt}^{f}forward_{jt} + \beta_{zjt}^{X}X_{jt} + \varepsilon_{zjt} \quad (1)$$

Where *horizontal* is usually defined as the ratio of foreign presence in firm z's own sector; *backward* is the ratio of z's output sold to foreign firms (foreign presence in downstream sectors) and *forward* is the ratio of z's output purchased from foreign firms (foreign presence in upstream sectors). Using the MRA approach, we evaluate and combine empirical results from different studies and test the null hypothesis that different point estimates, treated as individual observations (β_{jt}^{fdi}), are equal to zero when the findings from this entire area of research are combined.

The first step of the analysis is to build a point estimates database of the FDI–growth impact relationship. Then, we select papers using the following criteria:

(a) written in English;
(b) data based on EU countries;
(c) firm-level data;[6] and
(d) papers in the public domain between 2000 and 2012.

'Data points' are selected *via* an extensive search in Google Scholar (http://scholar.google.com) to identify studies in both unpublished and published papers, as well as in research published in peer-reviewed journals of the major commercial publishers using 'EconLit', 'Web of Science' and 'Scopus databases'. Table 13.1 contains information on mean, median, max and min of the 'effect' in the studies on the impact of FDI on domestic performance based on firm-level data for EU countries included in our meta-analysis dataset.[7] Table 13.2 adds a richer set of general information on each and every paper.[8]

---

[6] We exclude papers at the aggregate cross-country level.
[7] Detailed summary statistics for each estimate are available from the authors.
[8] This has to be considered when our search has been brought to an end. Other papers might have been published more recently.

DOI: 10.1057/9781137367204.0020

Table 13.1 Summary of firm-level studies on the effects of FDI on the performance of domestic firms

Paper	mean	p50	min	max	N
Altomonte and Pennings (2009)	−0.0231	−0.0373	−0.0549	0.0705	19
Añón Higón and Vasilakos (2011)	0.0351	0.0293	−0.0736	0.1536	90
Barbosa and Eiriz (2009)	0.0058	0.0058	−0.0456	0.1087	60
Barrios and Strobl (2002)	0.0012	0.0132	−0.1527	0.0587	44
Barrios et al. (2002)	0.0584	0.0382	−0.0417	0.3199	16
Barrios et al. (2011)	−0.0043	0.0022	−0.4662	0.0567	73
Barry et al. (2005)	−0.0219	−0.0272	−0.0467	0.0394	9
Bekes et al. (2009)	0.0058	0.0056	−0.0004	0.0101	9
Belderbos (2011)	0.0702	0.0590	−0.0437	0.2407	8
Castellani and Zanfei (2010)	−0.0186	−0.0177	−0.0593	0.0175	18
Crespo et al. (2009)	0.0042	0.0022	−0.0342	0.0365	16
Dimelis (2005)	0.0307	0.0330	−0.0466	0.0836	32
Djankov and Hoekman (1999)	0.0868	0.0868	0.0852	0.0884	2
Driffield (2004)	−0.0005	0.0004	−0.8835	0.7923	18
Driffield and Love (2005)	−0.0729	−0.0368	−0.3358	0.1336	12
Driffield et al. (2009)	−0.0376	0.1732	−0.5926	0.2592	9
Flôres et al. (2007)	0.2930	0.2696	0.2334	0.3701	7
Girma and Görg (2007)	0.0171	0.0266	−0.0787	0.1125	36
Girma and Wakelin (2000)	−0.0015	−0.0001	−0.0446	0.0364	34
Girma and Wakelin (2007)	0.0121	0.0042	−0.0678	0.1639	90
Girma (2005)	0.0061	0.0111	−0.0166	0.0201	30
Girma, Görg and Pisu (2006)	0.0027	−0.0009	−0.0544	0.0734	62
Girma, Görg and Pisu (2008)	0.0118	0.0105	−0.1411	0.1756	142
Gorodnichenkou et al. (2007)	0.0232	0.0203	−0.0015	0.0609	42
Görg et al (2009)	−0.0073	−0.0077	−0.0589	0.1019	128
Hagemeje and Kolasa (2011)	0.0140	0.0105	−0.0168	0.0575	72
Haller (2011)	0.0062	0.0086	−0.0270	0.0293	24
Halpern and Muraközy (2007)	0.0318	0.0011	−0.0233	0.1014	44
Jabbour and Mucchielli (2007)	0.0034	0.0008	−0.1374	0.1295	37
Javorcik and Spatareanu (2011)	0.0083	0.0070	−0.0081	0.0213	66
Javorcik (2004)	0.0337	0.0183	−0.0351	0.3221	80
Konings (2001)	0.0270	0.0082	−0.0257	0.1264	24
Lesher and Miroudot (2008)	−0.0036	−0.0032	−0.1390	0.0908	71
Liu et al. (2000)	0.1920	0.1705	0.0651	0.3821	10
Marcin (2008)	0.0076	0.0062	0.0056	0.0190	15
Mariotti et al. (2011)	0.0202	0.0130	0.0032	0.0756	7
McVicar (2002)	−0.0091	−0.0091	−0.0091	−0.0091	1
Monastiriotis and Alegria (2011)	0.0262	0.0099	−0.0202	0.1390	6
Nicolini and Resmini (2010)	−0.0112	0.0114	−0.3374	0.0263	24
Nicolini and Resmini (2011)	0.0794	0.0761	0.0104	0.1543	20
Proenca et al (2006)	0.0933	0.0616	0.0484	0.2017	4
Reganati and Sica (2010)	0.0302	0.0166	−0.0027	0.1191	6
Ruane and Ugur (2012)	0.0047	0.0038	−0.0003	0.0107	12
Stancik (2010)	0.0049	0.0080	−0.0379	0.0463	42
Vacek (2010)	0.0655	0.0492	−0.3445	0.2723	62
Vahter and Masso (2006)	0.0593	0.0637	0.0050	0.0816	10

DOI: 10.1057/9781137367204.0020

Table 13.2 Summary of firm-level studies on the effects of FDI on the performance of domestic firms

Article	Dependent variable	FDI Impact	Time spam	Industry coverage	Country	Data source
Altomonte and Pennings (2009)	TFP growth	Horizontal	1995–2001	Manufacturing and Services	Romania	Amadeus
Añón Higón and Vasilakos (2011)	TFP growth	Horizontal/vertical	1997–2004	Manufacturing	UK	ARD–ABI dataset
Barbosa and Eiriz (2009)	Output growth	Backward/ horizontal	1994–1999	Manufacturing	Portugal	Bank of Portugal
Barrios and Strobl (2002)	TFP growth	Horizontal/vertical	1990–1998	Manufacturing	Spain	ESEE
Barrios et al. (2002)	Labour productivity	Horizontal	1992–1997	Manufacturing	Greece, Ireland, Spain	Irish economy Expenditure survey (IEE)
Barrios et al. (2011)	Output growth TFP growth	Backward/forward/ horizontal	1983–1998	Manufacturing	Ireland	Irish economy Expenditure Survey (IEE)
Barry et al. (2005)	Output growth Labour productivity TFP growth	Vertical	1990–1999	Manufacturing	Ireland	Irish economy Expenditure survey (IEE)
Bekes et al. (2009)	TFP growth	Backward/forward/ horizontal	1992–2003	Manufacturing	Hungary	Hungarian Tax Authority APEH
Belderbos (2011)	TFP growth	Backward/forward/ horizontal	2000–2007	Manufacturing	Belgium	Amadeus/Belfast database
Castellani and Zanfei (2010)	Output growth	Horizontal	1992–2003	Manufacturing	France, Italy, Spain	Amadeus
Crespo et al. (2009)	Labour productivity	Backward/forward/ horizontal	1996–2009	Manufacturing	Poland	Portuguese Ministry of Employment and S
Dimelis (2005)	Output growth	Horizontal	1992–1997	Manufacturing	Greece	Confederation of Greek Industries (ICAP)

Continued

DOI: 10.1057/9781137367204.0020

Table 13.2 Continued

Article	Dependent variable	FDI Impact	Time spam	Industry coverage	Country	Data source
Djankov and Hoekman (1999)	Growth in sales	Horizontal	1992–1996	Manufacturing	Czech Republic	Czech Statistical Office
Driffield (2004)	Gross value added (productivity growth)	Horizontal	1983–1997	Manufacturing	UK	UK Office of National Statistics
Driffield and Love (2005)	TFP growth	Horizontal	1984–1997	Manufacturing	UK	UK Office of National Statistics
Driffield et al. (2009)	TFP growth	Horizontal	1987–1996	Manufacturing	UK	UK Office of National Statistics
Flôres et al. (2007)	TFP growth	Horizontal	1992–1995	Manufacturing	Portugal	Instituto Nacional de Estatistica – INE
Girma and Görg (2007)	TFP growth	Horizontal	1980–1992	Electronics and mechanical andinstrument engineering	UK	Annual Respondents Database (ARD), Office for National Statistics
Girma and Wakelin (2000)	Output growth	Horizontal/vertical	1988–1996	Manufacturing	UK	OneSource database
Girma and Wakelin (2007)	TFP growth	Horizontal/vertical	1980–1992	Manufacturing	UK	Annual Business Respondents Database
Girma (2005)	TFP growth	Horizontal	1989–1999	Manufacturing	UK	OneSource database
Girma, Görg and Pisu (2006)	Output growth	Backward/forward/ horizontal	1992–1999	Manufacturing	UK	OneSource database
Girma, Görg and Pisu (2008)	TFP growth TFP growth	Backward/forward/ horizontal	1992–1999	Manufacturing	UK	OneSource database

DOI: 10.1057/9781137367204.0020

Study	Revenue Efficiency	Backward/forward/ horizontal	2002–2005	Manufacturing	Central and Eastern Europe (CEE), Turkey	Business Environment and Enterprise Performance Surveys (BEEPS)
Gorodnichenkou et al. (2007)	Revenue Efficiency	Backward/forward/ horizontal	2002–2005	Manufacturing	Central and Eastern Europe (CEE), Turkey	Business Environment and Enterprise Performance Surveys (BEEPS)
Görg et al. (2009)	Output growth TFP growth	Horizontal	1992–2003	Manufacturing	Hungary	Amadeus
Hagemeje and Kolasa (2011)	TFP growth	Backward/forward/ horizontal	1996–2005	Manufacturing	Poland	Poland Central Statistical Office
Haller (2011)	Labour productivity TFP growth	Horizontal	2001–2007	Manufacturing and Services	Ireland	Annual Services Inquiry (ASI)
Halpern and Muraközy (2007)	TFP growth	Backward/ horizontal	1996–2003	Manufacturing	Hungary	Hungarian Central Statistical Office
Jabbour and Mucchielli (2007)	TFP growth	Backward/forward/ horizontal	1990–2000	Manufacturing	Spain	ESEE survey
Javorcik and Spatareanu (2011)	TFP growth	Backward/ horizontal	1998–2003	Manufacturing	Romania	Amadeus + Romanian Chamber of Commerce
Javorcik (2004)	TFP growth Output growth	Backward/forward/ horizontal	1993–2000	Manufacturing	Lithuania	Lith. Statistical office
Konings (2001)	Output growth	Horizontal	1993–1997	Manufacturing	Bulgaria, Poland, Romania	Amadeus + Chamber of Commerce
Lesher and Miroudot (2008)	Operating revenue	Backward/forward/ horizontal	1993–2006	Manufacturing and Services	EU15	Amadeus + OECD Input–Output Database
Liu et al. (2000)	Labour productivity Output growth	Horizontal	1991–1995	Manufacturing	UK	Fame
Marcin (2008)	Output growth	Backward/forward/ horizontal	1996–2003	Manufacturing	Poland	Poland Central Statistical Office

Continued

DOI: 10.1057/9781137367204.0020

Table 13.2 Continued

Article	Dependent variable	FDI Impact	Time spam	Industry coverage	Country	Data source
Mariotti et al. (2011)	TFP growth	Backward/forward/ horizontal	1999–2005	Manufacturing and Services	Italy	AIDA–Bureau
McVicar (2002)	TFP growth	Horizontal	1973–1992	Manufacturing	UK	OECD ANBERD data
Monastiriotis and Alegria (2011)	Output growth	Horizontal	2002–2005	Manufacturing	Bulgaria	Amadeus
Nicolini and Resmini (2010)	TFP growth	Horizontal/vertical	1998–2003	Manufacturing	Bulgaria, Poland, Romania	Amadeus database
Nicolini and Resmini (2011)	TFP growth	Horizontal/vertical	1998–2003	Manufacturing	Bulgaria, Poland, Romania	Amadeus
Proenca et al. (2006)	Labour productivity	Horizontal	1996–1999	Manufacturing	Portugal	Dun and Bradstreet database
Reganati and Sica (2010)	Gross value added (productivity growth)	Horizontal/vertical	1997–2002	Manufacturing	Italy	A.I.D.A and ISTAT
Ruane and Ugur (2012)	Labour productivity	Horizontal	1991–1998	Manufacturing	Ireland	Irish Central Statistics Office
Stancik (2010)	Growth in sales	Backward/forward/ horizontal	1995–2005	Manufacturing	Czech Republic	ASPEKT database
Vacek (2010)	Output growth	Backward/forward	1993–2004	Manufacturing and Services	Czech Republic	Czech Statistical Office
Vahter and Masso (2006)	TFP growth	Horizontal	1995–2006	Manufacturing and Services	Estonia	Balance of Payments of Bank of Estonia

DOI: 10.1057/9781137367204.0020

When a study provides multiple estimates of the effect under consideration, the assumption that multiple observations from the same study are independent draws becomes too strong; on the other hand, important information is lost in the grouping process and it is not clear which estimate one should choose as 'preferred' for each study (Jeppensen et al., 2002).

According to MRA practise (and wide-spread use in the literature) we collect all estimates and account for both the within-study and between-study heterogeneity. We can choose between a fixed-effect (FE) and a random-effect (RE) meta regression model. A FE model assumes that differences across studies are only due to within-variation. The single, 'true' effect ($\hat{B}_F$) is calculated as a weighted average of the individual estimate $\hat{\beta}_i$, where the weights are inversely proportional to the square of the standard errors, so that studies with smaller standard errors have greater weight than studies with larger standard errors (Higgins and Thompson, 2002):

$$\hat{B}_F = \frac{\sum_{i=1}^{n} \frac{\hat{\beta}_i}{se(\hat{\beta}_i)^2}}{\sum_{i=1}^{n} \frac{1}{se(\hat{\beta}_i)^2}} \tag{2}$$

The RE model assumes that the studies are a *random sample from the universe of all possible studies* (Sutton et al., 2000). In fact, a field of the literature showing high heterogeneity cannot be summarized by the FE estimate under the assumption that a single 'true' effect underlies every study. As a consequence, the FE estimator is inconsistent and the RE model is more appropriate.[9] The RE model assumes that there are real differences between all studies in the magnitude of the effect. Unlike the FE model, the individual studies are not assumed to be estimating a true single effect size; rather the true effects in each study are assumed to have been sampled from a distribution of effects, which is normal with mean zero and variance τ^2. The weights incorporate an estimate of the between-study heterogeneity, $\hat{\tau}^2$ (Higgins and Thompson, 2002).

Publication bias

Researchers, referees and editors tend to have a preference for statistically significant results so that a publication bias occurs, greatly affecting the magnitude of the estimated effect. In order to correct publication bias analysts use a MRA model that regresses estimated coefficients ($\hat{\beta}_i$) on their standard errors (Card and Krueger, 1995; Ashenfelter et al., 1999). Meta-regression errors are

---

[9] We use the RobuMeta command for this purpose.

DOI: 10.1057/9781137367204.0020

likely to be heteroskedastic when studies in the literature differ greatly in data sets, sample sizes, independent variables, so the ordinary keast squares (OLS) estimates of the MRA coefficients might fail to be unbiased and consistent. A weighted least squares (WLS) obtained by dividing the regression equation by the individual estimated standard errors corrects the MRA for heteroskedasticity and makes it permisable to obtain efficient estimates:

$$\frac{\hat{\beta}_i}{se(\hat{\beta}_i)} = t_i = \beta_0 + \beta_1 \frac{1}{se(\hat{\beta}_i)} + \varepsilon_i \tag{3}$$

Where t_i is the conventional t-value for $\hat{\beta}_i$ the intercept and slope coefficients are reversed and the independent variable becomes the inverse of $se(\hat{\beta}_i)$ (Stanley and Jarrell, 2005). Equation (3) is the basis for the Funnel Asymmetry Test (FAT): in the absence of publication selection the magnitude of the reported effect will vary randomly around the 'true' value, b_1, independently of its standard error, therefore β_0 will be zero. When the standard error of the effect of FDI is not significantly different from zero at any conventional level, the publication bias is not a major issue.[10] Another method to remove or circumvent publication selection is the Meta-Significance Testing (MST). It uses the relationship between a study's standardized effect (its t-value) and its degrees of freedom or sample size n as a means of identifying genuine empirical effect rather than the artefact of publication selection. When there is some genuine overall empirical effect, statistical power will cause the observed magnitude of the standardized test statistic to vary with n (Stanley, 2001). Alternatively, Card and Kruger's (1995) publication bias test assesses whether the key independent variable, the log of the square root of the degrees of freedom, has a coefficient of one in absence of publication bias. The results of publication bias will be analysed in the next section after a description of the main variables used in the MRA and the sample.

Meta-regression analysis (MRA)

Specification

In our meta-analysis all papers selected contain one or more equation which estimates the indirect effect of FDI on one of the following variables: a measure of firm efficiency (such as TFP), firm output, value added or labour productivity. The indirect effect of foreign firms is defined as the impact of foreign ownership on the performance of domestic firms. This effect may be measured as

---

[10] In such a case, the standard error can be omitted from the regression.

DOI: 10.1057/9781137367204.0020

a dummy variable for foreign presence or as the percentage of foreign presence in a domestic firm. This leads to the estimation of the following specification:

$$r_{ij} = \beta_0 + v_{ij} \tag{4}$$

where r_{ij} is the partial correlation coefficient, defined as $\dfrac{t}{\sqrt{(t^2 + df)}}$ with 't' being the t-statistic of the effect under study, 'df' being the degrees of freedom for the 'j^{th}' estimation in the 'i^{th}' paper. β_0 and v_{ij} are the average effect and the idiosyncratic (in this case, paper-estimate specific) errors, respectively. The partial correlation coefficient is chosen for two reasons: first, it allows direct comparison of studies with different dependent variables (e.g. TFP versus labour productivity); second, there is an important element of heterogeneity in specifications for firm-level databases, which makes it impossible to obtain an aggregate value that could easily be interpreted as an elasticity or semi-elasticity measure. In other words, limiting the reported estimates to a strictly comparable set of specifications would have excluded too many studies and as a result the findings would have been based on a very small number of observations (not to mention the obvious selection issues).

Data sample

Our final sample includes 46 papers either published in an academic journal or working papers series or released as an unpublished article between 2000 and 2012, providing 1643 point estimates. The period analysed ranges from 1973 to 2009. The countries selected in the sample are Belgium, Bulgaria, the Czech Republic, Estonia, France, Greece, Hungary, Ireland, Italy, Lithuania, Poland, Portugal, Romania, Spain and the UK.[11] Most of the observations involve the UK, Ireland (among EU-15 old member states), Hungary, Poland and Romania (among new member states). The studies are mainly organized in panel data.[12] The results are divided in to 'unconditional' and 'conditional' estimates. In the former we keep the most rigorous RobuMeta methodology as a specification but we do not control for any 'moderator' variables. In other words, we are unable to explain why there is heterogeneity in the results, even if we are fully accounting for such heterogeneity.[13] In the latter we insert a battery of FDI-growth effects, specification and paper specific moderator variables and we also test for the regression containing country dummies (or alternatively

---

[11] Three articles included in the MRA cover a group of countries instead of a single nation, namely Central and Eastern Europe; the EU-15; Bulgaria, Poland and Romania. They still perform a firm-level econometric investigation and have therefore been included in the MRA.

[12] This statistical property is quite important in guaranteeing less biased estimates. Cross-section estimates would be upwardly biased and would be less suitable for a MRA.

[13] See RobuMeta help on STATA 12.

DOI: 10.1057/9781137367204.0020

the EU-15 vs. new member state dummy). In the conditional regressions we explore why we see heterogeneity and we can also pinpoint the sources of such heterogeneity.

Econometric results: publication bias

Several meta-regression and graphical methods have been envisaged in order to differentiate genuine empirical effect from publication bias (Stanley, 2005). The simplest and conventional method to detect publication bias is by inspection of a funnel graph diagram. The funnel graph is a scatter diagram presenting a measure of sample size or precision of the estimate on the vertical axis, and the measured effect size (in our MRA partial correlation coefficient, PCC) on the horizontal axis. The most common way to measure precision is the inverse of the standard error ($1/se$). Here, the precision variable on the vertical axis is computed as the inverse of the standard error of the PCC, $1/se_{PCC} = (t^2 + df)$. Asymmetry is the mark of publication bias: in the absence of such a bias, the estimates will vary randomly and symmetrically around the true effect. The diagram, then, should resemble an inverted funnel, wide at the bottom for small-sample studies, narrow at the top for bigger samples.

An additional graphical method is the Egger test that detects funnel plot asymmetry by determining whether the intercept significantly deviates from zero in a regression of the standardized effect estimates against their precision. The funnel and the Egger tests for detecting the presence of publication bias are represented in Figure 13.1.

Even though the graph in Figure 13.1 (panel *a*) slightly resembles a funnel, it does not present the symmetry crucial to exclude publication bias. Estimates of FDI effects seem to indicate a positive effect, the plot being over-weighted

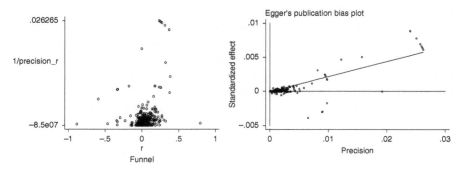

Figure 13.1 Funnel graph of individual estimates
Source: authors' computation.

DOI: 10.1057/9781137367204.0020

on the right hand side. Such direction is also confirmed by the Egger approach (panel *b*) showing the intercept deviating significantly from zero in a regression of the standardized effect estimates against their precision.

We also explore the publication bias more rigorously by implementing the FAT, the MST and the Card-Kruger test. Looking at the results of the FAT in Table 13.3, the statistically significant estimates of β_0 confirm the asymmetry of the funnel graph, since the reported effect is not independent of its standard error. The MST provides evidence of a genuine empirical effect of FDI on economic performance, since the β_1 estimate is statistically significant for the total sample, as well as for the old and new EU members. The Card-Kruger publication bias test leads to the rejection of the null hypothesis $\beta_1 = 1$, but we can however report a positive relationship between *t*-ratios and degrees of freedom, signalling a mild publication bias.

Econometric results: unconditional partial correlation coefficients regressions

Examining the entire sample, the average partial correlation coefficient between economic performance (e.g. TFP productivity) and FDI is statistically significant and positive. On average, its magnitude is 0.024 (both for the old EU-15 and the new member states): within the [–1,1] scale this translates in to a 2.4 per cent partial correlation. Therefore the correlation results between FDI and productivity for the EU-27 is positive and significant (though small

Table 13.3 MR tests for publication bias and empirical significance

Variables	Total sample			Old EU-15			New member states		
	FAT[a]	MST[b]	Card-Kruger[b]	FAT[a]	MST[b]	Card-Kruger[b]	FAT[a]	MST[b]	Card-Kruger[b]
β_1: 1/se (True)	0.003			0.003			0.001		
	(0.002)			(0.003)			(0.001)		
β_1: Ln(n)		0.237***			0.322***			0.108*	
		(0.073)			(0.091)			(0.062)	
β_1: Ln(Square Root DF)			0.474***			0.644***			0.215*
			(0.147)			(0.182)			(0.123)
β_0: Intercept	0.756**	−1.648***	−1.648	0.442	−2.391***	−2.391***	1.254**	−0.462	−0.462
	(0.351)	(0.650)	(0.65)	(0.440)	(0.817)	(0.817)	(0.592)	(0.538)	(0.538)
H_0: $\beta_1=1$			Rej***			Rej*			Rej***
Observations	1637	1041	1041	961	607	607	976	434	434
Cluster	46	45	45	28	27	27	18	18	18

Note: standard errors adjusted for studies/clusters are reported in parentheses;
*** p < 0.01, ** p < 0.05, * p < 0.1.
[a] Dependent variable: t-ratio; [b] Dependent variable: ln|t-ratio|.

DOI: 10.1057/9781137367204.0020

Table 13.4   EU-27 EU-12 unconditional RobuMeta-Analysis

RE model	Total sample	Old EU-15	New member states
Coefficient	0.024***	0.024*	0.024***
SE	(0.008)	(0.012)	(0.007)
Observations	1,643	962	681
N. Cluster	46	28	18
Tau^2	0.00249	0.00265	0.000323

Note: Standard errors in parentheses, *** p < 0.01, ** p < 0.05, * p < 0.1.

in magnitude), whereas there is no apparent difference between old and new member sates. As a first approximation, EU-15 countries make a crucial contribution to the positive impact of FDI on productivity as well as new member states, which seems to play a very similar role. In the next section we uncover some interesting caveats to this 'first approximation' conclusion.

Econometric results: conditional partial correlation coefficients regressions

We now turn to the conditional regressions. Table 13.5 presents an encompassing set of controls in column one: the type of FDI–growth relationship, the econometric model, the paper characteristics as well as country dummies.

There is a higher FDI–performance relation when using firm-level data (vis-à-vis industry regional or plant data). The OLS estimates (even if controlling for FE) overstate the FDI–performance relation with respect to more sophisticated econometric models. Studies including a higher number of observations (and therefore degrees of freedom) have less strong results. Finally, compared to the UK, Belgium, Estonia, Italy and Portugal are exhibiting a higher FDI–performance relationship.[14] Column 2 in Table 13.5 does not include country FE any more but just a country group 'old EU' dummy and this is insignificant (as already confirmed in the unconditional estimates). When omitting country dummies the results on moderator variables are only slightly modified and we can confidently state that the columns 2–9 are correctly specified.

Regarding publication 'impact', we distinguish published from unpublished studies. One of the main criticisms of MRA is that because the quality of studies included in the dataset can vary considerably, strong methodological or empirical analyses are lumped together with studies that may have serious methodological or empirical limitations (the 'garbage in, garbage out' criticism). It is argued that alternative selection schemes might be considered arbitrary and subjective. The inclusion in meta-databases of both published and unpublished studies is widely viewed as the best way to reduce the so-called

---

[14] For column 1, country dummies are available upon request.

DOI: 10.1057/9781137367204.0020

Table 13.5 EU-27 EU-12 conditional RobuMeta-Analysis

	1	2	3	4	5	6	7	8	9
	Country Ds	EU 15 D	EU 15 D*1995	EU 15 D*1996	EU 15 D*1997	EU 15 D*1998	EU 15 D*1999	EU 15 D*2000	EU 15 D*2001
Vertical FDI	0.006	0.008	0.007	0.007	0.007	0.008	0.008	0.007	0.004
	(0.013)	(0.01)	(0.01)	(0.01)	(0.01)	(0.011)	(0.011)	(0.01)	(0.01)
Firm-level data	0.057*	0.021	0.018	0.018	0.021	0.021	0.021	0.019	0.023
	(0.032)	(0.025)	(0.024)	(0.024)	(0.025)	(0.025)	(0.025)	(0.026)	(0.027)
Manufacturing	0.017	0.008	0.011	0.011	0.008	0.007	0.007	0.008	-0.005
	(0.019)	(0.023)	(0.023)	(0.023)	(0.023)	(0.023)	(0.023)	(0.023)	(0.022)
Non TFP as dependent	0.001	0.006	0.009	0.009	0.008	0.006	0.006	0.003	0.005
	(0.022)	(0.014)	(0.014)	(0.014)	(0.014)	(0.016)	(0.016)	(0.015)	(0.013)
Interacted FDI	0.005	-0.011	-0.012	-0.012	-0.012	-0.011	-0.011	-0.011	-0.014
	(0.018)	(0.01)	(0.01)	(0.01)	(0.01)	(0.011)	(0.011)	(0.01)	(0.011)
Not OLS estimator	-0.044**	-0.044**	-0.048**	-0.048**	-0.046**	-0.044**	-0.044**	-0.044**	-0.045**
	(0.019)	(0.02)	(0.02)	(0.02)	(0.02)	(0.021)	(0.021)	(0.02)	(0.02)
Data length in years	-0.003	-0.006**	-0.005	-0.005	-0.006*	-0.006**	-0.006**	-0.007**	-0.007**
	(0.005)	(0.002)	(0.003)	(0.003)	(0.003)	(0.003)	(0.003)	(0.003)	(0.003)
1995–2000 end year	-0.073	-0.080**	-0.082**	-0.082**	-0.080**	-0.080**	-0.080**	-0.081**	-0.076**
	(0.049)	(0.036)	(0.036)	(0.036)	(0.036)	(0.037)	(0.037)	(0.036)	(0.035)
2000–2005 end year	-0.073	-0.075**	-0.091***	-0.091***	-0.082**	-0.075**	-0.075**	-0.074**	-0.071**
	(0.047)	(0.034)	(0.032)	(0.032)	(0.032)	(0.034)	(0.034)	(0.033)	(0.034)
After 2005 end year	-0.083	-0.046	-0.065*	-0.065*	-0.054	-0.045	-0.045	-0.018	-0.015
	(0.051)	(0.037)	(0.037)	(0.037)	(0.034)	(0.033)	(0.033)	(0.024)	(0.028)
Published paper	0.000	0.001	0.003	0.003	0.003	0	0	-0.004	0.001
	(0.016)	(0.014)	(0.013)	(0.013)	(0.014)	(0.017)	(0.017)	(0.015)	(0.013)
Log square root DF	-0.027**	-0.020**	-0.021**	-0.021**	-0.020**	-0.019**	-0.019**	-0.020**	-0.021**
	(0.011)	(0.009)	(0.009)	(0.009)	(0.009)	(0.009)	(0.009)	(0.009)	(0.008)

DOI: 10.1057/9781137367204.0020

Table 13.5 Continued

	1	2	3	4	5	6	7	8	9
	Country Ds	EU 15 D	EU 15 D*1995	EU 15 D*1996	EU 15 D*1997	EU 15 D*1998	EU 15 D*1999	EU 15 D*2000	EU 15 D*2001
EU-15 dummy		-0.004	-0.022	-0.022	-0.011	-0.003	-0.003	-0.001	0
		(0.012)	(0.016)	(0.016)	(0.016)	(0.012)	(0.012)	(0.012)	(0.012)
EU-15 dummy*1995			0.037						
			(0.024)						
EU-15 dummy*1996				0.037					
				(0.024)					
EU-15 dummy*1997					0.016				
					(0.026)				
EU-15 dummy*1998						-0.002			
						(0.04)			
EU-15 dummy*1999							-0.002		
							(0.04)		
EU-15 dummy*2000								-0.048	
								(0.049)	
EU-15 dummy*2001									-0.098***
									(0.028)
Constant	0.129	0.206***	0.215***	0.215***	0.209***	0.206**	0.206**	0.218***	0.223***
	(0.102)	(0.072)	(0.074)	(0.074)	(0.073)	(0.076)	(0.076)	(0.078)	(0.076)
Country dummies	Yes***	No	No	No	No	No	No	No	No
Observations	1,643	1,643	1,643	1,643	1,643	1,643	1,643	1,643	1,643
N. cluster	46	46	46	46	46	46	46	46	46
Tau^2	0.572	0.115	0.136	0.136	0.136	0.148	0.148	0.131	0.115

Note: standard errors in parentheses, *** $p<0.01$, ** $p<0.05$, * $p<0.1$.
The omitted categories are UK (1st column), Horizontal FDI, not firm-level data, not manufacturing data, TFP as dependent variable, pure effect of FDI (i.e. not interacted), OLS (and panel FE) estimator, database stopping before 1995 (end year), unpublished paper, new member states (for the EU-15 dummy in columns 2–9).

DOI: 10.1057/9781137367204.0020

'publication bias' (Ashenfelter et al., 1999). Our sample includes 35 published academic journal articles (providing 1212 point estimates) and 11 working papers or unpublished studies (providing 431 point estimates). Since the conventional wisdom is that published and very specific studies tend to include more accurate econometric analyses, we introduce a dummy 'published paper'. Our results (Table 13.5) show that the peer-review process does not greatly affect the magnitude of the estimated effect, since the estimated coefficient of the dummy is not statistically significant.

Finally in columns 3–9 we introduce interacted variables, that is, the old EU-15 dummy with the relevant period of analysis (1995, 1996, 1997, 1998, 1999, 2000 or 2001 onwards): the stark result is that the new member states outperform the old EU-15 (interaction dummy for EU negative and significant) after 2001. This can be interpreted as an encouraging sign for new member states: on the one hand, the overall effect is similar to the old EU-15, but this becomes relatively more important in the last decade. This has interesting convergence implications in light of the last decade's catching-up process – new member states seem to have equipped themselves with a higher FDI impact potential and this might be the fruit of their continuous effort towards a more FDI-friendly environment (World Bank Group, 2010). However it is too soon to draw any general conclusions on the improved absorptive capacity of these countries.

Conclusion

The aim of this chapter is to combine, explain and summarize a large number of results on the impact of FDI on economic performance in the Enlarged Europe by using a MRA approach. This chapter discusses some of the more recent findings from the related empirical literature focusing on the Enlarged Europe FDI–growth relationship. Our results show three main findings:

(1) The existence of a positive impact of FDI on productivity and ultimately on economic growth in the Enlarged Europe as a whole.
(2) The existence of a limited magnitude of this positive relationship.
(3) The (relatively) more important role of New Member States in the contribution towards this effect after 2001.

In view of this analysis and previous results in the literature, we can argue that policies promoting the inflows of FDI can be a tool for productivity and economic growth, this result being particularly evident for the new members of the EU. From a policy perspective, this chapter provides evidence that policymakers' agenda should discuss the removal of the still large (explicit and

DOI: 10.1057/9781137367204.0020

implicit) restrictions to which the access of foreign investors is subject (World Bank Group, 2010).

The EU is thoroughly investigating the role of foreign investment in 'reaping the benefits of globalization' (European Commission, 2012) for policy purposes. At the same time the quality of available data for empirical estimation is increasing. It would appear therefore that we may be entering a favourable period for a rejuvenated effort in to the research on FDI and economic growth and this is particularly important given the conditionality of the results (e.g. role of absorptive capacity) and the not always beneficial direction of such externalities (positive spillovers vs. stealing effect externalities). More country studies using high quality firm-level data might be extremely useful, but also a better synthesis of the existing literature is essential too. This study falls in to the latter approach and we believe this has potentially very important policy relevance.

References

Alfaro, L., Chanda, A., Kalemli-Ozcan, S. and Sayek, S. (2004) FDI and economic growth: the role of local financial markets. *Journal of International Economics*, 64: 89–112.

Alfaro, L., Kalemli-Ozcan, S. and Sayek, S. (2009) FDI, productivity and financial development. *The World Economy*, 32: 111–35.

Ashenfelter, O., Harmon, C. and Oosterbeek, H. (1999) A review of estimates of the schooling/earnings relationship, with tests for publication bias. *Labour Economics*, 6: 453–70.

Barry, F., Görg, H. and Strobl, E., (2004) Foreign direct investment, agglomerations, and demonstration effects: an empirical investigation. *Review of World Economics (Weltwirtschaftliches Archiv)*, 140(3): 583–600.

Blomström, M. and Kokko, A. (1998) Multinational corporations and spillovers. *Journal of Economic Surveys*, 12: 247–77.

Blomström, M., Kokko, A. and Globerman, S. (1998) Regional economic integration and foreign direct investment: the North American experience. Working Paper Series in Economics and Finance 269, Stockholm School of Economics.

Borensztein, E., de Gregorio, J. and Lee, J.W. (1998) How does foreign direct investment affect economic growth? *Journal of international Economics*, 45: 115–35.

Bruno, R.L. and Campos N. (2013) Reexamining the conditional effect of foreign direct investment. IZA discussion paper no. 7458.

Bruno, R.L. and Falk, M. (2012) Theories of foreign investment and host country effects of FDI, background report on FDI flows and impacts on the competitiveness of the EU industry. *European Competitiveness Report: Reaping the Benefits of Globalization*, Annual. Luxembourg: Publications Office of the European Union.

Card, D. and Krueger, A.B., (1995) Time-series minimum-wage studies: a meta-analysis. *American Economic Review*, 85: 238–43.

Carkovic, M. and Levine, R. (2005) Does foreign direct investment accelerate economic growth? University of Minnesota Department of Finance working paper no. 314924.

Choe, J. (2003) Do foreign direct investment and gross domestic investment promote economic growth? *Review of Development Economics*, 7: 44–57.

DOI: 10.1057/9781137367204.0020

de Mello, L.R. (1997) Foreign direct investment in developing countries and growth: a selective survey. *Journal of Development Studies*, 34(1): 1–34.

Dunning, J.H. (1994) *Multinational Enterprises and the Global Economy*. Wokingham, UK and Reading, MA: Addison-Wesley.

Eichengreen, B. and Kohl, R. (1998) The external sector, the state and development in Eastern Europe. CEPR Discussion Papers 1904.

European Commission (2012) *European Competitiveness Report: Reaping the Benefits of Globalization*. EU Commission Staff Working Document.

Havrenek, T. and Irsova, Z. (2010) Meta-analysis of intra-industry FDI spillovers: updated evidence. *Czech Journal of Economics and Finance*, 60(2): 151–74.

Havrenek, T. and Irsova, Z. (2011) Estimating vertical spillovers from FDI: why results vary and what the true effect is. *Journal of International Economics*, 85(2): 234–44.

Higgins, J.P.T. and Thompson, S.G. (2002) Quantifying heterogeneity in a meta-analysis. *Statistics in Medicine*, 21: 1539–58.

Holland, D., Sass, M., Benaček, V. and Gronicki, M. (2000) The determinants and impact of FDI in Central and Eastern Europe: a comparison of survey and econometric evidence. *Transnational Corporations*, 9(3): 163–213.

Javorcik, B. (2004) Does foreign direct investment increase the productivity of domestic firms? In search of spillovers through backward linkages. *American Economic Review*, 94(3): 605–27.

Jeppesen, T., List, J.A. and Folmer, H. (2002) Environmental regulations and new plant location decisions: evidence from a meta-analysis. *Journal of Regional Science*, 42: 19–49.

Keller, W. and Yeaple, S.R. (2008) Global production and trade in the knowledge economy. NBER working paper no. 14626, National Bureau of Economic Research, Inc.

Kokko, A. (1992) Foreign direct investment, host country characteristics, and spillovers. Doctoral Dissertation, Stockholm School of Economics, Stockholm.

Liu, Z. (2008) Foreign direct investment and technology spillovers: theory and evidence. *Journal of Development Economics*, 85(1–2): 176–93.

Magai, A. (2012) FDI flows and EU industrial competitiveness, *European Competitiveness Report 2012: Reaping the Benefits of Globalization*, chapter 4. EU Commission Staff Working Document.

Markusen, J. and Venables, A.J. (1999) Foreign direct investment as a catalyst for industrial development. *European Economic Review*, 43: 335–8.

Martins, P.S. (2011) Paying more to hire the best? Foreign firms, wages, and worker mobility. *Economic Inquiry*, 49(2): 349–63.

Meyer, K. and Sinani, E. (2009) When and where does foreign direct investment generates positive spillovers? A meta-analysis. *Journal of International Business Studies*, 40: 1075–94.

Navaretti, B. and Venables, A. (2004) *Multinationals and the World Economy*. Princeton, NJ: Princeton University Press.

Pesola, H. (2011) Labour mobility and returns to experience in foreign firms. *The Scandinavian Journal of Economics*, 113(3): 637–64.

Rodriguez-Clare, A. (1996) Multinationals, linkages, and economic development. *American Economic Review*, 86: 851–73.

Rose, A.K. and Stanley, T.D. (2005) Meta-analysis of the effect of common currencies on international trade. *Journal of Economic Surveys*, 19: 347–65.

Smeets, R. (2008) Collecting the pieces of the FDI knowledge spillovers puzzle. *World Bank Research Observer*, 23: 107–38.

DOI: 10.1057/9781137367204.0020

Stanley, T.D. (2001) Wheat from chaff: meta-analysis as quantitative literature review. *Journal of Economic Perspectives*, 15: 131–50.

Stanley, T.D. and Jarrell, S.B. (2005) Meta-regression analysis: a quantitative method of literature surveys. *Journal of Economic Surveys*, 19: 299–308.

Sutton, A.J., Abrams, K.R., Jones, D.R., Sheldon, T.A. and Song, F. (2000) *Methods for Meta-Analysis in Medical Research*. Chichester: John Wiley & Sons.

UNCTAD (2012) *World Investment Report 2012: Towards a New Generation of Investment Policies*. Geneva: UNCTAD.

World Bank Group (2010) *Investing Across Border Report 2010*. Washington: The World Bank.

DOI: 10.1057/9781137367204.0020

14
Drivers of Technology Upgrading: Do Foreign Acquisitions Matter to Chinese Firms?

Sourafel Girma, Yundan Gong, Holger Görg and Sandra Lancheros

Introduction

Technology upgrading is a key element of industrialization in developing countries. While technology transfer through trade and FDI has for a long time been regarded as a major engine of technology upgrading, in recent years there has been a renewed emphasis on indigenous innovations as a means for building technology capabilities in developing countries. Many developing countries joined the competition for attracting FDI in the expectation that advanced technological and managerial knowledge embedded in FDI can build up technological capabilities in their country and drive technological upgrading in these economies. However the question is whether developing countries can rely on foreign technology to catch up with industrialized countries and whether foreign acquisition is one of the major drivers of technology upgrading in developing countries. China is a good example for investigating this question.

It is well known that one of the Chinese government's key goals in recent years has been to upgrade the technology capabilities of its industries. There are a number of drivers behind this strategy. Firstly, China's development focus is shifting: in order for China to transition from a developing to a developed country, its industry has to shift from low-value processing of relatively simple intermediate goods to the development and production of more sophisticated higher value goods. Currently, for export processing plants, value added in China as a share of total exports is estimated to be only 36 per cent whereas for the world as a whole, 75 per cent of exports consist of value added in the country of export (Hanson, 2012). A good example of the low value added in processing manufacturing are the cases of the iPhone and iPad, which are assembled in China, but for which less than 5 per cent of the total value is captured (Kraemer et al., 2011).

DOI: 10.1057/9781137367204.0021

Secondly, China's exports are getting more expensive: rising wages – which help increase domestic demand and achieve a rebalancing of the economy away from a mainly export-led strategy – and a stronger Renminbi make Chinese exports more expensive compared to low-wage countries such as Vietnam and Cambodia. For example, wages have annually increased by 14 per cent on average in the last decade (*Forbes*, 2011) and the Renminbi has appreciated by more than 30 per cent since 2005, putting pressure on lower value Chinese exports. It is therefore imperative for the Chinese government to upgrade technology in order to move from 'made in China' to 'made by China' and sustain high economic growth rates.

Over the past decades, China has continually received a large share of global inward foreign direct investment (FDI) and with $253 billion[1] was the largest FDI destination in 2012. It is therefore natural to ask the question of whether foreign investment in China is one of the main drivers for China's technology upgrading. However empirical research on the relationship between technology upgrading and foreign investment is so far limited in the literature (Guadalupe et al., 2012; Arnold and Javorecik, 2009).

This chapter investigates what kind of firm is more likely to be targeted for acquisitions by foreign firms and whether the injection of foreign capital will improve its innovation performance. The data used in the chapter contains information on a range of innovation and firm characteristics, as well as on firm performance and foreign ownership. The dataset covers more than 446,000 Chinese manufacturing firms over the period 2001–7. First, we use an ordered probit model to understand the determinants of foreign acquisition and then an approach combining the use of propensity score matching and difference-in-differences (DID) to isolate the causal effects of foreign acquisitions and to explore whether the share of foreign acquisition matters for a firm's technology upgrading. This approach, rather than establishing simple correlations between technology upgrading and foreign acquisition, can help to identify causal effects and deal with issues such as persistent firm heterogeneity and sample selection bias due to firm exit and selectivity in the acquisition process driven by firm performance.

By including a range of technology upgrading measures and different levels of foreign capital investment we consider not only whether the injection of foreign capital improves a firm's innovation performance, but also whether the increasing level of foreign capital has a direct positive impact on performance. Also, we are not only interested in the simultaneous impact taking place in the acquisition year, but also the impact in the following years. Technology upgrading measures considered include labour and skills training and new

---

[1] See FDI figures prepared by Ayse Bertrand and Emilie Kothe of the OECD Investment Division, available at: http://www.oecd.org/daf/inv/FDI per cent20in per cent20figures.pdf.

DOI: 10.1057/9781137367204.0021

product development (NPD). We find that younger, larger, more productive and exporting firms are more likely to be acquisition targets of foreign investors, while firms that are already engaged in technology upgrading don't have an advantage of attracting foreign capital. The results also show that newly acquired firms appear to invest and have better outcomes of new product development, but the positive effect only exists in firms where foreign investors control a minority capital share and only for the first two years post-acquisition.

The chapter is organized as follows. The second section discusses the theoretical framework on technology upgrading and foreign acquisition. We then go on to describe the firm-level data used and present some descriptive statistics. The fourth section outlines the empirical methodology and the following one presents the empirical evidence. We finish with a conclusion and discussion of policy implications.

Literature review

FDI may contribute to technology upgrading in the host economy in several ways. Firstly, advanced technology embedded in imported machinery and equipment can lift the production technology level of the acquired firms. Secondly, acquisitions might be used to access the specific know-how of target firms and to tap into the knowledge of the national innovation system. Therefore foreign firms are more likely to develop the innovation capability of target firms (Bertrand, 2009). Thirdly, FDI may contribute to local innovation activities by bringing in advanced management practices and thus improve the innovation efficiency of the local innovation system (Fu and Gong, 2011). Finally, the capital from foreign investors can help to improve the acquired company's absorptive capacity, and hence improve its technology level by either generating more indigenous innovative activities or 'absorbing' more of the knowledge transferred from multinational firms.

However foreign investment could also have negative impacts on a firm's technology upgrading. For example, property rights and agency cost problems could mean that foreign investors might wish to relocate innovation back to their parent companies or foreign investors are concerned that the local partner of the newly acquired firms might become a competitor in the future and therefore are reluctant to transfer technology to the acquired company (Child, 2009). Given the fact that foreign investors in China are mostly of the market-, resource- or cheap labour-seeking types, the impact on technology upgrading of domestic Chinese firms is likely to be limited.

Empirical evidence of post-acquisition effects focuses on the impact on productivity and employment. However results are still ambiguous. Arnold and Javorcik (2009) provide a comprehensive study of a wide range of firm-level

DOI: 10.1057/9781137367204.0021

outcomes, including productivity, output, employment, investment and average wages, following foreign acquisition using plant-level data from Indonesian manufacturing plants over the period 1983–2001. Their results suggest that foreign acquisition leads to significant productivity improvements in the acquired plants and these improvements exist not only in the acquisition year but also in subsequent periods. Using UK data from 1989–92, Conyon et al. (2002) find that firms that are acquired by foreign companies exhibit an increase in labour productivity and foreign firms pay employees 3.4 per cent more than domestic firms. However, with UK manufacturing data covering the period 1987–92, Harris and Robinson (2002) find negative effects of foreign acquisitions on productivity. Based on US firm-level data from 1978–2006, Chen (2011) concludes that foreign acquired firms' performance depends on the origin of the acquiring firms. Firms acquired by investors from industrialized countries lead to higher productivity, employment and sales. However firms receiving capital from developing countries are negatively affected by the acquisition in terms of firm performance. In a recent paper by Fabling and Sanderson (2011) using New Zealand firm-level data from 2000–9, the authors find that while recently acquired firms appear to increase both average wages and gross output, there is no evidence to suggest that acquisition improves productivity.

The direct existing literature on the impact of foreign acquisition on innovation is limited. Bertrand (2009) examines the causal effect of foreign acquisitions on the R&D activities of acquired firms using French data on innovative manufacturing firms over the period 1994–2004. Results support the hypothesis of a positive relationship between acquisitions and R&D spending. The authors further find that one of the resources of R&D growth is actually from external partners, especially parent companies. Another recent paper that studies the relationship between innovation and foreign ownership is by Guadalupe et al. (2012). The authors use a Spanish manufacturing firm-level dataset and develop a model taking innovation decision and potential sample selection biases into account. Their results suggest that multinational firms tend to acquire the most productive domestic firms and acquired firms are more likely to conduct more product and process innovation as well as adopting foreign technologies.

There is also very limited literature on the impact of foreign acquisition of Chinese firms, especially analysing technology upgrading performance. Using a survey dataset with more than 1000 Chinese firms, Liu et al. (2007) examine the performance impact of ownership change, distinguishing full and partial acquisitions and taking the Chinese political context into account. Woo (2012) studies sources of technological upgrading in China and India. Although he focuses on the impact of export bundles on technological upgrading, he discusses and provides evidence that inward FDI is significantly positively associated with TFP growth and FDI appears to be a main source of technology upgrading in China.

DOI: 10.1057/9781137367204.0021

One of the main issues in the foreign acquisitions literature is the potential selection bias due to the selection mechanisms and the diversity of FDI motivations. The theoretical channels through which FDI affects the performance of domestic enterprises are well understood in the literature and a wide range of empirical writing shows that foreign affiliates outperform domestic firms (e.g. Bandick et al., 2013; Greenaway and Kneller, 2007; Aitken and Harrison, 1999). The expectation of foreign firms having better performance is largely based on the belief that in order for foreign firms to be competitive they must have specific advantages to overcome the higher costs they face in entering foreign markets (Melitz, 2003; Dunning and Lundan, 2008). Greenaway and Kneller (2007) provide empirical evidence to support the notion. However it is difficult to distinguish whether the better performance is due to higher productivity before the acquisitions, or whether foreign firms indeed improve performance after the acquisition. The literature suggests that most FDI is positively selected, that is, foreign investors are more likely to select larger and more productive firms to invest (e.g. Guadalupe et al., 2012; Arnold and Javorecik, 2009; Fabling and Sanderson, 2011; Gong et al., 2007; Almeida, 2007).

This chapter differs from the existing literature in two respects. First, we consider the causal implications of foreign ownership on different measures of technology upgrading, namely labour and skills training, and new product development. Second, we not only look at the general impact of foreign acquisition, but also distinguish between minority and majority foreign acquired firms based on the level of foreign capital shares and different periods upon acquisition.

Data description

Our empirical analysis draws on the Annual Reports of Industrial Enterprise Statistics, compiled by the Chinese National Bureau of Statistics. The dataset covers all firms in China with an annual turnover of more than $800,000 and accounts for an estimated 85–90 per cent of total output in most industries. To estimate the causal effects of foreign acquisitions on technology upgrading we compare the performance of those firms that attracted foreign capital for the first time between 2001 and 2006 (about 8 per cent of our sample of organizations) and those firms that remained domestic during the observational period.

We defined two categories of foreign ownership according to the share of capital paid in by the foreign investors. The first category comprises those acquired firms with a share of foreign capital lower than 50 per cent (i.e. foreign firms with minority foreign ownership). The second category includes firms with a foreign share higher than or equal to 50 per cent (i.e. foreign firms with

DOI: 10.1057/9781137367204.0021

majority foreign ownership). Out of 3380 firms that received foreign capital for the first time between 2002 and 2006, 43 per cent were acquired with minority foreign control whereas foreign subsidiaries with majority foreign participation accounted for 57 per cent (Figure 14.1).

Summary statistics are given in Table 14.1. Overall it shows that acquired firms outperformed domestic firms in a number of dimensions in the pre-acquisition year. Compared to firms that remained domestic, acquired firms were on average younger, larger, more productive and more likely to export before being acquired. Foreign investors were also less willing to acquire Chinese firms with state participation. However in terms of technology investments, we did not observe that acquired firms always outperform domestic firms in the pre-acquisition period. For example, although we observe a higher fraction of firms engaged in new product development in the group of firms that were acquired with minority foreign participation, the differences between firms that were acquired with majority foreign ownership and firms that remained in domestic hands during the period of analysis was less evident. Also, while the fraction of firms engaged in training expenditure in the group acquired firms with minority foreign ownership was similar to that of domestic firms, the percentage of firms with training expenditure was significantly lower in the group of firms that were acquired with majority foreign control.

Figure 14.2 plots the initial productivity distribution for three groups defined already: firms that stayed domestics firms, minority- and majority-acquired firms. The figure shows that the distribution of acquired firms lies to the right of the domestic firms. It suggests that foreign-owned firms have

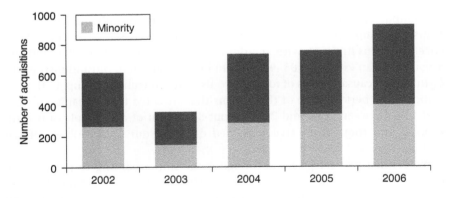

Figure 14.1 Number of acquisitions by foreign ownership structure 2002–6
Source: authors' analysis based on data from China's National Bureau of Statistics.

DOI: 10.1057/9781137367204.0021

Table 14.1 Summary statistics of pre-treatment characteristics

		Size	Prod.	Age	SOEs	RD	Training	NPD	Exports
Domestic firms	Mean	8.36	3.84	12.75	0.09	0.13	0.45	0.09	0.21
	Std. Dev.	1.63	1.20	12.72	0.29	0.34	0.50	0.28	0.41
Foreign ownership structure of acquired firms									
Minority	Mean	9.18	3.97	10.74	0.08	0.20	0.45	0.15	0.42
	Std. dev.	1.84	1.19	11.60	0.27	0.40	0.50	0.35	0.49
Majority	Mean	8.57	3.89	7.24	0.04	0.12	0.27	0.09	0.45
	Std. dev.	1.81	1.26	7.96	0.20	0.32	0.44	0.28	0.50

Source: authors' analysis based on data from China's National Bureau of Statistics.

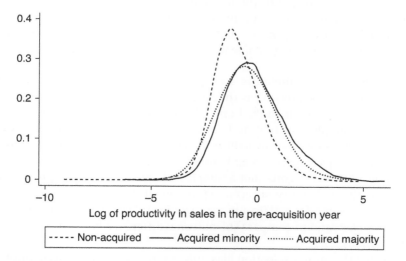

Figure 14.2 Distribution of initial productivity for majority- and minority-acquired firms and non-acquired firms

higher pre-acquisition productivity than those of non-acquired domestics firms. It indicates that foreign investors are 'cherry picking' highly productive domestic firms as targets for entry-by-acquisition. Interestingly in Figure 14.2 we notice that the group of acquired firms with a minority foreign share lie slightly to the right of the other two groups of firms. This suggests that firms with the highest pre-acquisition productivity are more likely to be targeted by foreign investors keen to engage with Chinese firms, but who don't want to or cannot acquire a majority interest in the company. It seems to be the natural choice for foreign investors who would like to access the specific know-how

DOI: 10.1057/9781137367204.0021

and local connections of target firms even if they are not able or willing to take a majority share (Bertrand, 2009).

Empirical methodology

We are interested in evaluating the effects of FDI on the population of firms that are acquired by foreign investors, compared to not receiving any FDI during the observation period. To compare the performance of acquired firms with the performance of firms that remained domestic, we combine a DID with a propensity score matching (PSM) estimator based on the nearest neighbour matching algorithm with replacement. This methodology has in recent years become an important tool of empirical studies in international economics (Girma et al., 2003; Girma and Görg, 2007; Bandick, 2011; Chen, 2011). The basic principle of the methodology is that as long as all the bias associated with differences in pre-treatment characteristics between the treated and untreated groups can be removed, then all systematic differences in outcomes are attributable to the treatment (Blundell and Costa Dias, 2000).

As discussed in the literature section, one of the major issues in evaluating the effect of acquisition is that the targeted companies are most likely not random. The combined PSM and DID approach allows us to address the problems of sample selection and control for observable and unobservable time-invariant factors that influence the acquisition decision. The approach includes two steps. The first step is to adopt the propensity score matching technique, which is to construct a sample of treated and control group firms and to use the probability of receiving treatment (foreign acquisition) as the basis for matching a treated firm to a control firm. The second step is to follow a DID approach and to compare the outcome difference between treated and control groups.

Regarding the sample selection bias, the PSM technique helps us to improve the comparability between acquired and non-acquired firms by adjusting for differences in observable characteristics in the pre-acquisition period; whereas the DID approach allows us to control for time-invariant unobserved factors and temporal trends other than acquisition that occurred during the period of analysis. In our empirical approach we evaluate the cumulative post-investment changes in the firm's technology in the acquisition year and in up to two subsequent periods. We use the firms that remain purely domestic firms as the control group and consider two types of technology upgrading, namely labour and skills training and new product development.

An ordered probit model of foreign acquisitions is estimated to determine which pre-acquisition firm characteristics predict foreign acquisition

DOI: 10.1057/9781137367204.0021

(treatment). Based on the probit model results, we can also compute the propensity score and match the treated and untreated firms[2] (Lechner, 2002).

$$F^*_{it} = \alpha + \beta X_{it-1} + d_t + d_s + d_r + v_{it} \tag{1}$$

Where F takes the value zero if the firm remains in domestic hands, 1 if the firm was acquired with minority foreign ownership and 2 if it was acquired with majority foreign control. Our control variables in the pre-acquisition period, X, include firm size, age, productivity and a set of dummy variables indicating whether the firm exports, produces new products or has state participation. We also include interaction terms between all variables in X and control for a full set of time (d_t), sectoral (d_s) and regional (d_r) dummy variables. The choice of these covariates is guided by the empirical literature on foreign acquisitions, such as Harris and Robinson (2002) and Conyon et al. (2002).

We also impose the common support condition in the matching algorithm. This involves dropping treatment firm observations whose propensity score is higher than the maximum or less than the minimum propensity score of the control group of firms. Finally, balancing tests are performed to ensure that the specification of the propensity score model 'balances' the pre-treatment variables between the treatment and control groups conditional on the propensity score (e.g. Dehejia and Wahba, 2002; Smith and Todd, 2005). We divide the sample by propensity score deciles and use a regression framework to test this for each sub-sample. The results reported in Table 14.2 indicate that the differences in covariates between acquired and non-acquired firms are not significant.

Empirical results

Determinants of foreign acquisitions

The distributions of initial productivity for majority- and minority-acquired firms and non-acquired firms shown in Figure 14.2 indicated that foreign investors are 'cherry picking' acquisition targets. Now we will turn to a more systematic regression analysis to explore the determinants of foreign acquisition. The results from the ordered probit model are reported in Table 14.3.

This model was estimated including interaction terms between all variables in this table and controlling for a full set of time (d_t), sectoral (d_s) and regional (d_r) dummy variables. Full regression results are available upon request.

---

[2] Each acquired (treated) firm is matched to one or more firms, which have similar scores but are not acquired (untreated).

DOI: 10.1057/9781137367204.0021

Table 14.2   Balancing condition: test for differences in observed pre-treatment characteristics

Decile	Size	Prod.	Age	SOE	Exporting	Training	NPD
			Minority foreign ownership				
1	0.7026**	12.4682	2.5160	0.0044	0.1153	0.2525**	0.0271
	(0.267)	(22.445)	(1.964)	(0.044)	(0.079)	(0.084)	(0.055)
2	−0.7946	14.1576	0.6577	−0.0043	0.0305	−0.1947	0.1505
	(0.423)	(45.670)	(3.032)	(0.060)	(0.111)	(0.123)	(0.095)
3	0.3040	−17.5692	−0.6422	0.0075	−0.0721	−0.0536	−0.0468
	(0.342)	(31.772)	(2.351)	(0.060)	(0.113)	(0.122)	(0.077)
4	0.2827	−36.5586	3.2227	−0.0002	−0.0178	−0.0934	0.0563
	(0.368)	(36.400)	(2.895)	(0.062)	(0.106)	(0.117)	(0.082)
5	−0.1112	−35.8213	−1.6547	−0.0485	−0.0541	−0.1551	0.0729
	(0.350)	(34.011)	(2.346)	(0.050)	(0.103)	(0.114)	(0.083)
6	−0.2757	−25.8427	−2.3625	0.0492	−0.0773	−0.1245	0.0054
	(0.338)	(32.383)	(2.338)	(0.063)	(0.099)	(0.112)	(0.076)
7	0.1211	−21.3602	0.3852	0.0809	−0.0340	−0.0878	0.1055
	(0.327)	(28.694)	(2.348)	(0.060)	(0.091)	(0.101)	(0.073)
8	−0.5499	−34.3816	−2.6387	0.0140	−0.0717	−0.2031*	0.0487
	(0.309)	(27.486)	(2.162)	(0.051)	(0.088)	(0.096)	(0.067)
9	−0.4568	−15.3823	−1.9665	−0.0082	−0.1166	−0.1753	−0.0257
	(0.295)	(30.637)	(2.139)	(0.049)	(0.086)	(0.092)	(0.060)
10	−0.2684	72.5955	−0.9177	0.0224	−0.0855	−0.1946*	−0.0211
	(0.284)	(65.954)	(2.075)	(0.047)	(0.082)	(0.088)	(0.058)
Observations	27627	27627	27627	27627	27627	27627	27627

Decile	Size	Prod.	Age	SOE	Exporting	Training	NPD
			Majority foreign ownership				
1	−0.1704	−27.1667	0.4992	0.0272	0.0652	0.0617	−0.0534
	(0.307)	(19.612)	(1.946)	(0.046)	(0.070)	(0.098)	(0.035)
2	−0.0472	46.6730	−0.1723	0.0029	−0.0694	−0.0901	0.1504
	(0.494)	(61.113)	(3.145)	(0.072)	(0.126)	(0.141)	(0.088)
3	−0.2150	−45.6327	−4.1281*	−0.0847	−0.2054	−0.0710	−0.0654
	(0.548)	(36.287)	(2.091)	(0.047)	(0.112)	(0.143)	(0.038)
4	0.3024	29.1918	1.0045	−0.0124	−0.0181	−0.0578	0.0008
	(0.368)	(29.481)	(2.435)	(0.064)	(0.096)	(0.121)	(0.050)
5	−0.0965	15.9725	−0.6942	−0.0258	−0.0227	−0.0335	0.0987
	(0.402)	(26.579)	(2.388)	(0.057)	(0.088)	(0.118)	(0.060)
6	−0.3612	11.6163	−1.9012	0.0116	−0.0709	−0.1192	0.0448
	(0.388)	(26.559)	(2.086)	(0.055)	(0.081)	(0.111)	(0.050)
7	0.0245	−6.0615	−1.0747	−0.0215	−0.0959	−0.1150	0.0431
	(0.356)	(25.434)	(2.214)	(0.053)	(0.081)	(0.108)	(0.048)
8	0.2559	44.6918	−2.1018	−0.0274	−0.1309	−0.0767	0.0265
	(0.332)	(50.982)	(2.023)	(0.049)	(0.078)	(0.104)	(0.042)
9	−0.0510	9.4747	−1.2612	−0.0432	−0.1110	−0.1602	0.0035
	(0.324)	(29.165)	(1.999)	(0.047)	(0.076)	(0.101)	(0.039)
10	0.1194	29.9243	−1.7900	−0.0471	−0.1204	−0.1250	0.0199
	(0.320)	(33.141)	(1.991)	(0.047)	(0.073)	(0.100)	(0.038)
Observations	21839	21839	21839	21839	21839	21839	21839

Note: * $p < 0.05$, ** $p < 0.01$, *** $p < 0.001$.

DOI: 10.1057/9781137367204.0021

Table 14.3 Determinants of foreign acquisitions

	Minority	Majority
Size	0.0046	0.0065
	(0.000)	(0.000)
Productivity	0.0000***	0.0000***
	(0.000)	(0.000)
Age	−0.0014***	−0.0020***
	(0.000)	(0.000)
State owned	−0.0098*	−0.0135*
	(0.002)	(0.004)
Exports	0.0184***	0.0259***
	(0.001)	(0.001)
Training	−0.0095	−0.0146
	(0.001)	(0.001)
New product development	−0.0028*	−0.0040*
	(0.002)	(0.002)
Observations	42789	42789

Note: * $p < 0.1$, ** $p < 0.05$, *** $p < 0.01$.

The results indicate the positive selection of target firms. We find that in general younger, more productive and exporting firms are more attractive to foreign investors. When we look closer at the results there are some interesting findings. First, productivity shows a positive and significant relationship with foreign acquisition, but economically it makes little difference for foreign investors to acquire firms with higher productivity. Second, there is also evidence that foreign investors are keen to target exporters because, for example, exporting firms have less exchange rate exposure and might also offer a better cultural fit as they are already engaging with overseas customers. Exporters are also more likely to be targeted when a foreign investor wants to take majority control of a company.

Foreign investors are less willing to acquire Chinese firms with state participation, especially those that were majority controlled by the foreign investors after the acquisition. In terms of technology investments however firms' investment in training expenditure or in new product development matters less for foreign multinationals. In fact, there is a negative relationship between the decision to undertake new product developments and the ability to attract foreign capital.

The impact of foreign acquisition

We use the marginal probabilities resulting from the model in Table 14.3 as our propensity score to carry out the matching procedure. The results of the post-acquisition technology improvement comparisons between acquired and

DOI: 10.1057/9781137367204.0021

matched domestically-owned firms are reported in Table 14.4. As before, we further divide our foreign-acquired firms into minority- and majority-acquired firms. Table 14.4 provides the effects of foreign acquisition on firms' technology upgrading in the year of the acquisition, while Table 14.5 consists of two panels that report the foreign acquisition impacts over the next two post-acquisition years.

In the acquisition year, we find that firms that have less than 50 per cent foreign share of capital have higher outcomes of new product development, but are less likely to invest more in labour and skill training. For example, Table 14.5 shows that a firm with minority foreign shares might achieve a 1.7 per cent increase in new product development, compared to a firm that stays domestic. In contrast, with the positive impact of minority-acquired firms, the effects on majority-acquired firms are less encouraging. There is no evidence that after acquisition foreign controlled firms conduct more skills training and have invented more new products. The results reflect our previous discussion that FDI might contribute to technology upgrading by importing machinery and equipment,[3] and accessing the specific know-how of local firms, but once the foreign investors majority-control the acquired firms they are more likely to have a global innovation strategy and relocate the innovation section to their headquarters, integrating the newly acquired firms in their international product networks, and hence have a limited contribution to technology upgrading after acquisition.

After the takeover, investing in technology in the newly acquired firm might not be the top priority for foreign investors, and it may also take some time to implement the new development strategy and see the outcomes, like the output of new product development. Therefore we also look at the impact of foreign acquisition on technology upgrading in the following

Table 14.4   Effects of foreign acquisition

Foreign control	In the year of acquisition		
	NPD	TRAINING	N
Minority	0.0172**	0.0012	40951
	(0.008)	(0.027)	
Majority	0.0034	−0.0123	41392
	(0.006)	(0.029)	

Note: $^*p < 0.10$, $^{**}p < 0.05$, $^{***}p < 0.01$.

---

[3] Arnold and Javorcik (2009) find that acquired plants invest between twice and more than three times as much in machinery as plants remaining in domestic hands, after taking into account of the initial difference between the control and treated groups.

DOI: 10.1057/9781137367204.0021

Table 14.5 Effects of foreign acquisition

One year after acquisition			
Foreign control	**NPD**	**TRAINING**	**N**
Minority	0.0299**	0.0068	40781
	(0.012)	(0.026)	
Majority	−0.0078	−0.0041	41219
	(0.010)	(0.024)	
Two year after acquisition			
Foreign control	**NPD**	**TRAINING**	**N**
Minority	0.0227	−0.0025	40256
	(0.015)	(0.024	
Majority	−0.0288**	−0.0436*	40541
	(0.014)	(0.023)	

Note: * $p < 0.10$, ** $p < 0.05$, *** $p < 0.01$.

two years after acquisition. The literature suggests that post-acquisition performance, such as productivity (Fabling and Sanderson, 2011), profit (Chen, 2011), employment and investment (Arnold and Javorcik, 2009), continue to increase for up to five years after acquisition. In terms of new product development, we find that, in line with the literature, foreign minority acquisitions tend to experience a statistically significant increase compared to the matched domestic firms in year one after the acquisition. For example, the increase in new product development is 2.99 points versus 1.72 points between the year prior and after the acquisition respectively. The impact of foreign majority-controlled firms on both measures of technology upgrading remains insignificant.

In year two after the acquisition the impact of foreign acquisition is different from the previous two years. We see no evidence for different measures of technology upgrading between minority-acquired firms and domestic firms. Given that minority-acquired companies are still largely controlled by Chinese partners, it is not surprising that the company might have similar innovative decision-making and innovative activities than domestic firms. Interestingly, when we pay attention to the impact of foreign majority acquisitions, which had little evidence of technology upgrading in previous years, we see that the acquisition is negatively associated with new product training. It supports our previous argument that the foreign parent might have a global innovation strategy and is relocating the technology development back to the parent company.

DOI: 10.1057/9781137367204.0021

In terms of labour and skill training, there is little evidence that it is associated with foreign acquisition. There are two possible reasons:

(1) The new foreign partners of acquired firms might rely more on hiring experienced workers and hence need less internal skills training upon acquisition.
(2) The expenditure of training data in China is also related to other management costs, such as hosting guests and so on.

Therefore it might be affected by tighter cost controls after the acquisition.

Conclusion

In this chapter we employ rich firm-level data from the Chinese manufacturing sector in order to explore whether foreign investors are mainly acquiring the best domestic firms and whether the foreign acquisition contributes to technology upgrading – one of the main priorities for the Chinese government. In order to identify a causal relationship and control for selection effects in acquisition, we use a combination of propensity score matching and a DID estimator, which is satisfied with the common support and balancing condition. We find that foreign acquisitions indeed are positively associated with younger firms and exporters, but negatively associated with state participation in the Chinese firm.

In terms of the effects of foreign acquisitions on Chinese firms' technology upgrading, it is not surprising that acquired firms are associated with higher levels of innovation due to the premium technology advantage of foreign firms, the potential technology transfer via imported machinery, access to international know-how and an increase in the absorptive capacity of acquired firms. However this positive relationship only exists for minority acquisitions and only for the first two years after acquisition. We do not find evidence that firms with majority foreign capital improve their technology levels, measured by new product output and skills training. This is in line with our argument that foreign investors who have majority control of an acquired firm are likely to relocate their innovation section back to their home land due to global development strategies.

The policy implications of our findings are very important for both the Chinese government and foreign investors. A Chinese government keen on upgrading Chinese firms' technology level, can guide foreign investors to work together with Chinese partners with less than 50 per cent of capital share in the company, and to encourage those newly acquired firms to invest in R&D and generate a higher level of new product outputs. For foreign investors, it seems likely that over time they will become more adept at growing their

DOI: 10.1057/9781137367204.0021

Chinese affiliates into full-fledged parts in their international development strategies and so ensure that the local firm fully participates in the technological resources offered by their parent company.

References

Aitken, B.J. and Harrison, A.E. (1999) Do domestic firms benefit from direct foreign investment? Evidence from Venezuela. *American Economic Review*, 89(3): 605–18.

Arnold, J.M. and Javorcik, B.S. (2009) Gifted kids or pushy parents? Foreign direct investment and plant productivity in Indonesia. *Journal of International Economics*, 79(1): 42–53.

Bandick, R. (2011) Foreign acquisition, wages and productivity. *The World Economy*, 34: 931–51.

Bandick, R., Görg, H. and Karpaty, P. (2013) Foreign acquisitions, domestic multinationals, and R&D. *Scandinavian Journal of Economics* (forthcoming).

Bertrand, O. (2009) Effects of foreign acquisitions on R&D activity: evidence from firm-level data for France. *Research Policy*, 38(6): 1021–31.

Blundell, R. and Costa Dias, M. (2000) Evaluation methods for non-experimental data. *Fiscal Studies*, 21(4): 427–68.

Chen, W. (2011) The effect of investor origin on firm performance: domestic and foreign direct investment in the United States. *Journal of International Economics*, 83(2): 219–28.

Child, J. (2009) China and international business, in Alan M. Rugman (ed.) *The Oxford Handbook of International Business*. Oxford: Oxford University Press, pp. 648–86.

Conyon, M.J., Girma, S., Thompson, S. and Wright, P.W. (2002) The productivity and wage effects of foreign acquisition in the United Kingdom. *Journal of Industrial Economics*, 50(1): 85–102.

Dehejia, R. and Wahba, S. (2002) Propensity score matching methods for non-experimental causal studies. *Review of Economics and Statistics*, 84: 151–61.

Dunning, J. and Lundan, S. (2008) *Multinational Enterprises and the Global Economy*. Cheltenham: Edward Elgar.

Fabling, R. and Sanderson, L. (2011) Foreign acquisition and the performance of New Zealand firms. Reserve Bank of New Zealand discussion paper: ISSN 1175-7576.

Forbes (2011) China faces years of double-digit wage increases, currency appreciation. Available at: http://www.forbes.com/sites/russellflannery/2011/03/18/china-faces-years-of-double-digit-wage-increases-currency-appreciation/ [accessed 19/7/2013].

Fu, X. and Gong, Y. (2011) Indigenous and foreign innovation efforts and drivers of technological upgrading: evidence from China. *World Development*, 39(7): 1213–25.

Gong, Y., Görg, H., and Maioli, S. (2007) Employment effects of privatization and foreign acquisition of Chinese state-owned enterprises. *International Journal of the Economics of Business*, 14(2): 197–214.

Girma, S., Greenaway, D. and Kneller, R. (2003) Export market exit and performance dynamics: a causality analysis of matched firms. *Economics Letters*, 80(2): 181–7.

Girma, S. and Görg, H. (2007) Evaluating the foreign ownership wage premium using a difference-in-differences matching approach. *Journal of International Economics*, 72: 97–112.

Greenaway, D. and Kneller, R. (2007) Firm heterogeneity, exporting and foreign direct investment. *Economic Journal*, 117(517): F134–F161.

DOI: 10.1057/9781137367204.0021

Guadalupe, M., Kuzmina, O. and Thomas, C. (2012) Innovation and foreign ownership. *American Economic Review*, 102(7): 3594–627.

Hanson, G.H. (2012) The rise of middle kingdoms: emerging economies in global trade. *Journal of Economic Perspectives*, 26(2): 4164.

Harris, R. and Robinson, C. (2002) The effect of foreign acquisitions on total factor productivity: plant-level evidence from UK manufacturing, 1987–1992. *Review of Economics and Statistics*, 84: 562–68.

Kraemer, K.L., Linden, G. and Dedrick, J. (2011) Capturing value in global networks: Apple's iPad and iPhone, available at: http://pcic.merage.uci.edu/papers/2011/Value_iPad_iPhone.pdf [accessed 19/7/2013].

Lechner, M. (1999) Earnings and employment effects of continuous off-the-job training in East Germany after unification. *Journal of Business & Economic Statistics*, 17: 74–90.

Liu, G.S., Sun, P. and Beine, J. (2007) The performance impact of ownership transformation in China. *Mimeo*.

Melitz, M. (2003) The impact of trade on intra-industry reallocations and aggregate industry productivity. *Econometrica*, 71(6): 1695–725.

Smith, J. and Todd, R.E. (2005) Does matching overcome Lalonde's critique of nonexperimental estimators? *Journal of Econometrics*, 125: 305–53.

Woo, J. (2012) Technological upgrading in China and India: what do we know? OECD Developing Centre, working paper no. 308.

DOI: 10.1057/9781137367204.0021

15
International R&D Spillovers, TFP and Institutional Distance

Dolores Añón Higón and Miguel Manjón-Antolín

Introduction

Research and development (R&D) activities are an important source of productivity gains and ultimately a source of economic growth. However these productivity gains may arise not only from the R&D activities performed by the firm but also from those performed by other firms. This is the case of the R&D spillovers from foreign-owned to domestically-owned firms through foreign direct investment (FDI). The argument is that foreign multinational corporations (MNCs) establish subsidiaries overseas and transfer the necessary knowledge to their subsidiaries for them to produce and sell their goods. But since the transferred knowledge has a certain public goods quality, it may spread through non-market mechanisms over the entire economy, thus leading to productivity gains in domestic firms (Blomström, 1989).

There is a large body of work investigating whether FDI inflows indeed bring about productivity spillovers for domestic firms. In fact, this has been a key argument used by governments to devote large sums of money to attract FDI. However the empirical literature using firm-level data is inconclusive regarding the magnitude and the direction of such foreign spillover effects. Some micro-level studies confirm positive productivity spillovers from FDI, while others find negative or no spillovers.[1]

This study extends the current empirical literature to analyse whether the R&D conducted by foreign firms leads to productivity gains in domestic UK manufacturing and service firms during the period 2002 to 2009. We follow the previous literature in that our approach relies on measuring the impact of foreign R&D spillovers from FDI upon the domestic firms' total factor

---

[1] Positive productivity spillovers from FDI are reported in for example Añón Higón and Vasilakos (2011), Girma et al. (2001), Görg and Strobl (2005) and Javorcik (2004); negative productivity spillovers from FDI are reported in Aitken and Harrison (1999) and Konings (2001).

DOI: 10.1057/9781137367204.0022

productivity (TFP). However we differ from previous studies in that we propose a two-step strategy that addresses both the potential pitfalls in estimating TFP (see e.g. Beveren, 2011) and the difficulties in measuring foreign R&D spillovers (see Görg and Strobl, 2001).

In the first step of our empirical strategy we use a Generalized Method of Moments (GMM) approach to estimate a Cobb-Douglas production function and retrieve the TFP (Wooldridge, 2009; Doraszelski and Jaumandreu, 2013). In particular we assume that firms' expectations about their future productivity depends not only on their current productivity but also on their lagged R&D expenditure (Añón Higón and Manjón-Antolín, 2012). In the second step, we use regression analysis to determine the impact of R&D spillovers on TFP. Moreover we analyse whether the magnitude of these spillovers may be influenced by the degree of internationalization of the firm by distinguishing between UK local and MNC firms.

Since our interest lies in studying 'pure' R&D spillovers (as opposed to output or other forms of investment spillovers), we propose a new measure of foreign R&D spillovers based on the institutional distance between the foreign and host country. According to institutional theorists (North, 1990), institutional distance reflects the extent of (dis)similarities between countries (Kostova, 1999). We argue that the larger the institutional distance between the country of origin of the foreign affiliate and that of the domestic firm, the lower the ability of the domestic firm to tap into the knowledge spilled out by the foreign affiliate. Factors such as different language, business culture, organizational practices or the institutional framework make up a physic distance that may impede or limit the spillover effect.

There is a large body of work investigating whether FDI inflows indeed bring about productivity spillovers for domestic firms. However previous micro-level studies on the topic are inconclusive regarding the magnitude and direction of foreign spillovers. This may be interpreted as evidence that there is no universal relationship between FDI and domestic firms' productivity. Differences in findings depend significantly on the research design, methodological approach, types of data used, estimation strategy and even on the construction of the spillover variable (Görg and Strobl, 2001). However some studies argue that the mixed findings may be attributed to domestic firms' characteristics or to the host countries' ability to absorb productivity spillovers (Görg and Greenaway, 2004; Smeets, 2008). Our approach addresses these issues by distinguishing the effects on domestic firms by industry and degree of internationalization, differentiating between UK MNCs and local firms. We find that UK firms benefit from FDI-transmitted R&D spillovers; with UK MNCs obtaining higher gains than local firms. Additionally, we show that not all foreign firms bring the same extent of positive externalities. In this respect, our results show that the

DOI: 10.1057/9781137367204.0022

(dis)similarities between the host and the home countries may be an additional factor behind the differences in these findings.

The rest of the chapter is structured as follows. The next section provides a review of the literature on international knowledge spillovers through FDI. The third section develops the empirical strategy. Then data and sources are described before a discussion of the results is presented. The last section provides concluding remarks.

Previous literature

The arguments for the existence of knowledge spillovers from FDI are based on the assumption that foreign MNCs possess firm-specific advantages, particularly in the form of intangible assets, that compensate for the higher costs induced by operating in foreign markets (Dunning, 2000). These superior advantages are transferred to their subsidiaries, but there is part of these benefits that spillover to domestic firms. The literature has identified several channels along which knowledge may spillover from a foreign firm to a domestic firm (Smeets, 2008): (a) demonstration effects (through imitation or reverse-engineering); (b) worker mobility from foreign firms towards domestic companies; and (c) upstream and downstream (inter-industry) linkages between the foreign firm and domestic suppliers and customers. Finally, competition in the domestic economy between foreign affiliates and domestic firms is an incentive for the latter to make a more efficient use of existing resources and technology or even to adopt new technologies. However the efficiency of domestic firms may also be negatively affected through this channel, as the presence of foreign subsidiaries may imply significant loss of market share, forcing them to operate on a less efficient scale, with a consequent increase in average costs (Aitken and Harrison, 1999).

The literature is vast and the results of previous studies analysing the role of knowledge spillovers due to FDI are inconclusive, ranging from negative to positive or insignificant depending on the methods and data used (for reviews on the topic see Blomström and Kokko, 1998; Görg and Greenaway, 2004; Smeets, 2008). In the empirical literature, we can identify two strands, one that focuses on the impact of horizontal (intra-industry) foreign spillovers, and the other that looks at the effect of inter-industry spillovers through customers (forward) and suppliers (backwards) linkages with foreign affiliates. The results of the former are rather mixed (Keller and Yeaple, 2003; Haskel et al., 2007; Barrios and Strobl, 2002); while there seems to be more consensus on the latter. In particular, there is evidence of productivity-enhancing backward spillovers to local upstream firms but no evidence for the existence of forward spillover effects (Javorcik, 2004; and Kugler, 2006).

DOI: 10.1057/9781137367204.0022

On the other hand, while most studies measure FDI-transmitted knowledge spillovers using a crude measure of the foreign presence (e.g. the share of foreign affiliates employment), there are few that use foreign affiliates' R&D activity as an alternative. Among those studies that focus therefore on 'pure' R&D spillovers transmitted through FDI, the results are also rather mixed. On the one hand, Todo (2006) for Japanese firms and Negassi (2009) for French firms find positive R&D spillovers, although relatively small in size. On the other hand, Barrios et al. (2012) find that the R&D undertaken by foreign plants that are active in Ireland has no significant effect on the productivity of Irish firms; but the presence of these foreign affiliates could induce the diffusion of global (i.e. beyond the national borders) R&D spillovers. Finally, Braconier et al. (2001) for Swedish firms and McVicar (2002) for UK firms find no significant R&D spillovers transmitted via FDI. In the same line, the study by Driffield (2001) using a cross-section of UK firms finds no evidence of 'pure' R&D spillovers from foreign-owned R&D in the UK.

Empirical strategy

Our empirical analysis involves two steps. In the first step, we estimate a Cobb-Douglas production function and obtain an estimate of TFP.[2] In the second step, we use regression analysis to study the effect of R&D spillovers on TFP transmitted through FDI.

Estimation of TFP

We assume that firms produce a homogeneous good using a Cobb-Douglas technology:[3]

$$y_{jt} = \beta_0 + \beta_k k_{jt} + \beta_l l_{jt} + \beta_m m_{jt} + \omega_{jt} + e_{jt} \tag{1}$$

where y_{jt}, k_{jt}, l_{jt} and m_{jt} denote the output, capital, labour and intermediate inputs of firm j at period t, respectively. The model is completed with two unobservables: firm's productivity (ω_{jt}) and an error term with the standard properties (e_{jt}). Our goal is to consistently estimate the firm's productivity.

We follow Olley and Pakes (1996) and Levinsohn and Petrin (2003) in assuming that the capital of a firm evolves following a certain law of motion that is not directly related to its current productivity (namely, it is a state variable), whereas labour and intermediate materials can easily be adjusted

---

[2] The Cobb-Douglas production function has been widely used as a conventional framework to obtain estimates of TFP (for a rcent survey see Van Beveren, 2011).

[3] We denote the log of a variable with lower letter cases and with upper letter cases a variable in levels.

DOI: 10.1057/9781137367204.0022

whenever the firm faces a productivity shock (i.e. they are variable factors). In particular, it is assumed that $k_{jt} = (1 + \lambda) k_{jt-1} + I_{jt-1}$, with λ being the discount factor and I_{jt-1} the demand of physical investments (buildings and equipment). Notice that this means that the decision of how much capital the firm uses in period t is made in period $t-1$. In contrast, the amount of labour and materials used is decided in period t, the period they are actually used.

To retrieve the firm's productivity from equation (1), estimation proceeds by defining a function that controls for the correlation between the variable factors and ω_{jt}. More precisely, the procedure lies on the idea of including as an additional regressor a proxy that 'controls for the part of the error correlated with inputs by "annihilating" any variation that is possibly related to the productivity term' (Levinsohn and Petrin, 2003: 320). To this end, it is assumed that the demand for intermediate materials is a function of firms' capital and productivity. Also, such demand for intermediate materials is monotonic and strictly increasing in productivity (the only unobservable in this function).

Under certain conditions we can then invert the intermediate materials demand function to derive firm's productivity as:

$$\omega_{jt} = h(k_{jt}, m_{jt}) \tag{2}$$

where h is an unknown function. Substituting equation (2) into the production function equation (1) we get our first estimating equation:

$$y_{jt} = \beta_1 + \beta_l l_{jt} + H(k_{jt}, m_{jt}) + e_{jt} \tag{3}$$

Notice that, in contrast to (1), this expression is not subject to endogeneity concerns. Observe also that we have included $H(\cdot)$ rather than $h(\cdot)$ to make apparent that plugging $h(\cdot)$ into the production function equation (1) results in the coefficients of capital and intermediate materials being non-identified (and a new intercept, β_1). But since we can only identify the labour coefficient from equation (3), we require an additional estimating equation to identify β_k and β_m (Wooldridge, 2009).

We consider two alternatives, depending on what is the assumed law of motion of productivity. First, we assume that productivity is governed by an exogenous Markov process with transition probabilities $P(\omega_{jt} \mid \omega_{jt-1})$. Second, we assume that productivity is governed by an endogenous or controlled first-order Markov process with transition probabilities $P(\omega_{jt} \mid \omega_{jt-1}, rd_{jt-1})$, where rd_{jt-1} is lagged R&D expenditures (Añón Higón and Manjón-Antolín, 2012; Doraszelski and Jaumandreu, 2013). These Markovian assumptions imply that:

$$\omega_{jt} = E(\omega_{jt} \mid \omega_{jt-1}) = g(\omega_{jt-1}) + \xi_{jt} \tag{4a}$$

DOI: 10.1057/9781137367204.0022

$$\omega_{jt} = E(\omega_{jt} \mid \omega_{jt-1}, rd_{jt-1}) = g(\omega_{jt-1}, rd_{jt-1}) + \xi_{jt} \tag{4b}$$

with E being the expectation operator, $g(\cdot)$ an unknown function and ξ_{jt} an innovation shock that is mean independent of ω_{jt-1} (and rd_{jt-1}). Also, it can be shown that:

$$g(\omega_{jt-1}) = g(h(k_{jt-1}, m_{jt-1})) = G(k_{jt-1}, m_{jt-1}) \tag{5a}$$

$$g(\omega_{jt-1}, rd_{jt-1}) = g(h(k_{jt-1}, m_{jt-1}), rd_{jt-1}) = G(k_{jt-1}, m_{jt-1}, rd_{jt-1}) \tag{5b}$$

Plugging this result into the production function equation (1) we obtain the second estimating equation:

$$y_{jt} = \beta_2 + \beta_k k_{jt} + \beta_l l_{jt} + \beta_m m_{jt} + G(.) + u_{jt} \tag{6}$$

where $u_{jt} = \xi_{jt} + e_{jt}$ is a composite error term and $G(\cdot)$ is given by either (5a) or (5b).

We estimate the system of equations (3) and (6) by GMM using (lagged) inputs and the lagged R&D expenditures as instruments. In particular, we use capital as an instrument in both estimation equations because our timing assumptions make it uncorrelated with ξ_{jt}. Also, labour and materials can be used as instruments in the first equation because they are uncorrelated with e_{jt}. In contrast, they cannot be used as instruments in the second estimating equation because our timing assumptions imply that they are correlated with ξ_{jt} (and thus with u_{jt}). Consequently we use their lagged values. Lastly, we also include lagged R&D among the instruments of the second equation when assuming an endogenous process for the productivity.

Thus we construct the GMM estimator using the following moment conditions:

$$E\left[\begin{pmatrix} l_{jt}, A(k_{jt}, m_{jt}) \\ l_{jt-1}, k_{jt}, A(k_{jt-1}, m_{jt-1}) \end{pmatrix}\begin{pmatrix} e_{jt} \\ \xi_{jt} + e_{jt} \end{pmatrix}\right] = 0 \tag{7a}$$

$$E\left[\begin{pmatrix} l_{jt}, A(k_{jt}, m_{jt}) \\ l_{jt-1}, k_{jt}, A(k_{jt-1}, m_{jt-1}, rd_{jt-1}) \end{pmatrix}\begin{pmatrix} e_{jt} \\ \xi_{jt} + e_{jt} \end{pmatrix}\right] = 0 \tag{7b}$$

where $A(\cdot)$ is a (second- or third-degree) polynomial function in its arguments. We take this expression to the data using (second- or third-degree) polynomial approximations to the unknown functions $H(\cdot)$ and $G(\cdot)$. This provides both coefficient estimates of the production function and firms' productivity estimates, which we compute as $TFP_{jt} = \hat{G}(\cdot)$.

DOI: 10.1057/9781137367204.0022

Foreign R&D spillovers

With the TFP estimates in hand we are now able to turn to the key purpose of the study, namely the estimation of the impact of the R&D activities conducted by foreign firms in the UK on the productivity of domestic companies. To this end we relate the estimated firm-level TFP to the foreign R&D spillover in a particular industry using regression analysis. More specifically we estimate the following model by OLS:

$$ln(TFP_{dt}) = \lambda_0 + \lambda_1 \ln S_{dit}^f + \sum_{d \in i, i=1}^{i-1} \delta_i I_i + \sum_{t=1}^{t-1} \delta_t T_t + \upsilon_{dt} \tag{8}$$

where d denotes a domestic firm, S_{dit}^f is a variable that captures foreign R&D activities at the (two-digit) industry i, υ_{dt} is the error term, and I_i and T_t are industry and time dummies that control for productivity differences across industries and macro productivity shocks, respectively.

The model is estimated for the sample of domestic firms to address the potential biases associated with the fact that foreign investors tend to acquire the most successful domestic companies (Djankov and Hoekman, 2000). Also, we correct for heteroskedasticity and cluster the standard error at the firm level. Lastly, we proxy intra-industry foreign R&D spillovers using a weighted average of the R&D conducted by foreign-owned firms in each industry:

$$S_{dit}^f = \sum_{j \in i} w_{UK}^f R\&D_{jt} \times FOREIGN_j = \sum_{j \in i} (1 / ID_{UK}^f) R\&D_{jt} \times FOREIGN_j \tag{9}$$

where $FOREIGN_j$ is a dummy that distinguishes foreign-owned firms and the weights w_{UK}^f correspond to the inverse of the institutional distance (ID) between the host country (the UK, in our case) and the home country of the foreign-owned multinational (f).

Notice that this variable measures foreign R&D spillovers under the assumption that the more institutionally distant two firms, the less able they are to benefit from the R&D performed. Yet, as suggested by Abraham et al. (2010), there may be different forces at work for firms engaged in international activities compared to those confined to local markets. Based on this argument, we assume that UK MNCs are able to reap higher gains from the R&D spillovers in contrast to local firms. Therefore, we extend equation (8) to include the interaction between lnS_{it}^f and a dummy distinguishing UK multinationals (UKMNC).

$$ln(TFP_{dt}) = \lambda_0 + \lambda_1 \ln S_{dit}^f + \lambda_2 UKMNC \times lnS_{dit}^f + \sum_{d \in i, i=1}^{i-1} \delta_i I_i + \sum_{t=1}^{t-1} \delta_t T_t + \upsilon_{dt} \tag{10}$$

DOI: 10.1057/9781137367204.0022

Empirical results

Data and statistical sources

The initial sample of firms was drawn from the 2007 R&D UK Score-Board and consists of the top 850 UK firms in terms of reported data on R&D expenditures in 2007. However our final sample is an unbalanced panel consisting of 599 manufacturing and service firms observed over the period 2002–9. The panel is unbalanced due to the existence of missing observations in critical variables. In particular, to construct the final sample we restricted to firms that provided information for three or more consecutive periods on turnover, number of employees, value of fixed assets, cost of sales and R&D expenditures. These were the variables required to implement the first step of our empirical strategy.

Information on R&D expenditures comes from the R&D Score-Board. This is an annual register published by the Department for Innovation, Universities & Skills (DIUS) and the Department for Business, Enterprise and Regulatory Reform (BERR), which covers a representative sample of the top R&D spenders in the UK. The remaining variables were obtained from the accounting information provided by Bureau van Dijk's database FAME (Financial Analysis Made Easy). In particular, deflated output (y) was obtained from data on turnover deflated by the Producer Price Index (draw from the ONS). To measure capital input (k), data on the book value of fixed assets was deflated by the Investment Price Index, which were obtained from the ONS. We use the firm's number of employees to measure labour (l), and to obtain a measure of intermediate inputs (m), where the cost of sales was deflated by the Intermediate Inputs Price Index. The firm's real R&D expenditure (r) was obtained by deflating nominal values of firm's R&D expenditures by the Producer Price Index.

As for the distinction between domestic and foreign companies, we use information on the ultimate owner of the firm (direct and indirect share of equity larger than 25 per cent) reported in FAME in the last year of the sample period, 2009. Also, we distinguish between foreign and domestic MNCs depending on whether the firm reports to have subsidiaries abroad or not in 2009. Moreover our sample of domestic-owned MNCs is restricted to those with at least a 25 per cent control over at least one subsidiary owned abroad.

Lastly, our measure of institutional distance follows Kogut and Singh (1988) and is based on Hofstede's (2001) national cultural scores. In particular, for foreign affiliates it was obtained as the estimated distance between the UK and the home country of the parent firm along Hofstede's (2001) power distance, uncertainty avoidance, masculinity/femininity and individualism scores:

$$ID^f = \sqrt{\sum_{r=1}^{4} (I_{rf} - I_{rUK})^2} \tag{11}$$

DOI: 10.1057/9781137367204.0022

where ID^f is the institutional distance for the *f-th* country and I_{rf} represents Hofstede's score along the *r-th* cultural dimension and country *f*.

Table 15.1 shows the main descriptive statistics from the sample of firms used in the first step as well as for the sample of domestic firms (i.e. excluding foreign affiliates) used in the second step. Figures show that about half of the innovative firms are foreign owned, while if we look at domestic innovative firms, three out of four are MNCs (i.e. UK firms that hold subsidiaries abroad). In general, our sample consists mostly of large, mature and internationalized firms. In addition, t–tests show that foreign-owned firms sell more, use more intermediate inputs and have higher R&D intensities with respect to domestic firms.

Estimates

Table 15.2 provides estimates of the production function equation (1) using alternative estimation methods: OLS, Fixed Effects and the GMM approach described in the previous section. Results from OLS and Fixed Effects are similar to those obtained in previous studies (for an overview see Van Beveren, 2011). In particular, figures in the first column of Table 15.2 show that, compared to the endogenous GMM estimator (fifth column), OLS tends to overestimate the effect of variable inputs (labour and intermediates).

Columns 3 and 4 of Table 5.2 provide GMM estimates when using an exogenous Markov process (i.e. without including R&D in the productivity process) and an endogenous Markov process (i.e. including R&D in the

Table 15.1 Descriptive statistics

	All sample		Domestic firms	
	Mean	Std. dev.	Mean	Std. dev.
Turnover*	11.337	2.284	11.013	2.646
Intermediates*	10.746	2.573	10.308	2.907
Labour*	6.422	1.859	6.401	2.183
Capital*	10.272	2.493	10.269	2.770
R&D*	8.307	1.565	8.35	1.667
TFP*	−1.026	0.485	−1.068	0.528
Spillovers*			13.645	1.635
UKLocal	0.120	0.325	0.261	0.439
UKMNC	0.339	0.474	0.739	0.439
FOREIGN	0.541	0.498		
Observations	3661		1681	

Note: asterisks denote variables in logs.

DOI: 10.1057/9781137367204.0022

Table 15.2   Production function estimates

	OLS	Fixed Effects	GMM Exog. Markov	GMM End. Markov (1)	GMM End. Markov (2)
l	0.2800***	0.2345***	0.3015***	0.2968***	0.2719***
	(0.011)	(0.017)	(0.017)	(0.017)	(0.016)
m	0.6331***	0.6696***	0.6354***	0.6382***	0.6263***
	(0.007)	(0.010)	(0.036)	(0.036)	(0.034)
k	0.0591***	0.0594***	0.0566**	0.0369	0.0538**
	(0.007)	(0.008)	(0.025)	(0.025)	(0.025)
Hansen			0.44	8.23	4.14
p-value			0.51	0.00	0.39

Note: standard errors in brackets. Level of significance: ***1 per cent and **5 per cent. The number of observations for OLS and Fixed Effects is 3661; whereas it reduces to 3062 in the GMM estimates because of the use of lagged variables.

productivity process), respectively. In both cases we used third-degree polynomial approximations for the functions $H(\cdot)$ and $G(\cdot)$. However the capital coefficient was not statistically significant in the second. In fact, results from the Hansen test indicate that the model is misspecified. We consequently reestimated equation (1) using a second-degree polynomial for the function $H(\cdot)$ in the first estimating equation. These estimates are reported in the last column of Table 15.2. There are now no signs of misspecification in the model and the coefficient of capital is statistically significant.[4]

Table 15.3 presents results from the estimation of equation (8) for the sample of domestic firms. In particular, the dependent variable is the logarithm of the TFP estimated from the specification reported in the last column of Table 15.2. Column 1 shows that when spillovers are measured as an unweighted sum of the R&D performed by foreign firms there is no significant effect. In contrast, when using as weights the institutional distance between the UK and the host country, results in column 2 show that, on average, UK innovative firms benefit from the R&D activities conducted by foreign firms in the same sector. More specifically, an increase of 10 per cent in the R&D activities of foreign firms increases the (log) productivity of UK firms by about 0.6 percentage points. However one may argue that spillovers in column 2 may be capturing geographical spillovers instead. As a robustness test in column 3 we present the

---

[4] We have experimented with other specifications, varying the degree of the polynomials from two to four. However the results we obtained are largely consistent with those reported in Table 15.2.

DOI: 10.1057/9781137367204.0022

Table 15.3   Intra-industry foreign R&D spillovers

	(1)	(2)	(3)
Spillovers (unweighted)	0.0485		
	(0.0341)		
Spillovers (CD weighted)		0.0588**	
		(0.0275)	
Spillovers (GD weighted)			0.0086
			(0.0263)
Constant	−1.4731***	−1.6037***	−1.1353***
	(0.3525)	(0.3110)	(0.2805)
Industry	Yes	Yes	Yes
Year	Yes	Yes	Yes
R^2	0.10	0.11	0.10

Note: OLS estimates, industry and year dummies included but not reported. The dependent variable is the TFP estimated from the last column of Table 15.2. Spillovers in column 1 are computed without weighting, while columns 2 and 3 are weighted by institutional distance (ID) and geographical distance (GD) respectively. Standard errors are in brackets. Level of significance: ***1 per cent, **5 per cent and *10 per cent. The number of observations is 1405.

results when spillovers are obtained by weighting foreign R&D by the inverse of the geographical distance between London and the capital city of the home country of the foreign firm. The results show that geographical proximity may not be the relevant channel of intra-industry knowledge transfer. Instead, institutional proximity appears as the significant one.

Additionally Table 15.4 shows the results from the estimation of equation (10) for the sample of domestic firms. The results in column 1 show that UK MNCs significantly benefit from foreign spillovers in contrast to local innovative firms. Even after controlling for potential competition effects, both in the domestic market (using industry market share) and overseas (using a dummy variable for firms that export), the results confirm the positive impact on foreign R&D spillovers (column 2 in Table 15.4). This suggests that UK firms with the highest degree of internationalization (i.e. UK MNCs) benefit more from R&D foreign spillovers. Lastly, it is interesting to remark that, given the measurement of the R&D spillover variable; domestic firms will obtain larger benefits in terms of productivity improvements from the R&D conducted by foreign firms that are institutionally close to domestic firms. These results are also robust when controlling for firm's own R&D effort, which appears significantly positive (column 3 in Table 15.4). In addition, in column 4 (Table 15.4) we test the assumption as to whether the degree of internationalization measured as firm's export intensity matters for the ability to absorb foreign knowledge. The results however do no support this hypothesis.

DOI: 10.1057/9781137367204.0022

Table 15.4   Intra-industry foreign R&D spillovers

	(1)	(2)	(3)	(4)
Spillovers	0.0456*	0.0531**	0.0532**	0.0639**
	(0.0274)	(0.0261)	(0.0265)	(0.0263)
Spillovers × UKMNC	0.0138***	0.0117***	0.0087*	
	(0.0044)	(0.0045)	(0.0047)	
Spillovers × export int				−0.0094
				(0.0073)
Exports		0.0608	0.0606	0.1391*
		(0.0517)	(0.0514)	(0.0829)
Market Share		0.8403***	0.4586**	0.4501**
		(0.2135)	(0.2314)	(0.2394)
Stock of R&D			0.4323**	0.5451***
			(0.1696)	(0.1749)
Constant	−1.5929***	−1.9980***	−3.4685***	−3.9313***
	(0.2997)	(0.2982)	(0.6733)	(0.7044)
Industry	Yes	Yes	Yes	Yes
Year	Yes	Yes	Yes	Yes
R^2	0.13	0.16	0.18	0.18
Observations	1405	1405	1402	1402

Note: OLS estimates, industry and year dummies included but not reported. The dependent variable is the TFP estimated from the last column of Table 15.2. Spillovers are computed weighting by institutional distance. Exports is a dummy variable, the Market Share is the share of industry sales, and the stock of R&D is obtained through the perpetual inventory method using a 15 per cent depreciation rate and a growth rate of 5 per cent to estimate the initial stock. Standard errors are in brackets. Level of significance: ***1 per cent, **5 per cent and *10 per cent.

Conclusion

In this study, using a panel of UK innovative firms over the period 2002–9, we have examined the impact of FDI driven R&D spillovers on the performance of domestic firms. Previous studies have ignored endogeneity concerns and/or imposed a linear accumulation of knowledge with linear depreciation rates. In contrast, our empirical methodology overcomes these limitations and consistently estimates a TFP measure controlling for endogenous R&D and allowing for a flexible accumulation of the stock of knowledge. Another advantage of our approach is that to obtain a measure of the R&D spillover we use data on the affiliate R&D spending instead of using a more general proxy for the presence of FDI (for instance, the share of foreign employment). Besides, assuming that institutional distance impedes to fully appropriate the benefits of foreign innovation, the R&D conducted by foreign firms in the same industry is weighted by the inverse of the institutional distance between the home country of the affiliates and the UK.

DOI: 10.1057/9781137367204.0022

The baseline result of our analysis is that UK firms benefit from FDI-transmitted R&D spillovers. However not all foreign firms bring the same extent of positive externalities upon their domestic counterparts. Our results show that UK firms tend to benefit more from the R&D efforts exerted by institutionally close foreign firms. Moreover UK MNCs obtain higher benefits in terms of productivity than local firms, suggesting that they enjoy a greater capacity to absorb foreign knowledge or a greater ability to narrow the negative effects arising from institutional distance. These results have important policy implications. If the productivity of UK innovative firms benefits from the R&D activities of foreign-owned MNCs, policies aimed not only at attracting foreign presence but also at increasing their innovation activities may, as a consequence, be an instrument to boost the productivity of UK innovative firms. Additionally policy explicitly aimed at boosting UK overseas investments, will help increase firms' ability to absorb foreign knowledge and improve productivity.

References

Abraham, F., Konings, J. and Slootmackers, V. (2010) FDI spillovers in the Chinese manufacturing sector: evidence of firm heterogeneity. *Economics of Transition*, 18: 143–82.

Aitken, B.J. and Harrison, A.E. (1999) Do domestic firms benefit from direct foreign investment? Evidence from Venezuela. *American Economic Review*, 89(3): 605–18.

Añón Higón, D. and Manjón-Antolín, M. (2012) Multinationality, foreignness and institutional distance in the relation between R&D and productivity. *Research Policy*, 41: 592–601.

Añón Higón, D. and Vasilakos, N. (2011) Foreign direct investment spillovers: evidence from the British retail sector. *The World Economy*, 34: 642–66.

Barrios, S. and Strobl, E. (2002) Foreign direct investment and productivity spillovers: evidence from the Spanish experience. *Weltwirtschaftliches Archiv*, 138: 459–81.

Barrios, S., Bertinelli, L., Heinen, A. and Strobl, E. (2012) Exploring the existence of local and global knowledge spillovers: evidence from plant-level data. *Scandinavian Journal of Economics*, 114 (3): 856–80.

Van Beveren, I. (2011) Total factor productivity estimation: a practical review. *Journal of Economic Surveys*, 26: 98–128.

Blomström, M. and Kokko, A. (1998) Multinational corporations and spillovers. *Journal of Economic Surveys*, 12(2): 1–31.

Braconier, H., Ekholm, K. and Midelfart-Knarvik, K.H. (2001) Exploring the existence of local and global knowledge spillovers: evidence from plant-level data. *Review of World Economics*, 137(4): 644–65.

Djankov, S. and Hoekman, B. (2000) Foreign investment and productivity growth in Czech enterprises. *World Bank Economic Review*, 14: 49–64.

Doraszelski, U. and Jaumandreu, J. (2013) R&D and productivity: estimating endogenous productivity. *Review of Economic Studies*, forthcoming.

Driffield, N. (2001) The impact on domestic productivity of inward investment into the UK. *Manchester School*, 69(1): 103–19.

Dunning, J.H. (2000) The eclectic paradigm as an envelope for economic and business theories of MNE activity. *International Business Review*, 9: 163–90.

DOI: 10.1057/9781137367204.0022

Girma, S., Greenaway, D. and Wakelin, K. (2001) Who benefits from foreign direct investment in the UK? *Scottish Journal of Political Economy*, 48: 19–33.

Görg, H. and Greenaway, D. (2004) Much ado about nothing? Do domestic firms really benefit from foreign direct investment? *World Bank Research Observer*, 19(2): 171–97.

Görg, H. and Strobl, E. (2001) Multinational companies and productivity spillovers: a meta-analysis. *Economic Journal*, 111(475): F723–F739.

Görg, H. and Strobl, E. (2005) Spillovers from foreign firms through worker mobility: an empirical investigation. *Scandinavian Journal of Economics*, 107: 693–709.

Haskel, J., Pereira, S. and Slaughter, M. (2007) Does inward foreign direct investment boost the productivity of domestic firms? *Review of Economics and Statistics*, 89: 482–96.

Hofstede, G. (2001) *Culture's Consequences: Comparing Values, Behaviours, Institutions and Organizations Across Nations*, 2nd edn. Thousand Oaks, CA: Sage Publications.

Javorcik, B.S. (2004) Does foreign direct investment increase the productivity of domestic firms? In search of spillovers through backward linkages. *American Economic Review*, 94(3): 605–27.

Keller, W. and Yeaple, S.R. (2003) Multinational enterprises, international trade, and productivity growth: firm level evidence from the United States. NBER working paper no. 9504, National Bureau of Economic Research.

Kogut, B. and Singh, H. (1988) The effect of national culture on the choice of entry mode. *Journal of International Business Studies*, 19(3): 411–33.

Konings, J. (2001) The effects of foreign direct investment on domestic firms. *Economics of Transition*, 30: 105–34.

Kostova, T. (1999) Transnational transfer of strategic organizational practices: a contextual perspective. *Academy of Management Review*, 24(2): 308–24.

Kugler, M. (2006) Spillovers from foreign direct investment: within or between industries? *Journal of Development Economics*, 80(2): 444–77.

Levinsohn, J. and Petrin, A. (2003) Estimating production functions using inputs to control for unobservables. *Review of Economic Studies*, 70: 317–41.

McVicar, D. (2002) Spillovers and foreign direct investment in UK manufacturing. *Applied Economics Letters*, 9: 297–300.

Negassi, S. (2006) International R&D spillovers and economic performance of firms: an empirical study using random coefficient models. *Applied Economics*, 41: 947–76.

North, D.C. (1990) *Institution, Institutional Change and Economic Performance*. Cambridge and New York: Cambridge University Press.

Olley, G.S. and Pakes, A. (1996) The dynamics of productivity in the telecommunications equipment industry. *Econometrica*, 64: 1263–97.

Smeets, R. (2008) Collecting the pieces of the FDI knowledge spillovers puzzle. *World Bank Research Observer*, 23(2): 107–38.

Todo, Y. (2006) Knowledge spillovers from foreign direct investment in R&D: evidence from Japanese firm level data. *Journal of Asian Economics*, 17: 996–1013.

Wooldridge, J.M. (2009) On estimating firm-level production functions using proxy variables to control for unobservables. *Economics Letters*, 104: 112–14.

DOI: 10.1057/9781137367204.0022

Index

DOI: 10.1057/9781137367204.0023

DOI: 10.1057/9781137367204.0023

DOI: 10.1057/9781137367204.0023

DOI: 10.1057/9781137367204.0023

DOI: 10.1057/9781137367204.0023

DOI: 10.1057/9781137367204.0023

DOI: 10.1057/9781137367204.0023

DOI: 10.1057/9781137367204.0023

DOI: 10.1057/9781137367204.0023

Indexed by Terry Halliday (HallidayTerence@aol.com)

DOI: 10.1057/9781137367204.0023

Printed and bound by CPI Group (UK) Ltd, Croydon, CR0 4YY